W9-BTJ-977

ISAAC HECKER

An American Catholic

David J. O'Brien

PAULIST PRESS
New York and Mahwah, N.J.

Library of Congress Cataloging-in-Publication Data

O'Brien, David J.
Isaac Hecker: an American Catholic/David J. O'Brien.
p. cm.
Includes bibliographical references and index.
ISBN 0-8091-0397-4
1. Hecker, Isaac Thomas, 1819–1888. 2. Paulist Fathers—United States—Biography. 3. Converts, Catholic—United States—Biography. 4. Catholic Church—United States—History—19th century.
I. Title.
BX4705.H4027 1992
271'.79—dc20
[B] 91-41545
CIP

Published by Paulist Press
997 Macarthur Boulevard
Mahwah, New Jersey 07430

Printed and bound in the
United States of America

Contents

TO

JAMES YOUNG, C.S.P.

Foreword

Orestes and Isaac: file it away, opera composers and dramatists, as a good name for a production. Such a title would fuse names of the Greek and the Hebrew traditions, the sources of the culture most accessible to most of us. The Orestes of the plot would not, however, be the mad son of Agamemnon and Clytemnestra but the driven offspring of a Stockbridge, Vermont couple in 1803. And Isaac, this time, would not be the bound potential victim of his father's sacrifice to God but a New York-born American who was Orestes' junior partner.

The plot? There would be plenty of love and death—not much sex, alas for plotters—in the careers of Orestes Brownson and Isaac Hecker, the two best known converts to Catholicism in America's nineteenth century, and no doubt the two most worth studying from any of the American centuries. Brownson's name comes up now and then throughout the plot of David O'Brien's biography of Hecker, but we have to leave him offstage henceforth here in order get the overture over with soon. Hecker is demanding enough.

Demanding, that is, of opera composers, dramatists, or biographers like David O'Brien, who shows a zest for his character, the priest who evidently welcomed the demands and challenges. Hecker is demanding of the reader, who almost never gets to sit back, relax, enjoy a Hecker achievement, and find an element of *stasis.* All this demanding goes on because Hecker was so demanding of himself, his contemporaries, his Church, his God.

One does not need to turn many pages to see that the lead in this drama was a tortured idealist who matched his time and place and used the raw materials of his environment and history, fused with the fire in his soul, to make something of the demands. While Brownson matched the stereotype of today's Protean-type Californian who is always spiritually shopping, even after he finds a home (in Catholicism), Hecker provides a countertheme by shopping, seeking, searching—and then finding a home with which to be at home. More or less. No less than Brownson he was tempted to keep on reforming the Catholic Church that he had found, but his soul was sufficiently quieted that he was able to be loyal no matter what.

There was plenty of "what" to matter. Hecker took plenty of buffeting, as we shall see. He dreamed of different outcomes than those which came with the First Vatican Council. He met opposition of hierarchs and leaders of religious orders who never knew quite how to contain the storms he generated or to accept the gifts he brought. For all his loyalty, he came to symbolize an "Americanist" heresy that he did not hold, thanks to the need some Europeans and American anti-Americanists recognized: to find a villain or a scapegoat that would make their heresy-hunting rewarding. Hecker knew frustration, thanks to the gap between his grand-scale dreams and the puny realizations of such dreams on a spiritual landscape as vast and thick-growthed as America's then was.

One gets the impression on these pages that Hecker knew everyone who shared his odyssey, his pilgrimage—let's keep our Greek and Hebrew imagery vivid here—in a turbulent time. Brownson and Hecker knew each other in that tangled thicket, and Hecker deals with Henry David Thoreau, the Brook Farm transcendentalists, the poets and politicians of his time. They seemed to see the environment as one which bid them to become almost anything; they could start history over again, or could reshape what the old had given, so they could make it new. They would all begin by remaking their selves.

Hecker had a complex and tortured self that needed remaking. It will disappoint some readers to know that, while he was capable of acquiring the sense of guilt that was requisite of Catholic converts in his time, he had perpetrated no great evils. At our house, Good Spouse and I ask each other a question about the subject of a biography, almost any biography, when the partner gets two-thirds through the book: "What was *her* cosmic flaw?" We assume that the titans have some cosmic flaw, took part in some event that made them mismatches with their times and their souls, knew some demonic thrust which threatened to overwhelm their creative energies. If Hecker had a cosmic flaw, David O'Brien covered it up or never discovered it, and I trust O'Brien. No, Hecker had to deal with a thousand nagging flawlets, tantalizations more than temptations, visions unfulfilled, good plans half-realized.

The Grand Plan after his conversion was a simple one: convert America. Why am I enjoying this plot? Hecker was baptized a Lutheran, as were so many of the violently spirited ones of his era (e.g. Karl Marx, Friedrich Nietzsche), and we Lutherans lost him to Methodism and then a whole sequence of "isms" until he found Catholicism or, as he would have put it, was found by God through the Catholic Church. People on his kind of odyssey or pilgrimage can never leave anyone else alone. (Comedian Jimmy Durante spoke for the millions who feel harassed by the tract-passing, lapel-grabbing evangelizer at the airport: "Why doesn't everybody leave everybody else the hell alone?") Hecker could not have conceived of letting anyone else the hell alone. What he found in Catholicism was so rich that he had to pester Protestants and criticize the faith which had half-nurtured him. He looked out at a nation in which the infidel seemed to be prospering, and he would woo and win the infidel to the truth, the Church.

To that end Hecker founded the Paulist order, into which he poured his best energies and through the love of which, and the hate of its enemies, he worked out his love-hate relationship with America and the citizens around him. The order gave him a singleness of purpose, though, as O'Brien tells it, there was a doubleness of plot, an ironic twist in his doings and dealings. He must commend America to Catholics; that is, this often inimical and Nativist Protestant set of surrounds had to be made potentially attractive to an often huddled, immigrant Church.

More important, Hecker must commend Catholicism to America. He must take this often foreign-seeming Catholic reality, whose European spokesmen and many of their agents hardly understood America, and make them understand and love it.

Though Hecker tried many things and never found rest even when he found rest—his soul still knew furies even as his Church offered solace—I have misrepresented him and David O'Brien if I suggest that he was "mad" like Orestes. He suffered breakdown of sorts; that fate seemed to come with the territory of odyssey and pilgrimage in the nineteenth century. But he also found steadiness of direction, and wanted to share it with others. He was not a dilettante of spiritualities, an esthete of quests, a hobbyist who pursued fads for fads' sakes, a virtuoso at not being able to decide or find. He found, in his own way. And he helped make that a way for other seekers, some of whom, I hope, will see elements of the drama of their own lives in the lively plot which follows.

Martin E. Marty
The University of Chicago

Preface

In the summer of 1978 I met with Paulist Fathers William Dewan, David Killian and Kevin Lynch to discuss the life and thought of Isaac Hecker. Anticipating the 125th anniversary of their community, which would take place in 1983, these leaders hoped that someone would undertake to write a one-volume life of their founder. Long a source of controversy in the Catholic Church, and even in the Paulist community, Hecker's life and thought had not been examined in full since an ill-fated *Life* published after his death by his disciple, Walter Elliott. Father Vincent Holden, C.S.P., began a biography in the 1940s, which resulted in the publication in 1958 of *The Yankee Paul*, covering Hecker's life to the founding of the Paulists a century earlier. However, for a variety of reasons, Holden made little progress on a projected second volume.

Recently, a number of younger scholars have written on aspects of Hecker's thought, while a handful of others are discovering some of his surprisingly modern ideas about prayer, spirituality and ecclesiology. Moreover, many of Hecker's ideas, which caused such controversy in the past, became the norm in the post-Vatican II church. A new biography would cause little difficulty for the Paulists.

The prospect of writing a life of Hecker interested me. For one thing, I had done little specifically historical writing since the publication of *The Renewal of American Catholicism* in 1972. Instead, I had spent considerable time and energy on various church-related projects and written numerous essays and papers on contemporary church affairs. I felt a personal desire to do some serious historical work again. In addition, Hecker's love for

America, his Catholic loyalty and his confidence in the providence of God corresponded to many of my own convictions. Most important, I thought Hecker's optimistic affirmation of human freedom, so unusual for a nineteenth-century Catholic, offered an essential message for the modern church. After agreeing that I would be able to spend some years on the biography so that I could continue to fulfill my responsibilities as a teacher and pursue other projects, I decided to take on this assignment.

The result has been a long search for Isaac Hecker, a search that proved more complex than I had anticipated. Hecker was a mystic, and I am not comfortable with mystical language or patient with descriptions of mystical experience. Moreover, there were flaws in Hecker's character that disturbed me, as they undoubtedly concerned Father Holden before me. There were times when Hecker seemed saintly; at other times he seemed unusually self-indulgent and self-pitying. Equally important, it was and remains extremely difficult to gather together the strands and patterns of his life, to draw out the themes of discrete experiences and events. I was led into some dead ends as I tried to understand this many-faceted, introverted, activist priest. In the end, I have tried to return to the framework and ideas I know best, those of American Catholicism and American religion in the nineteenth century, leaving it to others to impose upon the available evidence—Hecker's footprints in the sands of time—the interpretive tools they find most appropriate. In the end, even more than at the beginning, I am convinced that Hecker provides one important key to understanding American Catholicism, not just in his own time but in ours, when religion has become for us as it was for him, a matter of "personal decision constantly renewed amid perilous surroundings," to use Karl Rahner's words.

For Hecker, as for us, those "perilous surroundings" included even the church. Like many other religious figures of the modern era, Hecker regarded his life as in some immediate sense a failure, for he ended misunderstood and unappreciated, even by those closest to him. Neither his church, his American Catholic brothers and sisters, nor even his Paulist disciples were able to fully appreciate his vision. Yet, like so many other modern Christians—John Henry Newman and Dorothy Day come to mind—his failure may prove to have been only temporary. If the Catholic Church turns its back on the promise of renewal and reverts to the self-enclosed subculture of its recent past, then Isaac Hecker will remain an interesting but essentially irrelevant loser on those historical scales by whose measure Pius IX and William Cardinal O'Connell of Boston stand as winners. But if the church follows John XXIII in seeking to pursue "above all, and everywhere the rights of the human person and not just those of the Catholic church," if it fulfills the promise of Vatican II that "the joys and the hopes, the griefs and anxieties of the men [and women] of this age, especially those who are poor or in any way afflicted, these too are the joys and the hopes, the griefs and anxieties of the followers of Christ," then we may come to see Isaac Hecker, the condemned embodiment of "Americanism," as one of those who stood by the truth in a dark time, and we will find in him a kindred spirit.

No work of this sort is completed without the help of many people, only a few of whom can be thanked directly. In the footnotes are references to scholars from whose work I have benefited, especially those recent students and admirers of Hecker who shared their ideas with me so generously. They include John Farina, Susan Melia and, most especially, William Portier of Mount Saint Mary's College, whose brilliant insights into modern Catholicism and thorough knowledge of Isaac Hecker never fail to stimulate me. The Paulists previously named have been invariably helpful and always patient. Their calm acceptance of my delays in completing this work communicated a confidence in me which I regard as a great gift. Father Lawrence McDonnell was Paulist archivist when I was doing my research, and I remain extremely grateful for his assistance and cooperation. Professor Timothy Smith of Johns Hopkins gave me encouragement when I badly needed it, while Professor Francis Broderick of the University of Massachusetts at Boston lent his editorial skills to several chapters. Research and writing was aided by a faculty fellowship from Holy Cross College, a senior fellowship from the National Endowment for the Humanities, and a travel grant from the Cushwa Center for American Catholic Studies at Notre Dame. The latter's director, Professor Jay P. Dolan, is another friend who has always supported me and my work. Lynn Letourneau of Worcester typed notes and large portions of the early manuscript, while her mother-in-law, Barbara Letourneau, has been a friend and supporter throughout my years at Holy Cross. Barbara Fuhr did much of the later typing, struggling heroically with my scrawls and dealing with my disorganization with consistent kindness. Others who cheerfully helped with the typing were Aline Girouard, Bennie DeNardo and Kristy Nardacci, to all of whom I am most grateful.

It is commonplace to thank editors, so it is hard to make my gratitude to the people who worked with this volume entirely clear. Kevin Lynch, President of the Paulist Press, and Don Brophy, the editor for this text, have given new meaning to the word patience. They have been kind, generous, and compassionate. I hope that they will receive, I know they truly deserve, many blessings for what they have given to me by staying with this book.

My wife Joanne comforted me when things went badly, pushed me gently when I got distracted or lazy, listened to my confusion when it threatened to overwhelm me, and helped me appreciate the place of the Spirit of God in our own lives.

My children, Mary, Kenny, Joe and Dave, grew through high school, into college and beyond as I worked on Hecker. In ways I am only beginning to understand they have been an inspiration and grace to me. They will live in the future we create; we must try to build the kind of future for and with them that Hecker dreamed about. They have the faith and character to be the men and women of their age that Hecker thought the church and the human community required. The possibilities he saw are now enfleshed in their lives. I believe that under the guidance of providence they will be fulfilled.

Finally, there is Paulist Father Jim Young. He had been my friend for several years before I started this project and had much to do with bringing me together with his Paulist colleagues that day in 1978. He took a great interest in my work, provided hospitality at the Paulist camp at Lake George and their college in Washington, where he served as rector. As the guiding spirit of the North American Conference of Separated and Divorced Catholics he had as much as anyone to do with the revolution in Catholic consciousness on that subject in the last decades. Through his deep faith and love for people he empowered thousands of divorced Catholics to experience the persistent love of God and to find reconciliation with their church. He cared especially for the poor and powerless and was a consistent champion of the social ministries of the church. He was a person and a priest who deeply touched Joanne and me, and who provided a living example of what the renewal of contemporary Catholicism is all about. He loved the church, and he loved his country; he delighted in late-night discussions of church politics, which flowed easily into conversation about films and novels and the latest insanities of American public life. In the fall of 1986, as I was working on this manuscript, Jim Young died. He had looked forward to reading this book; he had twice invited me to talk about Hecker with the Paulist community in Washington, and he was deeply interested in Hecker and his legacy. I often wanted to tell him, but I did not, that he more than any Paulist I had met represented for me Isaac Hecker's dream for his community. He was a man of the church and a man of his age—intelligent, mature, self-disciplined, compassionate, hopeful, and altogether convinced that the spirit of God was at work in our history. I have dedicated this book to Jim Young, a friend, a Paulist, and a sign that Hecker's dream has lived in my lifetime and is alive still in many people touched by Jim's love.

Part One: An American Road to Rome

1

An American Life

Isaac Thomas Hecker loved to tell his story. Perhaps no American of the nineteenth century was as convinced that his own life embodied the meaning of the national experience. Hecker's journey took him from a German immigrant family in New York through the transcendentalism of New England's Brook Farm to Christianity to the Catholic Church and finally to the priesthood. Hecker then spent his priestly life trying to persuade others to follow his path. He wanted to build a "Catholic America," which would lead the way to a "Catholic World." In pursuit of that dream, he became famous as a preacher, lecturer, writer-editor, founder of an important religious community and, after his death, center of a major international theological dispute.

Isaac Hecker did not create a Catholic America, although he did help form American Catholicism. He combined orthodox faith with the simple conviction that the church had to learn to be at home in America. Hecker took for granted the value of freedom of conscience, self-reliance and democratic government. Indeed, he saw these as America's providential gift to the world. He hoped his Catholic Church would eventually come to appreciate and accept these gifts.

The Catholic Church had even more important gifts to offer Americans. Hecker cast himself as an American St. Paul, preaching to a doubting people the Good News that there was a goal for the aspirations of their nature, an answer to the questions of their souls. As Hecker saw them, his fellow Americans fit the image of the "American Adam." Free from the burdens of sin and history here in the bountiful garden of the New World,

Americans were innocent, open, sincere and ready to respond to the truth when it was clearly and honestly presented. Americans were beginning again, with a present and future, but no past. They gradually set aside the religious heritage of the Reformation, just as they rejected age-old axioms of monarchy and privilege. Might they not be receptive, then, to Catholic faith, the true Christian faith, if it was presented simply, without Old World, counter-reformation adornments, by "a real American," a man like themselves?

It is impossible to understand the life of any American of the mid-nineteenth century, and particularly the life of a born evangelist like Isaac Hecker, without understanding what it meant to be an American, "born free" in those exciting years of Andrew Jackson and Ralph Waldo Emerson. America has always excited imaginations, and never more than in the half century before the Civil War. First-hand accounts of the bold republican experiment across the ocean filled European journals. Visitors agreed that older forms of government, economic life, education and religion were giving way in the United States to new ones derived from "the people." Not everyone was included in the American democratic experiment, but more were than ever before seemed possible. Individuals of no great lineage became generals and politicians, lawyers and philosophers. Americans moved from place to place at a pace that seemed to explode traditional loyalties. Instead of looking to the past for wisdom, they looked ahead, replacing memory with hope, deference with defiance, order with progress. Literally nothing could be taken for granted; everything, from governments to personal lives, had to be constructed anew, and the process never ended.

Such intense self-consciousness produced an autobiographical strain in American culture evident in Hecker's never-ending preoccupation with the story of his life. Meaning, no longer reliably found in tradition or institutions, must reside in experience itself. The best evidence of truth was that it worked; the best evidence of that, a successful person. Successive generations of immigrants and inner migrants, "breaking loose" from traditions to seek their own new worlds, stood in the middle or at the end of their journey and gazed back, searching memory for the meaning of their lives. Biography and history became one.

New possibilities were exciting, but there was a cost, and at times it seemed too high. When everything, literally everything, was open, results might include the recurring loss of family loyalty, the decline of community life and the erosion of institutional authority. Farmers' sons seeking land and independence; their sons and daughters, more aware of their freedom, agonizing over decisions about career, family and faith, experienced both the pleasure and the pain of choice. For individual persons, the experience brought with it a continuing need to define identity, meaning, a basic orientation toward life, other persons and history. For society, it meant a seemingly unending struggle to develop structures, from the family to government, to channel the energy released by such freedom, and to give coherence, stability and order to the public world.[1]

The decades following the American and French revolutions witnessed a radical democratization of such experiences, evident in the rapid growth of voluntary organizations; heated political debates and the formation of political parties; multiplication of religious sects; sharp attacks on the professions, on slavery and sometimes on the rich; and new ideas about citizenship, representation, women's role and the place of youth in society. There occurred a "democratization of mind," an application of popular sovereignty, the rule of the people, to all areas of American life.[2] With it came the invitation to share responsibility for the shaping of the common life, the message of Jacksonian democracy, and to take responsibility for the direction of one's own life, the message of evangelical revivals and Emersonian transcendentalism. Isaac Hecker heard—and heeded—both invitations.

In fact, by the 1840s a large number of men and women, anxious to achieve economic success with some degree of moral integrity, were searching, as Isaac Hecker was, for saving knowledge and useful work, and they were inventing institutions to aid in the process. In 1846 Bostonians could choose among twenty-six different "courses" of lectures, while between thirty-five hundred and four thousand communities had a society to sponsor such programs. "Most Americans coming of age in these decades led a somewhat dislocated existence, and many of them were forced to strike out on their own, with scant resources to begin with or fall back upon, few clear cut institutions to guide them, and few unambiguous cues to follow," writes historian Donald M. Scott. "Life appeared to them less a matter of settling into an established niche than a process of continuing self-construction, as people had to decide how to begin, whether to move on in search of greater opportunities, when to seek out a situation with greater prospects or advantages, and, frequently, whether to go West or start afresh."[3]

Religion shared in the fluid, open, insecure condition of the times, but found meaning in the disarray. The early Puritans doubted that Christianity could survive severed from its historical roots. But Jonathan Edwards, a century after the founding of Massachusetts, argued that the separation of the church from its past, and the confusion of voices that resulted had a purpose. Here, in America, through the power of the Holy Spirit, operating through the free and enlightened consciences of men and women, the Kingdom of God would arrive.[4]

But the Puritan dream of a united Christian culture failed. Freedom, and therefore pluralism, were facts ratified in law and in the new constitution.

John Carroll, the nation's first Catholic bishop, thought the new nation's experiment in religious liberty more profound than its republican revolution. Never before had anyone tried to have a nation without at least outward recognition of one religion, which would provide a common identity and inspire common action. Religious freedom made such unity problematic. For the churches the experiment was equally radical, for they could no longer depend on public authority to coerce membership—or contributions. They must act through persuasion, in competition with other churches.

American Christianity, therefore, was invariably, if sometimes reluctantly, evangelical, accepting as given the autonomous self, the need for conversion, and the organization of the church as a voluntary association of like-hearted and like-minded men and women. Church leaders tried to limit personal autonomy by propagating shared Christian values through the press, schools and other forms of common instruction. They sought to persuade people to accept the authority of clergy or synods or bishops, and they tried, when they could, to limit the interaction, and particularly the intermarriage, of their members with those of other groups. Still, freedom and pluralism were facts; the availability of choice was the fundamental context within which the churches worked. It might mean stronger churches based on personal convictions, but it likely would also mean smaller ones. It might make religion a stronger element of personal faith, a firmer cement of family and community, but it might also confine it to private life and end by emptying public life of meaning.

For those concerned with the quality of public life, and with the success of the American experiment in self-government, religion was crucially important. Americans were generally a Christian people, however unchurched. They believed in the Bible as a divinely revealed guide to life, but they interpreted it differently and this diversity lent urgency to denominational efforts to define creeds which could gain as wide assent as possible. Americans were convinced that every institution, every aspect of life, could be improved, but they worried that this would become simply an unbridled pursuit of gain which would corrupt state and society. They also knew, however dimly, that there were victims—Indians, slaves, industrial workers—who had little reason to respect national pretensions or acquiesce in the prevailing distribution of wealth and power. So civic leaders looked to the diffusion of religion, with its "moral influence," to hold passions in check.

The heart of the problem was whether free men and women would voluntarily consent to the discipline required for the assurance of personal security, private property, and social order. One New England minister put it directly: "Unless true benevolence, and public spirit prevent, there is eminent danger that private interests will be pursued, at the expense, or built on the ruins of the public weal." To promote "true benevolence and public spirit," churches simplified creeds and organized missionary and reform societies. The result was a religious ethos that emphasized faith in Jesus, reliance on the Bible and on a few simple religious slogans, together with a lifestyle of thrift, self-discipline and hard work—all seen quite clearly as means to make the democratic experiment work.[5]

The evangelical churches were peculiarly well-suited to take advantage of the conditions of American culture in the post-revolutionary years. Uninhibited by rigid traditions or structures, bent upon bringing all people to confront the Jesus of scripture and to undergo conversion, they responded quickly to the religious needs of an expanding and mobile population still nurtured on the Bible but largely beyond the reach of the church. In the early nineteenth century a second Great Awakening swept the country, featuring massive revivals of religion. Methodists, Baptists and Presbyterians were soon at work bringing men and women within the life of grace. Evangelical Christianity supplied standards of personal behavior, brought some restraint to the rough life of the frontier, and to the new frontier of the industrial city. It instilled a sense of responsibility in the family, fought personal evils of intemperance and infidelity, and insisted on the need for each person to demonstrate sincere commitment to Christ by living an upright life. Most were convinced that America was a special nation and its people God's chosen, but this was less an assurance of the righteousness of the status quo than a continuing demand to challenge private vice and public sin by a personal commitment to moral reform.[6]

Evangelical leaders were fully committed to the democratic experiment; they felt a responsibility to sustain democratic ideals by a democratization of Christian faith. Free will and free grace were their watchwords, but neither the religious nor the political outcomes of these doctrines would be beneficial "unless righteousness—law rooted in what the teachings of both the Old and New Testaments declared was a covenant of holiness—could be internalized in the individual and corporate experience of Christians." Grace alone could purify the heart and strengthen the will to live by Christian standards in daily life. Committed to freedom, yet convinced of the dangers of selfishness and greed, they worked to spread "the experience of sanctification, of whole hearted devotion to the gospel law of love."[7]

But here again, it all began and ended with the self. Religion reflected —and sanctioned—the fundamental reality of the age for those who were not among the victims: the experience of personal autonomy. What evangelical Christianity did for the masses, transcendentalism did for the learned, and the would-be learned. Ralph Waldo Emerson became a popular guide for men and women nurtured in a religious faith more simple and scriptural than his own. They were united by an experience Emerson put into words: "the individual is the world." As much as any Baptist or Methodist, Emerson believed that God was immediately available, and that the inner experience of grace was the end and the means of holiness. Emerson translated autonomy into "self-reliance," a sturdy independence, a willingness to trust one's own experience. For the more conventional, Emerson seemed to promote an "anarchy of individual intuitions," but, as Perry Miller pointed out, Emerson believed that nature, flowing through the pure heart and open mind, produced a single truth, available to all.[8] It was closed minds and cold hearts, frozen reason and fearful interests, that created divisions, uncertainty and confusion. If each person would simply turn to nature, become a "transparent eyeball," the one spirit that blended man and nature would express itself in a new unity in freedom and truth. Spirit, like the evangelical's grace, was there for the eager, honest seeker.

The whole situation facing Isaac Hecker and thousands of young people of his generation was best summed up by Unitarian leader William Ellery Channing. He and his New England friends believed in the universal human capacity for improvement. They thought men and women could find in themselves "germs and promises of a growth to which no bounds can be set." By turning inward, by "self-culture," Americans could avoid the twin evils of a selfish plutocracy and an undisciplined mob. They could discover common ethical norms that would instill in each person a sense of virtue and self-restraint.

Self-culture, in Channing's view, rested on "two powers of the human soul." One was "the self-searching power," by which people had "the faculty of turning the mind on itself; of recalling its past and watching its present operations." By observing the operations of the soul, men and women could "learn in general what [their] nature is and what it was made for." They could learn "not only what we already are but what we may become." But it took the second power to go beyond the searching of self to the nobler stage of "acting on, determining and forming ourselves." Life was a project; in a setting of freedom, the ability to see and form the self, to determine one's own life, was a "glorious endowment . . . the ground of human responsibility."[9]

In Channing's generation more and more young men, and not a few young women, discovered something approaching that self-searching and self-forming power. The lives of Bronson Alcott, Orestes Brownson, Lyman Beecher, Charles Grandison Finney, William Lloyd Garrison,

Margaret Fuller—and Isaac Hecker—all partook of that discovery. Each one, and many others, felt emancipated from the constraints of custom and tradition; they read and listened and talked, and began to experience an exhilarating sense of possibility in themselves and in their world, a realization that they could become, or at least attempt to become, perfect, in harmony with nature and one another. The exact contours of their lives might be less clear, and a source of some anxiety, but it was certain that there was a truth to discover, that the path to that truth was an inward spiritual path, and that the result would be a work to do, even if it was only, and wonderfully, one's own work, like Henry David Thoreau's lonely but glorious work of looking around and within.

This was America, or at least an important slice of America in the early nineteenth century, an exciting place to live, a complex place to grow up. The signals given off by the culture, the patterns through which the young were invited to shape their lives, were at once exciting and baffling. One might become almost anything, but what one chose to become carried enormous weight, for it would determine the fate of the nation and, through the nation, the direction of history itself. Because there was everywhere to turn and almost every option available, there was nowhere to turn, save to the whole of reality outside and the voice of the spirit within. Opening out, one might find nature or God or Jesus, depending on the languages one learned and the companions one found; turning inward one might find corresponding voices. All one could depend upon was experience, filtered through the one inescapable reality, the self. The ongoing record of self-exploration and self-discovery—autobiography— was the surest form of theology, the most reliable form of social thought.

Creating a life was an intensely private matter, but it required continuing public expression in word and action. For those caught up in the romantic spirit of the age, it seemed cowardly to choose anything but the best. The invitation was direct: reach deep into the soul, reach beyond the chaos of experience, reach for the truth, for the good, for that reality which alone infused meaning and purpose, for God. In the record of that striving would be found the meaning of one's life, and the destiny of the nation. In such an atmosphere, mysticism and politics, biography and history, merged. Anyone might become a "representative man," in Emerson's phrase; anyone might embody the meaning of the nation and of history itself. Anyone might become an American St. Paul.

Isaac Hecker found his life filled with meaning. His recurrent autobiographical writing reflected the cultural landscape of his time. He, too, began life anew. Indeed, his stories of himself seemed like those of an orphan. He almost never mentioned his father, only rarely his mother. He provided little information about his life before the age of twenty, save to exaggerate his youthful involvement in reform politics. Life, it seemed, began in 1842 when he set out, or was driven by the spirit, to search for an answer to his own religious questions. In this way he confirmed that he was like other Americans, as he saw them, free from the prejudices and fixed ideas of the past, open to the possibilities of the future, self-directed, and determined only to respond to those ideas that met the yearning of his heart and the demands of his reason.

But Hecker was no orphan. He was the son of German immigrants who came to New York City at the end of the eighteenth century. His father, John Hecker, born in 1782 in Schwalback, seventy miles southwest of Bonn, spent much of his youth in Holland before leaving for the United States in 1800. His ancestors were Dutch Lutherans who for two hundred years had lived in Germany. A skilled metalworker, John found employment in a New York foundry and machine shop where he worked on Robert Fulton's steamship, the *Claremont*. He sailed on its maiden voyage to Albany in August 1807. On board with him was Frederick Friend, another German immigrant who had arrived in New York in 1797. Visiting the family, John met Frederick's sister, Susan Caroline, six years older than himself. They courted and finally were married on July 21, 1811, in "the old Dutch church in the swamp."[10]

John Hecker opened his own brass foundry and the young couple lived on Hester Street, next door to the Friends. Their first son, John, was born in 1812. A second son, Henry, died in infancy; a daughter, Elizabeth, was born in 1816; and then came two more sons, George, born in January, 1818, and Isaac, born December 18, 1819. The family's prospects seemed good in the early years. The business prospered, and their house was in a desirable neighborhood, close to the sea. Among themselves, the family spoke German. Isaac remembered in later years watching his grandfather Friend, a clockmaker as well as metal worker, work in a small shop in back of their house. Under his grandfather's eye, Isaac made a clock, which worked for forty years; all his life he was very proud of it.[11]

Yet mystery shrouds Isaac's childhood. Around 1824 John Hecker's foundry closed and the family moved five blocks away, to Eldridge Street. In 1828 the shop reopened uptown at 269 Broome Street; two years later it disappeared from the city directory, never to reappear. The father all but disappeared from the family's life. He was seldom mentioned in family records, though he lived until 1860. Years later, Hecker occasionally mentioned him in letters from Europe; once he wrote him directly, urging him to give up his "wicked passion."[12]

Despite the apparent tragedy of his father's "vice," Isaac Hecker seems to have had a relatively happy childhood. His mother was clearly the dominant figure in the household. Raised a Lutheran, she entered the Methodist church shortly after her marriage and remained a devout Christian all her life. A faithful member of the Forsythe Street Church, Caroline Hecker became immersed in the perfectionist movement. Based on John Wesley's call for "perfect love," perfectionism held forth an ideal of holiness which could be reached by ordinary people in daily life. In later years Hecker's correspondence with his mother indicated that she was a deeply committed, devout Christian who believed that her youngest son had been touched by God. Yet aside from passing references, which showed that Isaac was acquainted with some prominent preachers and familiar with the Methodist service and hymns, there is no evidence that Hecker or his brothers were exposed in any formal way to the fervor of perfectionism. In fact, there is no evidence that they even attended church or Sunday School. Still, the strength of Caroline Hecker's faith suggests that Hecker's later claim that he was raised with no positive religion at all was exaggerated.[13]

As the youngest in the family, Isaac was closest to his mother. He seems to have been a reflective, introspective youngster. Hecker recalled years later that he was once stricken with confluent smallpox and his family feared for his life. He is supposed to have told his mother not to worry: "No, mother, I shall not die now. God has work for me to do in the world and I shall live to do it." The smallpox left his face marked and damaged his eyesight, but he did not get glasses until he was twenty years old. On another occasion Isaac was lying on the floor when his mother spoke to his brother unexpectedly, "in a kind of unconscious speech": "John, let Isaac go to college and study." Her words "cut through me like liquid fire," Isaac remembered, but John was evasive and the subject was dropped.[14]

Clearly the father's failure left the Hecker family in serious trouble. John, the oldest son, worked as a baker, then opened his own bakery on Hester Street. Soon after, George left school to help in the business. In 1835 John purchased the building in which the business was located and, in 1838, opened a second shop. To get a steady supply of flour the brothers built their own flour mill and the business continued to expand. By 1843 they owned four shops and the Croton Flour Mill, the area's largest, a success due in part to the brothers' inventive genius. John invented a machine that mixed flour, water and yeast into dough, rolled it out and prepared it for the oven. In 1842 George invented a floating grain elevator. Later George invented an acid salt which allowed them to produce a very popular self-rising flour. By that time the older brothers were quite wealthy and George, who was Isaac's closest confidant, was able to help support his younger brother's many projects.

All that lay in the future when Isaac entered Public School Number 7 on Christie Street in 1826. This was one of a number of schools maintained by the Public School Society, a private philanthropic body dedicated to providing free education for the poor and open to others on a tuition basis. The school worked on the Lancaster System, in which older pupils assisted in teaching basic reading, writing and arithmetic. There was no specific religious instruction beyond daily readings from the Bible. At the age of thirteen, with his family in crisis, Isaac ended his formal education and went to work. His first job was as a messenger with the *Christian Advocate and Journal and Zion's Herald*, published by the Methodist Book Concern. Later he apprenticed in a type foundry before going to work with his brothers in the bakery. Here he stayed through his teens, sharing in building the business and eventually becoming a full partner with John and George.

It was difficult work. Toward the end of his life Isaac reminisced about those early years. "Thanks be to God," he said. "How hard we used to work preparing for New Year's Day."

> Three weeks in advance we began to bake New Year's cakes, flour, water, sugar, butter and caraway seeds. We never could make enough. How I used to work carrying the bread around in my baker's cart. How often I got stuck in the gutters and in the snow. Sometimes some good soul, seeing me unable to get along, would give me a lift.

Once, when walking with his disciple, Walter Elliott, Hecker saw a poor woman with a heavy basket and said, "I have had the blood spurt out of my arm carrying bread when I was a baker."[15]

Such statements were unusual, for Hecker rarely referred to his early life. Only one element of his youthful experience left an indelible imprint and came to occupy an important place in his autobiography. This was his teenage involvement in reform politics. In the mid 1830s a bitter split took place in the New York Democratic party. A dissident radical group, the Locofocos, broke with Tammany Hall and issued a Declaration of Principles calling for sound money, opposition to monopoly, free public education and "equal rights." John Hecker was one of the party's leaders. During the panic of 1837, when unemployment and business failures were very high, the Heckers made free bread available to the unemployed and campaigned hard for reform. During the height of the agitation, they purchased a hand press, and on each bill they received printed: "Of all the contrivances to impoverish the working classes of mankind, paper money is the most effective. It fertilizes the rich man's field with the poor man's sweat."

In the fall election of 1837 the Locofocos attempted to gain control of the Democratic party. Isaac and his brothers organized meetings, arranged for speakers and posted handbills. Defeated in the election, the radical faction was gradually reincorporated into the party. John Hecker remained an active Democrat for years thereafter, but Isaac seems to have been bitterly disappointed by the failure of their efforts.[16]

The experience came to play an important role in Hecker's understanding of his life experience. In 1858, in an autobiographical document written for his religious advisors, he described his interest in social reform as an important stage of his spiritual developments. He noted his response to the 1837 panic:

> A social reform was called for, and this led me into the examination of the social evils of the present state of society. The many miseries in modern society sprang, in my opinion, from the want of the practical application of the moral principles of Christianity to the social relations between men. How could a man love his neighbors as himself and then accumulate wealth by their toil? How can those who believe that all men were created in the image of God, and redeemed by the blood of Christ, and therefore equal before God, have them as servants, drudges, and slaves? Why should not those who profess Christianity imitate Christ in devoting themselves entirely to the spreading of the truth, the relief of the poor, and the elevation of the lower classes? Such like thoughts occupied my mind, and since a social reform was needed, it was my duty to begin with myself, and this led me to treat those in my employ with greater kindness, and to make important changes in my way of living. Abstinence from all luxuries, from all flesh meats, and from all drinks of water,—thus confining myself to what was absolutely necessary,—this was continued during seven years, until my entering into a religious order in the Church; and applying the same principles to my dress, my clothing was simple and common. Abstinence was necessary to bring the passions into subjection, and all superficialities should be devoted to the poor.[17]

This is the only evidence that exists of a turn to religion and self-discipline in the late 1830s. It contradicts other evidence that Hecker did not begin to explore religious questions until a sudden religious experience took place in 1842. What does seem clear is that young Isaac took these political events seriously; he read the literature, listened to the speeches and worked hard on the campaign. Undoubtedly this experience did familiarize him with some of the central symbols of American consciousness of the time, including the broadly Christian themes that informed the movement. The Locofocos, and other radicals in Jacksonian America, regularly justified democratic claims in Christian terms. They shared the widespread belief that the United States had a special role to play in bringing about the reign of God. And, most important, they trusted their fellow citizens. In later years Hecker may not have been fully democratic in his attitude toward his fellow Americans; indeed, at times he was something of a snob. Still, he never lost an almost instinctive love of liberty and a conviction that, at the basis of things, all men were indeed created equal and each possessed basic rights which no one, no state or no church, could infringe. On the other hand, there is no reason to accept at face value his claims about the significance of this experience. He was young, the excitement of political agitation attracted many young men like himself, and some began through that experience to get a sense that they could make some decisions about their life. It was not uncharacteristic to exaggerate such experiences in retrospect, investing them with meaning in light of what came later.[18]

The Heckers continued their interest in reform after the collapse of the Locofocos, reading reform papers and attending meetings and lectures. For Isaac, a crucial turning point came when he heard a lecture by Orestes Brownson, the famous Boston editor and reformer, in March 1841. Brownson was at the time the most prominent reformer in the country; only Emerson was more famed and respected as a writer and thinker. Born in Springfield, Vermont, Brownson was orphaned at an early age and raised by strict Congregationalist grandparents. The lonely Brownson became a living example of Channing's "self-culture." He rarely attended school, but read voraciously; by the time he was a teenager, he was deeply involved in the study of theology and philosophy. Converted to Universalism, one of the many enthusiastic Christian movements seeking a common faith and simple form of worship, he accepted a pulpit in New York state and became editor of the leading Universalist publication. Soon disillusioned with the anti-intellectual simplicity of that faith, he became a Unitarian, serving churches in New Hampshire before coming to Boston at the invitation of William Ellery Channing and George Ripley to serve as minister to a new church organized to evangelize working people.[19]

Brownson was passionately devoted to an activist democratic Christianity that would overcome injustice, greed and ambition. He established the *Boston Quarterly Review* in 1837 as an organ for his ideas. In 1840 he published a very controversial essay, "The Laboring Classes," which mercilessly dissected the class character of the emerging industrial society. He campaigned vigorously for Democrat Martin Van Buren, who lost to the "log cabin and hard cider" ticket of William Henry Harrison and John Tyler. Stunned by the election results, Brownson began to reexamine his political convictions and to focus more exclusively on religious questions while remaining in active contact with reformers like the Heckers.

Impressed by Brownson, the Hecker brothers hoped he could help revive the reform movement in New York. Isaac visited the directors of the New York Lyceum to arrange an invitation to Brownson to return to the city in the fall of 1841. The president of that body thought Brownson's views were no longer popular, so the brothers informed Brownson they would make arrangements themselves for his appearance. It is clear from that letter that they had met Brownson during his earlier visit and discussed with him some of the ideas then circulating in the city.[20]

Brownson did indeed return in January 1842, staying with the Heckers and delivering a course of four lectures. He emphasized in his talks the progress of humanity, the special role of America in that progress, and the need for a new, more democratic, Christian religion appropriate to the age. By this time Brownson was convinced that the hopes invested in America could not be fulfilled by people alone; they needed divine assistance. In his conversations with the Heckers, Brownson was clearly moved by the sincerity of young Isaac, who posed to him his "first and biggest question," how to be "certain of the objective reality of the operations of my soul." Brownson recommended readings in German philosophy, knowing Isaac was at home in that language. When he left, they began a correspondence.

In the late spring or early summer of 1842 something happened, something so profound that it shook the center of young Hecker's life and drove him into new and unexpected paths. The experience constituted perhaps the central moment of Isaac Hecker's life. Whatever else happened to him, he remained convinced that a power had touched his life, called him to something, he knew not what, and made him special in ways that startled him. Yet, the experience itself remains shrouded in mystery, the only evidence of it the concern of his family and the decision he soon made to leave home to explore large issues of meaning and purpose in life. Only one description of the experience itself remains, recorded by Hecker in May of the following year:

> Almost ten months ago, or perhaps seven or eight, I saw (I cannot say I dreamt, for it was quite different from dreaming as I thought I was seated on the side of my bed) a beautiful angelic pure being, and myself standing alongside of her feeling a most heavenly pure joy. It was as if . . . our bodies were luminous. They gave forth a moonlike light which I felt sprang from the joy that we experienced. We are unclothed, pure and unconscious of anything but

> pure love and joy, and I felt as if we had always lived together and that our motions, actions, feelings and thoughts came from one centre. When I looked toward her I saw no bald outline of form, but an angelic something I cannot describe . . . In my life previous to this vision I should have been married ere this, for there are those I have since seen would have met the demands of my mind, but now this vision continually hovers o'er me and prevents me from its beauty of accepting anything else. For I am charmed by its influence and I am conscious that if I should accept anything else I should lose the life which would be the only existence wherein I could say I live.[21]

One response to this event was the diary he began in October 1842. In early entries Hecker struggled for words to express the yearning that now filled his heart. "I have not yet attained the power to speak it," he wrote. "It rests in me yet undeveloped." Yet it was also an active force and he was always "conscious of its attempt to realize itself." Hecker thought this force would "be in a sense a new creation, a development of a deeper life, a new dispensation unfolding a new law of his being."[22] The sexual imagery of the initial experience, and the sense of helplessness before an active spirit, perhaps reflected anxiety about his own identity, complicated by the absence of his father and the warmth of his relationship with his mother and his brother George. Similarly, the language of newness, the conviction of the uniqueness of the experience, brought to a personal level the powerful images of new beginnings and providential expectation that informed the reform movement in which he and his brothers participated. Whatever its source, and whatever language came to the mind of this unschooled young man as he attempted to understand what had happened, he knew that his life had been permanently changed. It was a disturbing experience, for himself and his family.

The force of the experience was evident to everyone around him. Recalling those events a few months later, Hecker wrote: "My spirit overpowered me." He could not work, though his brothers at first told him that hard work would solve his problem. Probably at Brownson's suggestion, Isaac began attending a Unitarian church, which William Henry Channing, son of the founder of Unitarianism, served as pastor. At Channing's suggestion, Hecker went to see a physician, who told him the time had come to marry, advice he received regularly in the months that followed. But he had already made one clear—though secret—decision: to remain celibate. His brothers, unusually patient and caring, had difficulty grasping what was going on. In November John wrote Brownson, inviting him to stay with the family when he visited New York in early December. At that time Brownson apparently talked at length with young Isaac, explaining to him the ideas of Pierre Leroux, a French philosopher who argued that all persons seek communion with others and with God, and that their very hunger required the existence of an object for its satisfaction. Isaac found comfort in this doctrine, which he now understood to mean that there was a basis for his new yearning, and an object toward which that yearning pointed.

Brownson also invited Isaac to visit him at his home in Chelsea, outside Boston, and the young man responded gratefully. Relations with his family must have become tense by then, for Isaac left quickly, arriving in Boston on the morning of December 24. Writing to his mother that night, he apologized for being unable to express his feelings clearly, but he reassured her that, given time, things would probably return to normal. "There is no use allowing our doubts and fears to control us," he wrote. "By fostering them, we increase them and we want all our time for something better, higher than these."

The day after Christmas, Hecker more candidly sought to explain himself to his brothers. "If I have appreciated anything in life," he told them, "it is the favor and indulgent treatment you have shown me in our business. I know I have never done an equal share of the work." But an irreversible change had taken place, removing him permanently from normal life, directing him toward an uncertain future. He now had no attraction toward business and no desire to "keep company with females." All he had anticipated was gone; his life had escaped his control. "It lies deeper than myself and there is not power in me to control it." "I write this in tears," he added. "How this will end, I know not, but I cannot but trust God. . . . A new life has opened to me, and to turn back would be death." Now he stood at a moment of "crisis" requiring him to make a "decision"; he awaited their reply with "intense anxiety."[23]

Instead of awaiting their response, however, he wrote his brothers again two days later, emphasizing that the change he had described was "not a momentary excitement." He could conceive of no arrangement at home with which he could be content; he was subject to thoughts and feelings they were not interested in. With no one "to commune with" who might understand what had happened, he had felt that "the life that was in me . . . was consuming me."[24]

In one diary entry, written while visiting Brownson, there is evidence of Hecker's immaturity, but the power of his conversion is clear. The passage captures the anguish that had arisen as a result of this experience.

> Could I but reveal myself unto myself what shall I say is life dear to me No All my friends dear to me I could suffer and die if need

> be for them but yet I have none of the old attachment that I had for them. . . . I feel as life is too much for me it is indescribably painful for me to live and rather than go through the ordeal of living I would prefer to leave this life my spirit shrinks from contact with those that surround me there is none that I can commune with it is only by unuttered prayer that my bosom is unburthened riches I have given up what pleasure can I receive any more I would love but alas who will receive it my being is full of life but to whom shall I speak who understandeth my speech . . . when I think of turning back to my old life my spirit leaves my body what shall I do how can I work but in and by the spirit that controls . . . Who shall I cry to for help but he that has given me life and planted this spirit in me . . . if there is anything that is for me to do why this darkness all around me . . . I labored for riches but denounced them Friendship is gone love in its accustomed sense is gone and here I am left alone and I would cry with all my soul and heart What shall I do who will be unto me a friend a comforter . . . I cannot go backwards, neither would I if I could neither can I go forwards hence I would be glad if I was taken from this life in my present state, as I am, O Lord receive me Yet would I do my duty here establish thy kingdom here and while I pray O Lord, open thou my eyes to see the path thou would have me to walk in Thy spirit has led me in all my present judgements but I have not looked unto thee for light which I hope I may have the faith to ask in the right spirit so as I receive the blessing of wisdom.[25]

For all its scattered incoherence, the consciousness revealed in this passage is one of a young man who has been profoundly shaken from a settled way of life. He is a Christian, who knows that the spirit that moves within him is the spirit of God. He has enough Christian formation to find solace in inarticulate prayer, and he begins here to give "utterance," calling on God for light. He is alone before a God who is within. He knows he must respond, but he has no resources to define the response, no church, no form of prayer, no spiritual discipline, not even an ability to go to the Scriptures. While yearning for peace, and thus flirting with death, he sees in the experience a call to duty, to do God's will. So he asks the vocational question: I have been called, but called to do what? He is, in short a spiritual seeker, bereft of settled forms and institutions, on his own, forced to find the way himself, to be the spiritual equivalent of the self-made man.

Hecker ended his second letter to his brothers by saying that if it were agreeable to his family, he would go to Brook Farm, a community recently established by Brownson's friend George Ripley. John Hecker could be forgiven some reservations about this proposal. In his first letter from Boston, Isaac told his mother he was "much amused sometimes laughing and then almost weeping in reading some of the pamphlets of the Apostles of the Newness," a phrase often used to describe the New England radicals. Now, suddenly, he had decided to join some of these "Apostles" in their most notably new setting.

Quite naturally, John sought Brownson's counsel. On January 7 John wrote the famous philosopher to express the family's gratitude for his help. Isaac kept his feelings to himself, and John hoped Brownson could get more out of him. His worry was evident in his comment that Isaac's occasional despair "makes us feel bad for his sake." They had encouraged him, hoping that "some unknown circumstance" might "restore him to us as he once was." Isaac's mother thought he was under a religious change, preparatory to becoming a Christian, and that he only wanted to give up his whole soul to Christ. She hoped Brownson would be his "spiritual guide and father." John told Brownson the family approved of the Brook Farm stay, if Brownson advised it, worrying only that Isaac not engage in too much study.[26]

Returning to Chelsea from a brief visit to Brook Farm, Hecker was disappointed to find no letter from home. He wrote his family that he intended to move to Brook Farm in about three weeks and stay there until his mind "became perfectly settled in its present state or returns to its former state." He noted that board would be four dollars a week, reduced in proportion to the work he would do. He asked them to write if they approved and send his trunk with his working clothes, as "I may help them in our business." He added that a family friend, Mr. Ryckman, lived at Brook Farm: his wife was very kind and they "need not have any fears if I go there in any way." He wrote in his diary that he would go to Brook Farm to study French and music, hoping and praying he would "be studious and not waste my time."[27]

No orphan, no rebellious youngster angry at his family or his society, Isaac Hecker was nevertheless the embodiment of America's "new man." Unschooled and unchurched, shaken loose from a loving family and secure future, he was filled with discontent with the ordinary options set before him, driven by a new power he could hardly name, much less control; he was unsure of who he was or what he would do. For other young people, in other settings, the experience might be called alienation and might threaten despair. For Isaac Hecker these dangers were remote, for he loved and was loved by his family, he already had attained a remarkable confidence in himself and his own instinctive response to people and events, and he trusted the fundamental goodness of the public world in which he lived.

His anguish lacked the preciousness, the artificiality of so many young middle-class romantics; his previous experience of hard work and working-class politics contrasted sharply with the backgrounds of many he would meet at Brook Farm. He had read little romantic poetry and spent little time in cultural pursuits. Instead, he had been disturbed by the failure of reform, he was a bit dreamy amid the daily work of the bakery, and he had been profoundly shaken by a genuine religious experience. Occasioned by no external stimulus that can be identified, the religious experience's unique character was confirmed by Hecker's highly unusual commitment to celibacy. As he left for Brook Farm, he was conscious of his separation from his own past, intensely aware that he was indeed beginning anew. He was ready to learn from each new experience, but centered, and therefore rendered independent, by his own deeply personal engagement with a spiritual power as vivid and real for him as for any of the transcendentalists who would be his teachers in the next few months. His life, like so many American lives, was beginning again in the setting of self-consciousness and "self-culture" that was shaking the foundations of the new United States.

2

Ernest the Seeker

When Isaac Hecker arrived at Brook Farm in the cold New England January of 1843, he entered a utopian community that was an unusual mixture of school, church and reform movement. It was one expression of transcendentalism, itself a unique effort to remake the world, to begin again. That movement made an indelible imprint on the idealistic young baker. To understand that mark, it is necessary to get a sense of the movement as it had developed before Hecker's appearance at Brook Farm.

Transcendentalism in New England found its roots in the Unitarian rebellion against Puritan pessimism. The founders of Unitarianism built on earlier efforts to overcome Calvinist doctrines of human depravity, but they went much further, abandoning the Trinity and launching a search for moral perfection "such as cannot now be conceived." Gone were the days when one awaited the arbitrary gift of God's grace. Now, each person could find God "by effort, by reflection, by prayer, by resistance of the body, the senses and the outward world, by descending into [his or her] own mind, by listening to experience as it daily teaches that there is no true good which does not have its spring in the improvement of [humanity's] highest nature."

In its energetic youth, Unitarianism was a religious declaration of independence. As William Ellery Channing saw it, the new nation needed a new religion, or at least a new Christianity, "set free from unintelligible and irrational doctrines, and the uncouth and idolatrous forms and ceremonies which terror, superstition, priestcraft, and ambition have labored to identify with it." Emerging from the "darkness and corruption of the past," Christianity should have "but one purpose, the perfection of human nature, the elevation of men into nobler beings."[1]

The new emphasis on reasonable religion was very popular, yet few ministers of Channing's generation shared his view of democratic Christianity, even fewer his enthusiasm for social reform. But Channing's words, and the example of his personal warmth and idealism, awakened a radical spirit among the young that could not be easily contained. First, Unitarian moderates captured the key pulpits in Congregationalist Boston. Then, in the 1830s, the now Unitarian establishment was itself challenged by younger men who revered Channing but rejected his generation's confident rationalism in favor of romantic notions of intuition. They were soon called *transcendentalists*, a term derived from Immanuel Kant, whose thought filtered to New England through the French philosopher Victor Cousin and English writers and poets, especially Thomas Carlyle and Samuel Taylor Coleridge.

The radicals took literally Channing's contention that God was within, readily available, and anxious to perfect the human soul. Accordingly, they turned their back on the forms of religion, moving, as Channing's son put it, "from the idolatrous world of creeds and rituals to the temple of the Living God in the soul." Attacked as dreamers and mystics, the transcendentalists appealed for "religion of the heart" and denounced what Ralph Waldo Emerson called "the corpse cold Unitarianism of Harvard College and Brattle Street." Emerson, the most brilliant of the new generation, turned his back on the ministry and told a Harvard Divinity School audience to "go alone, refuse the good models, even those most sacred in the imagination of men, and dare to love God without mediator or veil." Yearning for God, "soul hunger," had long drawn New Englanders to look for God in the world around them, but a pervasive sense of their own sinfulness—and the consequent hiddenness of God —held them back. Emerson and his transcendentalist friends revived that hunger, now liberated from old worries about human pride and divine judgment. Union with God was possible.[2]

The development of transcendentalism can be seen in the life of George Ripley, the founder and guiding spirit of Brook Farm. Born in 1802 in Greenfield, Massachusetts, Ripley studied in Concord under his learned uncle, Ezra Ripley, then attended Harvard a few years behind his cousin Emerson. He arrived a quite conservative young man, but gradually was converted to liberal views, especially by his reading of Channing. In 1827 he married Sophia Dana and soon after was installed as pastor of a new church in Boston. At that time he saw himself as a Unitarian or in Channing's phrase, "a liberal Christian" but he was brought to challenge

Unitarian ideas by a controversy with Harvard theologian Andrews Norton over the miracles of Jesus.

Norton argued that Jesus' miracles were the foundation of Christian faith. Ripley disagreed. The truth of Christianity was demonstrated not by miracles but by the "correspondence" between the teachings of Jesus and the fundamental truths of human life known through what Emerson and Kant referred to as Reason, a basic intuitive power, present in every person. So the essence of religion was found in the inner life of spirit, not in doctrines, dogmas or empirical evidence. Ethical and religious conviction arose from within, from intense religious emotions and absolutely true theological doctrines, few in number but rooted in human experience. Christianity looked not to Jesus' miracles but to his humanity; Jesus differed from other men only in the clarity and force with which his religious "instinct" expressed itself.[3]

In 1836, Ripley helped found the Transcendentalist Club and announced the advent of the new philosophy:

> There is a class of persons, who desire a reform in prevailing philosophy of the day. These are called the Transcendentalists—because they believe in an order of truths which transcends the sphere of the external senses. . . . Hence they maintain that the truth of religion does not depend on tradition, nor on historical facts, but has an infallible witness in the soul. There is a light, they believe, which enlighteneth every man that cometh into the world; there is a faculty in all, the most degrading, the most ignorant, the most obscure, to perceive spiritual truth when distinctly presented; and the ultimate appeal on all moral questions, is not to a jury of scholars, a hierarchy of divines, or the prescriptions of the Creed, but to the commonsense of the human race.

Every person, literally, could intuit religious truths. Ordinary people, according to Ripley, had "a faith no less rational, no less enlightened, no less fervent, than that of the most profound antiquary, for they have the witness of their own hearts."[4]

This was democratic religion with a vengeance. The transcendentalists did not hesitate to pursue its logic to conclusions which would have seemed even more radical if those who propounded them were not so polite. Nevertheless, their views aroused the wrath of most Unitarians, to say nothing of the traditionalists who had long argued that liberal Christianity would lead to just such anarchy. Emerson referred to the struggle as one between the party of hope and the party of memory; Brownson described it as one between "the party of the hopeful and that of the fearful." For a brief moment it seemed that the hopeful were in command.[5]

By the time Hecker arrived at Brook Farm, however, the unity the transcendentalist group had achieved in the controversies of the thirties was fading. Emerson persisted in a radical individualism which made him sympathetic but aloof from reform movements. Ripley, in contrast, believed the time had come to put aside conventions and complete the democratic revolution. Reformers should demonstrate that individual values could be combined with democratic idealism. On an 1838 trip through New York State and the Midwest, he and his wife visited Shaker and Zoarite settlements, which stimulated their desire to create a community where this reconciliation could be achieved. Accordingly, Ripley proposed to the Transcendental Club that they construct a Utopian community.

Undismayed by their lukewarm response, Ripley raised ten thousand dollars and bought a farm in West Roxbury, to which he and Sophia moved in April 1841. The road leading to the farm wound through a rolling countryside dominated by two hills and bordered by a brook on one side and a dense pine forest on the other. A driveway led from the road to the base of one of the hills where the farmhouse was located, a two-story building they eventually christened the Hive. Along the slope between the brook and the Hive were terraced embankments planted with shrubs, flower beds, mulberry and spruce trees and a great lone elm that shaded the house. Across the street from the entrance to the farm, Ripley built another house he christened the Nest; later, houses were added on the second hill and just below it. By December most of the men and women who were to make the farm famous had arrived and settled into a pattern of life that continued for two years.[6]

Not all who came were unskilled teachers or literary people. Lewis Ryckman, the acquaintance of the Heckers, for example, was a cordwainer and had once been a fisherman. Bakers, carpenters and metal workers joined the intellectuals, most sons and daughters of Boston merchants. The work of the community centered around teaching in the community school, farming, working in the manufacturing shops, performing domestic tasks, maintaining the building and grounds and planning community recreation projects.

The young men helped in household tasks and the women took a full part in the life of the community. While performing household duties, the women wore short skirts with matching knickerbockers underneath; for leisure hours they changed to styles which were thought to be more conventional, but visitors were shocked by their long flowing hairdos, absurdly wide-brimmed hats, and adorning wreaths of vines, berries and flowers. The men almost always wore a costume developed by Ripley, a peasant tunic with a collar, hat, trousers and heavy farmer's boots. They also wore visored caps. Ripley adopted long hair and a beard and virtually every male followed suit, perhaps to demonstrate indifference to the demands of that clean-shaven era. Residents were allowed to hold any opinion whatsoever and arrangements were made for a free choice of jobs and a common wage for all. Ripley did not establish an entirely classless society, but he did establish one that was amazingly free of snobbery and in which there was a great deal of comradeship across varying social backgrounds.[7]

Isaac Hecker thus joined a community where the central questions of nineteenth-century American culture were actively engaged. At home he had been exposed to the Methodist quest for religious perfection, but in an unstructured way. He had experienced in the reform movement the language of evangelical democracy, which linked the Christian doctrine of the value of every human soul with the Jacksonian affirmation of the equality of all men. From Brownson he had learned something of religious philosophy, particularly the need to find some solid basis for personal religious experience. Yet, despite the variety of currents which touched his life, Hecker was to a remarkable degree the kind of open-minded, unprejudiced seeker after truth he later said he was. His formal education was extremely limited, his reading unsystematic, and his religious life undisciplined by any church affiliation. The dominant fact of his life was his own personal religious experience, a sudden, shocking encounter with what he took to be a spirit, at once frightening in its power and attractive in its promise. He was determined to remain faithful to that experience, to pursue the higher life to which he now felt called, but he had no clear idea of what that might be, no words with which to describe, and control, whatever was at work within.

The day Hecker moved in at Brook Farm, he wrote his mother, happily describing the setting: "A more pleasant situation could not be selected." The number in residence had now reached ninety. The Hive was the heart of community life, with a dining room, kitchen and sleeping quarters. Across the street from the farm entrance was a small house used as a school, with Marianne Ripley, George's niece, in charge. Hecker found a warm welcome. People were kind, he told his mother, especially Ryckman, "who would do anything for me with the greatest pleasure." A week later he had begun baking for the community. After baking he spent the rest of the day in his room. At night, there was recreation or entertainment. One night he attended a conversation with Bronson Alcott and his English friend Charles Lane, "one of the newnessites"; that evening there was also a singing class.[8]

Hecker's awkwardness was evident in those first days. He felt out of place, as his diary entries revealed:

> What judgment is formed of me in this community I know not but evidently I am not one of their spirits the tone of their speech to me is different Mr. Hecker is pronounced in tones different from the tones they address others. I don't know but that I will be unable to become one of the community.[9]

Such loneliness was understandable; what was remarkable was the degree of independence and determination Hecker showed throughout his stay at Brook Farm. Already he had questioned some of the ideas of his friend Brownson, one of the most powerful intellectuals of the day. So he was not likely to accept without question the advice of the residents of Brook Farm. Shortly after he arrived, William Henry Channing published in *The Dial* a brief short story, "Ernest the Seeker," about a sincere young romantic's search for truth and purity of life. Isaac's Brook Farm companions, impressed by his sweet disposition, evident sincerity and dedication to finding a truthful way to live his life soon bestowed the name on him. In one way, the comparison was misleading, for Channing's "seeker" was a pure romantic with few inner anchors to guide his search, while Hecker has a certain practicality, likely derived from the difficult economic circumstances of his youth. Moreover, he was completely convinced that his spiritual experience, awakened so suddenly a few months before, was a revelatory reality on the basis of which all options could be tested.

From the start the convictions that sprang from his experience led Hecker to resist ideas that did not meet his own instinctive sense of himself. After his busy boyhood, he had come to question the value of sheer activity, especially activity aimed solely at economic security, but he was by no means ready to abandon work altogether. "The Transcendentalist would say Thou art doing thy greatest work when thou doest not know that thou art consciously doing anything," he wrote. "To this I can only say I do not believe it." Quiet now, he felt that he was at a critical moment of his life, a period "just before positive action commences," although he was a bit afraid that his "ship may strike on a rock and be dashed to pieces."

Reviewing the experience of the previous nine months, Hecker felt bound by his dream and by its demand for submission. When he tried to resist it, he failed. He recalled how he had been unable to work at home as the spirit overpowered him. After his visit with Brownson, he came to the farm and began to improve until he again became "depressed and heavy in mind and body." He would have become ill if he had not changed his diet. He was desperately lonely, but he felt no regret, no desire for the churning of the spirit within to end. Unable to study, beset by feelings of unworthiness, he reached out more and more for Christian language to define his need and to name the force within: "Finally O Lord lead me to the Holy

Church which I am now seeking for by the aid I hope of Thy Holy Spirit."[10]

He regularly attempted to explain himself to his family. Unusually addressing both parents in a letter of February 22, for example, he described himself being led into a dark, uncertain future. "I feel that I am controlled," he wrote. "Formerly I could act upon intention but now I have no future to design." While his actions might "appear as designed," in fact they were "as unlooked for and unaccountable as it can be." Toward his parents he felt a sense of duty that was "a continued weight I cannot throw off." He asked them not to fret, but they could not have felt very comforted. Nor could his brother George when Isaac wrote a few days later describing the continued presence of "a dark irresistible influence which was upon me that led me away from home." When he struggled against it, "a spell comes over me."[11]

From the time he reached Brook Farm, Hecker began to study Christianity. More and more he referred to the spirit within as the Holy Spirit, and he regularly prayed that he might find a church. Brownson must have encouraged this interest, and his mother's Methodism undoubtedly provided a rough familiarity with basic Christian themes and perhaps a specifically Methodist concern to live fully under the influence of divine grace. The Brook Farmers themselves, for all their self-conscious rejection of dogmas, traditions and existing churches, were Christian to the core, deeply committed to the ethics of Jesus and in many cases to the God revealed in Jesus and the Spirit whose continuing presence they found confirmed by experience. Emerson, Ripley and more radical reformers like Alcott and Lane thought they were contending, not against Christianity, but for its soul.

The most controversial transcendentalist, Brownson, was now arguing strongly for a more systematic approach to the fundamental religious questions he and Emerson had raised but not answered. After spending a night at Brownson's so he could hear him preach, Hecker described to his mother Brownson's service. The congregation used Methodist hymn books while "the most scrupulous orthodox person might hear [his sermons] with pleasure." Brownson himself felt he would be better received by a Methodist audience than any other. Isaac then described a most untranscendentalist sermon in which Brownson used the scriptural reference to Christ as "a stumbling block to the Jews and foolishness to the Greeks" to attack those who denied the need for supernatural assistance, and those who admitted the need but rejected it when offered because it took an unexpected form. Brownson claimed it was a mockery to tell sinners, feeling the weight of sin, that they could save themselves. Rather, "Christ is the power of God unto salvation for those who believe in him." Hecker wrote favorably of this sermon to his mother, yet he seemed no more satisfied with such evangelical language than with the insistent optimism of the "newnessites."[12]

Despite his mother's Methodist faith and Brownson's Protestant style, Hecker was initially attracted to the Episcopal church, especially to the revival of ritual, authority and doctrine taking place in that Communion. He told his parents he was thinking about the *Tracts For The Times*, a series of papers advocating Catholic elements of the tradition produced by the Oxford movement led by John Henry Newman. Several weeks later he expressed pleasure that his brothers were reading them. He speculated that German theology, the Oxford writers in England and Brownson were simultaneously approaching a similar conclusion: the need for the church. Reflecting on this "providential" development, he suggested that it was "not absurd to contemplate the time when there will be but One Church, One Faith, One Baptism." Instead of being forced to give up any of their beliefs, the "scattered sects" would find them summarized in a larger church. Comparing Brownson to St. Paul ("I make the comparison with reverence"), Hecker noted that, once counted among the church's enemies, he was now battling in her defense.

Two weeks later Hecker received with pleasure the news that his brother John had decided to enter the Episcopal church. "Its History and its Doctrines present a better claim than any other church excepting perhaps the Roman Catholic with which it may assert equal claims for aught I know," he wrote. Still, at this point Isaac could not find his own answer. Among the Anglicans there was corruption and a lack of humility, he thought, while Protestants had missionary zeal, but at the expense of "consistency and good logic." Catholicism offered little more than the catechism of Trent, holy cards and the intervention of Mary. He hoped wistfully for the appearance of a truly "Catholic" church, which would settle all disputes on the basis of "The Bible, Tradition and the light of the Church."[13] Like Joseph Campbell, Joseph Smith, William Miller and many other of his contemporaries, Hecker could not find in the many churches an authentic expression of Christianity. So he grounded himself in his own experience of God's presence and drew upon commonly accepted Christian symbols to name that experience. Like Brownson, he concluded that he needed a Church, but to select any one church would cheapen his experience, compromise the Gospel, and perpetuate the scandalous divisions within what should be the body of Christ.

In late March Isaac made a brief visit home. On the way back he stopped once again to visit Brownson, who was studying "history and other things related to the Church." His friend showed a "greater affinity towards the Catholic Church than before" but he still was determined to avoid favor to "any sect." Perhaps inspired by Brownson's growing interest in Catholicism, Hecker visited a Roman Catholic church during Easter services in April. He found the physical setting "very impressively affecting," describing it in detail in his diary:

> The altar piece was Christ rising from the tomb this was the subject matter of the priests sermon. In the middle of the sermon the priest pointed to the altar piece, making the experience doubly affecting. . . . There may be objections of having Paintings and sculpture in the church but I confess that I never enter a place where there is either but I feel an awe an invisible influence which strikes me mute. . . . I stand dumb speechless a magical atmosphere that runs through my whole being scarcely daring to lift up my eyes for fear of being struck senseless, a perfect stillness comes over my soul and it is as if I were soaring on the bosom of clouds.

Writing to his family a few weeks later, he told them of the visit: "I was very much impressed with the services of the Catholic church which [I] attended [Easter] morning. Such joyful music, the spring like adornments, the imposing ceremonies, the unreserved devotion of the people, and in the midst of the priest's sermon he pointed to the altar piece of Christ bursting the tomb having a most sudden effect that after I came home I felt that it was good that I had been there." In this same letter he noted that Brownson was reading the Oxford *Tracts* and the *Dublin Review*, "which advocated the Catholic church." As for himself, the spring made him feel that "God is love," that he should lead a life of love and ask himself "whether I am now doing that which leads to this heavenly result."[14]

By April 1843, a full year before his entry into the Roman Catholic Church, Hecker had concluded that he needed a church, that the Protestant churches, partial and incomplete, could not satisfy his needs, and that the whole, truly "Catholic" church, full and complete, was the answer. On April 24 he wrote:

> The Catholic Church alone seems to satisfy my wants my faith life soul. . . . I may be laboring under a delusion . . . Yet my soul is Catholic and that faith answers responds to my soul in its religious aspirations and its longings I have not wished to make myself Catholic but it answers to the wants of my soul it answers on all sides.[15]

Yet, convinced as he may have been, he could not submit to "that which does not engage my whole being." He feared that entry into a church would cut him off from the inner experience of spirit, and thus from what had become for him life itself. "The Church is not to me the great object of life," he wrote. "Is it not best for me to live my own nature than attempt to mold it, like some object?" But he then reflected that the Christian church, formerly "Petrine" and "Pauline," was becoming more "love embracing, John like."[16]

In early May he again reported that Brownson intended "to preach the Catholic doctrines and administer the sacraments," but not become a Catholic. Brownson hoped "that by simultaneously proclaiming the Catholic faith and repudiating the attempt to build up a church," he might persuade Protestants in time to become Catholic in disposition, making Christian unity possible without submission or sacrifice. Hecker found that position "unsatisfactory" and Brownson's arguments "chimerical and illusive." If the Roman church is the true church, or even the church nearest to the true church, Hecker believed, there was a positive obligation to join it. As for himself, he was still uncertain, despite his earlier expression of Catholic sentiments. He "bought a few Catholic books in Boston which treat upon the Anglican claims to Catholicity," he told his brothers, but at the moment he knew only that he would "never join a Protestant Church."[17]

The church question remained unresolved, but Hecker was now a convinced Christian. While his Brook Farm acquaintances were breaking out of their religious backgrounds to pursue the spirit beyond the church, Hecker had been touched by the spirit with no previous foundation in church. Nevertheless, he gradually began to frame his reflections in Christian language, looking to Christ for guidance. In the midst of some of the nation's best-known intellectuals, intending to study, he heard disparagement of academic bookish knowledge in favor of a direct experience of truth. He now framed a similar attitude in Christian language:

> Christ is the foundation of all useful practical knowledge.... Should we do or attempt any thing from any other motive than a Christian one? Does not science advance by the motives Christianity inspires.... It is only through Christ we can see the Love and Goodness and Wisdom of God.... Christ is an active meditator who ... gives us the power to see by becoming one with him.[18]

He now felt more comfortable at the farm. When he returned from the brief trip home, his pleasure contrasted with his awkwardness only a few weeks earlier. "I was met at the door with numbers of the good people here," he reported to his family. "From all sides they met me with such cordiality and friendship that I felt like weeping. I cannot see how they can be so kind toward me." He now hoped that "the life I have been led to live these few months back may prove to the advantage of us all in the end."

Nevertheless, the inner struggle continued. Hecker filled his diary through April and May with a record of spiritual turmoil. One theme was unity, as the lonely seeker, still apart from others, in his inner life envisioned the unity of all things. Caught up for a time by romantic images of nature, Isaac echoed Emerson's mystical sense of communion with the earth. His spiritual yearning became an almost pantheistic emphasis on the unity of human beings and nature, open to and awaiting God's liberating action. But quiet moments in the fields could not resolve his intense inner conflicts. One night, "enticed by evil desires," he awoke conscious of someone protecting him. He tried to speak, but it was gone. The next night brought spirits he referred to as "advisers" and "impressive instructors," who were "as actual, nay more so, than my present activity." "When my natural strength is not strong enough," he wrote, "I find there comes foreign aid to my assistance," bringing messages warning against "false activity and its consequences" and promising God's help. Not all the spirits were benign. In May he awoke one night to see "a red fiery glaring eyed copper coloured singular dressed fiend." Reaching out to grapple with it, he awoke in bed with his arms outstretched. The next night he again woke suddenly, saying that the world was like a flower: "He who attempts to pick it pricks his finger."[19]

Despite the friendly, casual mood at Brook Farm, there was a certain formalism and coldness that seemed to reveal an absence of fire in the heart. The tolerant good nature of the residents, their respect for individuality and patience with eccentricity were good, but somehow those very virtues left each one alone, separate. Dimly Hecker yearned for a fuller, more complete union with all men and women. This had led him to respond positively to Brownson's talk of "communion," but left him discontented when he could not find that intimate union with others in family, friends, or a Brook Farm. "I meet with no one around me," he wrote. "I would that I could feel that some one lived in the same world that I now do. There is something cloudy that separates us. I cannot speak of my real being to them. There is no recognition between us."

He was not yet sure how to live in obedience to the spirit within, but he was sure there was another life available than the conventional, not by human initiative alone but by divine gift. He would not live as a "prudent man," benevolent but "existing upon the cause of the misery of his brethren." Such a man worships God "in his thoughts" but "practically denies him in his daily labor." Instead, Isaac determined to live as an "obedient one," always alive to "the presence of God." For such a person, "it is God in him who wills to think, to feel, to do." This unity of man with nature, with himself and with God would be restored when each person responded directly to the voice of God. But Isaac was not yet sure how to hear that voice or live in such obedience.[20]

Hecker's absorption in the inner life was complicated by the vocational questions for, unlike his upper class friends at Brook Farm, he needed work to do. The indecision, even paralysis, caused by his inner anxieties intensified whenever he began to move toward home, or toward action, leaving him feeling isolated, alone, misunderstood, and uncertain, unable to grasp any of the alternatives pressing upon him. So far, his only answer had been study.

After his return from New York, Hecker began to read more seriously. He was learning French and Latin, reading the Bible, Schlegel, Mohler, Kant, and books on the Anglican claims. He also found pleasure in the spiritual life, but both study and meditation left him feeling guilty for living "without an object." He was not baking any longer, as it had reduced his charge by only two dollars a week, so he depended on his family. In one warm letter to his mother, he expressed his indebtedness and promised to repay her "by living the way you wish."[21]

As the New England winter gave way to a warm spring, his loneliness eased a bit. He was pleased that the Brook Farm residents, men and women of education and talent, drawn from the "higher ranks of society," were now better able to understand him and respond to his feelings. Several women were attracted to him and he enjoyed their attention. The feelings stirred by Almira Barlow were particularly intense. She was a daring woman, separated from her husband and generally regarded as a flirt. She seemed fascinated by the awkward young man from New York, and he was flattered. On an afternoon walk, accompanied by "a soul susceptible of love and beauty," his "heart filled with love," and he "felt guilty of enjoyment." Three days later Almira came to his room in the afternoon and they had "a conversation, a communion." Later, Isaac, "full overflowing with Love Life," began to describe the episode in his diary, thought better of it, and scratched her name from the page. It was perhaps only coincidental that two weeks later the directors of the community decided to turn her quarters in the Hive, where Hecker shared a room with Charles Dana, into a parlor, forcing her to move to another building.[22]

Hecker also became close to Ida Russell, the Swedish-born daughter of an American diplomat, and to young Ora Gannett, who had left the community before Hecker's arrival but visited regularly. Ora formed a strong attachment to Hecker; her later letters to him were filled with romantic pledges of love and friendship. Hecker also enjoyed talking with

Ripley; the friendship they formed was life-long, strengthened rather than harmed by the fact that Sophia Ripley eventually followed Hecker and Brownson into the Catholic church. Among the younger men, Hecker became friendly with Dana, a serious young Harvard graduate who served as Ripley's assistant, and with the Curtis brothers, George and Burrill, sons of the president of the New York Bank of Commerce. All these young people pursued romantic dreams of unsullied idealism. The yearning for intimacy was so powerful, so pure, that it often prevented response to the care of real imperfect companions. Isaac reported to his family toward the end of May that he felt "a continued aspiration to sacrifice every connexion which brings me down to a life which checks or hinders my progress." One could not live either by bread or spirit alone, he admitted, but the question was "to what extent we can connect the actual to the spiritual and live." Spirit came first, and it led to "martyrdom and eternal life," the actual alone led to death.[23]

He longed for someone to "commune with," but drew back when anyone drew too close. Instead, he waited for "something to happen," believing that there were "spiritual laws" beneath events which, "if rightly believed and trusted lead to the goal of eternal life, harmony of being, and union with God. So I accept being led here."[24]

But he could not wait forever. Eventually he would have to choose a life's work. The values of hard work and self-discipline were an important part of the working-class community in which he had been raised. The Hecker brothers, Isaac among them, had been forced at a young age to leave school, to begin a business that depended on their own exertions, and to struggle through the depressions that punctuated the period. For the youngest to leave home with no clear end in view, no visible means of support, and no plans to become self-supporting, must have been very difficult for him and irritating to his hard-working brothers. Their love and concern was, therefore, quite remarkable; it must have intensified Isaac's impatience to find some direction for his life, at least leading to some form of work that would enable him to become financially independent of his family. Yet his spiritual experience had distanced him from the life around him. He read but did not really study, and he found the prospect of money making and ordinary employment distasteful, not because he was lazy or self-indulgent, surely, but because he was drawn to a higher life opened up by the spirit within and confirmed by his associates at Brook Farm.

At the end of May, Hecker cried out in his diary that he simply could not do the work normally done in the world.

> This is not work to me, it is death, it is no work, nay worse, it is sin, hence damnation and I am not ready to go to hell yet, friend; I

would rather beat my head against the wall, die in the battle, than accept plastically, indolently the slow, lingering annihilation of my soul. Accept things as they are! But I cannot. . . . Your work gives *me* no activity, no action. I am not *in* the work you set before me. It is dead, lifeless work for me, and to starve if I must is better than to do the profane, the sacrilegious labor you place before me. . . . I want God's living work to do. My labor must be a sermon.

The need to make choices, the inability to do so, the powerful passions stirring within, made him feel at times that he was "living in madness." He saw himself as both a religious person and a rationalist; he found the latter often soulless, but he was convinced that reason led directly to the negation of all things, the affirmation of one's own being and, once again, to God. Most of all, he now clearly acknowledged himself a Christian, finding in Christ the "brightest example of manhood." He was still thinking about the church, because it seemed the only available "channel" to God. Through it, "Christ's life has been continued through the past into this our time." Philosophers claimed to have achieved immediate communion with God, without the church, but history was against their case. Those "who rail against the Church? What are they?" Isaac asked. "Are they better than the church? That is the apparent assumption. . . . Do they have a superior life of disinterestedness and love than the church? Do they give up pleasures of wife and domestic bliss? No such sacrifice as this does their cause inspire."[25]

Still, it was one thing to value the church, another to choose a church for oneself. Isaac told John that he could accept neither Roman exclusiveness toward the Anglican church nor the Anglican hostility to Rome. The bigotry and fanaticism of the "strict orthodox sects" toward both put them out of the question. All had a "tendency of narrowing and hampering my sympathies in a more or less degree." So, it was his duty to labor to "do away with the sectarian tendency," but how could he do that? Church people said "join a sect and work within," but by joining, one became a sectarian.

By mid-June, the young seeker's anxieties reached a critical point. On June 12 he lamented he had found nothing to answer the void in his soul. Yearning for release from the agonies of indecision, he filled his diary with words of near despair:

At times I feel an impulse to cry out what wouldst thou have me to do. What shall I do. I would shout up in the empty vault of heaven ha ha why plaguest thou me so Great Heaven what wouldst though have me to do. Give me an answer unless thou wouldst have me consumed by inward fire drying up the living liquid of life. Would thou have me to give up all I have I have no dreams to realize I want nothing have nothing and am willing to die in any way starve give up now yes even now yes come now this moment I'd embrace thee death come come what ties I have are few those can be cut with a grand ha ha the world is nothing to me what care I if I go what is around may be beautiful to others but to me it is not so ha ha what care I if I go come death come now I have nothing here that binds me so humanly let us laugh and go Resign thyself to be nothing I shut up my hook ha ha ha ha[26]

By this time Hecker was thinking of leaving Brook Farm. He was stirred by a passage in Thomas Carlyle's *Past and Present*: "To make some little nook of God's creation a little fruitfuller, better, more worthy of God; to make some human hearts a little wiser, manfuller, happier, more blessed, less accursed! It is work for a God." In these words Hecker felt a prophecy; they seemed "an echo of my own soul." This was what he had left home, business, friends and prospective wealth to find. It required at the very least, sacrifice he had not found at Brook Farm. Life there was "not self-denying sacrificing enough for me, it is too much like society," he wrote. "It is not based upon the universal-love-principal. It is not Christ like enough for me." He determined to talk with Ripley and tell him his reasons for leaving: "I want to sacrifice more to live more for others than they do here."[27]

On June 18 Isaac told his family he was going to visit Fruitlands, the new community established at Harvard by Bronson Alcott and Charles Lane, those "newnessites" who had appeared on one of Hecker's first nights at the Farm. The next day he noted in his diary that he would visit them in order to "feel what sort of men they are," but he already believed that "my spirit leads me there." When he returned, he wrote his family that the farm was "sequestered, still, lonely from other places but not from heaven above or the beautiful earth beneath and scenery around it." There was one house on ninety acres of land. Lane had purchased the place but not taken a deed, as they renounced all property. They lived simply, avoided any flesh meat or food produced by animals, worked as their conscience led them, and searched for a more holy life. He planned to join them, noting the contrast with Brook Farm, where "their life is not deep holy self-denying." He promised to talk with George, who was to come for a visit the following week, before making a final decision.[28]

The move would again be temporary; eventually he would have to decide whether to go home. A week before his visit to Fruitlands he asked his brothers for their advice, hoping they could grow closer. "Our life in this state is very short," he remarked, "why should we not be more to each other . . . know, sympathize and love more intimately?" On June 24, when he was considering Fruitlands, he noted that the family might yet provide "the home my spirit is looking for," if "the life at home will be, or can be, lovingly, willingly, cooperatively, changed to a higher, a more self-sacrificing self-denying inwardly life." George arrived for a week's visit at the end of the month. He convinced Isaac that he and John were sincerely trying to live a more spiritual life and would try to adjust things at home so Isaac could return.

Again on July 7 Isaac wrote his brothers to explore his return. He asked them to examine their aims in life: what were they living for and what were they doing to attain that objective? If their aims were similar to his own, they sprang from a similar spirit and there was a basis for reunion, for building their "natural brotherhood' into a "spiritual brotherhood." Much had happened to develop the seeds which were in his mind when he left home; he expected that much had happened to them as well. So he asked them to answer frankly, that they might better understand each other. "We should sacrifice all that hinders us from the divine calling of the spirit," he wrote.

> If you desire to continue the way of life you have and do now lead be plain frank and so express yourselves explicitly. If not and you have any desire or intentions in your minds to alter or make a radical change in your external circumstances for a higher and better mode of life, be equally open and let me know all your thoughts and aspirations which are struggling for expression.

He ended by assuring them that it was his strong desire that they be united again. Before he mailed this letter, he received one from John filled with concern about the character of Alcott and the Fruitlands' community. John's concern was aroused by Brownson, who had little respect for Alcott. Isaac added a reassuring PS:

> Your fears and low opinion of the people I am now with I am happy to say [are] totally wholly erroneous. They are the most self-denying Christ like in spirit than any other people I ever met with. OAB gave a very wrong statement of Alcott. They are deeply religious and pious. They will be of very great benefit to me in that true spirit which you would wish me to have.

On the 11th he wrote again, asking for money to settle his accounts at Brook Farm and announcing that he would be at Fruitlands at least two weeks. Concerned as always about money, he thanked them for their help, "especially in the present state of business," and expressed his hope he might one day be able to help them as they were now helping him.[29]

Fruitlands was located in Harvard, almost forty miles to the west of Brook Farm. The community's spiritual leader Bronson Alcott was born of poor parents in Connecticut. He had left home at 17 to live as a "Yankee Pedlar" in the South, returning to teach school, first in Cheshire, Connecticut, then at the famous Temple School in Boston. There Alcott's experimental methods succeeded with the children, but his religious views and frank discussions of childbirth upset the parents. With the help of Emerson, Alcott went off to England, where he found disciples, including Charles Lane, who joined him on the return voyage with the intention of establishing a "new Eden in New England." Alcott was the great idealist of the age. He told Hecker's friend, Almira Barlow, that only "providential love" could bring happiness. Favorable external circumstances, such as those at Brook Farm, failed to touch the need for deep personal commitment and "the surrender of all individual and selfish gratifications."

He and Lane found Brook Farm too worldly, too relaxed, too filled with leisurely discussion. After one visit Lane lamented the spectacle of "80 or 90 persons playing away their youth and daytime in a miserable, joyous and frivolous manner." A strict vegetarian, Lane was particularly depressed by the "prominent position" occupied by the animals. Their new community in contrast, would emphasize hard work, simple living and good manners, and perhaps change the world. As Alcott told Mrs. Barlow, "we are not without hope that providence will use us progressively for beneficial effects and the restoration of the highest life on earth."[30]

Isaac Hecker was ready for a trial of such asceticism. He had fasted and experimented with diet since leaving home. In early July he wrote that he would move to Fruitlands to work, simplify his dress, and acquire lessons in "patient perseverance." He admitted he would miss Brook Farm, with its "refined amusements, cultivated persons and one whom I have not spoken of, one whom it is to me too much to speak of, one who would give up all for me." But by now his own inclinations corresponded at least in part with Alcott's. Hecker correctly analyzed the differences between the two communities. Ripley hoped to organize work, family life and recreation in such a way as to draw forth the highest qualities of men and women. Alcott and Lane argued that "a new race of persons" was needed; they would then "project institutions and initiate conditions altogether original." In short, as Hecker put it, Ripley would change people by changing conditions; Alcott would change conditions by changing people.[31]

Fruitlands was even more beautiful than Brook Farm. Indeed, it occupied one of the most attractive sites in New England, a farm of large meadows and woods with Mount Manadnock in view to the north and Mount Wachusett to the west. Hecker was welcomed on July 11 as "the first of all the recruits" for the "new Eden." He entered enthusiastically into the routine, working in the fields and joining the long conversations which took place periodically throughout each day. The day after his arrival, for example, they discussed the "Highest Aim" in life, which Hecker named "Harmonic Being." The next day they looked at obstacles to the realization of that aim, and Hecker said: "Doubt whether the light is light, not the want of will to follow, or the sight to see."

Hecker told his family that Fruitlands was "a place of self-denial, labor and aspiration after a holy life." When they put the first load of hay in the barn, Lane called for a period of silence for "holy thoughts at this first fruit." The basis of life was "Christ like," as the residents hoped "to purify the soul and body by the discipline of restraint," which seemed to Isaac a way "of bringing out and fixing that which has led me of late." Life at Fruitlands was more demanding than at Brook Farm; the self-centeredness of the latter contrasted with the emphasis on discipline, mutuality and love in the new community:

> Instead of "act out thyself" it is "deny thyself." Instead of liberty it is mutual dependence. Instead of the doctrine of let alone it is help each other. Instead of tolerance it is love. It is positive, not negative.[32]

Still, he retained his critical distance. Hecker admired "the strength of self-denial" in Alcott and the "unselfishness of Mr. Lane in money matters." In these things he would "sit at their feet that I might become as they are." "They will be a great deal to me," he wrote within a week of his arrival, but they would not "be what I am looking for." Hecker set a high standard and Lane and Alcott fell short. They "are too near to me," Hecker wrote. "They are not high enough to awake in me a sense of their high superiority which would keep me here to be bettered, to be elevated." Most important, they did not understand him, and he remained determined to be himself. He prayed to God to strengthen his resolution: "Let me not waver, and continue my life." Perhaps most important, Hecker rebelled at Alcott's impractical musings. Ten days after he arrived, Hecker was asked by Alcott what he thought were the community's problems. Isaac responded with characteristic honesty:

> I told him frankly 1. His want of frankness. 2. His disposition to separateness rather than win co-operators to the aims of his own mind. 3. His family who prevent his immediate plans of reformation. 4. The place has very little fruit on it, which it was and is their desire be the principal part of their diet. 5. I feared they had too decided a tendency to literature, to writing, for the success and immediate prosperity of their object.[33]

Sensing Alcott's disappointment, Hecker left the community soon after this conversation. Harsh and straightforward as his criticism was, Hecker felt no bitterness but only a peculiar blend of aloofness and affection which marked many of his relationships. Hecker had the ability to see the shortcomings of people, most especially the gaps between their words and their actions; at the same time he almost always felt genuine respect of the people with whom he disagreed:

> This morning I depart from Fruitlands. I have learnt much since I have come here. I have come in contact with some of the most prominent men of this school, the spiritualist-mystics. I feel that I could not get much more from them if I should stay any longer, They did not appear to me to be mystical nor so highly spiritual. But enough; I depart, perhaps not to return again.
>
> Farewell Fruitlands, birds, trees, hills, mountains, railways! Farewell, ye Inhabitants, Alcott, Lane, Barhama, Bower, Mrs. Alcott and All the Children. May Providence be in and with you.[34]

On the eve of leaving Fruitlands, Hecker seemed weary of community and even more alone than when he first arrived in New England. Resigned to a life "separate from those around me, one obedient to the spirit," he still did not know where the spirit was leading him.

Hecker's original religious experience had awakened a vision of a higher and better life. Among the romantic spirits of Brook Farm and Fruitlands his desire for that more challenging life was affirmed, but the romantic ideal intensified his sense of isolation. Hecker was not alone, surely, in sampling, then rejecting the dilettantish life of Brook Farm and the dreamy utopianism of Fruitlands. Unlike most other residents, he had come from relative poverty, he had already a considerable working life for a man of his age, and yet he had the native intelligence and intellectual independence to participate in the conversations with considerable insight. For one like himself, the impracticality was evident, but so was the idealism. The communities had not met his "wants," so it was his "duty to return" to New York and "let come what will come." Yet it was sad, for he knew that there was indeed more to life than what was available at home. It was unfortunate that the best of men and women lived so little, Hecker mused. Perhaps not three years out of the allotted seventy did a person really live "in the highest sense." Few lived even "an hour of the divine life daily": indeed, "many are there that do not even know what it is." People were not aware of their "godlike capacities." Though they knew it not, their destiny was in their own power to determine; this was the most exciting, and the most frustrating, discovery that Hecker had made:

> Man, thou hast thy creation in thy own hands. . . . He is a creator, A God in God. Every man I meet is an unconscious prophecy to me. I would awaken him to the wonder of his being. . . . Hence Christ said "Greater works than I do shall ye do" Who is a better authority than He who saw all that is in man?

Within himself Hecker sensed a Spirit now seen as the spirit of God, alive in every person. "Every human being strikes me as a wonderful becoming," Hecker wrote in his diary. It was "as if a God was struggling for birth in him. He is an imprisoned God. Like the young bird, fearful of venturing to fly, man appears to me not as a body but as a spirit-being, unconsciously giving utterance to God."[35]

As his own experience of working-class life in New York connected with the romantic idealism of New England, Hecker developed a powerful democratic vision. He saw in the awakenings around him the spirit of God at work; he caught a glimpse of the worth, dignity and possibility of every human being. Like many another questing spirit of his time, Hecker had concluded that personal conversion could unlock the power of God's spirit in the human soul. Under the influence of his transcendentalist friends, Hecker was convinced of the universal presence of "divine prophetic instincts implanted in the human soul." These instincts and aspirations, for union with God most especially, "will be realized as sure as there is a God above who inspires them," he believed. Fulfillment of these hopes, that "this world must become heaven," was the destiny of man.

Yet Hecker's desire for a work to do in the world set limits to his reliance on inspiration. He was a person whose bonds to family, community and nation were real and inescapable:

> I have been much impressed of late with the great effect the nation and Family progenitors have on the character of their

offspring. . . . Man is in much greater degree the creature of the past than he gives himself credit for. He reproduces daily the sentiments and thoughts of the dim and almost obscure before. There are certain ideas and aspirations that have not had their fulfillment but which run through all men from the beginning until now and are continually reproduced. There is a unity of Race called Humanity, one of place called Nationality, one of birth called Kindred, and one of Affinity called Love and Friendship. By all these relations we are greatly influenced. They all make a mark upon the Man.[36]

These were unusual reflections for one who had been immersed in transcendentalism, with its radical individualism and sense of separation from the past. Hecker drew these ideas from the idealism so much a part of the current philosophy, and he gave them an historic twist undoubtedly influenced by Brownson's contemporaneous exploration of the historical arguments regarding Christianity. For Hecker, they expressed a strong but still undefined yearning to be connected to real life, to find a vocation which would ground and enlarge the spiritual life while contributing to the fulfillment of the promise of the future so evident around him. But before he could find that vocation, he had to resolve the conflicts in his own mind and heart.

Personally, he still felt "wholly lost in the sea of the spirit, wholly lost in God." His soul would "fly to heaven" if not held back by the body. Anchored in reality, respectful, even reverential, toward the past, Hecker still believed that the way to God and to truth lay within.

Man should not think, feel, or act unless he is inspired to do so. Why is it that we cannot give the mind free play and let it utter itself on any topic it may be inspired to speak upon. . . . If men would act from the present inspiration of their souls, they would know much more than by reading or speculating.[37]

Hecker moved at times toward a deeper understanding of the inescapable historicity of all men and women, an insight which might have modified his and his contemporaries' feeling that world history rested on their personal decisions, but he left the thought hanging. Instead, he continued to struggle with the conflict between his need to surrender to the spirit and his equally pressing need to give some direction to this life. The issue, more sharply defined than ever, was even further from resolution than when he had arrived at Brook Farm.

On July 29, 1843, Isaac received a letter in which John said that "he felt at times the necessity of changing our circumstances and that he [was] willing to do all that can be done." Isaac responded affectionately. Since leaving home, he had become more aware of the profound meaning of family life; together they should strive to remove all the barriers, such as "keeping separate individual accounts," that prevented them from achieving "this union of life, this accord and harmony of being." "Let us set out to make our family fulfill this high ideal," he concluded.[38]

Yet he delayed a decision to return, for it must be "unwillful." "My spirit is daily drawing closer and closer toward home," he told his brothers. "It is most probable you will see me at home within two or in the highest three weeks and as much sooner as possible." However the same day he wrote these words, he described his state of mind and spirit in a way that suggested the return home would be a less than satisfactory conclusion to his spiritual quest.

He stayed at Brook Farm for a few weeks, eating little, keeping to himself. He was still trying to overcome the self, to be more like Christ and achieve union with God, as he told Charles Dana. The effort to "purify and refine" his life prepared him for death but also for the "transfiguration" of the body which would open the soul to "some agent acting within." The soul was sensitive to sense impressions, "a plate on which the senses daguerreotype indelibly the patterns of the outward world," so he should try always to be surrounded by things of beauty which would elevate the spirit. Because such a higher order had been present at Brook Farm, he had "improved and refined his being" and would return home "quite different" from when he had left.[39]

There was something more. Ripley, unlike Alcott, had established his utopia as an association rather than a community. He respected the individuality of each person who came, created space for those who would share in the work and those who would not. He trusted the maturity and good will of the residents, and for a time it worked, with the young men serving table, the men assisting the women with the washing and cooking. Conventional barriers did come down and the result was not chaos but a rough comradeship whose memory stayed with many of the residents for the rest of their lives. George Bradford, Hecker's sometime teacher, recalled the impact of the experience in terms that may well reflect Hecker's experience, for the qualities he mentions were Hecker's as well, later distinguishing him in the narrow, defensive world of nineteenth-century Catholicism. The experience, Bradford wrote, "had no small influence in teaching more impressively the relation of universal brotherhood and the ties that bind all to all, a deeper feeling of the rights and claims of others, and so, in diffusing, enlarging, deepening and giving emphasis to the growing spirit of true democracy.[40]

Finally, transcendentalism was a religious movement. While many of its leaders were philosophers, some given to very abstract speculation, others, like Ripley, were dedicated to reform; the heart of the movement evident in Emerson's poetry and Alcott's journals was a passionate desire for union with God. In the inner life of the soul, and in nature, God was present, available and receptive to human searching. Communion was possible. So the transcendentalists were able to confirm the validity of Hecker's experience, to offer sympathy and encouragement in his spiritual quest, and to remove obstacles to his examination of all religious options, including the Catholic.[41] The Brook Farm and Fruitlands communities strengthened Hecker's conviction that experience, not philosophy, provided the criterion by which alternatives should be measured and decisions made. The immediacy of God's presence and the priority of Spirit were transcendentalist themes that would never be erased from Hecker's life.

More personally, in the romantic spirit of the day, the young residents of Brook Farm were at ease with their feelings, indulging them to the extent of an often extreme sentimentality. It is doubtful that Hecker, if he had remained in the hard working, still quite German environment of his family, would have been able to express, much less become comfortable with, the feelings churning within him. Despite his family's loving indulgence, they would eventually have forced these feelings into his mother's Methodist channels or become impatient with them, and Hecker would never have been able to focus on them so directly and consciously as he was able to do at Brook Farm. The relatively untutored young baker had arrived at Brook Farm in the dead of winter, sponsored by the stormy, controversial and not very beloved Brownson, yet the residents had welcomed him, made no obvious demands, respected his independence, tolerated his silences, perhaps finding in "Ernest the Seeker" confirmation of their Emersonian hopes for the American people. For Isaac it had been a remarkable experience, for which he was very grateful. For the rest of his life he saw the United States through the lens of the New England experience, and it led him to believe that there was indeed a "special class" of Americans, noble minded and pure hearted, ready to devote themselves to truth and follow the spirit where it led. Years later he wrote that Brook Farm was "the greatest, noblest, bravest dream of New England. Nothing greater has been produced. No greater sacrifice has been made for humanity than the movement Brook Farm embodied." The community was "the realization of the best dreams these men had of Christianity." As he wrote in his diary the night before his departure, warmth and gratitude swelled within him:

> It is with no little emotion that I leave. Since I have been here I have become acquainted with some of the best minds in New

> England. Much very much has my character grown . . . many of my dreams and earnest aspirations have been met here. I do not ever anticipate such society and refined amusements again. . . . Alas I know not what to say my heart has such a strong attachment to these people and this spot. Where shall I be led. I return home like returning to a new world not knowing where I am alas what shall I say my future is dark but with a purpose in it I feel. Here I sit with pen in hand, book lying on the table by which I am sitting with a light tunic on and a drab velvet skull cap made with the hands of one who has come nearer to my heart than any other human being I have ever become acquainted with, and whose nearness I will feel most when I have left this place. Will I be drawn in the future to any of the persons I have met here. What purpose my destiny is educating me for I know not perhaps these are the last words I ever shall write at Brook Farm my heart is grateful inexpressibly grateful to the originator of this place Rev George Ripley, How much have I gained from his labor Oh may I be able to manifest my gratitude to him in a way which will satisfy my heart. To these I dare say friend Ripley my heart is grateful to thee from the very source of its life May heaven lead thee.[42]

The seeker was headed home, still uncertain. "Who is Isaac Hecker?" he had asked in his diary a month earlier. "If this world is not a mystery, and all things that are therein, then what is mysterious?"[43]

3

Searching for the Church

At Brook Farm, in surprise and anguish, Isaac Hecker exclaimed: "I am a mystic." He went there seeking understanding of the profound spiritual experience that had disrupted his life; he found much that strengthened him, but he did not find the answer. At home, the search continued. By now, there was a rhythm to it all: the absolute certainty of the initial experience, followed by twin impulses, one toward stillness and interior peace, the other toward action. When Hecker worked, he yearned for stillness; when he stopped and prayed, he yearned for a purpose to pursue in the world.

Nevertheless, when he arrived in New York Isaac seemed calm. John told Brownson that Isaac was working at the bakery again and, though too much "influenced by the transcendentalists," he would get over it. John was involved in local efforts to secure the 1844 presidential nomination for John C. Calhoun, and Isaac joined in. He asked Brownson to send an address for a mass meeting and later extended his friend an invitation from Calhoun supporters to edit a journal in New York. Brownson, interested at first, backed away. He now shared John's misgivings about the transcendentalist influence and was glad Isaac was home. "These communities are all humbugs," he wrote his young friend. "We must rehabilitate the Church and work under its influence."[1]

John and Brownson had reason to worry, for Isaac still turned inward and sought out the company of like-minded men. Dr. John W. Vethake, a Swedenborgian, became a friend, as did Edward Palmer, a "radical transcendentalist" Hecker professed to "love ... very much." In mid-

September Lane and Alcott spent five days at the Heckers' while visiting the city. Later Georgiana Bruce from the farm stayed for a month. Hecker visited with William Henry Channing, but found his preaching confused, even contradictory. Channing is "Catholic in heart, Protestant in head," he reported to Brownson. Despite such company, Isaac was lonely. Without bitterness, he classified friends and family along with work as distractions from the life of the spirit. A persistent attraction to "quietism" made things around him seem like shadows in a dream, "foreign." He saw himself as "a stranger in the midst of men." He was oversensitive to noise and "astringent tones," repulsed by the touch of others. He wanted "stillness, perfect voicelessness" and a "beautiful sweetness of heart." While others were busy until the end of life and then turned to God, he would "turn to him in youth and live heaven here." Hecker wanted to cease incessant activity, even to stop writing in the diary "because this is foolish." Rather than go to church to hear a preacher, he "would *be* at home what others go to hear."

Hecker's active dream life continued. One night, in November, he felt the presence of his grandfather. Another night it was Mrs. Ripley. Once, stirred while listening to a sermon, he imagined Christ preaching to the spirits. He was left with "profuse sweats" and "violent, nervous shocks." When still, an "unearthly feeling" returned: "By collecting its scattered rays" it would "burn in my soul so deeply, bringing forth deep sighs, groans and at times making me almost utter an unnatural howl which to repress takes all my energy." It was precisely this that had driven him from home the previous winter; if it came to that again, he would not wait for it to drive him away, but would leave immediately. Once again, these stirrings isolated him; his brothers had not had the experience and could not understand him. For his part, not wishing to be thought of as "desiring anything extra," he determined to "bear it until it is unendurable."[2]

Hecker shared his experience with his friends and received predictable advice. Ida Russell urged him to calm his spirit by avoiding "morbid books" and "morbid people." "Such a noble soul as yours must not be overwrought," she wrote. "Think how much one strong upright heart can do for the poor, the oppressed, the sorrow stricken." She added a gentle reproach to the shy Hecker, asking him not to begin his letters "Dear and respected Miss Russell." Richard Dana wrote invitingly of the continuing need for social reform, to which Hecker responded somewhat defensively that concern for others was indispensable, but each must choose his own way of assisting his fellow man. George Curtis took the opposite position, urging self-reliance and hard work and warning Hecker against reform movements; he hoped Isaac would remember that "the Individual life is the only life one knows." Charles Lane added a warning against study: "A soul born with genius equal to Shakespeare's could not go through any process more calculated to suppress it than that of reading and studying Shakespeare's works. I suppose it is because the Christian scriptures are so much studied that we have so few Christs."[3]

However strong his desire for quiet and prayer, Isaac remained interested in his friends. In September, when Alcott and Lane visited the city, Hecker joined them on visits to other New Englanders, including Channing, Margaret Fuller and Henry Thoreau, whom Hecker had not met before. Isaac wrote to George Ripley in early September, and Ripley responded affectionately. He was happy to hear that Hecker was "so happy in New York"; he had feared that in "common society" Isaac would "grow blind to the vision of loveliness and glory which the future promises to humanity." He hoped Isaac would come back to Brook Farm, though "not as an amateur, a self-perfectioner, an aesthetic self-seeker, willing to suck the orange of Association dry and throw away the peel." Rather he should "come as one of us, to work in the faith of a divine idea, to toil in loneliness and tears for the sake of the kingdom which God may build up by our hands."[4]

Lane and Ripley both asked Hecker to help raise funds for their projects, but he did not respond. Instead, he wrestled with his own problems. He showed more interest in women. In late August, before leaving New England, Isaac had written at the top of a diary page, "man requires a rebirth of the feminine in him." Back in New York the relationship between the sexes was much on his mind. He called on an old family friend who had written two articles on "Femality," which distinguished sharply between men and women, arguing that each sex should try to become more of its distinctive self, "truth" in the case of men, "love" in the case of women. Hecker disagreed, looking to Christ for a different understanding:

> I am inclined to think the two sexes should be in the same Individual being, that the same individual should unite in her being both sexes. He should be full of grace and truth the same as Jesus Christ. Whose life it was to do the work of his Father. Who had united in him the perfect lovefulness and tenderness of Woman with the wisdom and strength of man.

Hecker reflected on the manner of Christ's birth, "a male being born of a virgin." Christ must have been "filled with femality, with love such as no other being had ever been," with "light and warmth, head and heart, understanding and impulse" all in one. A week later he asked why men and women could not speak together, love each other and achieve intimacy. This was not all abstract, for, while Ora Garrett and Ida Russell continued to send chatty, affectionate letters, Isaac's thoughts turned to Almira Barlow, to whom he was "deeply attached," as he put it in his diary. One December night he could hardly keep from writing her. "I feel she is near to my heart," he wrote. "What position will we occupy in the future? I can scarcely think we will be so far apart as we are now."[5]

His hopes for his brothers were unfulfilled. Isaac found his responsibilities at the bakery not only interfered with the demands of his "higher life" but contradicted his desire to "live more for others," as he had told Ripley he wished to do. He felt that his diet was "all purchased and produced by hired labor, my dress, I suppose, by slave labor." He could not believe he would be "rightly conditioned" until "all that I eat and drink and wear is produced by Love." One possibility was to persuade his brothers to move to the country, with a farm perhaps linked to Brook Farm or Fruitlands. Another alternative was to transform the family's business and lifestyle, making love the rule. He started a reading room for the employees at the bakery and talked other ideas over with George, but he was not satisfied. "I feel I am not doing anything to ameliorate the social conditions of those around me, under my influence and partial control," he wrote in his diary in December. At Christmas time Isaac and George discussed some of this with John. The oldest brother desired more order in their business affairs, to be achieved by more centralized direction. They responded that they would accept if it was intended to realize a common object. Here they disagreed. As Isaac saw it, John favored treating the men as servants, George and he wanted to deal with them "as far as possible as brethren."[6]

Hecker's beliefs led him to discipline his body. He was a vegetarian, listing the reasons for avoiding "animal food": it was the "chief cause of the slavery of the kitchen, it generates in the body the desires the animals are subject to and encourages in men their bestiality; its odor is offensive and its appearance unaesthetic." His diet that winter consisted of apples, potatoes, nuts, and unleavened bread, sometimes replaced by a whole-grain bread he made himself, all with scarcely a mouthful of water.

Since his earliest days in New England, Hecker had shown an interest in the Christian churches, and he continued to explore the many churches in New York. He attended a Methodist "love feast" shortly after his return. Later, he visited local churchmen, including John's Episcopalian pastor and one of the leaders of the local Mormon community. More and more he thought about the Incarnation, with its claim that Christ provided a mediator between God and the individual soul. He was more interested in Christ than in the church, and he puzzled over how Christ continued to "commune" with humanity as he had promised. To the answer that the sacraments were the way, he responded that, if so, it should be evident in the "fruits" of such communication among those who shared in them, but the behavior of Catholics with their sacraments compared unfavorably with that of Quakers, who had none.[7]

Like Brownson, Hecker was convinced that the church was the object of his own aspirations and those of others expressed in utopian communities and reform movements. He was hopeful that his generation would come to see Christianity

> as the Soul Centre of all life and of reform, and as men and women become conscious of their own deep wants, and those of Humanity, so will they labor in and out of season for the realization of that Catholic Church foreshadowed in the past, lost sight of by Luther . . . reseen in our day by the inspired men.

Such views reflected those of his mentor, Brownson, who urged Hecker and other young men to join the Episcopal Church as the closest approximation to the fully Catholic Church available, though he himself could not join with a "fragment." But Hecker was looking for a heroic challenge that would call him to be more than he was and provide an object, a direction to his life. Transcendentalism did not do that, but at least its proponents were honest and dedicated. The existing church offered even less of a challenge to its members:

> There are those who have more of Christ's spirit out of the visible church than those in her bosom, in fact as a general rule reform has passed from the church into secular parties. The purest Gospel is taught out of the church. We do not say that the Church is not doing a work and that she has not done much for us that is the present church but she stops halfway. The church is a great almoner but what is she doing to ameliorate and improve the circumstances of the poorest and most numerous classes. She is more passive than active.

Hecker could not follow a church that, as he put it, "asks no more of me *practically* than what I am."[8]

As the year ended Isaac remained restless. He tried to organize his time in order to do good and "for self-culture," then criticized himself for devoting too much time to work, and, worst of all, for engaging in too much "frivolous conversation." In mid-December he was studying Latin and German daily, and he resumed his work on English grammar. He read, wrote letters to friends, and worked, leaving little time to retire to "a silent place where I can be perfectly still," although it was meditation that had the longest lasting and most beneficial effects on his soul. He resolved to speak less, to think less of his friends, and find the silence he needed.

A month later he had "a clearer vision" of things. Philosophy, he wrote in the diary, "looks at truth from a subjective standpoint" and leads to "idealism" or "egoism," while "theology or religion" sees truth as objective and leads to "quietism" and "self-annihilation." The next day he wrote of the divisions among spirit, soul and body, as the spirit tried to regain what had been lost by sin. This analysis helped Hecker understand what was happening to him. The life of the mind had its excesses, but one could also overemphasize the spiritual. He noted "the tendency of the human mind in all ages when utterly denying all physical instincts . . . to fall into the opposite extreme of spiritual licentiousness or intoxication. Such seems to be the fate of all modern spiritual cults."[9] He needed to find a proper balance.

He reflected again on the church question. Protestant countries seemed to him to express the "spontaneous elements of progressed humanity in an unorganized, unsystematic form." On the other hand, the "different societies, institutions and unions in the Catholic Church are the natural development of the needs of men under the influence of Christian inspiration." Protestantism had destroyed these institutions and people were now seeking them again, "in the shape of reorganizing society, Fourierism, communism, no property, universal reform," for the needs they met were enduring. He wondered that all the "founders of sects from Fox to Joseph Smith" had prophesied the downfall of the Catholic Church, but it still stood.

In March he once again knew he would have to make some decisions. He had little interest in business and found the effort to work and study at the same time filled with distractions. Suddenly he announced in his diary that he had decided to study "for the field of the church" and had written Brownson for advice. Brownson, touched by Hecker's appeal to him as a "parent," strongly endorsed his young friend's decision. He had always believed Isaac was destined for the ministry. They both knew that only through the church could they serve "our age and country." Brownson urged Hecker to study classical languages in order to prepare for the ministry, and, still worried about the transcendentalist influence, he gently warned Hecker against the anti-intellectual temptations of his mystical temperament.

Even before receiving Brownson's encouragement, Hecker wrote Rev. William H. Norris, an Episcopal priest in Carlisle, Pennsylvania, whose article on Anglican and Catholic claims had impressed him, to inquire whether Norris might accept him as a student. Norris responded sympathetically, but said he had not read enough theology to meet Hecker's needs. He invited Hecker to visit, then perhaps to try the Episcopal seminary in New York. Hecker also consulted New York's Episcopal bishop, Samuel Seabury, and was delighted by the distinguished churchman's candor and graciousness. The bishop asked him to name the obstacles that kept him from becoming either an Anglican or a Roman Catholic. Hecker told him he thought the Anglican church to be schismatic, while he disliked the neglect of discipline in that communion. As he reported his conversation in his diary, it was clear that Hecker, like Brownson, was tending toward Rome:

> I told him though the Church of Rome may commit errors in practice they had not committed any in principle and that it was easier to prune a luxuriant tree than to re vivify a tree almost exhausted of life.

At about the same time he called upon Archbishop John Hughes of New York—the first Catholic with whom he spoke. Hecker asked Hughes the requirements for the Catholic priesthood; Hughes told him, but he added some gratuitous remarks, and Hecker was irritated. Hughes said "the Church was one of discipline"; Hecker thanked the bishop "for the information." "He seemed to think I had inborn Protestant notions of the Church," Hecker wrote. He did not feel "in the least disinclined to be governed by the most rigid discipline of any church," but he was not thinking "at present" of becoming a Catholic. "The Roman Catholic Church is not national with us and hence it does not meet our wants nor does it fully understand and sympathize with the experiences and disposition of our people," Hecker concluded. "It is principally made up of adopted and foreign citizens." Later he told Brownson that he also disliked the power of Rome over local churches, though, like Brownson, he might yet someday join the Catholic Church.[10]

Still uncertain of which church to join, Hecker decided to go back to Concord to study Greek and Latin with George Bradford. He wrote for Brownson's advice again, suspecting he would not agree because of "the transcendental influence in Concord." The desire to study was deeply rooted, however, even though his efforts to date had been scattered and unsystematic. The new assurance evident in Hecker's decision to return to studies reflected a maturing sense of his place in the scheme of things. Surrendering to the powerful spirit within had become for Hecker a willingness to do God's will and to determine that will by humility before God and a clearsighted look at himself. The next step was to place himself within the framework of the Christian tradition, from which knowledge of the spirit was drawn. Hecker now saw himself in the context of the Christian church, although he had not yet determined, concretely, where that church was to be found. Nevertheless, placing himself inside it, he had an even clearer image of the goal toward which he should strive, one determined by Jesus Christ as the revelation of God to humanity and of humanity to itself.[11]

Hecker's decision seemed a bit anticlimactic after the passionate quest that preceded it. He had prayed and longed for an answer to his question about what to do, and it often seemed he anticipated a response as direct and unambiguous as his initial call from God. The decision to study for "the field of the church" seemed rather emotionless and cold, particularly when he remained ambivalent about which church to join. Yet his heart was now immersed in a warm sense of God's presence.

> I feel the presence of God wherever I am. I would kneel and praise God in all places. In his presence I walk and feel his breath encompass me. My soul is born up on his presence and my heart is filled with his influence. How thankful ought we to be! How humble and submissive! Let us lay our heads on the pillow of peace and die peacefully in the embrace of God.[12]

In April 1844 Hecker was back in New England. After a stop at Brownson's, he arrived in Concord. Hecker spoke with Ripley and visited Brook Farm, where he found his friends more sympathetic to his new interest in the church than he had expected. But reporting his visit to the family he added revealingly: "How sad it is to be always a seeker without ever being a finder."[13] Meanwhile, he talked with Bradford, and arranged to board, for three dollars a month, in the home of Henry Thoreau and his mother. After his first lesson, he felt grateful to his family for all they had done to allow him to search for the "true purpose of his being." "All we can do is be faithful to God and to the work he has given us to do," he wrote to his mother. "We must be fixed in God before we can do anything right." In contrast to his first days in New England a year earlier, Hecker was now confident and critical of some of the local heroes, including the great Emerson:

> I have had a few words with Emerson. He stands on the extreme grounds where he did several years ago. He and his followers seem to me to live almost a pure intellectual existence. They have no conception of the Church; out of Protestantism they are almost perfectly ignorant. They are the narrowest men and yet they think they are extremely "many-sided" and forsooth do not comprehend Christendom and reject it. The Catholic accepts all

> the good they affirm and finds it comparatively little to that which he has.[14]

The return to Concord did not shake his growing sense of peace. After two lessons in Latin and Greek with Bradford, Hecker wrote in his diary: "My spirit does not fail me, no doubts of my perseverance pass through my bosom. I am quiet and in peace. I hope I shall draw nearer and nearer to God daily. I feel that I am growing in his grace. To Him I look for support. Will he not impart wisdom as well as love?" Able to choose between "the things of the world" and the "things which belong to the Kingdom of God," Hecker had no doubt now of his choice and no fear that his choice would not receive a response.

It was in surrender that Hecker was finding the answer to his quest, in purging himself of willfulness that he was beginning to find direction:

> We must never forget that if we would give ourselves up to God that he is waiting and ever ready to give Himself to us! . . . Think of this—that all the love and light we have is from God and that it is our willfulness and that only that is in the way of our receiving more and more into perfect fullness.[15]

Submission seemed to fill him with strength. While it was still not clear where he was headed, he was serene and prayed simply for faith. His diary in late April and early May burst with statements of love, the closeness of God, even romantic eagerness for death in order to be with God. Writing home, he gave his family assurances, much more convincing than a year earlier, that he found conditions congenial. He welcomed solitude. He was "alone from early morning to late at night"; no one intruded, except Mr. Bradford between noon and one o'clock. His new life was ideal. His brothers could share that life if they would take less care of their "contemptible bodies" and more of their souls, he told them self-righteously. He added a long series of questions regarding their priorities, urging them to become true Christians: "This is Christianity, to take up the cross and follow Christ, that is, to deny ourselves and to submit wholly to the spirit of Love, and to this end was the church instituted." He was back at them two days later, informing them that the most important thing in life was "unconditionally submitting our wills to the influence of love." All the actions of self-will are delusions, he insisted; by fasting and self-denial one could shut the doors of the body and open the windows of the soul.[16]

Hecker was well along the road to a mystical communion with God. "Conscious of nothing but love," he struggled toward the spiritual world opening before him. By no means even now denying that he remained human and worldly, he was more conscious then ever of the yearning within, sure now that it had an object: "To live for this world for the good of this world is a duty but how much more does the soul desire to go to its house." One day Hecker took his Greek books and a copy of Shakespeare's sonnets and went to a part of the woods known as the Cliffs. He read "a few sonnets," translated two Greek sentences, and then "laid back on the dry leaves and looked up in the blue sky." Recording his thoughts later, Isaac finally felt at home in the world:

> Man's greatest act is obedience. His glory is in submission. He is most man when most divine. Man's spiritual eyes have been blinded by sin. He is not born with his spiritual sight. Spiritual sight is an after birth. The truths which should be his daily food he gropes about to find but seldom gets them.

How strange it seemed to think this way, and with such confidence: "The prophecy I was so eager to get from other lips some nine months ago is now uttered by my own." Isaac Hecker, mystic and seeker, had found something as certain and firm, yet still mysterious, as he had experienced in 1842.[17]

One unsuspected benefit of his new situation was the friendship of Henry Thoreau. In fact, Hecker regretted he had not asked Thoreau to be his teacher. "Mr. Thoreau has a better knowledge of languages, has more leisure, takes a delight in languages," Hecker wrote, while "Mr. Bradford comes here when he has been tired out by his school, simply hears me recite, gives me scarcely any valuable information on the structures and the nature of the languages and does not awaken any new interest in my study." On the other hand, "a few moments conversation" with Thoreau "gives me more instruction and delight than all that [Bradford] has ever said to me on the subject." However, after Hecker wrote these words in his diary, Bradford came for his daily lesson and "we had the pleasantest time since I came here." Like most complaints, Hecker reflected, his were uttered after the cure was at hand; still, he concluded, it was better to complain, it was a sign of life.[18]

The day following his happy experience at the Cliffs Isaac wrote that only true union with God could satisfy the soul, and that could be achieved only by "fasting, prayer and all kinds of self-denial." But the next day his old anxieties suddenly reappeared. He blamed himself for not trusting the spirit enough and felt sadness, even despair, "so deep no one could touch it." He again felt a void inside. Later he was more thoughtful, wondering if the cycle of pain and satisfaction was not part of a plan of spiritual growth.

"Man is a very restless animal," he reflected. "Scarcely is one hope realized than a new and wider one sweeps into being."

Once again he turned over the question in his mind: Was the answer to unite with the church? But the churches as they were did not seem to provide the way, so, again, it was best to wait and see where the spirit would lead. He turned once again to silence, describing the spirit as imprisoned, held by the self. Study was not important for "God is the true Educator, the Schoolmaster of the Universe and he will educate us all as we need and should be educated but his conditions are self-submission willingness to obey his Spirit and perfect reliance on Him." A few days later, he decided to put books aside for awhile and be perfectly quiet. He had hardly been overwhelmed with his studies, and probably needed little persuasion to give them up. He had become an uneasy mystic.[19]

But by now Hecker knew that, for him at least, there could be no salvation outside the church. He had none of the transcendentalist disdain for institutions, though he shared their desire to get at the spirit behind the form. To his brothers he wrote in May of his "reverence for the church, for the sacred and invisible life which it is the medium of. . . . The Church is really the Kingdom of God in fellowship with angels." Convinced of the need to submit to the will of God, he would be part of the church, but still could not determine which one to join. He was prepared to follow God's direction and stop attempting to spell out his own, but God until now sent no clear signals.

In another letter home he indicated that, as Bradford would be away during the following week, he would be going to Boston to see friends. He also planned to attend the convention of the American Anti Slavery Society and other reform meetings. On his return, he noted his disappointment; he had hoped mixing with others would open a new relation to his studies, but it was not to be. The conventions, visits and a concert by the popular violinist Ole Bull had no effect. "I feel that I move in an element as different from those around me as the bird does from the fish," he wrote. Instead of new activity, he was drawn to "doze and slumber more and more," even while in the city, for in his sleep "the dim shadows that appear in my waking state are clearer to me and my conversation is more real and pleasant." He confessed, "with a deep sense of humility," that his labors were useless and his ability to accomplish anything "Christian or worldly" was becoming "fainter and fainter."[20]

By the end of May the clear purpose that had led him to Concord, to study for the church, had disappeared. Study was "out of the question," he noted in his diary. He did not know what to do but "remain here for a time until something seems plainer to me than it now does." With others, "the man of Science, of Art," the method was clear, to move slowly and steadily toward the goal, learning what had been done in the past and adding one's own "original observations." For the man of spirit, things were different:

> But with the objective spiritual world of truth and goodness the process is not so tangible sure and progressive and the labor is of quite a different sort as the difficulties and rewards are of quite a different character. Man's spiritual senses are not so well trained and refined as his natural senses are, hence the former road is so much more difficult than the latter, and his labours, speaking from the worldly side, much less appreciated in this direction; in fact they are to a great extent derided and spoken of as vain foolish and mere delusive fancies of his own fertile brain.

One drawback was the body itself:

> It seems to me the body is a very costly machine at the cheapest rate to keep going in a healthy condition and as for myself its productiveness seems not to me to pay the cost of the expenditures for its sustenance, and so far it is a losing concern. But the tree requires some years before it bears its fruits and so I trust it may be with me. Patience and calm trust are godly fruits of life.

A few days later he noted that his meals consisted of "unleavened bread and figs, and my drinking water"; while he ate "no more than supports my body," he nevertheless felt "sinfully indulgent."[21]

Hecker had thought he would study for the clergy, but now felt attracted to no particular object. He had asked Brownson, expecting a different answer, and had been surprised by his encouragement. Coming from one in whose judgment Isaac had great confidence, Brownson's advice had temporarily given him a firmer resolution, but now it was gone and he found himself "once again afloat." He sent Brownson a long account of his recent experience. Brownson responded quickly, out of patience with his young friend's musings. The "dreamy luxury of indulging one's own thoughts" could destroy freedom, Brownson warned; he suspected Hecker had come to "mistake a mental habit" into which he had fallen "for the guidance of the All-Wise." There was no great victory in giving in to his natural tendencies but in overcoming them by disciplined study, even against his inclinations. To do this, he needed the help of grace through "appropriate channels."

Brownson then made the shocking announcement that he had begun preparations to enter the Catholic Church, and he urged Hecker to do the same. If he believed in the Holy Ghost and in the Holy Catholic Church, he must stop dreaming his life away and place himself under the direction of the Church. "Your devotion must be regulated and directed by the discipline of the Church," Brownson insisted. Later he could find a wide field of service among the growing numbers of German Catholics in the upper Midwest. Brownson drove the point home. "You must be a Catholic or a mystic." He should resist the temptation to mysticism, with its danger of self-indulgence, and come to Boston to see the bishop.[22]

Why hesitate? Hecker asked himself. After all, he could not say he "had anything essentially against her (the Catholic Church) and she meets all my wants on every side." Perhaps his hesitation was the last barrier of self-centeredness: "Is this not the self will which revolts against the involuntary will of the soul?" For once he resented all he had been through. The fundamental question had become why he would not "submit my will to the guidance and direction of the Church," having concluded that it was the Body of Christ, the channel of the Holy Ghost and necessary to secure "the favor of God and heaven thereafter." He could not answer his question.[23]

After completing this diary entry and writing his brothers, he went off to see Brownson, remaining in Boston four days. On his return, he wrote his family, admitting that his real intention on the trip had been to see Bishop Benedict Fenwick and his coadjutor Bishop John Fitzpatrick. He had talked with Fitzpatrick at length, he told them, and had made his decision. After visiting the new Catholic college in Worcester, Holy Cross, he would return home, there to "be united . . . to the Roman Catholic Church in our city." In his diary he wrote: "My mind is made up to join the Catholic Church and this soon." To his family he was less emphatic, despite the decisiveness of the original announcement: "Before I fully commit myself to the Catholic Church I wish to become acquainted to a certain extent with the practical effect of the doctrines and discipline of the Church." Besides, he added respectfully "before I make an unalterable step I wish to see you all and commune with you on this movement on my part."[24]

In explaining this step Isaac seemed defensive, going to some length to explain why the Anglican communion seemed inadequate. Worldly considerations certainly counted against Catholicism, he noted in the diary: "the Roman Catholic Church is the most despised, poorest and according to the world the least respectable on account of the order of foreigners which it is chiefly composed of in this country." His friends, he was sure, would regard his step "with astonishment and probably use the common epithets of delusion, fanaticism and blindness." He argued that the unattractive aspects of the church were evidence that he was not influenced by worldly considerations, while the derision of his friends would reflect their shortcomings, not his.

Hecker had read the Catechism of the Council of Trent months earlier and knew the formal doctrines of the church well enough to have argued vigorously with leading Episcopal churchmen in New York. He now urged his family to read the passage from the Catechism that contained the doctrine of the communion of saints to understand the wide difference between the two churches in "doctrine and life." That passage, which Hecker kept close to him for years thereafter, affirmed the solidarity of all believers, which Hecker obviously thought stood in sharp contrast to the respectable gentility of Anglicanism:

> In fine, every true Christian possesses nothing which he should not consider common to all others with himself, and should, therefore, be prepared promptly to relieve an indigent fellow-creature; for he that is blessed with worldly goods, and sees his brother in want, and will not assist him, is at once convicted of not having the love of God in him.

Despite the heroic, and now clearly unsuccessful, efforts of the Oxford reformers, the Anglican church had allowed "discipline and religious ceremonies and even sacraments . . . to fall into great almost total disuse." Convinced now of the divine origin of all seven sacraments, and acknowledging a personal need for them as practical means to secure union with God, Hecker asked his family, "why should one go to a weak and almost dried up spring when there is one equally as near always flowing and full of life"?[25]

A few days later Hecker described his feelings about his sudden decision:

> I feel very cheerful and at ease and in perfect peace since I have consented to join the Catholic church. Never have I felt the quietness, and immovableness, and the permanent rest that I now feel. It is inexpressible. I feel that essential and interior permanence which nothing exterior can disturb and that no act that it calls upon me to perform will in the least cause me to be moved by it. It is with perfect ease and gratefulness that I never dreamed of that I will unite with the Church. It will not change but fix my life. No interior relations, events or objects can disturb this unreachable quietness nor no event can break this deep repose I am in. I feel centered deeper than any kind of action can penetrate feel or reach.

The decision to enter the Catholic Church stimulated further critical reflection on the alternatives he had rejected along the way. In his diary he noted his judgment of transcendentalism, ironic in light of the movement's origins in reaction against "corpse cold" Unitarianism:

> The transcendentalist is one who has a keen sight but little warmth of heart. Fine conceit—but destitute of the rich glow of Love. He is in rapport with the spiritual world unconscious of the celestial one. He is all nerve and no blood, colorless. He talks of self reliance but fears to trust himself to Love. . . . He would have written a critical essay on the power of the Soul at the foot of the Cross.[26]

On June 13 he noted that the next day he planned to go with Emerson to Harvard to visit Lane and Alcott. He expected little from the Concord sage, whom he found distant. "We shall not meet each other," he wrote, "for on no other ground can I meet him than those of Love. We may talk intellectually together and remark and reply and remark again." Years later Hecker recalled that Alcott had been polite when he heard the news, but Emerson was less so. When Emerson suggested that he supposed it was the art and architecture of Catholic Europe which had attracted him to the church, Hecker snapped: "No, but what caused all that." As Hecker had not seen Catholic Europe or met many Catholics, the quick rejoinder, even if the invention of an old man's memory, was basically correct.[27]

Bishop Fitzpatrick had suggested Hecker visit with the Jesuits at Holy Cross before returning to New York. He did so, expecting to stay a fortnight or "as long as it seems pleasant to me." His stay lasted only three days. To his family he wrote that the teachers at Holy Cross were "men of good character, devoted to the church, innocent of the Protestant world of Literature, Philosophy, etc.," although the president was "a very social, frank, warmhearted man and of more extensive acquaintance with the world of letters." Writing to Brownson, Hecker was more candid about the shortcomings of his new brethren:

> The professors that I had the pleasure to speak to were well educated in the circle of Catholic Education which seems to be the Scriptural and historic grounds of their Church. As for its philosophic basis they seem to me profoundly ignorant and so long as the conversation was kept within their circle they were at home, otherwise they behaved as strangers. Their method is a very short one in settling difficult points, Scripture and the Church, not appreciating any other method however important and profound it may be to the welfare and success of the Church in her present position in the World. These men have done well

> to keep and preserve the Church but a new generation must take their place if Catholicism is to be reestablished in the World.[28]

Ten years later Brownson wrote publicly that he and Hecker had helped each other find the church. He recalled their conversations by the fire in his Chelsea home, the sincerity and honesty with which they had opened their hearts to one another, the "modesty and docility" that made Hecker regard him as the teacher when, in Brownson's view, "he aided us more than we him, for even then his was the master mind." Years later Brownson reaffirmed the view that it was Hecker who had led the way, even though by that time the two men had disagreed on many subjects. Hecker repaid the compliment, always claiming that Brownson was his chief guide and advisor. Toward the end of his life, after their many fallings out, Hecker nevertheless concluded: "He was the master, I the disciple. God alone knows how much I am indebted to him. To the channels of thought opened to me by Dr. Brownson, I owed, more than to anything else, my conversion to the Catholic faith." Hecker loved Brownson deeply, and the older man had certainly played an important role in Hecker's spiritual development. But Hecker's road to the church was his own; it led within, through deep and disturbing experiences of the spirit, and had little to do with Brownson's historical and philosophical speculations. As Hecker put it years later, he had found Brownson's arguments for Catholicism less compelling than his arguments against transcendentalism. In the search for God, "it was from the start a more personal affair with me than it was with him," Hecker wrote. Brownson "was occupied in working out the problem philosophically and for the universe. I was looking out for number one."[29]

While his actual movement into the Roman Catholic Church was indeed unusual, the motives which led Hecker to that step were far less so. Hecker was not alone in his desire for *a* church that would be *the* church and would embrace the full range of Christian experience. Christian language pervaded nineteenth-century America, providing the major symbols to give meaning to individual and national experience. The radical individualism and freedom of the early nineteenth century resulted in a democratization of religious life, as has been noted, and led to a proliferation of churches, movements and sects. Many of those churches aimed at Christian unity, either by forming a new church that would reduce Christianity to its basic elements and thus overcome divisions and fragmentations, or by uniting Christian energies in crusades for reform or evangelization, overcoming divisions by common endeavor. The yearning for Christian unity was intensified by the powerful millennial themes associated with American nationalism, envisioning the nation as God's chosen instrument for the redemption of humanity, a destiny that could only be fulfilled by bringing the sects and denominations together. The all-pervasive influence of the Scriptures, and the widespread sense of the immediacy of God's presence evident in revivalism and transcendentalism alike, suggested that the unity God desired, a unity which could secure one's personal faith from doubt, ought to be available.

Thus it was not unusual for religious seekers to confront the Catholic answer, especially when the Catholic question was posed by the Oxford movement and its American counterpart, by the obvious presence of Catholic churches, and by the growing number of immigrant Catholics. Most recoiled from the church, seeing in it a symbol of the past and of all that contradicted American values of freedom and independence.[30] But some, like Hecker, looked beyond the problems posed by the actual church to the idea of Catholicism, to the promise of one, holy, catholic and apostolic church. Probing that Catholic idea, with the help of European Catholic writers like Mohler and the English Tractarians, while at the same time noticing the shortcomings of the multiplying Protestant alternatives, a religious seeker might respond favorably to the church and even enter it. In the Boston of Bishops Fenwick and Fitzpatrick, from 1825 to 1846, there were two thousand conversions to the Catholic Church.[31] If a seeker, like Isaac Hecker, was relatively free of historical bias, unfamiliar with current church teaching and ignorant of how the church worked, the attraction of the Catholic idea might override what might be regarded as more human and worldly considerations. Hecker took the step quite innocent of what the church actually was, convinced only that it offered an answer to his basic religious questions. It alone seemed to offer the possibility that there was an object to his searching, a real, historical, visible object to which he could devote his life and in which he could find a way to live.

The reason for his conversion was primarily personal. It was a decision to submit fully and finally to the Holy Spirit within. All his future accomplishments and suffering in the Catholic Church arose from this central fact: Isaac Hecker considered the decision to become a Catholic and the decision to place himself unreservedly in submission to the Holy Spirit within as one and the same decision. The spirit in the church and the spirit who spoke from within were the same spirit. The journey inward led to Catholicism. Brownson had told him to choose between mysticism and Catholicism. Hecker was determined to be both a mystic and a Catholic. In the nineteenth century, perhaps in every century, that was a difficult combination.

4

The Land Promised Me in My Youth

Isaac Hecker's decision to become a Catholic marked not the conclusion of his search, but another beginning. He was now convinced that the object of his search was union with God, a union available only through Christ, present, here and now, in his church. Communion with God was secured by formal entry into God's church, which was the living expression of the same Holy Spirit who spoke in the depths of his own soul. Hecker had long suspected, and now knew with certainty, that the church of God was the Roman Catholic Church. He knew little of that church through personal experience, only a bit through reading and conversations with Brownson. The decision to become a Catholic created a new and radically different context for further explorations of the concrete meaning of union with God. But, at this point, that new context was abstract and theoretical. Conversion, it seemed, did not happen all at once, but needed to be deepened, renewed, reinterpreted, a process that would structure the rest of Isaac Hecker's life.[1]

On June 23, 1844, Hecker arrived home and two days later, as he had been instructed, he went to call on Bishop John McCloskey, coadjutor to Archbishop John Hughes. In his letter of introduction Bishop Fitzpatrick told McCloskey that young Hecker had found his way to the church "with no human guide but only the Spirit of God." Fitzpatrick had little doubt of Isaac's sincerity but some worry about his enthusiasm, for he wrote that Hecker needed "guidance, yet in many respects more for moderation than excitement." Hecker found McCloskey "a man of fine character, mild disposition and of a broader knowledge than any of the Catholics I have had the pleasure of meeting." He was particularly glad that the bishop knew the writing of Brownson and Emerson and had met Channing in Rome. McCloskey loaned Hecker some Catholic books but, as he was leaving town for two weeks, he told the young convert to await his return before taking any further steps.

While McCloskey was away, Hecker read and reflected. Perhaps recalling Hughes's warning of a year earlier, he asked himself: "Discipline, what is it? and what is its value?" Clearly there might be a problem reconciling his interior convictions, understood still in transcendentalist terms, with the demands of his new church. The young convert-to-be wanted to follow the inner promptings of the spirit which had led him to Catholicism. The only way "to happiness in this world and eternal felicity in the world to come," he believed, was to "express the divine life which stirs within" and "not to do anything which is not conformable to it." What held most people back was "in one word, the World . . . all that looks to time instead of heaven." Hecker prayed for strength for that "inward man" and now looked "to the Church of Christ for help: Oh, that I may find in the Church that which the apostles found in Jesus." The mission of Christ, Hecker believed, was "to infuse into the heart of humanity a divine life," and that was the life to which he was committed.[2]

In seeking a firm basis on which to pursue the inner life within the Catholic Church, Hecker again reflected on his own experience. This continuing process of autobiographical reflection, which became crucial in Hecker's career within the church, unfolded from a conviction that his experience, so personal and profoundly interior, was nevertheless not unique. He had been a seeker and had found an "object." To seek and never find was unreasonable and sad. Perhaps he could help others, seeking like himself, to find that same object. Indeed, perhaps in that insight lay the answer to his long, agonizing effort to decide what to do with his life.

If he was to give a "true narrative" of his life during the last two years, he wrote in early July, it would be "not uninteresting, I imagine, to a few." "It would be a story of the birth and youth of the Ideal," which, until two years earlier, had been "within my own bosom and had not exhibited itself in external action." Then it began to express itself, leading him to Brownson, to Brook Farm and Fruitlands, back to New York, then to Concord, and now, once again to New York, and to the Catholic Church. "There is material for one who could work this up for *Wanderjahre*," he thought. Hecker did not let the idea die; several months later he returned to it, resolving to write his autobiography for "his own satisfaction," as he put it, "for no other purpose than for the sincere reflection and beneficial emotions it may excite in my bosom." He wrote six pages, found it "like fiction," but was pleased that the "new position" he adopted writing about himself "gave rise to new thought." He laid the project aside, but he was far from done with writing and thinking about his life.

Hecker's sporadic venture into spiritual autobiography indicated that, while the church was giving him "deep eternal certainty" and "the interior consciousness of our true being's existence," becoming Catholic did "not necessarily indicate the color or tenor of all our future acts." For the moment, at least, Hecker was comfortable with uncertainty about the actual form his life would take, for he was near a safe anchor in the Roman Catholic communion.[3]

Hecker approached his baptism with a curious passivity. On August 1, 1844, he wrote simply in his diary: "this morning we were baptized by Bishop McCloskey. Tomorrow we attend the tribunal of confession." The experience of sacramental confession brought a more animated response, as he filled his diary with prayers of praise to God, but a few days later an old problem reappeared: the busy activities of everyday life. For reasons he could not explain, he had lapsed into an unconscious use of the plural pronoun in referring to himself. The "I" disappeared into the "we" "as shadows before the brilliant light of the Sun of Suns," he wrote. The "I was the negative of the we, the universal consciousness," an insight "so sudden it could not be retained without constant repetition." The use of the plural pronoun, perhaps, reflected this ambiguous struggle to merge the self with the ideal, to become one with another, with Christ.[4]

In the midst of these conflicting emotions, Hecker had an inspiration —he would go to Europe, and he would ask Henry Thoreau to accompany him. The circumstances which brought him and Thoreau to "commune with each other" in Concord rendered them "passive or cooperative instruments of profounder principles than we . . . dream of," Hecker wrote his friend. The idea of a walking tour of Europe had come to him in an instant; they would work their passage to Europe and "walk, work or beg if need be as far when there as we are inclined to go." They would immerse themselves in the old world before venturing further into the future with which their new world was identified. Along the way, he concluded good-naturedly, if Thoreau and his family did not "become great sinners," Hecker would call them "good Catholics." Two weeks later he wrote again, hoping to persuade Thoreau to accept the project. He was sure the feeling of others that the trip was impossible would persuade Thoreau to make it: "Tis impossible, sir, therefore we do it."

Thoreau's response passed Hecker's second letter in the mail. He had just returned from a "pedestrian excursion" through the Catskills and the principal mountains of Massachusetts and felt "a slight sense of dissipation." He was tempted by Isaac's idea and professed to "experience a decided schism between my outward and inward tendencies." As for

Hecker's proposed "method of travelling, especially to live along the road, citizens of the world, without haste or petty plans—I have often proposed this to my dreams, and still do." Nevertheless, Thoreau said he could not postpone "exploring Farther Indies, which are to be reached, you know, by other routes and other methods of travel." To ease the disappointment, Thoreau added a wistful note: "I remember you, as it were, with the whole Catholic Church at your skirts. And the other day, for a moment, I think I understood your relation to that body; but the thought was gone again in a twinkling, as when a dry leaf falls from its stem over our heads, but is instantly lost in the rustling mass at our feet."[5]

Hecker must have been disappointed. While writing to Thoreau, he had made a novena that the trip to Rome would come about as a "pilgrimage in the old middle age fashion." It seemed to him a better idea "than a monastery or any kind of seclusion." Obviously his restlessness did not end with his decision to enter the church. Conversion seemed the climax of a romantic quest for heroism, but now Hecker believed the certainty provided by the church should be the basis for the long-awaited life of action.

Hecker may have seen himself as taking a heroic action by becoming a Catholic, but by the time he actually was baptized the sense of heroism was evaporating. He had anticipated dismay and opposition, even ridicule, from his family and friends, yet his family apparently was tolerant, good-natured and supportive. As for his friends, Emerson was puzzled and Thoreau amused, but those who had become close to him continued to correspond and visit. George Curtis spent the fall and winter in New York, and he and Isaac attended lectures and concerts. When Isaac sent Curtis a religious magazine, his friend wrote that "it gives me some pleasure to read the records of these church doings. We infidels need to have our memories occasionally refreshed by the sound of the Trumpet, although we may persevere in our isolation and hug our hopelessness as a great treasure." George Ripley and Georgiana Bruce visited Hecker, while Ora Gannett wrote him warm and affectionate letters. In May and again in July Ora wrote of their friendship, which she valued highly, and her desire to learn more about Catholicism. "I feel perfectly much of its beauty," she wrote, "but it seems so loaded with shackles, though perhaps not more than other churches." Hecker noted in his diary that Ora was "the loveliest, most love natured being that has met my heart. . . . She is not lovely, but love itself." Nevertheless, perhaps frightened by the intimacy Ora invited, Isaac seems to have ended the correspondence. Earlier, Almira Barlow had ceased writing, and Hecker was hurt. Agonizing over the matter in his diary, he admitted he could only accept their separation with a struggle; "it will not diminish my attachment nor cool my love toward her, but stamp her image deeper upon my heart."[6]

Many questions remained unanswered. One was a problem which was a perennial in American Christianity and embodied in Hecker's own experience. If man was sinful and needed grace and if grace was God's free gift, as Hecker now believed, how could man be free? Even before the sinner can know he is a sinner, needing grace, must he not already have an experience of grace? Hecker confessed he could not yet understand how a person could be brought to see the truth in Jesus without "the operation of the grace of God a priori in his heart." Hecker, no Calvinist, could not accept answers of pre-election which restricted human freedom, but neither could he answer that grace came to all who sought it in Arminian fashion. Instead, he found an answer in the moderate doctrine he had perhaps learned in his mother's Methodism, an answer which would cause him many problems over the years:

> Every sinner of necessity must have the ability to supply the conditions of receiving God's grace, otherwise we do not see how he can be redeemed freely from sin without the destruction of his freedom. We do not say he has or possesses conditions that grace may enter and abide in his heart unto salvation. Thus the sinner who hears the Gospel preached partially perceives the truth of it and feels the power and has the power to submit himself to the conditions it requires of him that he may possess the power and grace of God unto eternal salvation, or he may if he so pleases continue the way of darkness, sin and death.[7]

However, this was clearly not Hecker's experience, his road to God and the church. Rather, he had been led by the spirit within, which he came to call the spirit of God. Instead of arguing like Brownson from conviction of sin to the need for grace and therefore for the church, Hecker argued again and again that the person began with intuitions of spirit, smothered by the daily cares of life, but available to all, as it had been to him. That spirit was the spirit of God. Because it was the spirit of God, it would lead each nearer to the church, through which that same spirit, incarnate in Jesus Christ, was manifested in history.

Hecker's decision to enter the church in no way shook his trust in his own experience of God, but confirmed it. Just as he had been moved by an inner spiritual experience and had been struggling for two years to direct his life away from selfish, material or worldly pursuits to a full and submissive response to the spirit, so he believed it was necessary for all people to put aside worldly preoccupations and respond to the invitation which arose from within. By now, however, it was clear to him that people could not do this alone; they needed God's help. "We must feel and possess the love and light from above before we have the disposition and power to deny the body and the wisdom of this world," he wrote. "If we have the Christ spirit we will fulfill the Christ commandment." Given the existence of sin, human beings required a redeemer, who necessarily had to be both divine and human, and a church to be the medium of the redeemer's influence, and that church must be universal, infallible and perpetual. Hecker was convinced the Catholic Church was "that divinely appointed medium by which man is saved from sin and given a new birth." So, the sincere inquirer could find in the church the answer to his or her needs, but it was not the seeker but the object of the search who initiated the process.

Hecker retained important elements of transcendentalism, elements not easily conformed to the Catholic Church, at least in its nineteenth-century manifestation. Transcendentalists argued that each person must harken to the voice within, the voice of "reason" as opposed to understanding, intuition rather than logic. Hecker identified the inner voice of the spirit with the spirit who spoke through the Roman Catholic Church. "In all our reasoning we must understand that the criterion of truth is not the individual judgement of our personal reason but the universal voice of the Catholic Church," he wrote. While individual reason could be trusted in some cases, "it is not competent to comprehend the universal truth hence no individual judgement is the criterion of absolute universal truth."

Hecker was drawn to search for universal truth by a native realism which made him aware of human limitations, his own as well as others, but also by a conviction that the world made sense, that, as Brownson taught him, the object world did exist. Conversion had allowed him to understand more clearly what had happened to him, but he knew he had needed God's help. "We are infants in Christ and need a mother as we have had a natural mother," he wrote. "Regeneration is a progressive work—tho' an act of an instant."[8]

So the quest was hardly over. His diary continued to be filled with speculation, illuminating some concerns which were far from settled. One clearly was a determination, grounded in his family experience, strengthened by his life in New England, and made sure by the gifts of grace he knew he had received from the spirit, to hold fast to a positive understanding of human goodness. Neither now nor later in life would Hecker accept an understanding of sin, redemption or church grounded in a pessimistic emphasis on human weakness.

On the other hand, the conviction that led him to the Church also reoriented his spiritual life. Now he had the sacraments, whose truth and efficacy he affirmed, but they seemed to overwhelm his old ability to be touched by God in prayer. A few days after his baptism he noted that since leaving Concord the gift of interior prayer had "been taken" from him.

"How hard has it been for me to go through with all these solemn mysteries and ceremonies without experiencing that great delight which I have felt," he wrote. Gradually the old sense of estrangement and loneliness reappeared, even though the mysterious spirit still came to him during his sleep. He concluded that God was testing him, trying his faith, and he should respond not by asking for "pleasant things" but by fasting, doing penance and trying "to be content, to be nothing," which he called "the highest state of perfection."[9]

Thoreau turned down his proposal for a pilgrimage to Europe in favor of the interior pilgrimage he could pursue at home. Hecker, almost in spite of himself, made a similar choice, seeking to retrieve the ecstasy of the spiritual life and regain a sense of assurance through self-discipline. He became a spiritual athlete, though his choice of metaphors suggested that the "Love Spirit" was being complemented, if not replaced, by a more stern and demanding God. "As we [teach] some animals to spring up in the air for the food we hold up for them to catch, and hold ever higher that they may learn to spring farther," he wrote, "so does God entice us with heavenly food, Love, that we may rise to a higher state of perfection." Hecker embarked upon a series of personal disciplines designed to overcome sin and achieve a closer union with God. In addition to working and sleeping, he determined to give three hours a day to spiritual exercises, two to intellectual work, and one to his physical well-being, a schedule he thought reversed the world's priorities.[10]

Throughout August his discouragement deepened, as he wrote in his diary, "one day passes after another and we seem to remain where we were." He reflected with uncharacteristic pessimism that little seemed to be added to the progress of the human race. "There is nothing surer than that we are born to war, struggle, suffer," he wrote. His diary became an almost Puritan record of introspective assessment of his spiritual state. In September he decided to record "the many smaller venial sins which beset my path, which form a net to keep me down to Earth," and prescribe "remedies . . . fit for these thorns in my flesh." Omitting the "many unworthy thoughts and feelings" which passed quickly, he began a daily record of faults and remedies, beginning by taking credit for expressing disapproval of "an unprofitable story" and refusing to join in "frivolous" singing. The next day he noticed that he had upset his brother by a critical remark and, to respond, he proposed to read and meditate on St. Frances DeSales' advice for dealing with "certain sins."[11]

Hecker, once remarkably innocent, was now beset by guilt. He accused himself of the sin of forgetfulness and promised to begin rising early to "meditate on the consequences of one little sin" and to attend daily mass. His most common fault was his supposed "desiring the attention of others" and failure to resist gossip and "idle chatter." He worried about such talk at the dinner table and complained that someone in the family "eats like a beast and talks like a heathen." He would have preferred to read while others were eating, but knew his family would not accept that. Instead he promised himself to try to elevate the tone of the conversation, but he did not seem overly optimistic. More pressing was his apparent enjoyment of the company of friends, which always stirred in him a sense of remorse. One evening, after visiting the seashore with friends, he felt spent by the gaiety of the party and promised to be "grave and solemn from this moment forth."

Later he accused himself of loving the company, not of those who gave the greatest pleasure or "highest benefit," but of people who engaged in trivial conversation and frivolous activity. Yet, when he tried to be more "grave and solemn," he felt self-righteous, accusing himself of "peevishness." Even after he had resolved to abstain from meat, coffee and tea, to "fast, fast," he continued to believe that indulgence had "crept upon us with its soft noiseless unobserved march like the sly tiger who hides himself until it's prey is sure and escape hopeless." He recognized that he did many things that were innocent, but his conscience would allow "nothing but the absolute," giving rise to intense feelings of guilt that seemed to be relieved only temporarily by confession.[12]

In November Hecker returned to his studies and began to neglect his book of faults, remarking that his spiritual life had become "stationary." Nor was the vocational issue any closer to resolution. While determined still to follow the path set by the spirit, he believed he should not expect that "anything providential will happen to me." Everyone had to do something to "recompense the world for that which he consumes from its store," but he did not believe he had "any talent or genius in any direction in particular." His mind was "of a general and ordinary capacity." If the family owned some land, he would work it for a while; if he were in Europe he might find Catholic institutions "wherein I could enter for a time until this period of my life either fix itself permanently or give place to another." He had only a "slight hope" that the "advice and influence" of the Catholic Church would provide the remedy. Brownson urged him toward the priesthood and so did Bishop Hughes. Bishop McCloskey thought Hecker's experience would lead him to "a contemplative life," but in the United States, where circumstances required the church to be more active, that option was not yet available. Hecker thought he might go to Europe and find a setting suitable to his needs, but he was still uncertain.

Once again the alternative was study. Although he really had little interest in languages, by mid-October he was again studying Latin and Greek. He did so "with weakness of heart," distrusting education, for "we learn to live, not live to learn." He remained certain he was being led to "some unknown, objective, invisible end." He pursued his studies at a private school, "the Cornelian Institute," where he was invited to participate in a literary society. He hesitated, for the other students were Protestant, "some of them well-informed and talented young men." Hecker worried that "if he openly expressed his opinions," it might cause "a state of things" which would upset others, although "mixing," conversing and sharing an interest in "their objects" would "not be unprofitable." He discussed the matter frankly with a teacher and soon was actively engaged. In early December he read a paper on "the subject and object" and was planning essays "on whether the animal creation have an after existence or no; and one on the characteristics of the American people and the tendency of their civilization."[13]

On December 18 Isaac Hecker noted the beginning of the "twenty-fifth year of my conscious existence on this globe." The doubts of the previous year passed for the moment, and he faced the coming year with a characteristic mixture of hope and uncertainty: "Ah thou eternal, ever blooming virgin, the Future, shall I embrace thee. . . . Shall I see next year this time that my hopes have been fulfilled? My past hopes have been more than fulfilled!" The key to the past year he found in faith, something he had little discussed before. "Faith is the great magic power," he wrote. "This is the great miracle worker. Whatsoever thou believest with all thy might is thine already."

Isaac Hecker had come, almost without knowing it, to the life of faith: faith centered on the twin poles of the interior life of spirit and the exterior life of the church, itself an expression of the same spirit. Only if "union with God results in slavery" could there be truth in the charge that union with the church reduced true liberty. Because Christ promised that his church would never fall into error, Protestantism was nothing less than a denial of Christ's promises. For this reason, too, every protest against the church was false: "There is no half way house between Catholicism and infidelity." In matters of faith, all that popes, councils and priests had done was truly Catholic "if received by the Church of Christ." Of course it could "not be taken for granted that all that professed Catholics have said is Catholic":

> Catholic Truth *is*; it depends not upon Scriptures, neither Councils, bulls nor sermons. If there had been no opposition to its introduction, none of these would have been needed.

No, anyone who came to a clear perception of "the Beautiful True and Good is Catholic," even if they did not know it. "Popes, Councils and

Priests bow to that [to] which the simplest and least member of the church bows and all their authority is in it, not in them." None of these officers would be needed "if men would unconditionally submit themselves to the Universal Love Spirit," who was the real authority in the church, "as much binding on the Pope as upon the least member of the Church."[14]

Hecker came first to the *idea* of the church, "what caused all that," as he put it to Emerson, and only later, from the perspective of faith, did he come to grips with "Popes, Councils, Priests," with "Bulls and Sermons." Still later, when he realized that many of his fellow Catholics, including many who worked closely with him, had come first to "all that," he gently tried to guide them to, and persuade them to put their trust in, what lay behind it all. When he found Catholics, even men in the highest offices, relying too heavily on the forms, he tried to point them to the power of the "Universal Love Spirit." That he would come to play such a part, or that it would even be necessary, he did not yet suspect.

But his early encounters with "all that" were not all positive. He had been put off by the parochialism of the Holy Cross Jesuits. He was troubled as well by the system of pew rentals at the Cathedral in New York, and in other Catholic churches. He consulted McCloskey, who explained the reasons for this practice, and Isaac was "more at ease" but hardly satisfied with the "system of hiring out the Temple of God for gold and silver." McCloskey had explained the "side of necessity and prudence," but Hecker thought that "providential and unconditional faith in God would be the true and only course for the Church to pursue." Deciding that the arrangement was temporary, he agreed to "rest awhile." Still, he "never sat in the pew from principle" while a Protestant; "how much less would one tolerate it as a Catholic." Like his comment on Holy Cross, his response to pew rentals indicated that Hecker's inner road to the church, and his continuing trust in the not always responsive spirit, would make him an independent and, from the point of view of church leaders, a somewhat troublesome, Catholic.[15]

Like so many nineteenth-century converts, Hecker sought certainty. His first conversation with Brownson had centered on the question: "How can I be assured of the reality of my experiences"? Unable to settle the question on strictly intellectual grounds, and humble enough to doubt the wisdom of relying exclusively on his own consciousness, he was led first to Christ as God's self-revelation, then to the church as Christ's presence in the world. For the church to provide the ground he sought, to meet the needs of his soul, it necessarily had to be gifted with infallible authority. If the church and its councils could make errors, as individuals clearly could, then, as Hecker saw it, it would not be possible to have "any settledness and security in our faith. . . . We are left orphans and have no guide." The issue was not whether people differed in their religious opinions, as they clearly did, but to know the decisions of Christ's church and submit to them: "The Church is the pillar and ground of truth, not the Bible as interpreted by private judgment." That the church was infallible was demonstrated, to Hecker's satisfaction, by "the promises of its founder, its own uniform doctrines and its continuous faith."

The other pole of Hecker's faith was more personal, more uniquely his own. At the beginning, as at the end, of his Catholic life, he could say: "This supports me, and I know of nothing else: the faith in me of the guidance of a superior wisdom." This set him apart to wrestle throughout his life with the sometimes terrifying realization that he was free and, under divine inspiration, called to choose. "Man possesses to a fearful extent the power of directing the course of his own destiny," Hecker wrote. This left each person, thus free, with awesome responsibilities, for "thy choice of ways is one of eternal consequences."

Like so many of his generation, he experienced the world as something apart, a dim, misty arena in which he stood, profoundly alone, the master of his destiny. But, where others concluded that their own consciousness was the only sure ground of being, the only thing really real, Hecker was always aware of another reality which transcended and embraced his own:

> I am not worthy of the place I occupy. Yet it is my impression that it is my place as naturally as the flowers appear in time for the wants of the bees. I have not sought it. It has come involuntarily. It is the land promised me in my youth. . . . Often it seems to me that man's destiny is in his own hands, and then it seems equally true and to me profoundly more impressive that we are ruled by an irresistable [sic] mystic force.[16]

Despite the power of his faith, Hecker could not shake the old melancholy. Again in January he pledged to fast, promised to intensify his devotion and filled his journal with prayers for mercy and forgiveness. Sin was a "disease," and he felt sick, relieved only by confession. Again, his associations seemed dim and unreal. Even a visit from Brownson in mid-February did not still his uneasiness. He professed a desire to surrender more fully to God, yet studies and daily affairs interfered and in them he felt sinful, with no real control over his actions. He needed the advice of someone older and more experienced but McCloskey, his spiritual director, while open and candid, did not command his confidence. His family gave him their "deep friendship" and would not "be the slightest cause of hindering me from treading the path of my duty," but he felt "in doubt and scrupulous" about their relationship. For days his diary was filled with self-condemnation. Even attendance at Holy Week ceremonies in April, while "not . . . without some fruit," seemed only to deepen his "certainty" that he was "a great sinner, a weak, ungrateful and cowardly Christian, doing nothing."[17]

In the midst of this he saw McCloskey and placed himself entirely in his hands. He seemed calmer after the visit. "All that we can do in this life is very little and this of less importance than it seems," he wrote in his diary. As a rule "we deserve nothing and therefore all that we have is given to us from God's mercy, for which we ought to be profoundly grateful at all times." Still, he remained perplexed. He felt "safer" now, but he had lost "much that was mine" in Concord, perhaps because he had little time for prayer and meditation. Not wanting to take up too much of the bishop's time, he still yearned for someone in whom he could confide.

McCloskey persisted in his suggestion of "sacred ministry," taking Hecker to visit the Jesuits, who had recently been installed at Rose Hill, and directing him to read the lives of Ignatius Loyola and Francis Xavier. A short time later Hecker received a note from a Catholic he had met some years before, informing him that "a German priest" wanted to see him. On April 24 Hecker visited Gabriel Rumpler, a Redemptorist stationed at that order's New York parish. Convinced that Hecker was called to the priesthood, Rümpler urged the young convert to make a retreat to determine what community he should enter. Redemptorist discipline seemed strict and its men of a high character, but Hecker was skeptical, for Rumpler was "a very zealous person and too much so it seems to me." Reluctant to place himself in hands other than McCloskey's, he refused the German priest's invitation, a decision confirmed by the bishop, who suggested he make a general confession and retreat at the Jesuit college. Determined to make a decision by July, Hecker prayed and practiced self-denial, hoping that if he pushed himself now he would not find the rigors of religious life too difficult. The first lesson was to be willing to be nothing, to purge himself of "self will" and the desire to "be thought more than I really am."[18]

By spring Hecker was on the verge of entering the seminary to study for the priesthood, a decision arising less from strong conviction than from a continuing inability to find an answer to his vocational question and a readiness, at least in part arising from confusion and self-doubt, to place himself in the hands of another. McCloskey, the closest thing to an immediate representative of the church's authority, was convinced he should become a priest. Rumpler seemed to appear mysteriously to confirm this call, and Brownson was enthusiastic. As with his conversion a year before, other options had failed to win his enthusiasm, waiting had become intolerable, no inner inspiration gave clear direction, and the advice of those he trusted became decisive. There was a sense of inevitability, even resignation, in his decision, which by May had become simply a question of choosing between the diocesan priesthood and a religious order "of severer discipline." He recognized that such a life demanded "great self-denial, humbleness and self-forgetfulness." On the other hand, he thought himself unqualified for such a vocation because of his "want of talent and culture." In addition, he was dissatisfied with McCloskey's spiritual direction. He tried very hard to open his soul to the mild, unassuming bishop, but he felt little consolation after their conferences.

He worked at being perfectly obedient, attributing his failings to self-will and his inability to be quiet and calm before the will of God. "All our anxiety, troubles and uneasiness arise from our own willfulness," he wrote. "If we would wholly submit to God, we should enjoy such peace, love and quietness that is His." He yearned for that experience, his hunger again distracting him from studies, confirming his conviction that they did not matter much in any case. Books were not profitable "until we had no need of them," he wrote one day. "We must come to depend more and more on what those who wrote depended on, rather than on what they wrote. Shall we depend upon the Bible when we have Jesus Christ himself?" The Bible, after all, was a guide, not the way itself.

But how to find the way? Here Hecker showed how far in spite of himself he departed from the direction of the church and his appointed spiritual director, whom he had pledged to follow. The problem of discovering what would aid a person's approach to God could "only be solved by each individual soul," Hecker thought. In matters where there was no infallible judge, "we have no higher ground of action than our conscience and reason to follow," and each one must work it out for himself:

> The Bible, the Lives of the Saints, and the ascetic and spiritual writers are in this matter no infallible rule—nor do they pretend to be. The thing itself is impossible. For how could such rules be laid down for each individual soul which is different from all others and should be as well adapted to it in its peculiarities as it is to those of very unlike characteristics? New diseases require new remedies. New times new measures. New masters make new laws. Hence it is each individual so far as he is truthful to the character bestowed upon him by his Creator must tread upon untrodden ground and sail in a different course. To make that similar which in the wisdom of God is dissimilar as the characteristics of man are would be sacrilegious not religious. Hence the true Church is Catholic. It meets all the wants of each individual of the Race.[19]

So he could not expect his director, or anyone else, to decide what path God wanted him to follow. Through willfulness or weakness, he might follow one to which he was not "assigned," but if he asked with the same sincerity as St. Paul, he might get an answer that would be plain.

Brownson was no more dependable a guide than McCloskey. In late June when Brownson arrived for a visit, Hecker noted in his diary his most detailed evaluation of his mentor to date. While Brownson had been his sympathetic friend and adviser, he "never moves my heart," Hecker admitted. Though himself "a man of heart," Brownson was "so strong and intellectually active that all his energy is consumed in thought. He is an intellectual athlete. He thinks for a dozen men." Sadly, Isaac noted that Brownson seldom took time for "contemplation and interior recollection." He was, and would probably remain, "a controversialist." In transcendentalist terms Brownson's "temperament" was not that of a "genius" but of "a rhetorician and declaimer," who "arrives at his truth by a regular and conservative system of logic." His mind was more "historical" than "practical" and he never "startled" Hecker with "profound truths rushing forth from his brain." Whatever there was of art or poetry "running through his nature," it was not enough "to tincture the whole flow of his life." Hecker had met no one so dedicated or self-sacrificing—Brownson's love of truth was supreme and his great enemy was bad logic—but it also was an important flaw, which made him "peevish and often rules his temper." As a result "he defeats but will never convince an opponent." "No one loves to break a lance with him because he cuts such ungentlemanly gashes. He is strong and he knows it." Some wondered why Hecker could "have such a friendship with Orestes Brownson," for "they imagine him to be so harsh and dictatorial," Hecker admitted. "We have not felt this. His presence does not change us. Nor do we find ourself [sic] where we were not after having met him." Hecker thought all Brownson's faults arose from his "nature," so that he was "genuine and we love him for this."[20]

On July 16 Isaac attended commencement ceremonies at Cornelius Academy. He had made no close friends, for the students he met there lacked "that deep earnestness which is a characteristic of a mind of any value." In fact, he concluded from his experience there that Protestantism had not the resources to move the world or put sin to rout. There was so much "ignorance, prejudice and such a want of humanity in the Protestant community" that Isaac was "glad to get free of its disagreeable presence." From his experience at the school he felt he had seen deeply into Protestantism and discovered "its want of deep spirituality, its superficiality and its inevitable tendency to no religion." Still the question of what he should do persisted. His "good advisors" told him to "accept things as they are," have faith in God, study, and help his brothers. But work in the bakery was "sin, damnation and death," he blurted out in his diary," and he was "not ready to go to hell yet friend." Instead, he must find his calling, a fit response to that summons he had first heard two years before:

> I want God's living work to do. My labor must be a sermon and every motion of my body a word, every act a sentence. My work must be devotional. I must feel that I am worshipping. It must be music love prayer holy to me my field must be the Kingdom of God. Christ must reign in me. What I do must be Christ in me doing and not me. . . . My work must be work of inspiration and aspiration. My heart cannot be in heaven when my head and hands are in hell. I must feel that I am building up Christ's Kingdom in all that I do.[21]

In June McCloskey had again raised the possibility of the diocesan priesthood, suggesting that he might begin his studies and transfer to a religious community later if he wished. However Hecker was still seeing Father Rumpler, despite his earlier reservations. He desired a sharper break from his past, his family and his surroundings than the diocesan priesthood required, he told Brownson, and he also wished to study in a "Catholic atmosphere," which he thought he would only find in Europe.

Hecker was not the only young convert meeting with the German priest. Earlier in the year New York's General Theological Seminary had been rocked by a conflict between young Episcopal seminarians influenced by the Oxford movement and church authorities determined to break the back of what they saw as a Catholic-tending rebellion in their ranks. When the Church's General Convention repudiated the reformers in May, two of them, James McMaster and Clarence Walworth, left the seminary and began taking instructions with Father Rumpler. By mid-June they were baptized and applied for entry into the Redemptorists. McMaster wrote a friend that the Redemptorist Provincial, Father Gather de Held, and their most eloquent preacher, Father Bernard Hafkenscheid, were in the country. If they accepted them as candidates, he and Walworth hoped to sail with the two priests at the end of July, stopping to visit "our Oxford friends" in England before proceeding to the Redemptorist novitiate in Belgium.[22]

Sometime that summer Hecker met the two young men and decided to join them. As late as July 25 he told Brownson he would probably follow Archbishop Hughes' advice and go to Paris to study with the Sulpicians, a move which would allow him to observe several religious orders. But four days later he told Hughes he would join his new friends and enter the Redemptorists. He needed the permission of Father de Held, who was in

Baltimore, so, leaving his brother George to pack his bags and arrange his tickets, Isaac took a night train and arrived at the Redemptorist house in Baltimore at four in the morning. Meeting de Held as he emerged from Mass a short time later, Isaac satisfied the provincial that he had adequate preparation in Latin and his request was granted. Rushing back to New York on a morning train, he arrived barely in time to bid a fast farewell to his family and join McMaster and Walworth aboard ship.[23]

He left with the pledge of prayers, and a not too subtle warning from his oldest Catholic friend. Brownson gently urged him to overcome his still strong tendency toward mysticism. The old "notion" of communion, which had "wrought revolution" for them both could become dangerous and heretical if taken too far, he argued. Hecker should distrust all modern Catholic writers, for even the best had been influenced by Protestantism. Instead, he should remember that "the Church is objective. It proposes truths to be believed and acts to be performed. It concerns almost exclusively the reason and the will." In the year since their conversion, Hecker had held fast to the central ideas and experiences that had drawn him to the church. There is little evidence he heeded, then or later, his friend's advice.[24]

Once again a central question had been answered, almost impulsively. For all his talk of inspiration, Isaac Hecker was not an outwardly emotional man, and he was little given to irrational action. Indeed, throughout his life he was noted for attention to detail, careful planning and methodical work. Yet, at the most crucial moments of his life, leaving home, entering the church, joining a religious order, Hecker acted suddenly and decisively and never turned back.

He was now on board a ship headed to a new life in a Redemptorist novitiate in Belgium. His American road to Rome had taken a new turn, now to Europe, as a way station on a new journey which would lead, he already knew, back to America.

Part Two: The Promise of American Catholicism

5

In Another Country

The little group arrived in London on August 26 after a "pleasant and very quiet" passage of twenty-five days. While McMaster went off to visit John Henry Newman at his retreat in Littlemore, Hecker and Walworth remained in London, impatient to move on to the seminary at St. Trond in Belgium. On Saturday Hecker wrote his family, reassuring them of his happiness: "I am going towards that point where secretly I have always been tending. The nearer I approach it, the happier I am." On receiving this letter, George wrote Brownson that the novitiate was "the goal that he has for years secretly wished for," although his brother's departure had been difficult for his mother, who could "hardly overcome it."[1]

The three young Americans joined thirty others from Holland, Belgium and Germany at St. Trond, where they immediately began a retreat prior to donning the habit on October 15. The language of the novitiate was French, so Hecker began studying the language in every free moment, of which there were few. The novitiate lasted one year, during which the applicants studied the Redemptorist Constitution and Rule and lived a Religious life, surrendering their wills to that of their superiors, eradicating their faults, and testing their vocation. More than two weeks after arriving at St. Trond Hecker told Brownson "conditions here are perfect." He wrote his family: "All my seeking is now ended. . . . You can scarce imagine the happiness I felt on my arrival here. For three days my heart was filled with joy and gladness. It was like one who had been transported to a lovelier, purer and better world."[2]

After the anxiety of his long search for God, for the true church, and for a vocation, Hecker found rest and security in the beauty of the physical setting of the novitiate, in its Catholic atmosphere, and in the routine of its life. Hecker describes the daily schedule to his mother. At 4:30 A.M. the seminarians woke to an alarm bell. One seminarian entered each room, saying in Latin, "But Thou, Oh Lord, have mercy"; the student responded, "Thanks be to God and Mary." At 5:00 the bell rang again, summoning the students to the oratory for meditation and reciting of the breviary. At 5:30 they heard Mass and received communion, then returned to their rooms to say acts of thanksgiving or to read the Rule. Breakfast was at 7:30, followed by manual labor, if they were assigned, or relaxation in the garden. At 8:30, they were back in the chapel for the rosary, a reading from a spiritual work, and the stations of the cross. At 10:45 they had their first free time for reading or meditation on spiritual matters. During dinner at noon they listened to a reading from a spiritual work. At 1:30 in the afternoon they went back to the chapel until 2:00, when they had some more free time. The recreation periods after dinner and supper were the only times the seminarians were allowed to break silence. At 2:45 they visited the Blessed Sacrament; at 3:00 they went back to their rooms for a half-hour reading about the life of a saint and another half-hour meditation. At 4:00 they returned to the Oratory to recite the breviary. At 5:15 there was recreation until 6:00, when they worked on memorizing the Redemptorist Constitution. They then recited what they had memorized and at 7:00 returned to the Oratory for meditation. Supper was followed by a brief recreation period, evening prayers in the chapel and retirement at 9:00. The routine varied a bit; Thursdays and principal festivals of the church were recreation days, in which their spiritual exercises totaled only about two hours. On those days the students often took a walk in the neighborhood. Friday, on the other hand, was a day of strict and total silence.

Hecker told his family that he found these exercises quite delightful. The changes prevented them from becoming monotonous, and the variety made them "agreeable." Time passed rapidly and there were diversions. In the time set for recreation they could have music, and many of the brothers could play the piano or sing. There were twenty novices in the house; with the fathers and lay brothers the community numbered forty or fifty in all. Much of the conversation took place in German. In March 1846 Hecker reported he had not had a half hour's English conversation in over a month. The year-long period of novitiate was designed to test the vocation and form the character of the Religious. Following that, they would proceed to the studentate, about thirty miles away in Holland, where the education was much more thorough.[3]

During Hecker's first months in Europe a new note of Catholic militance appeared in his writings. His letters to his family were filled with pleas that they leave their Protestant churches and enter the one true church; only in that way, he insisted, could they avoid eternal damnation. In his first letter from London, written three days after his arrival, he told them: "The truth is, with me the unsafeness of your position gives me more trouble of mind than anything else except it be my own salvation." Apparently his father had reentered the family; Isaac urged him to put his life in order. "You must not give up seeking but get George to get some German books for you to read from Father Rumpler," he wrote in mid-September. "Remain not where you are if you would overcome temptations, the world, and gain heaven." He urged his Episcopalian brother John and sister Catherine to read the works of Newman and the other Tractarians who had entered the church, insisting that as long as he loved them he would pray for their conversion. He continued in this vein throughout 1845 and 1846. To his mother he constantly insisted that only if she were converted could they be reunited in heaven. His respect for non-Catholic communions had all but disappeared as he pleaded with his mother to leave her Methodist "assembly without sacraments, founded by a man who fell, as he himself confesses, into the grossest errors." When he heard that his mother was visiting the Redemptorist fathers, he expressed his pleasure and returned to the attack: "You know, too, dear mother, that the principal motives which led and moved those who separated themselves from the Roman Catholic Church were self-will, personal ambition, pride, lust, and the spirit of error, which delights in separation and controversy. And these are still the motives which keep a number of their followers from submitting to the Church of Christ."[4]

By this time Hecker's zeal was clearly focused on converting not only his family but his country to the Catholic faith. Even at the very beginning of his introduction to institutional Catholicism, he had visions of his future career. In an early letter to his family, written from St. Trond, he told his mother he would never return to America "otherwise than as a poor missionary priest to labor and suffer for the salvation of the most abandoned souls . . . and for the conversion of our country." Commenting to his family on the statues and crucifixes placed along the foot trails through the woods and fields near the novitiate, he lamented the absence of such a visible Christian presence in American life. He hoped the time would come in the United States when similar shrines would appear "at the crossroads and other places." He wanted a Catholicism for American culture, as well as for the American people.

> Religion must become an everyday business and a public affair if souls are to be saved and sanctified, and the people made peaceable and happy. It must be in the closet but also in the family, in

> society, in trade and commerce; its spirit must pervade our public assemblies and penetrate our legislation. Its spirit must be everywhere, for out of Christ there is no way, no truth, no life. But alas this never can exist in our land so long as there are such a number of sects, isms, and schisms.[5]

In his appeals to those he cared for Hecker was providing evidence not only of his own personal faith but of a conviction which would more and more shape his life. He believed that his own course had been guided by the Holy Spirit toward a true end, God, found in the church. He believed as well that this was the end of all human aspirations, all those yearnings for a higher and richer life he had felt among his friends in New England. If this was so, if the salvation found through the church was the natural and necessary answer to the questions arising in every honest heart, then he needed to announce that good news. By now he was so convinced of all this that the truth seemed self-evident, if people would only look and listen. What he had found, they too could find, and at no more sacrifice of personal integrity than he had made. This unwavering conviction, that he must preach that good news, eventually would guide him to seek out an audience and, when that audience proved less than responsive, to explore the barriers which prevented honest and earnest people, so like himself, from hearing the message. That in turn would lead him to new forms of evangelization and, even later, to efforts to make that evangelization more effective by making his church a more credible witness to the truth it wished to convey.

All that lay in the future. What preoccupied him now was the need to deepen his own spiritual life amid the seminary's regular routine of work, study and prayer. The novitiate was a congenial environment.

Hecker found in the Redemptorist Rule and exercises, and in Catholic spiritual writers, a conceptual structure to make sense of his own experience. In mid-October, when he took his vows as a member of the Redemptorists, he wrote his mother and used his new resources to explain himself. He admitted that his life during the past few years must have seemed strange to his family and friends; until recently, it had seemed equally strange to him. The road that led him to God was not an ordinary road, he believed, but one which few traveled. Hecker explained that when God saw a soul sincerely desirous of finding the truth and uniting itself to him, he prepared the soul for this "by infusing into the heart a secret love which consumes its inordinate human affections and pleasures of the senses." This love is hidden even from the person while God weans the heart away from things of the world; the person was conscious of this change, but ignorant of its cause. "The more that the heart was attached to these human and worldly pleasures, the more rigorous and severe will have to be this trial and this purgation," Hecker wrote. In becoming detached from family and friends, the person suffered "inexpressible pain." Instead of loving company, he loved solitude, even expressing himself toward loved ones "in a cutting and cruel manner." Almost without knowing why, the person mortifies his senses of eating, drinking, sleeping and clothing. "Who would believe that it is the love of God which is the hidden and secret cause of this cruel suffering?" Hecker asked. He was convinced that this was what had happened in his life.

In order that his soul could attain union with God, it had first to be "purged from all its imperfections, its disorderly affections, and worldly attachments." Once the soul was freed from these "defects," God infused a love even more subtle and penetrating than the first in order to cleanse the soul of its "will, its judgment, its memory, in a word, the use of all its faculties." This "second purgation" was even more rigorous and severe than the first: "The soul is as it were chained down upon a rack and suffers inexpressible tortures." In this period the individual can do nothing intellectually or physically and seems to suffer "the torments of hell." God at this point is demanding "a complete submission, subjection, and subjugation of his whole being" and is "unrelenting until this is accomplished."

He knew he had caused his family much pain, but he thought himself "blameless," for he acted "involuntarily." Having freed his soul from its imperfections, God infused into his heart "the Christian virtues and graces" in the third stage of his spiritual development. God enlightened Hecker's soul and poured in upon it "sometimes in torrents, His divine love, in order for the soul to embrace the truth that He gives it . . . and to be united to Him most intimately." It was at Concord that Hecker experienced this third stage, and it was "the cause of my sudden return and entrance into the holy Catholic church."

Hecker said his life now was all that he could ask. The lives and writing of Catholic saints and the grace of God had "made my experience intelligible to me." In a similar, detailed letter to Brownson, he noted that the writings of St. John of the Cross and St. Catherine of Genoa had helped him to understand his spiritual journey. He had followed the "passive" rather than the "active" way to God; and had been led from Egypt, through the desert, to peace in Israel. Perhaps most influential were the writings of the seventeenth-century French Jesuit Louis Lallement, whose particular brand of Ignatian spirituality struck a responsive chord in Hecker's own experience. Lallement emphasized the need for each person to recognize the presence of God in the human heart and in the events of daily life. Holding forth an ideal of contemplation and action, of the pursuit of holiness in the midst of strenuous activity, and reconciling the voice of conscience with the authority of the church, Lallement confirmed many of Hecker's instincts and gave a direction to his spiritual life for years to come.

Still aware of the reservations his family might have, he concluded their letter, written just before taking his first vows, with words of comfort addressed to his mother.

> Dear mother: in a half an hour I go to the chapel to consecrate my whole being forever to God in His service. What peace! What happiness! this gives me. To live alone for His love and to love all for His love, in His love, and with His love! We leave nothing in leaving all for God.[6]

That same day he informed Bishop McCloskey, who had been so important in his conversion, that he had passed through the novitiate without doubts regarding his vocation. The next day he would leave with eight others for Witten, fifty miles away, to pursue his studies. Once again, he expressed the conviction that he had a particular, perhaps providential, role to play in the future. "Perhaps it is not simply for the salvation and sanctification of my own soul that our Blessed Lord has bestowed upon me so many favors," he told the bishop. "It would be my greatest delight to be, with his grace and in his time, an aide to you, Right Reverend Father, in converting our country to the holy church of our Lord and the honor of our Blessed Virgin Mary."[7]

Returning from the ceremony of consecration Hecker wrote yet another letter, this one to his brother John. He had taken the "holy vows of the Catholic religion which are obedience, poverty, chastity, and final perseverance," he wrote, and these vows bound him solemnly to the Redemptorists for the rest of his life. It was the custom, when one was received into the congregation, for the family to give "a certain sum" for his support. Ordinarily families of European students gave five hundred francs a year; some gave more and others less according to their means. Nothing was required; even if no gift was received he would be treated equally, but John would be doing him "a very great favor and merit and receive the prayers of the order daily" if he was able to make such a donation. But, he added quickly, "our love will not be affected one way or another."[8]

These affectionate letters to his Methodist mother and Episcopalian brother brought no change in his passion for their conversion. He was also pursuing his friends, including Henry Thoreau. Interest in Thoreau's "greatest welfare" compelled him to write. "The Catholic church is the ideal of every individual of the race, the universal ideal of humanity," Hecker insisted. When one reached that ideal in communion with the church, a new life began, "a higher, sublimer, supernatural career." Sustained by supernatural love, the soul reached "the end of its creation, the perfect union with an immediate vision of God." Wherever Catholic influence was strong, therefore, people acted from a higher inspiration and entered a "life of art, of poetry, of social happiness, of political freedom." Hecker concluded: "We don't want the middle ages, but we want its inspiration. It is here my friend, it is here. *Mon Dieu* could you see and feel it once!"[9]

During his novitiate, Hecker flourished, aided by the hours of prayer and his first exposure to the Catholic mystics. In the studentate at Witten, however, some old problems reappeared, most notably, his aversion to systematic study. This may have arisen from his relative lack of experience with formal classes, but it also apparently derived from the distracting spiritual turmoil hinted at in his letters home. Fr. Michael Heilig, his confessor and spiritual director, was sympathetic, but Heilig was made provincial, replacing Father de Held, in December 1847. In the spring the seminary was hit with an outbreak of typhus, and Hecker served tirelessly in the infirmary. When the faculty and students returned, Hecker found study impossible. On May 25, 1848, Heilig instructed the faculty to relieve Hecker of formal classes and assign him to the infirmary, and he told the young American to prepare a written account of his spiritual life, which Hecker did, submitting it on May 30.[10]

Since entering the novitiate Hecker had abandoned his diary, probably at the direction of his superiors, who undoubtedly would have considered such a practice self-indulgent. That judgment is supported by the introduction to his report, in which he expressed "the utmost repugnance" at setting forth the "sentiments or inspirations which I have felt more or less strongly for some time past," even though he had done just that in his letters to his family and Brownson six months earlier. Nevertheless, in order to "satisfy my sentiment of duty, and also that you may be able to direct me securely by seeing whether my sentiments are illusory or real," he recorded his spiritual experience up to and including his year in the college. He began by stating that, from his youth until his entry into the Catholic church, he was unable to avoid an awareness that his ways "had been singularly directed by providence." He believed, and had always believed, that providence called him to "an active life," although some advisors thought his vocation was contemplative. He believed in both: "I have always felt a strong and even irresistible attraction for the interior life and nevertheless I never lost sight of an active life—but supernaturally active."

Entering the studentate, he intended to apply himself to "solid and general learning" and had "not the remotest inclination to interrupt the regular course" of studies, but he now doubted whether he could apply himself. Before his conversion, whenever he had begun to study, he was "forced by some non-material cause or other" to stop. Similarly, during his first year in the studentate, he was at times drawn away from "scientific subjects." He feared submitting, for he was "sensible of a certain remnant of natural activity." Nevertheless, in spite of himself, his "faculties were more or less suspended." He then described his spiritual experiences in more detail. "I would see God as a brilliant sun in the centre of my soul," he wrote. The result could not be described otherwise "than by saying that it is some sort of participation of the life of the blessed—for I can hope for nothing further after death than its perfection and continuance."

If asked how all this was to end and what could be done, Isaac could only answer that God was directing him. Since entering religious life he had "tried to acquire a total indifference to all states and places, thinking that otherwise I could never be a true disciple of Him who became a servant of all in order to save the world." For a considerable time, "all power to think was taken from me and my soul seemed like a blank surface before God." Now things had become clearer and Hecker thought he knew what God had in store for him.

> I believe that providence calls me to an active life: further that He calls me to America to convert a certain class of persons among whom I found myself before my conversion: I believe that I shall be the vile instrument which He will make use of for the conversion of a multitude of those unhappy souls who aspire after truth without having the means to arrive at and possess it. But to convince me that this work will not be mine and that I shall be only the mean instrument for the accomplishment of His designs He wills me to be deprived of all human means, so I shall not attribute His glory to myself.

Hecker went on to argue that, contrary to what he had believed earlier, God had now shown him that it was not by learning or eloquence that he would convert others, "but solely by His grace and power." If this were true, he could only follow God's direction. He requested permission to study on his own: "I have the conviction that God will permit me to apply myself sufficiently to arrive at the end to which He seems to call me. Thus I think could I be permitted to set myself to acquire what is absolutely necessary, chiefly the practical knowledge required to exercise the sacred ministry, God would abundantly supply all else of which I have need."[11]

Surprisingly, Hecker's request was granted. Walworth, who had studied for the Episcopal ministry before his conversion, was ordained after two years, in August, 1848. He was then sent to serve with the newly established Redemptorist community of St. Mary's at Clapham, outside London, where Father de Held served as rector. Hecker, not yet ready for ordination, was also assigned there so that he could be close to de Held. Hecker arrived in September, but a short time later de Held was transferred; Louis de Buggenoms replaced him and became Hecker's confessor and life long friend.

In December 1848 Hecker learned that his mother was seriously ill and had only narrowly escaped death. Once again, he begged her to think of the great pain he would feel if she died outside the church, but he added an affectionate thanks for her prayers and for those of his father and asked forgiveness for his own lack of faithfulness: "How much more I might have done for father than what I did. Alas, I did scarcely anything." That same day he wrote to his Aunt Betsy, expressing gratification that she, too, had escaped death and, in that same letter, he addressed himself to his father: "Dear father, I know of nothing that gives me more pain than when I think of the habit that has governed you for so many years past. Surely if you do not conquer it you can not expect to see heaven. God has expressly declared in the Bible that those who are given to this custom can not, shall not, enter the kingdom of heaven." He insisted that he would continue to pray that his father would be able to resist this temptation and he asked John, George and his mother to help him.[12]

Isaac's enthusiasm for their conversion irritated some of his friends. He must have written the Curtis brothers jointly in early 1849, for they responded within days of each other in mid-February. George Curtis expressed appreciation for Hecker's affection, but he was less happy with Isaac's zeal. "As by nature and observation I have long since declared for the heart," he wrote, "I am not disturbed by the opposition and condemnation of your head." Burrill Curtis believed Hecker's "almost exclusive religious bent" had led "to a degree of inexactness in his judgment of character." He had always respected the Catholic church, but "the only thing likely to prejudice me, more than some things do, against it, might be too great zeal on the part of some of its members to convert."

Hecker's correspondence with the Curtis brothers ceased, but he tried again with Thoreau. In the summer of 1849 Isaac urged his friend to recognize that "the gate out of the present era of folly is close; the gate lies at your feet." Another object of Hecker's evangelizing zeal was Charles Lane, who responded good-naturedly: "If my soul is not expanded in the way you desire, your own is warmed in the act of missionarizing me."[13]

Hecker's efforts to convert his family and friends were not having favorable results. His continuing struggle to integrate his spiritual life into a life of action was not resolved either. He remained in close contact with Heilig, whose support had been so important in the spring. The older man was encouraging but invariably cautious. In October Hecker once again tried to communicate to his advisor his ongoing experience of God. Hecker thought his experience similar to those described by the major figures in the Catholic mystical tradition. To illustrate this claim, he described an event that took place during the latter part of his novitiate. One day, when giving thanks after Holy Communion, he found himself unable to make his customary prayer. He felt the Lord telling him to cease activity, as if to say, "I have no need of your thanks or words when I have your will. It is I and not you who should act. I cease to act when you begin, and begin to act when you cease. I wish you to be still, tranquil, to listen and suffer me to act. Abandon yourself to me and I will take care of you." This spirit of abandonment now dominated his life; he thought it the state described by the mystics as "the first degree of supernatural prayer." His mind was more and more fixed upon God and his heart absorbed in "his infinite love." In silence and stillness "an extraordinary light" came into his soul, bringing him "a filial affection for God." In this state, he felt a "constant and continual hunger and thirst for our Lord in the sacrament of his body and blood." If it were possible, he would "receive no other food than this, for it is the only nourishment that I have a real appetite for." The doctrine of the real presence had become for him a conviction "arising more from experience than from faith." Even when visiting the Blessed Sacrament, he was "seized with such a violent love" that his soul seemed to be "in the same sphere as our Lord in the Sacrament, where there appears no time nor space." At times, as during his retreat before taking his vows, he was "as it were inebriated with love," so that he "scarcely knew what I said or did."

This was the state of his interior life when he entered the house of studies at Witten. For over a year Hecker slept on boards, rarely for more than five hours, wore the large cilice constantly, and took the discipline of self-administered flagellation for fifteen minutes or longer every day except Sundays and Thursdays: "Often the blood would flow from the affects [sic]." For many months he ate no meat and often little else. He even considered requesting permission "to make a coat of mail with points to cover my whole body." Instead, he frequently fastened the small cilices upon his breast. "The vilest habits and things that I was allowed to wear and to use gave me the greatest pleasure," he reported. "The thought of not having wearwith to cover my nakedness, of being condemned, ridiculed, and spit upon, gave me extreme joy." He threw off all possessions he thought superfluous, including manuscripts that were in his possession and books that he could do without: "It was as though I had scarcely need of a body in order to live, or in other words, it seemed that I lived for the most part independent of the body."

During this period God gave him the grace that he had longed for to suffer without any idea of recompense. Feeling himself "a slave and hireling in the service of God," he had been "mortified" and "much ashamed of myself" but, when this grace was given unexpectedly, he experienced a new sense of joy and freedom. At the same time, he began to feel a close communion with certain of the saints, such as St. Francis of Assisi, St. Bernard, St. Thomas and St. Alphonsus, founder of the Redemptorists. At one time he was given a special devotion to the Holy Cross, which enabled him to understand how "when St. Thomas demanded of St. Bonaventure what books he read in order to write, he simply pointed to the crucifix." During a year or more, in his spiritual exercises, he was "gently seized with a species of slumber." This "suspension of the faculties" had long been regarded as "one of the most singular in the history of the interior life, for the soul doubts whether it is asleep or awake, but returns to a wakefulness with a consciousness of more lively and universal love, a greater joy and peace." Yet it was never so complete that it left him without doubts, even scruples.

At the beginning of his second year of studies, Hecker reported, his faculties were concentrated to such a degree toward the center of his soul that he was bereft of his exterior senses. He could not resist the "attraction towards interior recollection." Heretofore, Hecker had been conscious of having the freedom to exercise his will; that gave him "more or less liberty to apply myself to the studies." But now he was even deprived of this and it was out of his power to make any resistance; he could only resign himself. Again turning to spiritual writers, he explained this experience as "a certain participation of the beatific vision." His soul could hope for nothing else after death than its continuation. It caused a great and living thirst within his soul, a weakness, an emptiness that yearned for love. From this flowed "rivers of brotherly love, longing to do good to one's neighbor as to creatures of God," and "desires for the conversion of the nations, leading back of heretics and sinners, a tender love of the innocent, and zeal for helping souls detained in purgatory." At this stage Hecker experienced a new incapacity to engage in penance and even the slightest touch caused "inconceivable pain." With St. Teresa and St. Mary of Jesus, he shared a sense of horror at those penances in which he had previously taken pleasure. Hecker ended this report with quotes from several spiritual writers on this "languor of love." He was confident that this change meant for him, as it had for St. Teresa, a final extinguishing of the effects of sin, laying "the basis for regeneration of a new life and for activities more agreeable to God's pleasure."[14]

Unfortunately, Hecker's spiritual directors were not entirely sympathetic. Somewhat testily, Hecker charged that "scarcely one" had read the important books of the mystical traditions. He believed that those who had not made a special study of mysticism, or had not shared such experiences, could not direct others "with wisdom and profit." St. Teresa and St. John of the Cross had deplored "this almost universal ignorance" in their time and it was no less true today. So Hecker lacked the unquestioning submissiveness expected of new-comers to religious life. No wonder his superiors had difficulty determining what to do with him. They were forced to judge the genuineness and sincerity of his reports, unusual in themselves and even more subject to skepticism when coming from a convert, and an American at that. They could be forgiven some irritation at his criticism of spiritual direction, and some skepticism at his claim to have experienced the spiritual gifts of the church's greatest saints.

Heilig, for his part, encouraged Hecker's passion for God but warned him against the dangers of self-indulgence and delusion. He knew Hecker had suffered a great deal, performed many acts of virtue, and was destined "to do a great deal one day for the salvation of souls." He assured him, too, that he was not in any danger in his present state as long as he would "remain docile to the advice" of his superiors. If he was in the world, Heilig feared he would fall into the "most terrible faults," but in the congregation he would risk nothing by pursuing his spiritual calling. However, he warned him that "this state of impression and suspension of faculties so varied and so violent—does not befit you and consequently you ought to strive to rid yourself of them gradually." Spiritual ecstasy was "like a great garment that can be good for a man of large stature but if a small man put it on he will have indeed the mien of a tall man but he is nonetheless troubled and embarrassed." Of course persons at different degrees of spiritual development could have such experiences, "but you are not there," he warned his young charge. In the spiritual life, Heilig told him, people must, as in all affairs of life, "begin at the beginning and not at the end, backwards." Hecker's misfortune was that he had passed too quickly from "lower degrees to higher degrees of the spiritual life."

Most strange to European ears was Hecker's intense self-consciousness, the "self-forming" power described by Channing. Like diary keeping, it seemed dangerous, an expression of self-centeredness and pride. In humility, and in all sincerity, Hecker had been seeking the Lord and had been given great graces, Heilig admitted, but he was "mistaken in stopping to examine the divine operation and in attaching himself rather to the gift than to the giver." Reading mystical books, he discovered that others had had similar experiences and applied these to himself, a way of proceeding that might be good for those well-advanced in the spiritual life, but not good for a beginner like Hecker: "The demon and self-love have come upon you unawares and have confirmed you in false application of some spiritual principles to your own state." He recognized that Hecker could not suddenly change his feelings, but he insisted that he could change his conduct "in regard to those impressions and operations which you experience within yourself." What was he to do? Heilig's answer was clear:

> You must first believe blindly that you are not in *via extraordinaria perfectionis* but only in *via ordinaria* and act in consequence as much as it will be possible for you. Second, despise all these impressions, however holy and strong they may be, and pay them no more heed then does a man with the noise children make on the street. Do not speak—and write of them except with a supreme contempt. Almost never think of them and if you do think of them let it only be with scorn.

Heilig understood that such a practice would be painful, but it was necessary and was "founded on very holy and sound principles." By proceeding in this direction, Hecker would not move away from God but come closer to him. He urged Hecker to apply his greatest attention to "interior mortification, to the ruses and seekings of self-love." He insisted that he had not written such harsh words without consideration for Hecker. He remained convinced of Hecker's sincerity and holiness; nevertheless, he warned him that he would risk great dangers if he did not humbly submit himself to the direction of those responsible for his spiritual welfare.[15]

Two months later Heilig told Hecker once again to trust in his spiritual director. He was confident that one day Hecker would be "very useful in the congregation. You stand well with your superiors and that is an argument I am advancing."[16] That Isaac accepted his friend's advice is evident in the fact that from this point on he seems to have kept no further record of his spiritual experiences, at least for many years. Heilig's reference to the "argument I am advancing" undoubtedly referred to continuing controversy within the congregation regarding Hecker's unusual method of preparing for the priesthood. No one doubted his sincerity, and his spiritual directors testified both to his intense devotion to God, the Blessed Mother, and the Rule, and to his at least outwardly docile acceptance of their advice. Moreover, when he felt ready, he took oral examinations in the required areas of study and received good grades. Indeed, his over-all record compared favorably to that of the more academically experienced Walworth. Accordingly, in the fall of 1849, Hecker was judged worthy of ordination and, on October 23, he received the sacrament of Holy Orders from Nicholas Cardinal Wiseman.[17]

Years later, when an old man, Hecker told his disciple Walter Elliott that he had "blundered" into the Redemptorists. Because he "craved" intimate and careful spiritual direction, in order to forward his pursuit of "a perfect life," he had believed it necessary to join a religious community. He had indeed found at least some sympathetic directors, notably Heilig and de Buggenoms, and had submitted to their advice, though only after more give and take than his directors were accustomed to. Hecker found confirmation of his experience and legitimation of his mystical yearning in the Catholic spiritual writers, but his directors, wary of premature ecstasy and the subtle workings of human pride, regularly tried to confine his spiritual life within conventional forms. Hecker seemingly accepted their advice, though he remained remarkably independent; he no longer kept his diary, he turned more attention to apostolic work, and he became a zealous priest and cooperative religious. That he was less happy than appears is suggested by the fact that he continued to seek out writers, like Lallement, who offered alternative approaches to spiritual direction, developed innovative methods himself when dealing with individuals, and complained later of the rigidity of the direction he received during his seminary years.

Now he was a priest, attached to the little Redemptorist community at Clapham. They gave missions throughout the city of London and received a trickle of converts. Hecker told his mother that they were slandered by Anglican and Presbyterian preachers but were building a beautiful, large, Gothic chapel, the foundations of which had been laid in August of 1849.

In early 1850 the Redemptorists decided to make some changes in the American province, placing a famous mission preacher, Bernard Hafkenscheid, in charge and establishing a new English-language mission band with Hecker, Walworth and two other American converts who were being trained at the new American seminary in Maryland, Abraham F. Hewit and Francis Baker. Elated by the news that he would be returning home, Isaac wrote his mother in September that he would embark the following month, but in November he was still in London, promising to see them soon. Isaac had written the congregation's vicar general asking if he might call on him to discuss American affairs before leaving, but Father Smetana responded in early November, giving several reasons why such a meeting was impractical. He told Hecker to write to him, promising to make no decisions about the United States without reflection and prayer.

On January 11 Heilig wrote from Liege with the news that Father Bernard had been again delayed. Father Heissberger had only then arrived from Bavaria with formal notification of Bernard's appointment as American provincial. Heilig, himself slated for a year's reflection and then a term as consultor for the community, bid Hecker goodbye. Finally, arrangements were made and Hecker could write his mother that they would be sailing from Le Havre for New York on January 28, 1851.[18] The vocational question, like that of faith, had been answered, it seemed; he was a priest, a missionary, with new work to do. That work, as the Redemptorists understood it, was to enliven the faith of Catholics in the United States, still regarded as a missionary country. For Hecker, who knew the country better, it was a work which pointed further, toward the conversion of a "special class" he had known well, and with them the conversion of the nation, so that its people might, as he had done, find the truth which was the origin and the object of their dreams and aspirations.

6

American Evangelist

Isaac Thomas Hecker was thirty-one years old when he returned from Europe a Redemptorist priest. There had been a curious pattern to his personal life. Everywhere he went he aroused warmth and affection, even among people who had good reason to be irritated with him. His brothers might have been impatient, even angry, when Isaac abandoned the family and their business to pursue his dreamy notion of a higher life. Moreover, Isaac regularly questioned his older brothers' work and criticized their way of life, at times sounding arrogant and self-righteous. Yet there was never the least doubt of their love; they seemed ever ready to consider changes at home, to provide financial assistance, even to examine their religious views in light of his changing ideas. Similarly, at Brook Farm and Fruitlands, Hecker maintained a sturdy independence and a critical spirit remarkable for one of his background; he did not hesitate to challenge even the great Emerson or to offer candid criticism of Alcott only days after joining him. Yet, with few exceptions, his companions seemed to find him refreshing and many of the friendships he made survived even Hecker's triumphant Catholic pleas for their conversion. Once again, in the novitiate and seminary, he pursued his own course, listened to criticism, submitted without surrendering his own ideas, and won the confidence, respect, even love of most of his superiors.

One explanation is that young Hecker was a transparently sincere idealist in an age which valued "earnestness" above all. At times his ideas were vague and impractical, but they obviously arose from a lively spirit. He was a hard worker, as his companions at Fruitlands discovered, and once committed, he gave his all to a cause, as his fellow novices learned in the seminary. Freed from formal studies, he must have worked very hard to win approval for ordination and earn a good academic evaluation. Among the few descriptions of his personality was one written by Brownson in the middle 1850s, a decade after their conversion. It offers a portrait of a man whose warmth and enthusiasm made many tolerate his unusual ideas and overlook his implicit criticism of others:

> No one can commune with him for half an hour, and ever be again precisely what he was before. He is one of those men whom you feel it is good to be with. Virtue goes out from him. Simple, unpretending and playful, and docile as a child, warm and tender in his feelings, full of life and cheerfulness of manner, he wins at once your love, and infuses as it were his own sunshiny nature into your heart. From his youth he has been remarkable for his singular purity of heart, the guilelessness of his soul, the earnestness of his spirit, his devotion to truth, and his longing after perfection. We owe personally more than we can say to our long and intimate acquaintance with him.[1]

A young man who could write, days after deciding to become a Catholic, though having almost no acquaintance with Catholics, that the nineteen-centuries-old church needed "a new generation" to fit it for the modern world, might have irritated people and made them ignore his seemingly extravagant and visionary proposals. That they did not, but on the contrary came to respect the man, admire his vision and support his work is further testimony to the unusual personality described by Brownson.

When Hecker arrived in New York in March 19, 1851, he was on the threshold of the busy, active life he had sought for a decade. He would need all the charm he could muster if his hopes were to be realized and his enthusiastic faith given space for its exercise. Establishment of an English-language mission band proved a wise stroke, for Hecker and the other fathers were soon hard at work, with more invitations than they could possibly handle. They worked first under Father Bernard, assisted by Hungarian-born Father Alexander Czvitkovitz, who became their superior when Father Bernard was transferred in 1853. They began with a highly successful mission in New York, the first organized mission given in English in the United States. Hecker reported that six thousand people went to confession and received communion, while sobbing filled the church at the renewal of baptismal vows.

On April 27 they were at a mission in Loretto, Pennsylvania. Almost all the people in the area were Catholics, and most of the three thousand

Catholics were native-born Americans; only three or four hundred were Irish and German immigrants. "It is like a green spot in a great desert," Hecker wrote his brother George. The German priests delivered a mission nearby, but the English fathers needed their help to administer the sacraments to the great crowds. After eight days in Loretto, the band moved on. In the cities, Hecker, whose previous contact with the American church was minimal, found the large numbers of Catholics everywhere they preached "a constant source of surprise." They gave fourteen missions during their first season; at some they distributed as many as four and five thousand communions. Hecker told his English friend, Richard Simpson, that he found the "country missions particularly gratifying." He described the enthusiasm stirred by one mission event:

> We planted an immense cross near the church; the congregation was composed of backwoodsmen. At the conclusion of the ceremony we gave three cheers for the Holy Cross, and then made the welkin ring with their stout voices, and it gained their hearts for us.[2]

Hecker seemed to thrive on the work. They were a group of priests who traveled the country "preaching penance and doing good," and he could imagine "no life so like the life which our Savior lived when upon earth." The mission sermons themselves were designed to awaken among the Catholics of the area a sense of their need for the sacraments; success was measured in terms of the numbers who made their confession and received communion. But the mission records also mentioned the improvement of Catholic behavior, especially in reducing drunkenness, and the consequent increase in respect for the church among non-Catholics.

Father Walworth's book of mission sermons outlined the typical schedule. After the opening ceremonies, the main sermons proceeded through the topics of salvation, mortal sin, the necessity for penance, death, judgment, hell, the mercy of God, the sacraments, the Blessed Virgin Mary, the unity, apostolicity, sanctity, and catholicity of the church, and the "means of perseverance." Walworth ordinarily gave the scarier sermons; he was universally acknowledged the nation's most powerful Catholic preacher, able to arouse fear and contrition in the hardest sinner. Hewit, a scholarly, reserved man, gave the sermons on the church, while Hecker gave only a few mission sermons, taking major responsibility for the instructions offered after morning Mass. His short instruction on the rosary was so impassioned he was dubbed "Father Mary" by his colleagues. These were catechetical talks, designed to offer a rudimentary religious education, and were invariably short, lively and simple. Years later Hecker told a friend that he "could never have helped men to a better life by preaching hell," for it was "against both my nature and my training." In the novitiate, he recalled, Father Ottman called Walworth "the blacksmith" and Hecker "the silversmith." Later, on the missions, Hecker "could only deal with topics of a more generous and noble kind," while Walworth "could pound away at any sinner on any subject."[3]

Caught up in the work of the missions and bound by Rule to a strenuous daily series of prayers and spiritual exercises, Hecker had not forgotten his friends in New England. He wrote Thoreau in July that he had been in Boston and tried but failed to visit Concord. "I should like much to see you and Mr. Emerson, to see where you are," he wrote. His assault on Thoreau's conscience remained relentless. He attacked Thomas Carlyle, a transcendentalist guru, for a recent assault he had made on the Jesuits, the "meanest" of whom was "more of a hero" than Carlyle, in Hecker's opinion. Heroism required "something that shall add to or complete our nature," Isaac argued, and the Catholic church alone "possesses this power—the grace to sustain the soul to live a life above nature."[4]

Thoreau may have proved unresponsive, but Hecker did not swerve from his convictions. Less than four months after his arrival from Europe, he shared his dreams with Brownson:

> Often my mind is seized with the idea of a future development of our holy faith in this country. Our people are capable of great enthusiasm, and if once this is turned into the right channels, it must and will produce effects worthy of our faith. . . . Our people are young, and not like Europeans, and were they filled with a lively faith, new ages of faith would spring up on this continent. . . . The Catholic young men of our country have no Catholic religious ideal future. We are so scattered that we seem not to be a body and have no common life. Our young men therefore, as a matter of course, fall into . . . unholy pursuits . . . or if they dream of an ideal future, it is pagan, like all Protestants. We as Catholics have a future, we alone have an ideal, by this I mean a bright and glorious future. Our young men need to be told this, inspired with it, and shown the means to attain it. We are a young people, a vast, immeasurable field is before us, and (we) have no overpowering monuments of the past to check our fresh enthusiasm or to dishearten us in our youthful attempts.

Tension would soon develop between the work of the missions, addressed as it was to Catholics, and Hecker's urgent desire to evangelize among non-Catholics. But in these formative years of the American church, the two goals seemed to go hand-in-hand. Everywhere they went the missionaries reported that their work was followed by evident improvement in the behavior, and therefore the status, of the Catholic population. Alcohol abuse was checked, the churches were filled, families were united, and the non-Catholic view of the church was transformed. Nothing could be more valuable in light of the desire to bring the faith before the non-Catholic public. As Hecker told Brownson:

> Until we have a higher tone of Catholic life in our country we shall do nothing. We shall make some progress in material things, and perhaps in numbers, but in the end we shall do little for the greater glory of God, the good of souls, or for our country.[5]

Nothing seemed to slacken Hecker's enthusiasm about the future of the church in the United States. "We must make Yankeedom the Rome of the modern world—or at least work hard to make it Catholic," he wrote Simpson in January 1853, asking for prayers that he might become "the first Yankee saint in the calendar."[6] And, as Hecker saw it, the road to sainthood lay among non-Catholics.

The English Fathers were interested in the impact of the mission on non-Catholics and, from their experience, they saw the need for literature which would ease prejudices. Hewit, Walworth and Hecker worked hard at their mission talks, and during the summer of 1854 they prepared some "controversial discourses" for mixed or Protestant audiences. By this time Hecker had formed his own project, the first step on his road to convert that "certain class" of Americans. He disclosed his plan to Hewit, his spiritual director, in June 1854. "There is a class of minds who by nature are inclined to asceticism and mystical life," he wrote, probably with Thoreau and his Brook Farm friends in mind. Protestantism could not meet their need for heroic sanctity because it offered no encouragement to self-denial and spiritual growth. Hecker wished to write a book "to expose these wants of the heart," demonstrate that asceticism was "an essential feature of the Gospel," that "voluntary poverty, obedience, chastity and mortification" were taught in the church by word and example. "Christian asceticism and supernatural life is found nowhere except in the Catholic church, " he argued; the proof was contained in her religious orders and the lives of the saints. He would conclude with a description of such a life and an invitation to follow the path of perfection, hoping that the book would meet the needs of a "class of men" and be "sort of a guide to the Church for them."

Encouraged by his superiors, Hecker worked on the book that summer and fall, suspended his labor during the mission season, then rushed it to publication in the summer of 1855. To that point, Hecker was a pious, hardworking, almost totally unknown priest who had a passing acquaintance with some of the leading literary figures of the day. *Questions of the Soul*, however, established him as a nationally prominent spokesman for the growing Roman Catholic Church. Hecker enjoyed a growing reputation among Catholics who had been exposed to the missions, and many bishops had become warm admirers of the earnest young priest. But only with his books did he come before a wider public and begin to establish himself as one of the most prominent Catholics in the nation.

The book was an almost perfect expression of contemporary American self-culture. It was filled with the confused excitement of that American sense of innocence of the past and openness to the future. The freedom to choose, to define for oneself the terms of life, was the fundamental context for Hecker's argument, an argument he did not frame in traditional apologetical terms, refuting Protestant errors and defending the church on historical grounds. Instead, he raised fundamental questions about human nature and history, all arising from that sense of the American, beginning anew, free from the prejudice of the past, prepared to follow reason and trust intuition. All of this Hecker explained by references to his own experience. As he told Brownson:

> My object in view is to bring minds similarly constituted as my own to similar convictions and results, by the same process I passed through. The leading idea is to expose the wants of the heart and demand their proper object, rather than a logical defense of the church. . . . The affections of the heart, when pure, are no less unerring guides to truth than the logic of the intellect.[7]

He began with the fundamental question of human destiny, claiming that everyone "has for his task to find his destiny, or to make one." Hecker portrayed a situation in which all was flux, doubt and uncertainty. As soon as the "eye of reason opens," he wrote, each person confronted the question of destiny, and all answers were open to consideration:

> The idea of God himself, and the world around him, strikes him at that moment as separate and independent facts. . . . He asks: "Who am I"? "Whence did I come"? "Whither do I tend"? "Who is God"? "What are my relations to God? to man? to the world around me"? "Have I a destiny? A work to do? What is it? And where? or is all ruled by fate? or left to what men call chance"?

These questions sprang up most directly for those who had "no fixed notions of religion," Hecker argued, and this was "the condition of the great mass of American youth," citing Emerson in support of this claim. Like himself, "the greater part of those born in the United States" had "no positive religious instruction" and were left to decide religious questions for themselves. The question of destiny had to be settled "satisfactorily to the intellect and heart," before a man could truly live. But, Hecker wrote, the answer was clear, alive in the consciousness of each man and woman. In transcendentalist fashion, Hecker argued as self-evident that human intelligence desired to know the truth, and the human heart desired to love the good, indeed the absolute true and absolute good, God.

Hecker had always believed his own experience was not singular to himself; what happened to him happened, or could happen, to all people. Humanity had a destiny, God, and each individual had "a special destiny, a definite work to do." Every soul had moments "when the iron hand of its destiny is laid upon it with irresistible power" and one knows that to resist is death. Among these were some persons who, like himself, could not "satisfy their natures with the common modes of life." They sought a deeper and fuller spiritual life, to be holy and perform "heroic deeds of sacrifice." They challenged those who sought mere wealth and power, they passionately desired to live life to its fullest. This class existed in the United States in large numbers, Hecker believed; indeed, "one might almost say that this desire after a more spiritual life is one of the chief characteristics of the American people."

In the history of Brook Farm, Fruitlands, and the Brotherhood of the Cross, a short-lived Episcopalian experiment in monastic community life in North Carolina, Hecker saw evidence of this yearning among a large class of Americans for "a better, purer and holier life." For his description of Brook Farm, he used a long citation from Nathaniel Hawthorne, contrasting the high ideals of the founders and the tragic failure of the community. He drew from Alcott a description of Fruitlands, while he probably drew from his former Episcopalian associates his brief account of the Brotherhood of the Cross. For Hecker, each was evidence not of "idle fancies and splendid insufficiencies" but of the persistence of the highest and noblest capacities of humanity, of deep wants and sacred needs, springing from the heart of human nature. Emerson was right to insist that man could see to a life more clear and truer than lived around him, but he was wrong to offer no path to reach it.

Hecker then turned to the past for an answer to the question of what path should be followed. God offered the ideal, but as pure spirit, far above humankind, he could not provide the perfect pattern of life. Nations needed a fuller revelation, the coming of a God-man who would reveal the way. Slipping into transcendentalist language, Hecker argued that because "the universal convictions of the conscience of humanity are the voices of the Divinity," this expectation could not be in vain. So, yes, one did come who made plain the way, who became the model man, Jesus. He was a man like others, he suffered as others did, and as such he could stand as the full and completely credible model of what life should be. Having made this revelation and provided this model, God could not leave people alone. To be a living model, Christ had to be present "not in a dead book, or in an indefinite and abstract manner," but "really and personally." He had to leave some extension of himself that would answer "the wants of man for all generations."

Hecker then examined what he took to be basic human wants. One was the desire for "unerring and divine guidance" on which people could rely and to which they could submit. Hecker insisted that the need to submit to truth and obey real authority was fundamental to human nature, but only a submission to a divine, not a human, authority, for submission to purely human truth was indeed degrading. As he had seen before his conversion, any religion that did not lead people to obey, that confined its demands to what people would ask of themselves, and offered nothing to which to aspire, was insufficient, for it did not raise people above themselves.

The church must attract the child, and bring out the childlike in adults, especially the childlike virtues of "purity, sweetness, cheerfulness, docility and obedience." Further, because from the moment of consciousness the person thought of God and would live for God, each needed, as Hecker had needed, a friend, a counsellor and guide, a spiritual mentor. The desire for such guidance and friendship was evidence of the soul's desire to free itself from self-love and self-deception, to anchor its destiny beyond illusion and the subtle working of pride. Prayer and Bible reading alone were insufficient, for they easily bent to one's own individual purposes. Because sin was real, each person needed to unburden the self of guilt in order to achieve union with God.

Hecker then examined Protestantism to determine whether it met these needs of the human heart. He found that it did not. Its clergy were no sure guide because they were subject to those they would direct. Protestant churches offered no certainty and no call beyond that which already existed, no sacraments, no penance, no eucharistic expression of love and communion. To the yearning of young idealists for guidance, affirmation and heroism, Protestantism offered an argument of human sinfulness and then left people on their own, with nothing but their private judgment to rely on. Before these questions of the soul and needs of the heart, Protestantism was "stony, heartless and unconcerned as a sphinx." To those, especially, who yearned for perfection, who had gone to Brook Farm and Fruitlands, it offered only the charge that they were sinners, that there was no authority to obey, no guide to follow, no friend to turn to, no possibility of attaining that which they sought, no gift of grace which would enable them to pursue their ideals.

For those who remained constant, who would go forward, the path grew narrower, and what was left? Rome! Rome spoke with authority, God's authority, not human authority, an authority to which the pope and the humblest Catholic alike were subject. It attracted children and brought out the childlike in adults. It offered guidance and spiritual direction by men who were independent, disinterested and impartial. It offered sacraments, especially penance and Eucharist; it eased the passage to death. In its religious communities it offered the means by which men and women could respond to that special call to holiness and perfection by yielding up their whole selves to God and to their highest ideals. On each score, the Catholic Church answered the questions of the soul and invited the consideration of the American people.

It remained for Hecker to return to New England and offer his Catholic reflections on the aspirations so clear to him a decade before. He praised Emerson for his work of destroying the "false and narrow dogmas, the hollow forms, and the hollower cant of Protestantism" and taking his "stand upon man's simple nature." But Emerson stopped there, leaving "no future, no aims but false ones." Emerson's message was "obey thy instincts," which would be satisfactory only "if man were a bee, a cat or a pig." "Self-culture," taken alone, made man "feel more keenly and painfully his wants and deficiencies," it "did nothing to satisfy or supply them." To Margaret Fuller's exclamation that the "only object in life is to grow," Hecker responded: "A melon, a pumpkin, or a squash could say the same, if they could only speak." Reversing Emersonian slogans, Hecker substituted "humility to obey" for "self-reliance," "courage to believe" for "trust thyself," self-denial, self-sacrifice and surrender to God for self-culture. For those who could overcome their pride and prejudice, there was a way to heroic self-realization, to God, the way of the Catholic Church. "The class of men" at whose conversion Hecker aimed were brave and earnest; if only they would listen:

> Once we were their companion and bosom friend; but we are changed. Changed not in our aspirations, not in our heart's affections, not in our purposes in life; no, these are not changed, but exalted, purified and enlarged! Our change was this: to pass from a natural to a supernatural basis of life, thus giving to our nature a new and extraordinary participation in the Divine Nature. . . .

> For Jesus Christ did not come down from heaven to contradict or destroy man's nature, but to rectify and restore it, and to give to man a new, superior divine mode of life and activity.

Believing that Catholicism was the answer to the questions of the soul, Hecker did not hesitate to affirm that Catholicism was not one choice among many, but *the* answer, the only complete answer to those questions. Unfortunately the church, though in the midst of Americans, was still concealed "by ignorance, misrepresentation and calumny, as effectively as if it were once more buried in the catacombs." But the time would come, and soon, when a practical and inquiring people would no longer rest content with Protestantism, when the scales of inherited prejudice would vanish, and Catholicism would stand forth once again as the full expression of Christian faith and life. The American people, "young, fresh and filled with the idea of great enterprises" would, if Catholic, "give a new, noble and glorious realization to Christianity, a development that would go beyond the past in achievements of zeal, in the abundance of saints, as well as in art, science, and material greatness." Hecker called for nothing less than a Catholic America, for the sake not of the church but of the nation and its people.[8]

Publication of *Questions of the Soul* established Hecker as a national figure in and out of the church. Letters of praise came from around the country, most expressing confidence it would have special impact on the young. Historian George Bancroft wrote that the book was one of the "signs of the times"; men were beginning to look inward, and "desire with a loftier earnestness to solve the great problems of existence." Letters like this, and sales of *Questions of the Soul* to non-Catholics, confirmed Hecker's conviction, as he put it to a friend in 1856: "our work, or a large part of it, is with outsiders."[9]

So did Brownson's review, which was extravagant in its praise, claiming that it "is one of the very few original and genuine American books our country can boast." He emphasized that *Questions of the Soul* "could have been written only by an American "to the manner born." Brownson recalled their long friendship and argued that Hecker had a mission of great importance to the country. The American character was still in the process of formation, it was oriented toward the future and not the past, and its direction could be found in that small minority of New England men and women who had shucked off the baggage of the past and were seeking something entirely new and original. This was the "class" to which Hecker addressed himself. Hecker was correct to understand that it should not be addressed in the old controversial style of refuting Protestant errors, the style Brownson himself had adopted "for it suited best our peculiar temperament." His contentious arguments, Brownson admitted, were better designed to win debates than hearts; they presented Catholicism "under its least amiable and most repulsive aspect." Hecker, in contrast, presented Catholicism in its "affirmative and positive character," rested his argument on the "innate cravings of the soul, finding itself abandoned to simple nature, on that inward need which all men feel even by nature, for truth and goodness."[10]

Hecker was especially encouraged to learn that he was not alone in his views that "something special" should be done for conversion. Earlier he had formed a small "circle" to pray for conversions; he and others also arranged for Brownson's move to New York so he could work more actively for the cause. In 1855, when *Questions of the Soul* appeared, Brownson, James McMaster, now an influential editor, and "several other talented men," mostly converts, were urging the same views. According to Hecker, their position was that "up to the present time the Church has been almost exclusively devoted to provide for her own children, and this has been almost too great at task for her." Now, as immigration had "to some extent ceased . . . we are a little freer, and can be thinking of extending our holy faith among the American people." Explaining all this to a Redemptorist in Rome, he asked him to bring Brownson's *Review* and McMaster's *Freeman's Journal* to the attention of Vatican officials; he (with George Hecker's help) would gladly bear the expense of getting them mailed to Redemptorist headquarters.[11]

Hewit, who was closest to Hecker among the Redemptorists, was in sympathy with his objectives. He told Brownson that the young Redemptorist students had "a strong love of country and an ardent desire for its conversion." He had long believed that history was approaching its end, but he thought there would be "a brilliant though brief period of the triumph of Catholicity before the appearance of the anti-Christ." Like Hecker, he hoped to devote his life "to the noble end of the conversion of America." He also hoped that God would give the Redemptorists the opportunity for acting more directly on the American people and working for their conversion.[12]

McMaster was another friend pushing for a more aggressive policy. By 1855 his *Freeman's Journal* was the nation's most widely circulated Catholic newspaper. Hecker was convinced that the paper, read by so many priests, could be a vital instrument in the program to turn the church's attention outward toward the nation and toward non-Catholics. In November 1855 he praised a recent issue and told McMaster of his growing conviction that God was "preparing the way by special graces to converts of the faith for the conversion of our country." He urged the editor to "let this idea predominate in the *Freeman's* columns."[13]

In the 1850s then, Hecker and Brownson were working in tandem. Hecker thought that he and Brownson had "a double work to do: to labor to bring up the Catholic body to Catholic truth intellectually and morally, and to open the way to the American people to see the same truth in all its beauty." It would be hard to convert the "special class" until the cultural tone of Catholic life improved, but, as converts themselves, they had to proceed cautiously. At this stage it was Hecker who had to warn the editor to go slow and beware of offending the sensibilities of the Catholic people. In June, Brownson told Hecker the great obstacle to a fair hearing for Catholicism was "the real dislike of the American people and character felt by a large portion of our bishops and clergy." If they used forms of expression that would render the faith "intelligible," they risked attack by the Irish. Hecker agreed, but after Brownson's effusive review of *Questions of the Soul* appeared, Hecker warned him that his earlier articles on Native Americanism, in which he admitted that problems existed among the immigrants, had upset many Irish-American priests. If Brownson had known the "first dose" was still operating, he might not have added the "second dose" of the review so quickly. Hecker worried about a "collision" within the church. As the "American element" was increasing and circumstances gave the converts a "certain prominence," they should be sensitive to the "unpleasant feelings" stirred by these developments and "bide their time."[14]

The American bishops particularly valued the work of the Redemptorist mission band. They had long been anxious to insure that new bishops were drawn from priests who, if not American born, at least had extensive pastoral experience in the United States. It was not surprising, then, that the names of Hecker and Hewit began to appear on lists of candidates submitted for consideration as bishops. Still, as Hecker's warning to Brownson indicated, there was also a growing concern about the enthusiasm of these converts, especially the prominent Brownson. Talk circulated as early as 1851 about an "American party" growing within the church, with the names of Brownson and convert bishop James Roosevelt Bayley of Newark among those mentioned. This concern arose in part from the different priorities of the converts, especially their concern about the image of the church and its attractiveness to non-Catholics, a concern heightened by clashes between native-born Catholics and the immigrants. Know Nothing agitation in the 1850s increased the pressure for Catholic solidarity, making self-criticism within the church seem like disloyalty. It also put the converts on the defensive, both in dealing with their fellow Catholics and in explaining themselves to non-Catholics.

Hecker was no nativist; he had little desire to please Protestants, and he wished only to present Catholicism in a way designed to bring a favorable response from fair-minded, often unchurched, Americans. But he was very serious about this work and deeply convinced of its providential character. Despite his commitment to the missions, which were primarily aimed at bringing immigrant Catholics to practice their faith and support the church, he showed little concern with the need to defend the church against attack, even less with preserving the faith and loyalty of Catholics themselves. As he told his Roman correspondent, the church's work of providing "for her own children" was pretty much accomplished, parish work could be left to the secular clergy, and religious communities could turn the church outward toward the country and give younger Catholics a vision of the future to inspire them to action.

The American bishops, faced with the financial and pastoral problems of an expanding, largely uninstructed and poor Catholic population, could be forgiven if they detected unjustified criticism in this appeal, especially when made less deftly by Brownson or McMaster. Irish and German Catholics, stung by bitter nativist attacks, might regard Hecker's generous description of Americans as naive at best, disloyal at worst. Brownson's effort to combat parochialism among Irish-Catholics aroused just such charges. It was a mark of Hecker's winning personality, and of his ability to arouse pride among Catholics as an attractive American convert, that little criticism was directed at him or his work, at least in the church at large.

Within the Redemptorist community, however, serious problems arose. Tensions between the Americans and their German colleagues were present from the beginning. Hecker and Walworth, trained abroad, seemed to have less difficulty with Redemptorist life than did their fellow Americans trained in the United States. Four years after Hecker, Walworth and McMaster went to Europe in 1845, Hewit entered the Redemptorist novitiate in Baltimore. Later, George Deshon joined the group. A West Point graduate and military engineer, Deshon had been converted in part through the friendship of McMaster, who pointed him toward the Redemptorists. A man of wide experience, Deshon found it hard to accept an approach to religious life which emphasized unquestioning submission to authority. He was not alone.

The Redemptorists had come to the United States in 1832, serving in northern Ohio and Michigan before establishing their first permanent foundation in Pittsburgh in 1839 and another in Baltimore the following year.[15] Despite their history of mission work in Europe, they were prized by the American bishops for their work among German immigrants, for whom they were invited to establish parishes. The houses which were set up for this parochial work were the centers of Redemptorist life in the United States and there the missionaries lived during the winter months when mission work was suspended. Tensions inevitably arose between the missionaries, anxious to spend their time in prayer, study and preparation for their next mission season, and the parish fathers, hopeful for some help with parochial duties. In addition, the American fathers occasionally complained about the use of the German language and food, and the sometimes disdainful attitude of the German fathers toward them. The Germans, on the other hand, worried that the Americans were too inclined to emphasize the importance of their work as missionaries over the more tedious tasks of the parish. Charges were heard that the Americans failed to appreciate the commitments which had been made to the bishops to serve German immigrants. Moreover, some Redemptorists worried that the Americans, with their spirit of informality, threatened to relax the discipline of the houses. As long as Father Bernard remained provincial, problems were minimized, not only because he shared the American's enthusiasm for the missions but also because he was a talented leader. In 1853, however, he was ordered back to Europe and replaced by Father George Ruland, a far weaker man.

Among the most critical of the German-American fathers was Father Rumpler, Hecker's first Redemptorist guide. He was never at ease with the work of the converts among English-speaking congregations or with non-Catholics. Frustrated in dealing with American seminarians, he told Hewit: "I know the German devil and I know the French devil, but the American devil puzzles me"![16] When Hecker showed him the manuscript of *Questions of the Soul*, Rumpler feared that Hecker's "general thoughts and sentiments" were "too far on the easy side," especially on the question of whether salvation was possible outside the Catholic Church. Like many Redemptorists, Rumpler felt the community's first concern should be for German immigrants, especially for staffing the parishes which they had agreed to take on at the request of the bishops.

With Father Bernard's departure and the election of Father Ruland as Provincial, the peace of the American fathers was lost, as it turned out, forever. As Hecker and his friends saw it later, Ruland was very much influenced by Rumpler, who had charge of the novitiate. Though his friends denied it, Rumpler's behavior was erratic, at times cruel. The rigorous discipline which had bothered Deshon became more arbitrary. Some American recruits left the novitiate; others became ill with consumption and tuberculosis. At least two seminarians died, and some fathers, including the Americans, believed Rumpler was responsible. Yet, despite these warning signs, Ruland left Rumpler in charge of the entire community when he left for a General Chapter in 1855. Rumpler summoned an aide to Annapolis, then behaved strangely when he arrived. Before long, Rumpler broke down completely and was placed in an asylum. He was released in two weeks, but the news spread to New York, where a group commissioned Walworth to go to Baltimore, obtain the relevant papers, consult with the archbishop and, if necessary, place Rumpler back in the asylum, which he did.

By the summer of 1856 Father Rumpler had to be kept chained. Hewit told Hecker that he was constantly crying, howling and tearing at his clothes. Hecker proposed that Rumpler be removed to New York and placed under the care of a family friend, Dr. Watson, but Hewit reported that all the fathers believed that plan impossible; they regarded Hecker's confidence in Watson as "an infatuation." Hewit ordered Hecker to end all association with Watson immediately. Yet, in October, Rumpler was in New York, apparently sent there by Ruland on his return from Europe; a lay brother was sent to care for him and Watson was in charge of the case. A certificate of insanity was issued in Baltimore and, in November, Ruland gave Hecker formal powers of superior over Rumpler. At the same time, Ruland expressed amazement at the change in Rumpler's condition; he did not doubt his being cured and expressed great thanks to Hecker for the trouble he had taken.[17] Nevertheless, Rumpler died shortly after.

Yet, despite these signs of the provincial's confidence in Hecker, differences persisted in the community. The American fathers believed that Ruland, who had been a Redemptorist only a few years before becoming provincial, lacked Father Bernard's missionary zeal. Irish-born John Duffy had been detached from the mission band to serve a parish in New Orleans and Ruland kept him there, despite the need for more missionaries. Under Father Bernard, German-speaking priests with parish responsibilities were ordered to assist the missionaries with confessions when they were nearby; under Ruland those requests were often ignored. Moreover, the Americans had little respect for Ruland's abilities and had written Rome to complain.

And there were, of course, cultural differences. Hecker and his American colleagues were generally optimistic about human nature, and they took it for granted that a democratic way of life was desirable and the wave of the future. They also believed that American Protestantism was in decline, giving way to indifference and infidelity, opening up new opportunities for evangelization. While not all shared Hecker's optimism about the prospect of conversions, they generally shared his conviction that their countrymen would give Catholicism a hearing if misconceptions about the church, particularly the widespread belief that Catholicism was incompatible with democracy, could be cleared away. They respected the European-born clergy, but felt they could not carry out this work of explaining the church to Americans because they were unfamiliar with American ideas, they did not encourage their people to mix with non-Catholics, and many of them were personally suspicious of democracy and personal liberty.

Even more important, the zealous Americans thought acceptance of parish responsibilities not only made their work unnecessarily difficult, but that it violated the spirit of the Redemptorist missionary vocation.

Apparently Hecker expressed these concerns in a letter to Father de Held as early as 1855, for the latter wrote in February of that year expressing hope that the forthcoming General Congregation would introduce reforms. De Held believed that no more houses should be started with the care of a parish, nor should present parish responsibilities be expanded. There should be "serious and continuous efforts to do away with parochial burdens." Where parishes had been taken, priests should be detached for that work, but the remainder should be left free to live as Redemptorist missionaries. Unfortunately, he feared that only "partisans of the existing system" had been elected as delegates to the congregation, so they could only pray that Providence would insure the election of a superior general who would understand the problems and bring about "necessary and salutary reforms." Instead, Father Nicholas Mauron, a protege of the previous superior general, was chosen. The Germans were delighted; de Held, Hecker and his colleagues were severely disappointed.[18]

The missions continued, of course, but the American Redemptorists were more determined than ever to place their work on a secure foundation. In March 1856, in Norfolk, Virginia, for the first time they addressed a non-Catholic audience directly through public lectures following a mission. Attendance was good, press reports were favorable, and Hecker was delighted. The event marked "the commencement of a new field of labor, the application of the system of missions to the conversion of heretics," he told Brownson. Walworth, now superior of the mission band, told Hecker that this was indeed his real vocation. Coming on the heels of his book, the Norfolk lectures confirmed Hecker's confidence in his mission at a time when events in the country and in his own community were erecting new obstacles. He was now an American evangelist, but he was also an American Catholic priest, and the two vocations might not grow easily together.

7

Risking Everything

Elated by reception of *Questions of the Soul*, Hecker moved ahead boldly on his campaign to evangelize his fellow Americans. No sooner was his first book in the press than he was at work on a second, this one to show "the road of reason to the church," complementing the "way of the heart" described in *Questions of the Soul.* Here again Hecker hoped to show "on what basis controversy is to be placed in this country if we are to convince the American people of Catholicity and convert them." Because, as Hecker saw it, most Americans, or at least his special class, had no positive religious beliefs, the basis of controversy must be human nature, which "alone can be taken for granted." For Hecker, this conclusion, which was to cause him great difficulty, was inescapable:

> The Religion, therefore, that is to meet the wants of the age, and answer its demands, must take its starting point from man's nature. It is, therefore, upon the essential and indestructible elements of Human Nature that Religion, particularly in this country, has to raise the foundations of its temple. The sanctuary of religion must be restored to the place where the God of nature placed it, in the human soul.[1]

In *Aspirations of Nature* he again described his contemporaries by returning to his own experience. The typical American was an "earnest seeker" as he had been, sincere, unblemished by prejudice, or indeed by any historical legacy whatsoever. People began life with no positive religious convictions and, when their natural religious aspirations awakened, they set out to find a religion which would fulfill these aspirations. Some, raised in a religious atmosphere, found that many of the doctrines taught them in childhood contradicted the "clearest convictions of conscience." They then tried to find, or construct, a religion agreeable to their intelligence. Others discarded all religions and tried to satisfy their religious instincts in "the different movements of the day," such as transcendentalism or one or another reform.

Americans, as Hecker saw them, were a people open to religious impressions but, for the most part, without firm Christian beliefs. The reason was that they were usually presented with a choice between religious convictions that violated their reason, such as those presented by enthusiastic evangelists, and no religious beliefs at all. But there was little infidelity, "and that little is of foreign importation." "Famished" for constructive, positive religion, the earnest seeker was determined to accept no authority which would interfere with the sacred space between God and the human soul. Given such honesty, true religion never had "so glorious a field," false religion "so much to dread." American civilization was "young, fresh, and in the vigor of its manhood":

> We cannot repeat the past if we would. The new world promises a new civilization. And in this unfettered civilization, true Religion will find a reception it has in vain looked for elsewhere and a development of unprecedented glory. For religion is never so attractive and beautiful as when connected with intelligence and free conviction.

Accordingly, Hecker argued that the time was ripe to present that "true religion." "No people ever became great without religion," Hecker claimed. A religion for Americans would have to be a religion superior to themselves, providing a lofty inspiration which would "break the ordinary bonds" and call forth genius in poetry, painting and music. Free now from history, with the false claims of the Protestant past exploded, Americans and America could choose a new faith.

> Our destiny as a nation hangs on this moment. For no nation, as no individual, becomes fully conscious of its capacities, discovers its divine destination, until it is wholly under the influence of religious inspiration. No people becomes properly one nation, acts as one man, unfolds its highest capabilities, displays its true genius and utmost strength, until it becomes not only politically and socially, but religiously, of one mind and heart.

Religious pluralism, it seemed, was necessarily temporary; in the long run, America would require a common faith to realize its promise. National energy would be in proportion to the intensity of the unity of the people and that in turn depended on the development of common religious belief. All humanity waited on the choice, for America was "the Country of the Future."

In this exciting, millennial, setting, Hecker placed his argument for Catholicism. He examined heathen philosophy and the work of contemporary German, French and English thinkers, and found all unable to affirm God, the soul or the future of humanity. Philosophy, as in Emerson, could pose but not answer the fundamental questions of life. A divine light, a revelation, was needed, and Hecker drew upon a whole list of past and present writers to demonstrate the universality of that assertion. True religion did not contradict or degrade reason but opened it to its divine origin. The only religion adequate to the claims of reason was Christianity.

He then examined the two branches of Christianity, first subjecting Protestantism to a professedly objective analysis. For the earnest seeker, all creeds and systems of belief which contradicted reason or the convictions of conscience had to be repudiated. Going back to Luther and the Reformers, Hecker argued at length that Protestantism held human nature degraded, reason flawed at its roots, and human beings incapable of doing anything good without the aid of divine grace. To be a Protestant Christian, one had to "cease to be rational creature and become a ninny."

Having sounded the depths of Protestantism's reliance on a theory of human depravity—and ignored the development of Protestant theology over the previous two centuries—Hecker concluded that the Reformation "was nothing else than the rebellion of the unregenerate passions of man under the guise of the emancipation of the human mind." Fortunately, the criticisms of Channing and Emerson were liberating Americans from the inhuman teachings of the Reformers. Further accelerating the Protestant downfall was the increasingly obvious antagonism between American institutions, based on the essential goodness of human nature, and a religion which denied it.

Having shown that Protestant Christianity could not meet the aspirations of nature, as it had failed to answer the questions of the soul, Hecker, always as the earnest seeker, turned to Catholicism. He recognized that the key would be what Catholicism taught regarding human nature. Quite simply, Hecker argued that, with original sin, humanity fell from divine grace and was deprived of the supernatural gifts possessed in the garden. While humanity lost its original integrity and was deprived of sanctifying grace, the natural gifts of reason and free will were left "unimpaired, uncorrupted, uninjured." These essential elements of human nature were

Above: The Croton Flour Mill, a principal element in the Hecker family flour business.
Right: George Hecker supplied constant support to Isaac during the latter's lifetime.
Unless noted, all photos courtesy Paulist Archives.
Below: Brook Farm in West Roxbury, Mass., pictured before the buildings were destroyed by fire in the 20th century. *Photo courtesy Illinois Historical Survey.*

Above left: Isaac Hecker, around the time he lived at Brook Farm. **Above right:** Orestes A. Brownson, Hecker's mentor, from a lithograph of 1843. **Below:** Fruitlands, scene of Bronson Alcott's experimental community in Harvard, Mass. *Photo courtesy Fruitlands Museum.*

Above left: Chapel of the Redemptorist novitiate at St. Trond, Belgium. **Above right:** George Ruland, C.SS.R., provincial of the American Redemptorists. *Photo courtesy Redemptorist Provincial Archives.* **Below left:** Nicholas Mauron, C.SS.R., Redemptorist General in Rome. *Photo courtesy Redemptorist Provincial Archives.* **Below right:** Hecker, 1858–60.

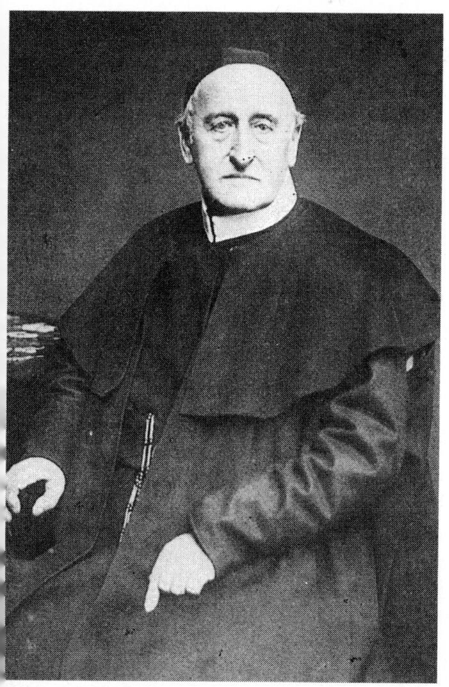

Above left: Cardinal Alessandro Barnebò, prefect of the Congregation of Propaganda. **Above right:** Hecker pictured around 1870. American priests at the time rarely wore clerical garb in public. **Below:** The Paulist Fathers' first chapel and living quarters on West 59th Street, New York, around 1858.

what was meant by "made in God's image and likeness." Original sin thus left "no positively evil quality, depraving the substance of our common nature."

The Catholic Church, free from a doctrine of essential depravity, taught that reason could know with certainty the existence of God, the immortality of the soul and the liberty of persons. Reason could uncover the principles which underlie religion, morality, social order, political economy and human rights. The exercise of reason preceded the truths of religion; it was the responsibility of each person to inquire into the reasonableness of religious truths. Catholicism affirmed reason, stimulated its exercise and respected its results.

He went on to explain Catholic teachings in such a way as to affirm reason, free will and human dignity. Church teachings were always consonant with human worth and adapted to various ages and circumstances in such a way as to affirm natural truth and beauty. Its teaching on justification upheld both God's free grace and human freedom to respond, so that justification became a mutual work of God and human beings. Grace operated in the realm of conscience and spirit, strengthening natural gifts and aptitudes. It called forth the individuality of each person, providing a remarkable array of alternatives through which men and women could respond to the call from God.

As for the church, it spoke with divine authority. Reason, the Holy Spirit dwelling in the heart, "exterior divine revelation," and the church, all worked in harmony, never conflicting with each other, to produce conviction which was both free and certain. Sanctification was "an intrinsic work of grace," for God alone had power over the human heart. Each person was expected to respond with fidelity to the interior promptings of the Holy Spirit, fortifying them with the aids the church made available. Emphasizing the indwelling of the Holy Spirit, Hecker insisted on this interior character of sanctity and upheld the authority of the Holy Ghost within the soul. But he insisted as well that the promptings of the spirit within corresponded with the teachings of the church.

In summarizing his argument, Hecker noted that the aspirations of reason distinguished human nature, that religion alone addressed the question of human destiny, and Christianity was the only religion which reasonably could claim the attention of humankind. Protestantism contradicted reason and shocked conscience, while rationalism, unitarianism and infidelity denied humanity's religious nature and convictions. To be Christian and at the same time loyal to reason, one had to become Catholic. The doctrines and practices of Catholicism were consonant with reason, in harmony with moral feelings and "favorable to the highest conceptions of the dignity of human nature." Nations could not realize their collective destiny without powerful religious influences, so that the question pressing upon Americans was "to determine our Religion as our fathers did the character of our political institutions" which, under the guidance of Providence, were themselves based on Catholic principles.[2]

Aspirations of Nature was, at first glance, a more controversial book than *Questions of the Soul.* Not until later would Hecker's spiritual ideas arouse suspicion, but his effort to reconcile Catholicism and reason projected him into some of the most complex and difficult problems of nineteenth-century Christianity. Of course Hecker was aware that his effort to ground a Catholic apologetic on human nature ran counter to much of what he had learned in the seminary. Accordingly, he was careful to submit his chapters to others for advice, delaying publication. Hewit, his confessor, had approved his decision to write. A learned man and an excellent critic, Hewit was not at all unsympathetic, confessing that he was fascinated by "the idea of Catholicity divested of the accidental forms of the past and presented to the intellect in a way suited to the advanced intelligence." Still, he was confused by Hecker's rather unsophisticated treatment of nature and grace. Father Ruland, the provincial, was far more critical. He disliked Hecker's starting with natural man, before the infusion of supernatural gifts. The church had not rendered a decision on the question of whether man was created first and only subsequently received supernatural gifts to be lost at the Fall, or was endowed with them at the moment of creation and later deprived of something essential to human nature. Ruland thought it better to start with those truths the church did teach regarding the Fall and its consequences, with fallen, not with natural man. The problem was a crucial one, for Hecker's emphasis on natural human capacity was central to his argument. Ruland, like Brownson, drew on the common Catholic approach, which, by emphasizing human sinfulness, suggested that Catholic faith required submission first; reason was enlisted only later to explain why such submission was necessary.[3]

The debate was not new to Hecker, for while he was composing the book he was corresponding with his English friend Richard Simpson, who was wrestling with a similar problem. In 1856 Simpson wrote an article on original sin which brought difficulties with church authorities but led Hecker to good-naturedly charge Simpson with stealing his thunder.[4] The exchange with Simpson, along with the comments of his superiors, might have suggested to Hecker that his second book would not bring the universal approval which greeted his first. By the time *Aspirations of Nature* appeared, however, he was, embroiled in a dispute and badly needed the support of a favorable reception. Unfortunately, he was not to get it; the book was far less noticed than the earlier volume and it drew criticism even from Brownson, who had been his closest ally to this point.

Hecker might have anticipated these problems, but the ever optimistic priest seemed to write with almost no reference to events around him. The middle 1850s were marked by a resurgence of anti-Catholic animosity through the Know Nothing movement, which not only challenged the reasonableness of Catholic belief and the sincerity of Catholic professions of patriotism, but made Catholics themselves more defensive and less inclined to celebrate a work intended to appeal to the reasonableness and good will of non-Catholic Americans. Brownson, already having problems within the church and anxious to be noticed as her defender, had his antennae more attuned to changing currents in the wider world. Accordingly, he received *Aspirations of Nature* in a mood of defensiveness regarding church authorities and at a time when his combative instincts were aroused by the resurgence of nativist prejudice.

Brownson's review appeared in the October 1857 issue of his *Quarterly.* He began and ended his lengthy commentary with warm praise for Hecker as a Catholic, a writer and controversialist. He affirmed much that Hecker has written, insisting that his own reservations extended not to the orthodoxy of the work, for it was above reproach, but to its wisdom and expediency. But he then took issue with Hecker on almost every point, in the process reversing positions the two had once held in common. First, he believed that the number of "earnest seekers" was far less than Hecker thought. Many Americans, as Brownson saw it, had simply exchanged Protestant belief for religious indifference. Furthermore, according to Brownson, the transcendentalists, regarded by Hecker as central to his new class, had always been a somewhat exotic minority, less American than German. Evangelical Protestantism, on the other hand, the religion Hecker dismissed contemptuously as irrational and emotional, was growing stronger, and Brownson thought this all to the good. Unlike Hecker, Brownson now believed that conversions to Catholicism were more apt to be based upon the remnants of Christian belief found among active Protestants than from "earnest seekers" freed from Christian belief altogether.

Second, Brownson feared that some would think Hecker had gone too far in affirming the transcendentalists' belief in the natural aspiration for God. While acknowledging the orthodoxy of Hecker's view, and agreeing that original sin left intact the reason and dignity of man, Brownson felt it important to emphasize that the will was impaired and hampered by the absence of grace. Instead of subjecting the passions to reason, people became the "vile slaves" of their "lower nature." In principle, nature aspired to God and reason could prove God's existence; in fact, because of sin, they rarely did so. In his eagerness to demonstrate that reason was able to apprehend and conduct persons to their appointed end, Hecker had failed to give the other side of the picture: "With its innate ability, reason in fact accomplishes little even in the order of natural truth and virtue, without the aid, direct or indirect, of divine revelation and grace."

Equally important, Hecker underrated the importance of the supernatural. What Hecker meant, Brownson argued, was that Catholicity presupposed, respected, addressed and satisfied reason, not that the soul aspired of itself to Catholicity, but that Catholicism met and secured its aspirations. He was concerned that in the artifice of his argument, Hecker studiously avoided use of the word supernatural, seeking to lead his earnest seeker to Catholicism without informing him in advance. Yet, at some point, he would have to ask him to make a further step, to submit to the supreme teaching authority of the church. Brownson believed that at that point the seeker would pull back. Why? Because the clear, open, honest seeker was a myth; actual persons were Americans, bred in a Protestant society and culture. As such, they might be brought to Catholicism to salvage the sometime inarticulate Christian beliefs of their youth, but not as pure seekers, abstracted from time and place—and prejudice.

It was here that the two men's paths most sharply diverged and Brownson did his old friend most damage. Brownson spent the last portion of the review demonstrating that in working for conversion one had to avoid "everything which looks like accommodating Catholic teaching to the tastes and temper of the country." At length he argued the need for the laity to be subject to hierarchical authority and warned against the American practice of lay domination. He admitted he had far less confidence in the Catholic potential of American culture than Hecker, whose attitude led Catholics not of American birth to suspect converts "of a design to Americanize Catholicity." While he agreed there was a great future for Catholicism in the United States, he believed conversions would be difficult, not least because there was "scarcely a trait in the American character as practically developed that is not more or less hostile to Catholicity. Our people are imbued with a spirit of independence, an aversion to authority, a pride, an overwhelming conceit, as well as with a prejudice that makes them revolt at the bare mention of the church." Conversion would come about not by taking American peculiarities as the starting point, but by appealing to those things Catholics held in common with other Christians and which the universal church recognized and raised to a supernatural level. Equally important, the souls of Catholics themselves were not less dear than those of non-Catholics, and the bishops who could hardly provide for the religious needs of those already in the church should not be expected to endorse visionary schemes to make converts.

Brownson concluded with a characteristically personal apology for his own actions during the fifties. He had been criticized by Catholics, even bishops, for defending the church against the attacks of the Know Nothings by appealing to American ideals; in the process, he seemed to some to be an enemy of immigrants, even a Know Nothing himself. This slander had hurt him deeply, and he insisted at length on his disdain for "an American party" in the church, his respect for the different nationalities within the church, his confidence that all groups would eventually Americanize and his opposition to all efforts to force them to do so. To prove his fidelity and loyalty, he promised to close his *Review* if any in authority should conclude that he was not serving the Catholic cause. By placing his defense in the review of Hecker's book, Brownson was clearly trying to distance himself from his friend's tendency to affirm native-born Americans.[5]

In part, the review reflected a deep ambivalence in Brownson's relationship to the church. Shortly after their conversion, Hecker told the older man that Bishops Hughes and McCloskey regarded his entry into the church as "an era in Catholic America." Brownson responded with sincere humility that he saw the church as the means of his eternal salvation: "I go into the Church because I need it, not because it needs me." This remained the strongest conviction of his Catholic life. Yet, like so many converts of the day, he was drawn to the idea of the church, and he found much in American Catholicism distasteful. "The mass of our Catholics are not Catholics," he told Hecker in 1845. He admitted he did not like the Irish, who were rapidly taking charge of the churches of Boston; their priests either seemed Irish first, or they were preoccupied with raising money.[6] Brownson badly needed the Church but he had difficulty with the church.

So did Hecker, but disagreement between the two converts was fundamental and long-standing, foreshadowed in Brownson's earlier criticism of Hecker's mysticism. Simpson had attempted to explain the problem of nature and grace, which had caused him so much trouble with the English bishops, but Hecker had made light of it. Now Brownson, an even closer friend, was taking him to task. If Hecker's position was correct, that the goal of the most basic human aspirations was the Catholic Church, then the whole stance of the church would be clear: to evangelize at the heart of culture, to witness to a church at the service of persons, to see that every reasonable, humane and liberating action in history was anonymously Catholic but Catholic nonetheless.

Brownson saw things differently. One first came to the church through the route of human failure and the need for grace and for authority, and only then was an authentic humanism possible. In the one case, human persons, guided by the Spirit of God, were the center of human history; the church existed for humankind. In the other, the church, in practice the organized, hierarchical church, was the center of human history and, for their own good, persons must come to that church. This conflict, now with Brownson, later with others, although often masked by Hecker's obvious holiness, would dominate the remainder of his public life.

Not only were Brownson's views in sharp contrast to those he had expressed in public and private over several years, but they seemed to contradict a letter he wrote on Hecker's behalf only two months before the review appeared. On August 5, 1857, on the eve of Hecker's departure for Rome to resolve problems which had arisen among the American Redemptorists, Brownson wrote him a long letter to be used to support Hecker's cause in Rome. He argued that a new, American congregation was needed to evangelize among non-Catholics, as the Redemptorists, hard-pressed by their work among German immigrants, could not take on such work. Moreover, he described the prospect for American conversions in glowing terms.[7] Brownson's review thus came to the attention of church authorities at a particularly difficult moment in Hecker's life, and because it seemed to contradict Brownson's earlier position, it took him completely by surprise. He was hurt, even angry, and their friendship, though it survived, was permanently damaged.

Whatever the merits of Brownson's criticism, Hecker's books marked a new turn in American Catholic life. When they entered the church, Brownson and Hecker were hardly peers, but with his books of the 1850s, Hecker established himself as a leader of the American church in his own right. He did so while bringing to his discussion of Catholic subjects some very American assumptions, none more striking than his use of American symbols of the "redeemer nation." Millennial language, filled with the promise that the new nation would be the agent of God's final triumph, was common among evangelical Protestants and infused the reform movements with which Hecker had associated in his youth. No American Catholic before Hecker had adopted that language, but here was a Catholic priest arguing that, indeed, America had a cosmic role to play, and it could and would do so through the Catholic Church. Just as the Holy Spirit spoke within the individual soul, so that an open mind and sincere heart could not but lead the earnest seeker to God, so the spirit spoke in historical events, guiding nations, in spite of themselves, to their collective destiny in God's kingdom.

The person who would speak to this people, then, must be alert to the signs of the times. He or she must constantly search events in the world for signs of God's saving presence. Others might challenge Hecker on the abstract, theoretical questions, like original sin, but he hardly understood what they were saying. He was alive to an entirely different mode of discourse, concrete, historical, empirical, experiential. As one student of Hecker has noted, he was an "American Catholic empirical theologian" and as such a "typically American religious thinker."[8]

A simple fascination with the signs of God's action in the contemporary United States was evident in his apologetic method. Most nineteenth-century Catholic apologists focused on the question, "Is the Catholic Church the Church of God?" Their writings featured biblical and historical arguments on behalf of the church and took up issues like the role of the papacy and the church's claim to monopolize the means to salvation. Hecker, in contrast, offered what theologian Joseph Gower describes as "a non-scholastic fundamental theology that was self-consciously American."[9] Like so many romantic Americans of his generation, the idealistic Hecker felt an "aversion to petty religious problems," and instead searched for "first principles." Assuming that his countrymen were naturally religious, admiring their "earnest" moral character, and convinced that people like Channing and Emerson had all but destroyed what little positive theology Protestantism has possessed, he argued that religious controversy had become philosophical, and the locus of debate had shifted from abstract dogmatic propositions to the subject of belief, the human person. As for evangelical, revivalist Christianity, also responsive to these changes, Hecker simply ignored it.

Hecker's enterprise was risky both as Catholic and as American theology. Americans of all schools were bound to wonder at the claim that the Catholic church, and it alone, would answer their religious needs and political hopes. Catholics were bound to be startled by the argument that American individualism and freedom could provide a proper foundation for Catholic belief. "What we call our Americanism does very well in the political order," Brownson wrote in his review, but "it cannot be transferred into the Church without heresy and schism."

Nor could it be transferred into the Redemptorists without conflict. Despite their disappointment at the outcome of the Redemptorist General Congregation of 1855, the English-speaking American priests were by no means resigned to the difficulties posed by parochial responsibilities. What was needed, they now argued, was a separate house for the English-speaking mission band, a proposal considered earlier by Father Bernard but rejected as impractical. In the winter of 1856–57, while engaged in a highly successful mission tour of the south, the American-born priests revived the idea, convinced that their own house was an "absolute necessity" for the continued health of their missions. Their determination was fueled by rumors that the Redemptorists were considering establishment of English-speaking parishes in Quebec and on the island of St. Thomas. They feared that the demand for priests to staff these foundations could well terminate their mission work.

But the problem was less one of accepting parishes than of affirming the missions. In the spring of 1857 Archbishop Bayley of Newark offered them a parish in his diocese; Walworth treated the offer as fulfilling their hopes for a mission house of their own. Hewit, a member of the provincial council, took up the idea with Ruland. The provincial was worried, Hewit found, that they would only receive native-born Americans in their proposed house and, as the German Fathers died out, the young "Anglo-German Fathers would be stranded and left high and dry." Hewit reported that he assured the provincial that they would "take all his young Americanized Germans off his hands," and Ruland then promised to support the project and write to Rome in its favor.

Hecker had been in Cuba that spring, recovering from pneumonia caught during the southern tour. When he returned to New York, Hewit sent him the news and urged Hecker to "get us a good place, for our happiness and perhaps our salvation depend on it." As these words suggest, the group was not satisfied with the Newark offer. Hecker preferred to locate the house in New York, where he was assured of financial support from his now-wealthy brother George. He spoke with Archbishop Hughes, who responded favorably. When Ruland learned later that Hecker had discussed the matter with Hughes, and even selected a possible site, without informing him, he was incensed.

Despite Hewit's report, Ruland in fact was not fully persuaded. His letter to Rome was indecisive and contained some remarks critical of the nationalism of the American priests. Reaction at Redemptorist headquarters in Rome was decidedly negative. On July 23 Walworth passed along the "disastrous news" that the new general, Father Mauron, opposed any kind of separation; he had called their motives into question by expressing his "abhorrence of every symptom of nationality." According to Walworth, Mauron had also suggested that fathers would be needed for Quebec and St. Thomas, making some of the English-speaking Redemptorists "expatriates." Walworth was angry, writing that the general was "ignorant as a bat of all our affairs in this country, and looks upon us as little children, that don't know what we want and can be kept quiet by a whip." They should try to persuade Archbishop Hughes and Bishop Bayley to write directly to Rome in support of the new house. Most important, Walworth argued, they should keep in as close communication as possible with the provincial; otherwise "we shall always be going on with schemes and hopes, while mines of which we are perfectly unconscious are preparing to explode under our feet."[10]

After writing Mauron that the new house was required by the needs of the church in the United States, not because the American missionaries were discontented, Walworth consulted Hewit and then wrote Hecker that both men heartily approved the suggestion that Hecker go to Rome to explain "how fatal these new establishments" abroad "would be to our missions and how necessary [is] a mission establishment here." This was a remarkable suggestion, for on June 12, 1857, the provincial had notified Redemptorist communities that, as a result of an earlier incident involving an American-based Redemptorist, personal trips to Rome were forbidden. The circular, signed by Mauron, read: "I hereby make known to all that it is allowed no one to leave America on his own authority under penalty of automatically-incurred expulsion from the Congregation."[11] Nevertheless, Father Deshon wrote Ruland that the provincial had the right to send a subject to Rome. Individual members of the order also could not be denied the right to go there on a personal matter; much less could they be denied appeal on a matter so crucial to the welfare of the Congregation.[12]

The four conspirators agreed that the situation had reached a crisis point. An English-speaking house was needed, Hughes had promised the necessary support, and the project, and the mission work itself, was threatened by the prospect of new establishments, which might be ordered from Rome at any moment. To a man they were serious, responsible, not given to emotional decisions, yet their correspondence was filled with a talk of "grave dangers" that made the admitted risks of the trip worth taking.

Even before Deshon wrote the provincial, Hewit had written Hecker as if the trip were a foregone conclusion. He warned Hecker to give no information in Rome on bishops or on ecclesiastical affairs in the United States; they must retain the confidence of the hierarchy and secular clergy. He further recommended that Hecker make no comment on other internal Redemptorist disputes unless he was forced to appeal to the pope, in which case additional displeasure within the congregation would make no difference. In fact, the English-speaking fathers were extremely upset; Hewit told Hecker to do what he could to encourage appointment of a consultor general to investigate Redemptorist affairs in the United States. The solidarity of Deshon, Walworth and Hewit, and their trust in Hecker, was impressive. All put in writing their authorization of him to make the trip on their behalf, their belief in the absolute necessity of an English-speaking house, and their confidence that Hecker, faced with difficulties, should consult "God and his own judgement." In doing so, they took a risk, and they knew it.[13]

To prepare for the trip, Hecker rounded up letters of testimonial to the importance of the missions and the prospects of vigorous mission efforts among the English-speaking, and personal testaments to his character and zeal. James McMaster wrote of the obstacles placed before the mission work and the gaining of new vocations by the exclusively German cast of the Redemptorists. He wrote Hecker: "From the special gifts and providence in your history [you] have in a particular manner the confidence and love, as well as respect, of Bishops, priests and the best of the laity." Bishops' testimonials were equally glowing, none more fervent than that of John Hughes. To Cardinal Alessandro Barnabò, head of the Propaganda, the Vatican office in charge of U.S. affairs, he described Hecker as a "laborious, edifying, zealous and truly apostolic priest." Hewit and Walworth were gathering similar letters from other bishops.[14]

Until the last moment the fathers tried to win Ruland's approval of the trip. He was unpersuaded by Deshon's argument and feared offending the general, but he agreed to state that he concurred in the object of the trip and would have approved the journey "without the slightest hesitation" if he thought he had the authority to do so. A few days later, on the eve of Hecker's departure, he backed away, supplying a letter of testimonial for Hecker personally, but expressing his disapproval of the trip as contrary to the will of the superior general and undertaken without sufficient reason. He indicated, however, that he supported establishment of an English-speaking house and had promised to help secure permission for it. Father Helmpraecht, rector of the New York house and Hecker's immediate superior, at first promised to grant permission, even if Ruland did not, but at the last minute refused to do so.[15]

The four fathers again debated the wisdom of taking the trip without the provincial's endorsement; they all agreed that, if Hecker had any doubts about the matter, he should not go. If he felt the trip was justified, they unanimously pledged themselves to his support. Hecker himself had no doubts and quickly made arrangements. While the rector of the New York house and the provincial were kept fully informed, most of the other fathers knew nothing and undoubtedly wondered at the preparations being made. Hecker departed on the *Asia* for Liverpool on August 5, 1857. He asked Hewit to write an account of the missions for publication in the Roman journal *Civiltà Cattolica*, in which he already planned to insert Brownson's article on the "Mission of America."

Throughout the controversy the convert fathers were at pains to show that their request did not constitute a schism in the congregation and was not motivated by anti-German feelings. Nevertheless, there is considerable evidence that among the German fathers, even those most friendly to them, their plans were looked upon in this light. At Ruland's request Father Helmpraecht wrote Father Mauron of the controversy in terms that confirmed the general's suspicions. He charged that the American fathers wished to have a provincial chosen by the province, that they did not want

English-speaking students to have to learn German or to have German fathers give English-language missions. He added that the American fathers were upset by their perception that the congregation government was German, that none of their number had been elected to the General Chapter nor did any of them sit on the General Council. Furthermore, they argued that "America should be converted by Americans," to which Helmpraecht added "the principle of the Know Nothings is: that America should be ruled by Americans." Finally, Helmpraecht, with whom the Fathers had often lived, claimed that the Americans did not have the same zeal for German souls that the Germans had for the English-speaking. He opposed the English house as laying the basis for "schism" and because its residents would be freed from parish work to which the Germans were devoted. Helmpraecht was particularly critical of Hecker, who had taken this "daring step" to promote the idea that "only through an *English* house in *New York* can the Congregation become permanent and of value to America," to remove from himself and his companions "the suspicion that they are national and revolutionary" and because of his "complete distrust of the Provincial."

Ruland was at the same time writing a long secret letter to the general, laying more "mines" under Hecker's feet. Unknown to the fathers, the letter traveled to Europe on the same ship with Hecker and arrived in Rome well before he did. In it, Ruland gave a full report on the negotiations regarding the English-speaking house in a way which cast grave doubt on the motives and character of the English-speaking fathers. Ruland admitted he had communicated to them Mauron's earlier letters regarding their project, omitting a paragraph in which the general noted the impression that the English-speaking fathers seemed to give insufficient weight to the authority of the Rule and wanted to judge for themselves what was demanded of them. Yet the Americans were aroused by what he did read them, and he soon was "exchanging harsh words with Father Hecker," who demanded permission to go to Rome. They argued that Mauron's letter indicated they were regarded as "partisans and rebels" in Rome, a prejudice which could not be overcome by writing. In the discussions, it became clear to Ruland that the four fathers had concerted together regarding the new house. Under heavy pressure, he held to the position that all they wished could be accomplished by mail, that if they insisted he would write for permission for one of them to go there, but under no circumstances would he give permission for the trip on his own authority. Citing the political slogan "America should be ruled by Americans," he charged that their behavior showed that "something similar seems to stick in the heads of our English Fathers."[16]

Ruland also was worried that a New York house would be difficult to maintain in the Redemptorist spirit. Already there was too much visiting with family and friends, especially by Hecker, who associated with other converts there and took up "eccentric" ideas, many of which had merit but were too novel and flexible to accord with the spirit of religious life. Hecker was prepared to "risk everything and do everything" for the success of the project, approaching bishops, planning to win support in Rome, and even to go further should he find no sympathy among his superiors. Reports of these plans surprised Ruland and gave him "a new insight into Father Hecker's character."

With this letter from his superior on its way to Rome, the unsuspecting Hecker was approaching the first great crisis of his Catholic life. He was, indeed, prepared to "risk everything" for his vision of a Catholic America, pursued by a body of religious men committed to it. Confident that this vision came from God, he left with little apprehension, sure that this was another step toward "the land promised me in my youth."

8

Catholic Innocent Abroad

When Isaac Hecker embarked for Europe, Brownson's critical review of *Aspirations of Nature* was about to appear. Letters were on their way to Rome suggesting that Hecker's ideas arose from a fevered imagination and his project was a manifestation of American nationalism which could disrupt the unity of the Redemptorist community, perhaps even that of the American church. Unaware of all this, Hecker stopped in England to visit old friends and share his ideas about the future prospects of the church. In London he saw the noted converts Edward Manning and Frederick Faber, both of whom he had met briefly while at Clapham. Hecker heard Manning express sympathetic views regarding "the adaptation of Catholicity to the non-Catholic community." Nevertheless, Isaac wrote his brother George, who was paying his expenses, a rather depressing account of his meetings:

> Strange to say I find no men animated with a view of a better future. I did my best to excite it, but somehow or other men's heads in Europe are turned quite around. They see the past but cannot fix their gaze on the future. But they all admit that for us in the U.S. there is a prospect of something better. . . . The Church now stands pretty much in status quo. No one is actuated by hope and the energies which ought to be directed to her interests are wasted in great measure in private bickerings.[1]

Unfortunately for Hecker, the "bickerings" had only begun. Since the French Revolution, the Catholic Church in Europe had been deeply divided. Many Catholics rejected the Revolution's fruits as the product of the poisoned springs of Protestantism and its daughter, the Enlightenment. For this group, republican government, modern liberties, independent intellectual life and secular culture all arose from rebellion against the church, religion, God himself. A dwindling minority disagreed, arguing that a new era of human liberty, economic progress and social equality would bring many benefits for humanity and new opportunities for the church. Instead of simply denouncing modernity, the church should seek out the elements of good, show their relation to Catholic truths, and attempt to renew the faith in order to bring human life once again to its full realization in Christianity.

When Giovanni Mastai Ferretti became Pope Pius IX in 1846, hopes were high among the latter group that such a renewal had begun. They were encouraged by the new pope's efforts to reform the government of the papal states and his apparent sympathy with political liberalism. Their hopes were dashed two years later, however, when revolutions spread across Europe, the pope was driven from Rome and returned only with the aid of Austrian troops. Pius IX then turned sharply to the right and placed the church on a course of all-out opposition to liberalism that would climax in the *Syllabus of Errors* in 1863. Missionary enthusiasm of the kind Hecker searched for had become dangerous, regarded with suspicion by churchmen and with disbelief by the Church's enemies.

The alternative policy, associated with an increasingly self-conscious group within the church, was Ultramontanism, a word which was coming to suggest both devotion to the pope and opposition to modern society. National churches were to be brought under Roman supervision, the autonomy of religious orders checked by Roman centralization, the orthodoxy of belief guaranteed by the authority of Rome and the infallibility of the pope. The laity were to be bound to the church through popular devotions, a variety of confraternities and associations, and loyalty to the one teaching church, the source of certainty in a changing, unstable world. This stance particularly appealed to those most threatened by the political and economic revolutions of the day—aristocrats, peasants, petit-bourgeois artisans and shop-keepers. The clergy were to be renewed as a more loyal, disciplined body under the authority of the bishops, while the bishops, in turn, were to be made loyal to the Holy See by challenging governmental involvement in their selection and by weakening the role of national and other episcopal bodies which might mediate between the diocese and Rome.

The heart and center of this new church lay in Rome. As most Catholics saw it, the authority of the pope stood as the only guarantor of tradition, even of truth. His government of the papal states, even if upheld only with foreign armies, seemed necessary to his independence. Papal supervision of local churches alone insured that they did not get swallowed up by the passions of nationalism. In the new differentiation of Western culture into nations, classes, and ethnic groups, Catholicism stood forth as a transcending ideal, above the passions and conflicts of the day, the custodian of truths older and wiser than any others, a symbol and ideal of unity, coherence, and a spirit that stretched beyond the present. The papacy, above all, embodied this romantic ideal, one which appealed to all those threatened by modernity.

In the 1850s the triumph of Ultramontane Catholicism was far from complete. There was growing popular devotion to the pope, but his infallibility was not yet defined and the scope of his authority remained open to question. Vatican centralization still struggled against traditional national institutions and the historic autonomy of many religious orders. Communications were improving, but it still took months to deal with problems in churches outside Italy. More important, it was not clear that papal authority need mean political reaction or intellectual intransigence. Conflict and debate were present, even in the Vatican.

It was in this context that Isaac Hecker arrived in Rome on August 26, 1857, to face a Redemptorist general already warned by his American provincial about Hecker's "enthusiasm," "eccentric ideas" and divisive concern for non-Catholic Americans. Father Mauron received the provincial's letter only a few days before Hecker's arrival. He summoned Hecker to his room and told him that Father Douglass, the only member of the council who spoke English, would return to Rome in a few days, a council meeting would be held, and Hecker could explain why he had come. He should put his reasons on paper; Douglass would translate them and give them to the general. Before Douglass arrived, however, Hecker met several times with Mauron and explained his case, emphasizing the opportunities for conversions. Mauron, according to Hecker, took his words "in the wrong way," again and again "insinuating" that the English fathers had acted from "low and ambitious motives." The council meeting was called for August 30, and Hecker begged Douglass to arrive early so he could show him the documents he had brought with him. Unfortunately, Douglass arrived only a half hour before the start of the meeting and was summoned away before Hecker could complete his explanation. An hour and a half later, Hecker was called in and told bluntly that the council had already decided his trip was in itself reason for dismissal from the Redemptorists. They need not hear his explanation. Nevertheless, the general asked his reasons and Hecker began by citing the provision of the Constitution which gave subjects the right to appeal. Mauron, according to Hecker, took the document, and read the passage in question, "slurring over what regarded the right and emphasizing the other." Then he launched into a series of accusations against Hecker and his colleagues. Hecker remained silent, fully expecting to be allowed to continue. To his surprise, the general handed the secretary a document and told him to read it; it was a decree of dismissal from the congregation. Hecker was accused of ignoring the circular prohibition on trips to Rome, "procuring money from outsiders," and having a "way of acting and thinking in general . . . by no means in harmony with the laws and spirit of our Institute." He was formally dismissed from the congregation and released from the vows of poverty, obedience and perseverance.

After the decree was read, Hecker begged to be heard but was denied. He withdrew to a nearby chapel to pray, then returned to the council hall to again beg on his knees for a hearing. Denied once again, he asked: "You condemn me then, without hearing?" and the assembled consultors nodded in the affirmative. After expressing the purity of his intentions and those of his colleagues, he withdrew. That afternoon he met with Mauron, hoping to insure that the others would not be punished. Reporting on these events to his American friends the next day, he concluded with surprising equanimity: "My mind is tranquil, my conscience does not accuse me of having acted as I am accused." While his journey was considered "a great scandal," Hecker told them, Mauron was also upset with them for seeking a location for the house without permission. Most important, Hecker thought Mauron and the other Redemptorist leaders were prejudiced against them as Americans. Nevertheless, he was determined to fight on in Rome as long as "there is a spark of hope."[2]

Hecker's calm response seemed to indicate that, by the time he reached Rome, perhaps even before he left home, he had given up hope that his goals could be achieved through the Redemptorist community. Brownson's letter, with its mention of a new congregation of native origin; Hecker's earlier comments to George; his conversations in England, and his behavior in Rome together suggest that he was enthusiastic about his program of evangelization, skeptical that it could be carried out in a European-oriented community, confident that a way would open for the work, and at ease with the uncertainty about the exact form that way would take. Subsequent events indicated that, while his colleagues were generally familiar with his goals, they had not discussed pursuing them outside the Redemptorists. That is not to say that Hecker deceived them, or that he would not willingly have joined in the work of an English-speaking mission house if that proved possible. He was candid about his objectives, and the reasons for them, but less so about his means, partly because he had no clear idea what means would be placed before him by church authorities and divine Providence. Accordingly, when he found himself dismissed, and presumably in disgrace, he was neither surprised nor angry.

On September 1 Hecker wrote his brother twice, expressing confidence that he was pursuing the right path and that God would guide him. At the very least he would do his best "to get some American ideas understood and appreciated here in Rome."[3] Meanwhile, Mauron was passing the news along to Ruland back in the United States. Failure to dismiss Hecker, he said, would have destroyed the American province and ultimately the "entire congregation" by "loosening completely the bonds of authority and discipline" and introducing, "a democratic system" at odds with the spirit of religious life. Reviewing the grounds for his action, he said that Hecker and the others had associated "in a kind of conspiracy and a plot" by sending Hecker as a representative of a dissident group. Mauron added that he would not attack Hecker for "his further utterances that the Congregation in America is not what it ought to be, that one ought to adjust oneself to the needs of America," because these views had been communicated to Mauron in their private meetings before the Council session. Mauron ordered Ruland to communicate the news to the other three fathers, but not to show them the decree. If they wished to be dispensed from their vows, they should write him. He, in turn, would not grant a simple release but "expulsion, since they are equally guilty." He anticipated that they would wait, as Hecker had taken rooms and was planning an appeal. As for their proposal, he would never recognize an exclusively American house, but expected eventual establishment of a house in which the ministry would be carried on in English.[4]

For the fathers at home, the results were distressing. Brownson and George Hecker called at the New York house, "greatly excited," to give the news to Hewit, Walworth and Deshon, who wrote quickly to assure Hecker of their support. They indicated that they would quietly avoid conflicts with the provincial, lest they seem rebels against authority. Walworth saw it as an internal Redemptorist conflict. The new constitution, with its excessive centralization, was the source of the difficulty; only revision would solve their problem. A week later, he wrote on this subject in greater detail. The new system, he argued, made the Redemptorists resemble the Jesuits, stripping the rectors of authority, reducing consultors to a strictly advisory role, and placing all power in the hands of the provincials, who, in turn, were entirely dependent on the general. Walworth's interpretation seemed confirmed by the formal notification from Ruland a week later in which he quoted at length from the decree of expulsion and the general's letter, with its accusations of disobedience. Ruland told the fathers he had been severely, and properly, reprimanded by the general for his indulgence.[5]

On September 8 Hecker reported a most cordial reception by Cardinal Allesandro Barnabò, head of the Congregation of the Propaganda, which supervised American affairs, and his assistant, Archbishop Gaetano Bedini, who had previously visited the United States. The way had been well-prepared by the testimonial letters solicited from the bishops. Barnabò told Hecker that the general had been to see him; he urged Hecker to report to his religious house and try to work things out. When Hecker told him he had been in Rome "better than a week" and reported on what had happened, Barnabò was shocked, for Mauron had not mentioned the expulsion, or even Hecker's arrival in Rome. Expressing his displeasure with the general, Barnabò urged Hecker to draw up a petition requesting permission to say Mass, which would be presented to the Cardinal Vicar of Rome. He then should prepare a report giving his reasons for coming to Rome. Both prelates gave Hecker "every encouragement." Bernard Smith, former rector of the Irish College in Rome and the Roman agent for several American bishops, had also been asked for help; he told Hecker he had never seen even a bishop treated with such cordiality by Propaganda. In this initial meeting Barnabò expressed one reservation: theirs appeared to be an "American movement." Bedini, on his visit, had been publicly attacked by anti-Catholic nativists. He undoubtedly alerted Barnabò to the charge. Hecker pointed to their support by Hughes and other prominent Irish-American clergy and the cardinal seemed satisfied. Hecker was delighted with Barnabò, calling him "a Father, a Counsellor, a Protector."[6]

Having come to Rome to win approval of an English-speaking house, and thus forward the dream of conversions, there was no turning back. If the decree of expulsion were allowed to stand, Hecker and his friends would not be able to continue the missions, much less form an alternative community. He asked his colleagues what he should do if the cardinal, once the dismissal was removed, should tell him to return to the United States and devote himself "to the English-speaking Catholics and to the conversion of non-Catholics." Clearly, he argued, they could never work effectively among the American people until they found some vehicle more conformable than the Redemptorists to the American character.[7]

Accordingly, he launched himself immediately on a course that seemed designed, at the very least, to free him, and give him official sanction, for the work he had in mind almost from the beginning of his Catholic life. The call for a "new generation" after his visit to Holy Cross, his statement to superiors in the seminary, and his labors since 1851 all led in the same direction; the conflict with the Redemptorist leadership seemed but one more obstacle to be overcome. If the fathers agreed with him, the first step was to prepare their own memorial to be sent to Cardinal Barnabò, stating their grievances, outlining the needs of religion in the United States, and requesting permission to be allowed to labor to meet those needs. In this document they should ask for release from their obligations to the congregation with an eye toward placing themselves under "a Bishop as our superior" who would favor the work and give them "full liberty to work for the conversion of the country." For the moment, Bayley seemed to be the best hope, though they should solicit support from Hughes and Kenrick, who carried great weight with Rome.

Hecker seemed worried that his colleagues might think their situation did not justify release from their vows. For himself, the disposition of their superiors and the "hindrances in the Congregation" in the way of the work seemed to provide sufficient grounds. Before ending his letter, he urged them to open this possibility to all the English-speaking fathers, inviting their participation. He was confident that Father Baker, another convert who had joined the mission band, and Father Cornell, an Irish-born preacher, would join them, though he doubted that the Irish-American Redemptorists in New Orleans would follow. Most important, they should exact secrecy from all, as it could become a matter to be used against them. He concluded with another idea. An American studying for the priesthood in Rome had visited Hecker and told of how attending their missions had inspired his vocation. This young man recommended that they join the Oratory, the community of priests bound by promises, not vows, founded by St. Philip Neri in the seventeenth century and recently introduced into England by John Henry Newman. Bedini had also recommended this option, and Hughes had long considered trying to bring the Oratorians to his diocese. This would have to be investigated. For now, the memorial should be prepared and backed by episcopal authority.[8]

In early October Hecker wrote George that his health and spirits were good, though "if I had to fight the enemies of the church it would be sport, but to have to do so with my own brethren, this is afflicting." He was learning more of church procedure. There seemed to be three options: a personal decision by the pope, appointment of a special commission, or reference of the case to the Congregation on Bishops and Regulars, a step which would mean long delays. On Barnabò's advice he drew up a memorial requesting appointment of a special commission. He wrote his colleagues of this step, indicating the chances were not good it would be followed; it was more likely to be referred to the congregation, which had jurisdiction over religious orders. The cardinal was highly critical of the general's action because it was made without reference to the interests of religion in the United States, which was his responsibility. Legally, however, a dispute between a subject and superior fell under the jurisdiction of Bishops and Regulars, which was probably why Mauron had not mentioned his decision to Barnabò on his earlier visit.[9]

Well before receiving these letters, Walworth wrote that the fathers at home all agreed that "if things remained as the general and his party have determined neither F. Hewit, Deshon or myself can find any vocation left to us in the Congregation." They wanted to let Hecker know he was free to act for them all, that they wished him to pursue the object of his trip to Rome and not leave "until *all our affairs* are settled." They would prefer to be restored to the Congregation and their "true vocation"; failing that they would hope to receive permission "to separate and form a distinct band or society without relaxation of our vows" and, as a last resort, to "procure from the Holy Father the relaxation of our vows." A few days later, Hewit wrote in a similar vein. On October 20, they wrote as a body, indicating not quite accurately that their views coincided perfectly with Hecker's: they had a special vocation, the Redemptorists could be happily adapted to the needs of the country, but present policies hampered the work of missions. If they could not get the decision reversed, they repeated, they should seek new arrangements to work under new superiors as vowed missionaries. Even after receiving Hecker's letter of October 3, with its explicit reference to work beyond the missions, Walworth wrote again of their agreement.[10]

While Hecker was making his plans, the Redemptorist superiors were also taking action. Mauron saw the pope and felt reassured that the Holy Father recognized that he had acted to preserve congregational discipline. He wrote a stinging letter to Ruland, telling the provincial that the personal testimonials to Hecker's virtue, supplied by him and by the New York rector, had almost proven fatal. He urged him to discuss the matter with Hughes, Kenrick and Bishop Neumann of Philadelphia, a Redemptorist, all of whom had fallen into the trap of providing personal testimonials. He should point out to them that Hecker, who Hughes said deserved all confidence, had "not scrupled" to say that the German fathers did not learn English, that only German was spoken in Redemptorist houses, and that the Germans could not converse with the bishops or educated Americans; he had shown himself to be "a bad and dangerous religious." The general also ordered the provincial to end the "abuse of massive correspondence" among the dissidents. All letters from Hecker, even those marked personal, should be opened "and only those which contain no deceit may be handed to the Fathers," who were to be "forbidden to carry on any correspondence with him." Father Douglass reaffirmed this directive a few weeks later, reminding Ruland that Hecker was not "a simple stranger" and the provincial had the right to open and read his letters, even those addressed to provincial consultors, of whom Hewit was one.

Ruland, for his part, was caught in the middle. He accepted Mauron's initial reprimand, admitting it should have been harsher. He and Helmpraecht had been bombarded by the American fathers, he argued; if they had completely resisted, it would have been attributed to personal motives and worsened suspicion and distrust. He accused Hecker of being "a dreamer and enthusiast" and claimed that the American fathers were more concerned with "a special class of people" than with "the masses." Nevertheless, he urged the general to readmit Hecker to the Redemptorists, for his dismissal would have a bad effect on the American fathers and on Hecker's many friends and admirers. After receiving Mauron's instructions, he wrote Hewit that the fathers should discontinue all correspondence with Hecker. At the same time he expressed his personal hope that Hecker would be reinstated and said he had pleaded for his re-admission in his last two letters to Rome.[11]

Hecker had rushed to complete *Aspirations of Nature* and have it published as part of his plan to organize support for missions to non-Catholics. His strategy brought substantial benefits. In September, while he was beginning his long struggle to overcome his expulsion, Archbishop Purcell of Cincinnati wrote Archbishop Kenrick of Baltimore:

> What a book for the times is the "Aspirations of Nature" by Father Hecker. I had a chance of reading it while on my last visitation. Thanks be to God who raises up such men to illustrate his holy truth and vindicate his Church—by life and pen.[12]

Purcell became one of the group's most influential supporters, writing Rome to praise Hecker's value to the American church, to support the missions and to argue for action to prevent the scandal that would be given by Hecker's disgrace.

From the beginning Hecker had taken every step possible to win such support from the American bishops. When he left for Rome, he carried testimonials to his good character and to the work of the missions from at least fifteen bishops. After the expulsion, when he came to depend so heavily on Barnabò, such support was even more critical, for the cardinal's standing in the case rested on its impact on general religious affairs in the United States; internal problems of religious orders lay outside his jurisdiction. In November Hecker was still urging the fathers at home to solicit letters of support, emphasizing that they should center on the need to continue mission work and the damage that would be done to the church if it was known how Hecker had been treated; he did not tell them to mention convert work. Walworth worked hard, informing friendly bishops of what had taken place and urging them to write Barnabò. On Christmas day, for example, Walworth wrote an admittedly "not very entertaining" report to Purcell. Again, Walworth did not mention conversions but emphasized the missions, which he said were threatened with ruin because of "the indifference not to say hostility of our Superiors." He explained Hecker's expulsion and their conviction that the grave circumstances in which they were placed justified their reliance on the Redemptorist Constitution in making the appeal. He asked Purcell to send Propaganda a message of satisfaction with the work of the missions, together with a request for their protection.[13] Purcell did write Barnabò, praising the work of the missionaries and indicating that all the bishops believed that Hecker sincerely thought he was within his rights in going to Rome. In addition, he indicated his respect for the "heroic obedience" of the missionaries and expressed his hopes that their work would be allowed to continue. Over two months later, Bernard Smith told Purcell that Barnabò and Bedini appreciated his letters and, while it was a difficult question, Propaganda was determined to carry out the views he had expressed.[14]

Many bishops who had written earlier also responded quickly to Walworth's appeals, including Bishops Barry of Savannah, de Goesbriand of Burlington, McFarland of Hartford and James Wood, coadjutor of Philadelphia, who was supposedly highly thought of in Rome. Bishop Lynch of Charleston wrote a warm testimonial and suggested to Hewit that, if things did not work out in Rome, the mission band would be welcome in his diocese. Perhaps Bishop Bayley of Newark was closest to the case; a fellow convert, he knew the fathers personally, had actively supported their work, and made the original offer of land for an English-speaking Redemptorist house. Walworth noted that Bayley was "to every intent and purpose a *brother*." He repeated his offer of a house in his diocese, even if they were separated from the congregation, while telling Walworth they could "count on him always for anything in his power."

Some bishops were doubtful. Kenrick, who had been familiar with their problems and was consulted during the crisis occasioned by Rumpler's insanity, wrote a personal testimonial for Hecker when he went to Rome. After the expulsion, the Redemptorists, whose headquarters were in Maryland, took pains to win Kenrick's support, with some success. In February 1858 Kenrick told Martin John Spalding, Bishop of Louisville, that he would have attempted to dissuade Hecker from making the trip if he had known its object, for it was bound to displease his Redemptorist superiors. Eventually the Redemptorists would become Americanized as they received more American candidates, but it was imprudent to press the matter, Kenrick thought. His close friend, Bishop O'Connor of Pittsburgh, agreed; he thought very highly of Hecker and even suggested Hecker come to work in his diocese, but he professed to know nothing of the disagreement that led to his expulsion. Later, Kenrick passed along his views to Purcell, who replied that, if he had known of Kenrick's reservations, he would have hesitated in registering his strong endorsement.[15]

The most important, and most difficult, prelate was Hughes, who had written a warm personal endorsement of Hecker when he left for Rome. When news of the affair reached him, he quickly wrote Barnabò that he welcomed establishment of an English language house in New York, but regarded the consent of Redemptorist superiors as essential. He did not have reason to suspect tension between English and German-speaking fathers and had no complaint against either group. He wrote the next day to Mauron, insisting that he had not encouraged Hecker's trip. He pointed out that he always supported religious authority and would have accepted a house only with the consent of Redemptorist leaders. Hughes received several visits from the fathers in New York, who tried to keep him posted of events. In December, when letters of support were needed, Hecker sent Hughes a letter, which he had drafted as early as September 30, giving a detailed description of the events which had led up to his expulsion and his dealings with Barnabò since that time. Shortly after this letter was written, the bishop received an oral report on the state of affairs from George Hecker. He then wrote Hecker a warm personal letter, for use in Rome. He claimed to know Hecker and the other missionaries better than any other bishop and no word of criticism had reached his ears. "I have always looked on you as a model of religious obedience," Hughes wrote. Hecker was pleased, promising to use this letter if the general attempted to use Hughes' earlier letter against him.[16]

The same day he wrote Hecker, Hughes also wrote Bernard Smith, his American contact in Rome, who ordinarily communicated the contents of his letters to Propaganda. Hughes claimed he could not find a copy of his letter to Mauron, but he knew he wrote in "the spirit of one who recognized the legitimate exercise of ecclesiastical authority . . . but no word of mine could be interpreted to the disadvantage of Father Hecker." Indeed, he regarded Hecker "as a most excellent priest, learned, zealous, edifying and energetic in all his ministry." It appeared he had been dismissed without a hearing and Hughes argued that he and the priests associated with him were "entitled to receive the respect so far as I know of the Catholic bishops, clergy and laity of this country." Hughes professed himself unable to judge the dispute within the congregation, but he did know that Hecker considered himself acting in good faith in going to Rome. It was only "on the basis of a well founded conviction on my part that he was acting in good faith" that Hughes had supplied an introduction "and to some extent a recommendation." Never one to avoid a lesson, Hughes added that the relationship between religious orders and bishops should be examined by those "charged with the government of the church." He himself never interfered with religious, but he required them to adhere strictly to the ecclesiastical discipline of the diocese, "the same as if they were . . . secular clergymen." Smith had the portions of this letter which dealt with Hecker translated into Italian and shown to Barnabò and Bedini, who were glad to know Hughes was not opposed to Hecker; they had the letter read to the pope.

Reporting all this to Hughes in early March, Smith noted that the problem had "now assumed a gigantic aspect." While the general had powerful support, Propaganda was determined to prevail "over a religious superior who has little knowledge of the meaning of religion in your country." However, Hughes' vacillating course disturbed the priests, especially Walworth, who reported they had little success in getting the archbishop's help until George Hecker went to see him. "George has money, which gives him a prominence in his Grace's eyes, and the appearance that you have made powerful friends in Rome also helped," he wrote Isaac.[17]

Meanwhile Hecker solicited support among European Redemptorists. His earlier superiors were sympathetic. Fr. de Buggenoms was not surprised by the general's action; he expected that Hecker would not win out. De Held wrote Barnabò, praising Hecker as "a model, and a pillar of the Congregation." He told the cardinal the previous general had governed with excessive severity and still exerted great influence. The step taken against Hecker was extreme and deplorable, he argued, and he reported that de Buggenoms and Fr. Deschamp, present or former officials in England, shared his disapproval of the expulsion. Hecker's correspondence with de Held must have revealed something of his drive for independence, however, for in February de Held warned him that complete obedience to religious superiors had to be upheld, despite the fact that this rule of religious life was sometimes not taken seriously by Propaganda. Nor could he accept Hecker's criticism of the Redemptorists for taking parishes, for this was often the only way to become established in mission situations.[18]

In addition to winning a hearing from powerful officials and making contact with knowledgeable Romans who could help, Hecker wanted to strengthen his case by encouraging public discussion of American affairs. For this reason, he presented Barnabò with *Questions of the Soul* and urged George to speed him copies of *Aspirations of Nature* as soon as they became available. In this context Brownson's review arrived, and it was a serious blow, for it not only hurt Hecker personally but jeopardized the cause as well. Hecker was very upset, writing George that Brownson might at least have delayed publication, especially as George had been his "warm friend" and had offered to pay the expenses of the *Review*. He told his brother to see McMaster and ask him to keep all notice of the article out of the *Freeman's Journal*. Hewit attempted to reassure Hecker with news of Brownson's reaction to events in Rome: "Whatever coldness may have arisen in his mind toward you is now gone and the ill treatment you have received has aroused all the noblest and most generous parts of his nature."[19]

At home, Brownson was well aware of the damage his review might do in Rome. He wrote Hecker a long letter, expressing his sincere concern that Hecker's dismissal would set back the cause they both had at heart. The problems of the American church arose, he told Hecker, from foreigners who arrived badly instructed in their faith. Hecker's experience was one more sign that this problem was not understood in Rome. Associating himself with Hecker, he argued that the issue was whether Americans could become Catholics without becoming "foreigners in this our own land." He then offered a lengthy apologia for his review, which he described as "long, elaborate and not unfriendly." He had hoped to protect Hecker against the charge that he was part of an American party or clique. Rightly understood, nothing in the article should embarrass Hecker. Brownson also thought Roman publication of his "Mission of America" article, as planned originally, would probably not help. In replying, Hecker agreed on the last point and noted that he was instead preparing two articles himself. Still, he did not shrink from expressing to his friend the pain he felt at the review: among other things, it would further poison the minds of the already suspicious Ruland and Mauron. It was regrettable, he wrote sadly, that men who shared the same "noble and divine work" should have so many differences. Nevertheless, he promised to show the explanatory portions of Brownson's letter to Barnabò; he hoped it would do some good.[20]

Hecker's worries, however, proved exaggerated. As so often happened in his life, his personal warmth and magnetism seemed to overcome skepticism about his ideas. Barnabò, Bedini, Smith and others had become his advocates, though none had reason to appreciate his vision. On October 13 Hecker informed Smith that he was leaving for Naples for eight days, travelling with Bedini's secretary. Bedini had met with the pope, who noted that he and the cardinal had taken up Hecker's defense. The general's explanation had arrived; Hecker was "surprised at its weakness and even the silliness of some of its passages," but recognized that it was "adroitly calculated to convey a false impression to those who are not fully posted."[21] On his trip, Hecker visited the tomb of St. Alphonsus and met with Neapolitan Redemptorists, who had been separated from the general's authority some years before. They hoped the Belgians, French and Americans would unite against "the military rule of the Germans." Transfer to Neapolitan jurisdiction was considered, but given up when Hecker learned that the pope regretted the earlier decision to divide the congregation.[22] In early November, Hecker wrote the fathers of his satisfaction with their unity of views and indicated that he was exploring all possible solutions. At Barnabò's suggestion he had paid yet another call on the general, presenting him with a copy of *Aspirations of Nature* and chatting about the weather before taking up the general's report. Hecker told him that the provincial had been fully informed and there was no conspiracy involved. Mauron agreed Ruland was weak, but they could reach no agreement on whether or not Hecker had been allowed fully to present his case.[23]

By November, his first article was ready for publication in *Civiltà Cattolica*, the Jesuit journal favored by the pope. It outlined the prospects for successful conversion work in the United States, emphasizing Catholic growth, Protestant decline and the sincerity and good will of non-Catholics. Hecker told the fathers at home that Barnabò was pleased, the editor promised to call the pope's attention to the article, and it was causing much comment, conveying a better idea of American conditions. He noted as well that the same journal had attacked a speech by the French liberal Catholic Charles de Montalembert, whose paper did not say "a thousandth of what these contain." An Italian had told him that if one of his countrymen had written it, he would have been called in for explanations.

Apparently, Barnabò thought the article too optimistic, so Hecker suggested he could easily describe the difficulties facing the American church and the means of overcoming them in the second paper he was writing. But that paper was even more optimistic than the first. "God in his Providence has prepared in our time the American people for conversion to the Catholic faith," Hecker wrote. He then repeated the arguments of his books, the decline of Protestantism, the inadequacy of liberal religion, the hunger of "high-minded" Americans for positive religion, and the resulting opportunities for Catholic evangelism. American constitutional arrangements, themselves shaped by Providence, "left the church free as the sun in her heavenly course to exercise upon earth her divine mission." The freedom of the church contrasted sharply with its restriction in Europe both by Catholic monarchs and anti-Catholic revolutionaries. American political institutions rested upon the assumption that human beings could govern themselves, but Protestantism saw human reason as corrupted and the will bound by sin. Protestant Christianity was simply incompatible with American political institutions, and, Hecker believed, more and more Americans recognized that fact.

The obvious question was how to square this assessment with the rising popularity of the anti-Catholic Know Nothings. As Hecker saw it, recent events, far from giving reason to postpone a campaign for conversions, confirmed the "growing conviction" that American institutions required Catholicity for their foundation and fulfillment. The association of immigrant Catholics with the Democratic party had aroused Protestant fears, so that anti-Catholic "political parsons" enjoyed momentary success. But the blatant bigotry of the movement created a backlash among many fair-minded Americans. Democratic party leaders, out of self-interest, were forced to defend Catholics and to learn more about Catholic teaching and beliefs. Know-Nothing excesses exposed the absurdity of many widely held myths about Catholicism, while American opposition to prejudice and to the intrusion of Protestant ministers into politics enhanced the respectability of Catholicism and spread knowledge of Catholic teaching. Furthermore, the behavior of Catholic clergy, tending to their pastoral work, contrasted sharply with the political activities of many ministers. As the Protestant churches split over the slavery issue, often under the influence of radical ministers, more and more people were looking to the Catholic church as perhaps "the only conservative body in the union." If the union was to be preserved, America's diverse people blended into a single nationality, and its promise fulfilled, Americans would eventually have to turn to the church, and the church should be ready. Hecker ended with the enthusiastic rhetorical flourish that marked his books. The church had only to address the intelligence of Americans and they would respond. The glorious prospect for the church was to seek to win the allegiance of a civilized, free and intelligent people. Let every means be employed, Hecker pleaded—colleges, religious orders, missionaries, literature and the press—to win "this young nation of a virgin soil" to the Catholic Church.[24]

In contrast to the articles, with their emphasis on the unique possibility of conversions, Hecker's negotiations in Rome stressed the importance of continuing the missions among Catholics. In his report to Cardinal Barnabò, Hecker repeated his conviction that a providential moment had arrived for missionary work among non-Catholics, but he went on to emphasize that the basis for his trip, and the immediate problem, was to continue their work among English speaking Catholics.[25] This was also the theme of the memorial prepared by the fathers at home. They explained their missionary work and told how Redemptorist decisions to increase parish work had dealt a "mortal blow" to their plans to expand the missions. They feared they would be forced more and more to become parish priests rather than missionaries, as had already happened to many of the German and Belgian fathers, and that their mission band would be broken up. They then indicated that the provincial was not competent to inform the general correctly. He was hostile to them, although they had given no cause for complaint despite "gross and culpable mismanagement." They admitted they had intended to appeal to the Holy See if their petition to the general was denied, because the "evils" they "dreaded" were "pressing and imminent." The circular prohibiting trips to Rome was inapplicable in their case. They responded in detail to the charges levelled against Hecker in the decree of expulsion. On the basis of the impediments placed in the way of the missions, the unjustified hostility of their superior-general, his "violent and unjustifiable conduct" against Father Hecker, the fatal policy of substituting parochial for missionary labors, the maladministration of the American province, and the "introduction of a system of despotism and cruelty," they asked the Holy See to separate them from their superiors, and place them either under the pope, the Congregation of the Propaganda or such other administration as the pope should judge expedient. They did, however, wish to retain their Redemptorist vocation, vows and rule. As a last resort, if this should not be expedient, they asked for "relaxation of our vows of religion" and counsel regarding their future course. They ended by requesting that Hecker be accepted as their representative.[26] Clear, forceful and marked by the American candor in which men like Walworth took such pride, the documents were all that Hecker could ask for. Together with yet another report from Hecker, they began to work their way through the Vatican bureaucracy. The future of Isaac Hecker and his convert friends was in the hands of the pope and his counsellors.

9

All We Had at Heart

The central problem of American Catholicism was the relationship between the church's responsibilities as a Catholic community subject to the authority of the Holy See and its pastoral responsibilities as an American church growing in conditions of freedom and pluralism. After a near disastrous series of episcopal appointments in 1820, the American bishops united to insure that in the future Vatican authorities would be well-informed about American affairs and would not act without consultation with those closest to the scene. Throughout the nineteenth century, however, American church leaders were continually upset by Rome's misperceptions of American culture. Isaac Hecker and the other convert Redemptorists thought their local superiors grudgingly understood the need to adapt to some degree to American conditions, but centralized Roman control of the congregation prevented them from working out American problems within the American community.

When Hecker arrived in Rome, he quickly concluded that Father Mauron and the other members of the Council misunderstood, even disliked, Americans. He turned to Cardinal Barnabò for help because he was the Roman official in closest touch with the United States and the one most subject to the influence of American church leaders. But his case soon became embroiled in Vatican ecclesiastical politics, subject to the power of men who remained unfamiliar with the peculiar religious characteristics of his country. Hecker set out to educate them on these matters, hardly recognizing that his perspective was unique. His *Civiltà Cattolica* articles reflected an optimism which seemed almost quixotic in the context of the

Know-Nothing agitation of the 1850s. His enthusiasm for the conversion of the country had never been shared by more than a few other converts, and of these the most influential, Brownson, had already become skeptical. Yet, in some strange chemistry generated by Hecker's personality, his evangelical views passed almost unnoticed. Instead, his case was discussed in the more modest terms of the needs of the American bishops both for English-language missions and for Redemptorist services to German immigrants. On that basis the case was finally resolved, though not before Hecker himself had faced what at times seemed an unbridgeable gap between the ways of Rome and the ideals he associated with his country.

As the eventful year of 1857 drew to a close, Hecker understood clearly the options the fathers might pursue and the Vatican might permit. He knew Rome would not force them back into the Redemptorists, allow their affiliation with the Neapolitan group, or arrange their establishment as an autonomous group of missionaries under Redemptorist rule, for any of these steps would embarrass the general and multiply Redemptorist divisions. What was more likely, and Hecker thought "perhaps best of all," was that they start entirely anew and "on our own hook." This was the prospect he had held out from the start, and the one he consistently seemed to prefer, for reasons he made clear to a friend in Ohio: "My own conviction grows stronger that the old religious orders, with their superiors who have so little sympathy with the nature and spirit of things in the United States, will either be inefficient or a source of serious difficulties."[1]

If any doubt remained of where Hecker was heading, it was removed in a letter of December 9 urging the other fathers to get further episcopal support for their Memorial. "We need as broad and unconstrained a basis to act upon as we can get," he wrote, "for there is no reason why we should not adapt ourselves to accept what is good in our social and political customs and institutions, as other religious Orders have hitherto done in Italy and elsewhere in Europe." Redemptorist allies had "stirred the waters" and created an impression that theirs was an exclusively American movement and they would need the help of bishops to overcome that suspicion.[2] At home Hewit and Walworth worked hard to generate this support, and Hecker was deeply grateful for their loyalty and trust. At the end of a long letter explaining the complex negotiations in Rome, he burst forth: "How I should like to give each one of you one of my old hugs if only for a moment."

Nevertheless, some cracks began to appear in the group. Hecker's November letter arguing that a new, independent community, under episcopal authority was the most likely outcome upset Walworth, who wanted to live by the Redemptorist rule, even if outside the congregation. He immediately responded that Hecker had jumped from their simple, straightforward approach to speaking of "a new foundation," previously treated as a last resort. Walworth claimed that Baker and Deshon agreed with him; they should avoid all expedients, even those suggested by cardinals, for they were "thrown out to get rid of you," and stick with the desire to carry on the missions under the rule of St. Alphonsus. Bishop Bayley agreed, he claimed; they should stick to their mission work and show that they were prudent men, "not visionaries."

Arrival of copies of the *Civiltà Cattolica* articles upset Walworth even more; Hewit told Hecker the fathers unanimously agreed that he should not publish the second, as the matter contained in it was "too delicate." Walworth wrote again in early January; many of their friends disliked the articles, he claimed, and Bayley felt they would do more harm than good. Walworth bluntly warned Hecker he should avoid identifying his ideas with their cause, allowing the general to use those ideas as weapons against them. "Besides," he warned, "it must be remembered that the rest of us do not altogether sympathize with you in some of these things." The fathers were concerned, Walworth claimed, about Hecker speaking of his "mission" to Rome to open its eyes about America. "We had no idea of this," he argued, but simply wanted to save the missions. They were prepared to accept defeat but wanted the issue decided on "its real and original merits"; he should not give the general any opportunity to charge that they entertained views beyond their vocation as religious.[3]

In February, calmer, Walworth told Hecker that he, too, expected they would be released from their vows, but in that case they should still live as Redemptorists. The fathers at home were as anxious as Hecker to work for conversions, but there was nothing in the Rule to prevent it and only the "blindness and ignorance" of their superiors had impeded that work earlier. However, nothing would be gained by "dedicating a new congregation to the conversion of the country, for labors of such a kind are only impeded and thwarted by blowing horns." Hewit wrote a similar letter the next day, urging prudence so that they would retain the confidence of priests and bishops. Unlike Walworth, Hewit felt they could make changes in the Rule if it seemed appropriate, but "we all wish to continue the same life we are living on the missions, and *substantially* the same in the house, and, even without vows, to preserve the spirit and the virtues of a religious and apostolic life." All wanted to undertake any work for conversions that would open to them, but all wanted as well "to preserve a continuity of life and action" and "make the missions our nucleus and basis." "We need our little Congregation, and it needs each one of us," Hewit said. He gently reminded Hecker that the "little band" could not spare him. Equally important, it would be "a great misfortune" for Hecker personally if he separated himself from the rest: "I think you need the restraint of obedience, and still more of that moral and intellectual influence which a community of your compeers and associates will exert over you."[4]

Disturbed by Walworth's letters, Hecker hastened to reassure his colleagues that he always regarded continuation of the missions as central; he only asked that they be open to reaching non-Catholics as possibilities might arise to do so. He was prepared, he insisted, to sacrifice anything to keep them together; he was their servant, not their leader. Servant he might be, but at the very time he was assuring the fathers he would not lead them into any paths they had not chosen, he was writing George praising him for working closely with Hughes, keeping the offer of land open and raising the possibility of establishing a new religious community in New York.[5]

There was good reason for the fathers at home to be nervous. Hecker's report of his long-awaited audience with the pope made clear that he did have his eye upon conversions, not upon missions to Catholics. It revealed as well his wit and charm, little evident in his private diaries and correspondence. Upon entering the room, he kissed the pope's slipper, and when he rose, the pope said he was informed about his problem and asked what he wished. Hecker responded by asking the pope to examine the purpose of his coming to Rome, "since it regarded the conversion of the American people, a work which the most intelligent and pious Catholics have at heart." The pope indicated that Cardinal Bizzarri of the Congregation of Bishops and Regulars would make his report and he would render his decision, to which Hecker replied that he would regard that as "God's decision" and humbly submit to it. This seemed to satisfy the pope, who then launched into a discussion of America.

The pope said the American people were "engrossed in worldly things, and in the pursuit of wealth, and these are not favorable; it is not I who say so, but Our Lord, in the Gospel." Hecker replied that "the United States is in its youth, and like a young father of a family who is occupied in furnishing his house, and while this is going on, he must be busy. But the American people do not make money to hoard, nor are they miserly." The pope agreed they were generous, for they contributed to churches, concluding: "You see, I know the bright as well as the dark side of the Americans!" But, he said, there was too much freedom in America: "All the refugees and revolutionaries gather there and are in full liberty." True, Hecker agreed, but that, too, had a good side for "many of these, seeing in the United States that the church is self-subsistent, and not necessarily connected with what they call despotism, begin to regard it as a divine institution, and return to her fold." "Yes," the pope responded, "the Church is as much at home in a republic as in a monarchy or an autocracy." The pope was not finished: "Then again you have the Abolitionists and their opponents, who get each other by the hair." Hecker was quick: "There is also the Catholic Truth, Holy Father, which, if once known, would act on these parties like oil on troubled waters; and our best informed statesmen are becoming more and more convinced that Catholicity is necessary to sustain our institutions and enable our young country to realize her great destiny. And allow me to add, *très Saint Père*, that it would be an enterprise worthy of your glorious pontificate to set on foot the measures necessary for the beginning of its conversion." Hecker then rose to retire, and as he did so the pope imparted his blessing and "repeated in a low voice as I kneeled, 'Bravo! Bravo' "! Noting the event a few days later, Hecker wrote that the pope, "a man of the largest size head," was "moved more by his impulses than by his judgement—but his impulses are large, noble, all-embracing."[6]

As happened so often in Hecker's life, a time of crisis was also a time for retrospective assessment of his own spiritual history. During the winter of 1857–58, at the greatest crisis of his Catholic life, he was once again filled with thoughts about the providential significance not just of American Catholicism, so evident in the *Civiltà Cattolica* articles, but of his own life. In January he formalized the fruit of considerable discussion with Roman friends in an autobiographical reflection prepared for his new spiritual director, a Passionist, Barnabò, Bedini and two other priest friends. The document clearly indicated the intimate relationship, even identity, between Hecker's understanding of his own life and of the larger experience and prospects of Catholicism in the United States.

In this lengthy paper Hecker made some revisions in earlier autobiographical accounts. Now his involvement in Locofoco politics played a crucial role. Failure of political reform had led him to social reform and charitable business practices. He then concluded that personal moral reform through religious conversion was needed, and he had tested all religions on the basis of reason and conscience. Once a Catholic, he became more and more convinced that he was called to work for conversions, a conviction that produced his books and his present struggle to serve the needs of the church. He now believed that Americans required "an institution which shall have their conversion to the Catholic faith as its principle aim." He asked his readers whether his experience was not evidence of his "special vocation" for such work.[7]

No record of the response of his friends exists, but the document deserves comment. The fundamental argument that his attraction to the work of converting Americans had persisted since his entry into the Redemptorists was unquestionably true. Yet Hecker revised his life story in a way that obscured some important elements of his own religious experience. He did not mention the powerful spiritual experiences that had launched him on his religious quest. Instead, he exaggerated the role of his early political involvement and his commitment to social reform. In fact, there is no evidence of special concern with lifestyle or the needs of the bakery employees until his return from New England in the summer of 1843. Furthermore, the argument of *Questions of the Soul* that innate religious need, a hunger of the soul, motivated his own religious quest and provided evidence that even the unchurched and apparently irreligious were good prospects for conversion, was subordinated in this paper to an argument of utility: that religion is the road to social reform and Catholicism the surest expression of real religion. Finally, the paper contended that there was a widespread conviction of the need for new methods to reach non-Catholics and a belief that the times were ripe for American conversions. Even his English-speaking Redemptorist brothers had only mild convictions on these scores, and they had repeatedly expressed opposition to making conversions the central aim of their work.

This autobiography was undoubtedly shaped by his changing understanding of his own prospects, but it reflected as well the basic direction of his aspirations toward evangelization. Moreover, if his old allies at home were wavering under the impact of nativism and the parochialism of strong bishops, new supporters were being won in Rome, some, like Barnabò, men of immense influence; they were attracted, as always, less by his ideas than his personality. In addition, Hecker befriended a number of expatriate Americans. Several were on their way to conversion under his influence. Their admiration for the American priest enhanced his standing in the city.

In early January, whether by luck or Providence, another important ally appeared unexpectedly on the scene. Bishop Thomas Connolly of St. John, New Brunswick (in 1859 he would become Archbishop of Halifax) was already familiar with Hecker and the missionaries. On his way to Rome for an *ad limina* visit, he was assaulted and robbed in the papal states. This established him immediately as a person with the pope's favor. Before meeting the pope, he saw Hecker, learned of his problem and became his enthusiastic supporter. He went with Hecker to call on Barnabò; they discussed the widespread fear of eventual domination of the American church by native-born Catholics. When Barnabò indicated he shared these fears, Connolly told him that, while the Irish and German Catholics took care of their own, in twenty-five to fifty years there would be grass growing in front of their churches unless special efforts were made to attract the English-speaking, native-born Americans. This gave the cause a "boost," as did a similar conversation between Connolly and Bizzarri. Bizzarri had recently seen the pope, who said that authority must be maintained. Yes, Bizzarri had replied, but what if an injustice had been committed? Then, the pope replied, there must be an investigation. Hecker rejoiced in Connolly's presence, reporting to the fathers the bishop's statement: "I am ready to die for your cause." Connolly reported after his conversation with the pope that the latter had asked why they did not form themselves into a new company of missionaries. When informed they were ready to do so, the pope reportedly said that when the case came before him he would examine it and, if all was in order, give his consent.

Later Hecker must have gotten a fuller report, for he told the fathers that Connolly had "a regular tussle with His Holiness about us and our cause." When the pope repeated some of the accusations made against them, Connolly was said to have responded: "Your Holiness, I should not at all be surprised if some fine day you yourself would have to canonize one of these Yankee fellows!" The pope had then suggested relaxation of the vows and formation of a new company, but they would have to make the proposal; he could not take the initiative. On leaving Rome, Connolly left a long letter with Barnabò and asked Bernard Smith to let him know if any other document was needed.

If there was ever any doubt that Hecker would somehow be vindicated, Connolly's letter, coming on top of the other testimonials from American bishops, eliminated it. Connolly told Barnabò that because of "the holiness of his life and through the excellence of his preaching," Hecker was "perhaps the man who enjoys the highest and respected esteem of the bishops . . . revered also by Protestants, many of whom he has converted and continues to convert daily." It would simply never be believed in the United States that "a man who is regarded as the most distinguished among the entire American clergy suddenly became the worst and incorrigible." If action were taken against him, Connolly concluded, it would "result in a great chill toward Catholics" and be "a triumph for the bigots," causing "great harm to Catholicism throughout the country."[8]

After Connolly's departure Hecker reported that "the Propaganda is identified with our success." The general had called on Barnabò, claiming that he had told him of the action taken against Hecker on his September visit. Barnabò, certain he had not, characterized the general to Hecker as "a man without mind, without memory and without a conscience." To the general's claim that the priests at home were content, Barnabò said that documents before him indicated "there is a terrible earthquake under your feet." Still, Hecker explained, it was not yet time to propose the step suggested by the pope, as it would make them appear as renegade Redemptorists.[9]

The long delays began to wear on Hecker. "The procrastination here is beyond all measure," he reported, describing daily requests to have the Memorial sent to the general for his comments. He promised to "push, push, push." If the officials concerned about Americanism could have seen some of Hecker's comments, which grew increasingly nasty as his case was delayed, they would have been convinced their concern was justified. Despite the help he received from Barnabò, Bedini and others, he lamented the absence of one "honest official" who could clear up their case. He told the fathers: "You cannot imagine how volatile and impressive the Italians are; they have the character more like children and women than men." He found Italians impulsive, more responsive to instinct than reason, avoiding decision, seeking compromise, swayed less by arguments than "external impressions." They "never do today what may be done tomorrow" and "if there be a round about road [they] never take the direct one."[10]

Hecker was by this time fighting a two-front war. In addition to working daily to win a favorable decision in Rome, he had problems at home. Walworth wanted him to settle for a simple dispensation from the vows, which would allow them to continue to live and work as Redemptorists, perhaps under the protection of Propaganda. But by this time Hecker was wary of Roman ways and his long-standing conviction of the need for autonomy, in order to adapt to the needs of the country, was accentuated by his loss of respect for Vatican procedures and personnel. At the heart of it all was "ignorance, suspicion and prejudice" about the United States. People in Rome, though they would not admit it, held the same ideas about America as prevailed throughout Europe. "We are regarded as rebels, without any true conception of Christian principles or virtues, or sound political principles, who do not care for either God, man or the devil," Hecker wrote. "In a word, the U.S. has *no* status in Europe, either religiously, socially or politically. And it is imagined it never will until it becomes like the old rickety monarchies and aristocracies of Europe." If such views were only those of the general, things would not be so bad, but they affected even the pope. Hecker's supporters in Rome saw clearly only occasionally, and always hesitated whether to trust him. Hecker told the fathers: "I have to be constantly on my watch that our best friends do not in some unlucky moment, by some word or act, sell us out completely."[11]

Hecker seemed to become more militantly American the longer he remained in Rome. He told George and the fathers that most of their problems arose because, from the pope down, European officials distrusted Americans. For his part, he was more convinced than ever of the need for the church in the United States to put aside European ways and adapt to American conditions. As he told his colleagues:

> So far as it is compatible with faith and piety, I am for accepting the true American civilization, its usages and customs; leaving aside other reasons it is the only way in which Catholicity can become the religion of our people. The character and spirit of our

> people and their institutions must find themselves in religion, in the way those of other nations have, and it is on this basis that the Catholic Religion alone can make progress among us. I am in favor of no sudden changes, but am in favor of that liberty which will leave the way open to the application of these principles as the case may demand and the Providence of God direct. That many important changes will be required is a fact that I do not wish to conceal. Such at least is my opinion. So far from my devotion to religion being diminished by recent events, it has, thank God, greatly increased; but many other things have changed in me. On many points my intelligence has been awakened, experience has dispelled much ignorance; on the whole I hope that my faith and heart have been more purified. If God spares my life to return, I hope to come back more a man, a better Catholic, and more entirely devoted to the work of God.[12]

From his arrival in August until February, Hecker's spirits and health remained remarkably good, but the strain was beginning to tell. He was laid up for two weeks with pneumonia early in the month and, even after recovery, continued to complain of being "under the weather," weighed down "by the bungling way Italians managed things and their want of what we call character." To the fathers he wrote that never in his Catholic life had he felt such "oppression and anxiety of mind." Rome was "a crucible in which one's faith either becomes wholly supernatural, or disappears entirely."[13]

Yet, behind the scenes the way was clearing for a settlement. Father Mauron had his own case to make, but he did not close the door to a resolution which would satisfy Hecker. The decree of expulsion relied entirely on the circular, with its explicit denial of the right of subjects to go to Rome without permission. Subsequent documents submitted by Mauron to the Holy See continued to emphasize this point. As Mauron pointed out, the recent reforms in the congregation, carried out at the behest of the Holy See, had been aimed at centralizing authority and limiting the autonomy of local houses in order to insure fuller commitment to the religious life and to the Rule of the Redemptorists. As Mauron saw it, any other course of action in Hecker's case would have undermined his authority; any reversal of his action would do the same.[14]

In a private letter to Bizzarri, Mauron provided personal reasons for his action, reasons he did not wish to include in the formal documentation. Here he contradicted his testimony in the public letters to Hecker's good conduct and zeal as a missionary. He charged that Hecker was "a bad religious and a dangerous subject." He incorrectly reported that Hecker's conversion had been due to Father Rumpler, recounted his difficulties with studies during his seminary days, attributing them to enthusiasm and "false mysticism," and criticized his superiors for not dismissing him or at least handling him with greater rigor. At the time of his own election in 1855, he had been informed of the "dangerous inclinations" of these fathers, but had tried to encourage them, especially by appointing Father Hewit a provincial consultor. Nevertheless, Hewit, Hecker and Walworth had formed a clique, attracted Deshon to it and used Father Hewit's privileges as a consultor to forward their scheme, which he called "a war against their superiors." They were associated, he believed, with "a new party" in the American church, led by converts like Brownson, who believed the church should be more American and that only Americans could convert other Americans, and who upheld a notion of religious obedience which emphasized the rights of subjects rather than their duties toward superiors. He feared that the new house was intended to forward such an American movement, and thus he could have little confidence in it.

Yet Mauron was not unaware of the difficulties confronting the Holy See, and he offered an alternative which could uphold authority while providing the fathers with a means of meeting the supposed expectations of the bishops. In his letter to the holy father on February 11, and his simultaneous letter to Bizzarri, he proposed that the pope allow the expulsion to stand, give Hecker the title of missionary apostolic, allow him to return and establish the proposed house under the authority of Archbishop Hughes. The other three fathers might be granted a dispensation from their vows, either by the Holy See or through the usual procedures of the congregation. The bishops would have a missionary house and four subjects in whose training they had no expense, the fathers would have the basis to continue the work they had at heart, and the discipline of the community would be preserved.[15]

The prospect of the departure of the whole group was more easily considered in Rome than back in the United States. Writing on March 2, Ruland reported rumors that "several American Fathers" had asked the Holy See to be dispensed from their vows. He emotionally urged the general to do all in his power to prevent this, for, given the confidence which the English-speaking missionaries commanded among the bishops, the younger members of the community and the other fathers, it would be a "blow from which [the congregation] could not recover" and "would rock her very foundations."[16]

In February the pope was presented with all the documents in the case, Barnabò intervened several times with Bizzarri to push for a report, then spoke at length with the pope, reporting to Hecker that he had defended him against many charges. At mid-month the pope was still awaiting Bizzarri's report; the latter claimed to be ill. Hecker was forced to go regularly to his office to request action and often was met unpleasantly. At the end of a letter to George, dated March 2, Isaac told his brother that Bizzarri kept saying that, if Hecker would join the others in asking for a dispensation, it would be granted. Hecker feared, in that case, that the general would argue they had wanted separation all along and had always been against authority. On the other hand, the general was threatening to abdicate if forced to accept Hecker back into the congregation. Hecker did not mail the letter, for he appended a postscript dated March 6 indicating that the pope had rendered his decision, but it was still secret.[17] In the intervening four days Hecker had in fact sent a message to Andre Balzani, Bizzarri's secretary, authorizing him to inform the archbishop that "if his Holiness deigns to cancel my illegal expulsion and if he gives dispensation to the other American fathers, I will be satisfied, seeing the circumstances that have supervened in my affairs, to accept my dispensation as well as they."

While awaiting the final decision, Hecker wrote the fathers that the general, while praising him in public documents, had attempted to blacken his reputation in private conversations and correspondence. Such machinations "have opened my eyes a *little*," he wrote; "once freed from the present meshes, I shall be jealous in the future how I place myself in the power of another." On March 4 Barnabò met with the pope, who told him that the general had "a hard head," while the Americans did not understand religious obedience. Nevertheless, the expulsion would have to be set aside and the fathers granted dispensations. Two days later the decree of dispensation was sent to Barnabò and the general by Archbishop Bizzarri. The decree simply dispensed all the fathers from their vows. No mention was made of the earlier expulsion. They were now secular priests, to work "under the direction and jurisdiction of the local bishops" for the salvation of souls. Hecker interpreted the fact that he was named with the others as *de facto* setting aside the expulsion, while the Redemptorist leadership took note of the fact that no explicit rejection of the expulsion was made. Both sides could claim victory.[18]

Hecker, for his part, was delighted, writing George that associating him with the fathers "supposes that my expulsion was worthless, illegal." To the fathers he wrote that the pope had granted them "a *clean* and *complete* dispensation," leaving them "entire liberty to act in the future as God and our intelligence shall point the way." He explained that Barnabò had warned against asking for a dispensation before the decree was reversed. "He told me to tell Bizzarri that if the decree annulled and others dispensed I would join them. The pope then associated me with the dispensation, wording the decree to cast favor on the Fathers."

Mauron, in contrast, notified Ruland that the fathers had been "dismissed" from the congregation. He was surprised that the matter had ended so satisfactorily, "for it is unbelievable how many powerful protectors Hecker and his friends found here and in America." He was pleased he had expelled Hecker when he did, for now he believed that otherwise he and his friends would have "followed their separatist purposes" and led the congregation to ruin. He urged Ruland to give Kenrick and Hughes an account of events, including how the Redemptorists had been slandered. As for the four fathers in America, the provincial should "try to get rid of them in a friendly fashion," making sure they left without delay and with no further communication with other members of the community.[19]

On leaving the climactic meeting with Barnabò, Hecker met the general waiting in the ante room. Hecker told the fathers, with uncharacteristic cruelty, that he seemed "a moral and physical wreck." Hecker thought the general was especially bitter because, in granting Hecker dispensation, the pope "put no value on his expulsion." Barnabò and "several friends" were not satisfied, Hecker reported, because the general was not made to withdraw the expulsion, but Hecker felt this "would only be a personal gratification" and, with the way now open, he was "far from desiring this; I feel for the General." Later Hecker called on Mauron and reported the visit to his colleagues. The general admitted he had been forced to back down, Hecker wrote, but he warned Hecker not to broadcast the results through the newspapers. They parted amicably, with Hecker offering to carry out some errands for the general in New York and presenting him with some engravings for his house in Rome.[20]

According to Hecker, Barnabò had made it clear that the group should stay together, choose a bishop, any that they pleased, inform him of their intentions and, if he approved, make arrangements with him to continue their work. Barnabò and Bedini both suggested location in New York. When Hecker asked what they should do if Hughes set difficult conditions or attempted to divert them from their work, they responded that they should "tell him frankly before hand that you will not be his blind instruments." Barnabò warned them not to take on too many responsibilities and suggested they use his name if difficulties arose. The pope, too, when Hecker met with him on March 16, asked if they intended to stay together as a community, a question which Hecker took "to show clearly that such is the expectation of Rome." The pope also took the "rare" step of imparting a plenary indulgence to the fathers and about forty lay friends. Finally, the pope indicated that, by associating Hecker with the dispensation, "he considered me a member of the Congregation," a statement Hecker took to involve the "illegality of the expulsion." In December Hecker had written that everyone predicted his "ultimate success," but he was unsure they knew what that meant. "In my mind the question is one of the conversion of the people of the United States," he wrote, and "to be successful in the sense I understand things is to obtain from the pope his sanction and blessing for the American fathers to form themselves in a company with this object in mind." His conversations with the cardinals persuaded him this had been obtained, but the decree was less clear, merely returning them to the authority of their bishops.[21]

Nevertheless, Hecker appeared triumphant. He told George to inform Hughes that they had "gotten all we had at heart," explaining to his brother that they had won the "liberty to devote ourselves, *and that without any restriction* to the great wants of religion in our country." "Our success is complete," he crowed, "and I leave Rome to return to the United States without having any desire or wish unfulfilled or unanswered." Boarding ship in Le Havre, he wrote the fathers, mailing the letter before leaving Southampton on March 28 for home:

> The seven months past here in Rome seem to me an age, and taxed me to that extent, that I look forward to home as a place of rest and repose. When I think of the kicks and cuffs received, the fears, anxieties and labors undergone, I say to myself: "Boys, that's fun enough for this time." On the other hand, when I remember the warm and disinterested friends God has given us through these difficulties and the happy issue to which his providence has conducted them, my heart is full of gratitude and joy. To me the future looks bright, hopeful, full of promise, and I feel confident in God's Providence, and assured of His grace in our regard, to realize this. I feel like raising up the Cross as our Standard, and adopting one word as our Motto: "Conquer."[22]

Ruland had taken steps at the very beginning of the crisis to intercept mail from the American fathers. With receipt of the decree, Ruland feared that other priests would join the new band. Under pressure from Mauron he attempted to reinforce community solidarity. In a circular letter to superiors of all American houses, he charged that the problem had arisen from the disobedience of the dissidents, who had conspired to force the general to adopt their policies. They won dispensation only by maligning the congregation with charges that their fellow Redemptorists had nothing to do with Americans and did not understand or preach in English. They had really wanted an exclusively American house, which would have created a schism in the Province. Hecker and his associates had stated that, even among the German fathers, there were many who wished separation. To maintain their honor against such "vile imputations," he demanded a letter to the general, written in Latin and signed by each father, expressing "unconditional and unbreakable devotion" to their superiors. Writing Mauron three weeks later, Ruland admitted that he had presented the matter of the separation "in its most terrible aspects," but he was pleased that no other fathers or students were leaving. Hewit had approached Father Duffy by mail, but the Irish-born priest "tore the letter into shreds, unopened." He still worried about the bishops' reaction, and reported indications of episcopal support and friendship for the departed fathers. If they did stay together and continued their missions, they would become formidable "rivals" for the Redemptorists, as "ambition together with will power is common to the American more than to any human being on earth."[23]

Father Baker's inclusion in the dispensation greatly disappointed Ruland. He had worried that Baker might be collaborating with the American fathers, but hoped he would not go so far as to identify with their rash actions. A remarkably sweet-tempered man, Baker was popular throughout the community and was thought to be especially close to Archbishop Kenrick of Baltimore. When the decree arrived, Baker was summoned to Ruland's presence. There he explained his concern about the missions, his loyalty to his fellow missionaries and his judgment that Hecker had been treated unfairly. Reporting the meeting to Mauron, Ruland indicated that Baker's departure would be particularly damaging because of his reputation within the community and in the Baltimore area. Shortly after his departure, Ruland wrote Baker a personal letter in which he stated that, while he had long regarded the movement of the Americans as dangerous, he felt no personal animosity toward the fathers and had petitioned for Hecker's readmission. If they had been candid with him about their intentions, he might have been able to avert the unhappy outcome. Most important, he now feared that God would not bless their work, begun as it was in disobedience. Writing his farewell to Walworth, Hewit and Deshon, he stated more bitterly that at each step they had been led by "the evil one."

Ruland would have been less worried if he had been able to read the letters Walworth was quickly sending out to friends in the hierarchy. Far from reviling the general or rehashing the problems that had led to the dispensations, he simply told each one that he and the others had been released from their vows in order to go on with their work as before. He reported their enrollment temporarily as priests of the Newark diocese, their continuation with two scheduled missions, and their intention to gather to make plans on Hecker's return. In addition, Hewit wrote the provincial expressing on behalf of the entire group their respect and love for the congregation and their hope for a fraternal relationship in the future.[24]

Perhaps the best commentary on the whole affair came in a remarkably candid private letter sent to Mauron in early June by Father J. Geisen, a

Redemptorist stationed in Buffalo. While he had never accepted the plans of the five departed priests and believed they had been led into error by excessive zeal, Geisen had studied with several of them, regarded all as fine priests, and loved them. He noted that, as Americans, they had made great sacrifices to enter the congregation. They were forced to live with German fathers, eat German food and follow German customs. Sometimes, on return from missions, they were forced to do too much work; other times they were given no work at all. They were even ridiculed at times for making a stir about such things. In such conditions it was hardly surprising they would request an English house. Geisen felt that, given a house with prudent superiors, and a few exceptions to the Rule as were frequently granted in other countries, they would have been satisfied. Such concessions were minor, especially when considering how important these men were to the future well-being of the congregation.[25]

This was a balanced assessment, but there was more going on than Geisen suspected. As Redemptorist historian Michael J. Curley has pointed out, Hecker's own interpretation of events was less than fair. Mauron and the Redemptorists, having experienced the separation of the Neapolitans and faced with opposition from the Belgians, had good reason to worry about further divisions in their community. The order forbidding appeals to Rome was clear and the fathers well knew the risks they were taking. While Hecker was denied a chance to make his case to the Council, he did have several long talks with Mauron, during which he emphasized the non-Catholic apostolate. Pressed by demands to staff parishes and other missions to Catholics, Redemptorist leaders were within their rights to discourage new undertakings aimed at conversions. In addition, Mauron was aware that Hecker had already considered a new congregation before coming to Rome. Through Father Douglass, he was familiar with Brownson's letter, the last line of which spoke of a new congregation should the Redemptorists prove unable to respond to the need for missions to non-Catholics. Finally, the decree simply returned the fathers to the status of diocesan priests, under their respective bishops; forming a new congregation to carry on the missions was given oral approval by Barnabò, and perhaps by the pope, but, formally, none of Hecker's objectives had been secured.[26]

In addition, there are several issues that remain unclear. One is the mystery of Hecker's success. Clearly his personal warmth, sincerity and piety were impressive and, in Rome as everywhere he went in life, he made friends quickly and easily. At Brook Farm, the lonely, brooding young man of his diary appeared to others as a rather dreamy and pleasant fellow who got along well even in that rather anarchic community of independent personalities. In Rome Hecker once again showed a keen wit, was alert to the concerns of others, read situations of human interaction with considerable skill, and conducted himself throughout with evident grace, charm and dignity. Nowhere was this more evident than when he visited the pope for the first time. He learned quickly the political requirements and adapted to them. "Everyone has an axe to grind, and has trimmed his course in view of this," he told George. "Priests are looking to be bishops, bishops to become archbishops, archbishops to be Cardinals, and Cardinals to become Pope." In contrast, he said innocently, "I want nothing, so I can afford to speak openly and to the point." Of course he did want something, and he was ambitious, and he learned to use the ambitions of others, especially Barnabò and the bishops, to forward his goal.[27]

In February Hecker saw the dilemma in which the pope was placed. "Which ever way the Pope turns, he is in a fix," he wrote the fathers. On the one hand, he could not force a reversal on the general without risking the overthrow of Redemptorist leadership. The general was reported to have threatened to withdraw all his subjects from the United States if the fathers were allowed to separate as Redemptorists. On the other hand, the pope could not decide in Mauron's favor without disregarding the argument of many prominent bishops that the interests of religion in the United States would be damaged, and without giving a blow to Barnabò and the Propaganda. Bizzarri was reported to have told Pius IX that the issue had now become "immense" and "a matter of the American episcopate."[28]

Then, as later, the Vatican was not noted as a bureaucracy sympathetic to the plight of holy and sincere enthusiasts. Something more was at work. At first glance, a lone American priest of no great reputation outside his native land would seem ill matched against the leaders of one of the church's most successful religious orders. But Hecker had come well-prepared, especially with endorsements from prominent bishops and lay leaders, some, like Louis Binsse, Vatican Consul-General in New York, and Levi Silliman Ives, a converted Episcopal bishop, well-known in Rome. When Hecker appeared in Barnabò's office in September, he posed a problem, and all the delays, reports and discussion could not make the problem go away. So a compromise had to be worked out, one which would allow the mission work, which the bishops valued so highly, to continue, would avoid besmirching the reputation of this priest, whom everyone liked so much, but which would also insure sufficient control to avoid problems in the future. What better solution than to throw responsibility back to the bishops by releasing Hecker and his friends from their Redemptorist vows? If they organized as a mission band, they would be subject to the jurisdiction of an American bishop, probably Hughes, known for his tight control over religious orders, and any future changes would require Roman approval as well. Hecker's skillful work in organizing support and sharpening the dilemmas of his new-found friends should not obscure the fact that the result was hardly revolutionary.

A second major point is that the American fathers were far less united than they seemed. Hecker quite clearly dreamed of converting the nation, or at least that certain "class" on whom he had long cast his eye. He was convinced it was possible, that he had a call to do it, and that his life moved under providential guidance in that direction. His colleagues, on the other hand, were primarily concerned with continuing the mission work; they merely found Redemptorist conditions intolerable. They were less interested in conversions than in more energetic mission work, and more active, efficient operation of the American church at large. Even among Americans, they were more concerned about the small, emerging Catholic middle class than with the New England intelligentsia or the masses of Protestant or unchurched Americans beyond the church.

Hecker, of course, believed in the value of the missions; he shared in the work and wished to see an English house organized so that more men would be attracted to it. Further, he knew that a more vibrant, educated and respectable English-speaking Catholic population would enhance the work of evangelization. But he also had clearly indicated that his own direction was toward the conversion of non-Catholics. It was to them that his books were addressed, to them that he hoped a greater portion of his energies could be directed, and it was from them that he drew the inspiration to "make American ideas known at Rome." The petition he submitted to the curia was firmly anchored in the mission work and received the unanimous endorsement of his colleagues. But the *Civiltà Cattolica* articles were another matter altogether, causing Walworth to write a stinging rebuke. The others were in fact faithful, devoted Redemptorists, anxious if at all possible to continue their work within the congregation. As Father Geisen saw, reasonable changes would have satisfied them. With Hecker, restless and ambitious for his church, convinced of the need for a "new generation" of leadership, the case is less clear. As he wrote George in January 1858, he had realized shortly after his return to the United States in 1851 that the introduction into the United States of religious orders "founded for different places and times" would result in a contradiction between adaptation, which would be seen as rebellion, and submission, which would perpetuate inefficiency. As a result, he had always "been in hot water" and "one or two fathers thought I lacked the spirit of the Congregation."[29] By 1858 it was clear to Hecker that "the course of our affairs" had been "providential," but, providential or not, Hecker had done his share to bring about the separation the others did not want.

Finally, critics of the American fathers were right in charging that they were a national group seeking an American policy. Converts, all well-educated and still bound by personal and family bonds to people outside the Catholic subculture, they were necessarily anxious to improve the church's image and achieve for it a degree of respectability, if not through conversions then at least through more intelligent leadership and effective policy. They were not nativists, surely, but they were loyal Americans, excited about the nation, devoted to its unity and progress, anxious to win respect both from non-Catholics and the small but growing Catholic middle class. Inside their religious community, this meant gradually displacing German language, priorities and leadership; outside it meant supporting the development of a better organized, more vigorous church. They did not need to share Hecker's confidence about converting the nation to believe that their church could only benefit by putting on a more American face. In this they may have been a bit ahead of their time, but they were hardly radical.

The support of Hughes, cautious as it was, showed that they merely represented one dimension, an important but not exclusive one, of the American church at mid-century. For Hughes, and for all the more sophisticated American bishops, the problem was not to choose between the immigrants and the Americans, for both provided important resources for the church. Nor was it a problem of choosing between pastoral work and evangelization, for a successful church would have to do both. A group of respectable, intelligent and progressive priests could be extremely valuable, for they would serve not only the missions, but the needs of the important group of Americanized Catholics and converts who were providing money and respectability for the church in New York and beyond. The trick was to have them do all this while at the same time taking care of the even more pressing needs of the immigrants and finding the means to support the burgeoning array of separate Catholic educational and charitable agencies. Similarly, it was necessary both to defend Catholic rights and interests against attack, requiring the unity and morale of the Catholic bloc, and to win greater respect and security by serving the public interest and the common good. Hecker and his friends were ideal, for they were American, they spoke the language and built the morale of the American portion of the population; they were popular among respectable Catholics and respectable among powerful non-Catholics, and, best of all, they were loyal. They accepted episcopal authority. Allowed to carry on their missions, to develop other projects and work for conversions, while clearly subject to the jurisdiction of the bishops, this was the ideal solution. In many ways New York's Archbishop John Hughes was the real winner of the crisis of 1857–58.

What all this also indicates is that many of the problems which later beset Hecker and his Paulist community were present at the creation. The tension between convert work and missions to Catholics, between evangelism and parochial duties, between respectability in the American world and influence in the smaller Catholic world, between nationalism and ultramontanism, were all part of the dynamics of Paulist formation. Hecker compromised throughout, as when he responded to criticism of his *Civiltà Cattolica* articles by insisting he was prepared to give up everything for the sake of the group's unity, yet he never surrendered his vision or lost his enthusiasm. He returned delighted with the outcome, excited by the prospects, prepared in New York as in Rome to bring them as close to fulfillment as he could in the human, historical circumstances in which Providence placed him. It had taken a unique combination of faith, courage and skill to get him this far. If there was a cloud, it arose from the fact that he was still, in the things dearest to him, traveling alone.

10

The Paulists

As soon as the news of the dispensation reached America, Fathers Walworth, Hewit and Deshon left the Redemptorist house in New York. Hecker had already asked his brother George to place some money at their disposal and "guide their steps." George Hecker's family was in the country at the time, so he invited the priests to take up temporary residence at his home on Rutgers Street. Baker, given the news at the provincial's home in Baltimore, hastened to New York to join his colleagues. Together, the four decided to live according to the Redemptorist Rule, with Walworth as interim superior. After arranging with Bayley to serve temporarily as secular priests of the diocese of Newark, they continued preparation for two missions scheduled before Hecker's return. Permission to impart the papal blessing, a standard part of the closing ceremony, arrived just in time for the first mission at Watertown, New York. Hecker wrote regularly, urging them to find a house in the country, free from urban distractions. He insisted that they stay together, do nothing in haste, and particularly that they accept no commitment to serve a parish, which would be "the grave of our little band and the death of our hopes." He urged these views on George in even stronger terms, but told him to be cautious "lest they may think *you* would influence them to have things in *your* direction."[1]

Hecker had no doubts about their status; they were free to form a new community under the authority of a bishop of their own choosing. When Walworth notified their supporters of the Roman decision, he told them that separation from the Redemptorists had taken place "charitably and kindly," and the pope had given them "encouragement to go on and form a new society."

Hecker, far more than Walworth, desired some changes in community life. As early as December 1857, he told his colleagues he was in favor of seeking "as broad and as unconstrained a basis to act upon as we can get," so they could adapt themselves to what was good in American "social and political customs and institutions." While proposing no specific changes in the Redemptorist Rule, he insisted that, as long as there was opposition between the "character" of their religious order and the political order in which they had been born and bred, there would be endless occasions for misunderstanding as there had been with the Redemptorists. Because American institutions rested on a basis "totally different" from those in Europe, old orders might try to adapt to New World conditions, but Hecker doubted it was possible. As for themselves, they should "live our natural life if we would do something for our countrymen." Hecker repeated these views in January, but when Walworth responded critically, he pulled back a bit, stating that he would defer to the group. Nevertheless, in late January he told George he would not confine himself "to the limited and special character of the Redemptorists." He recognized that Walworth wished to remain to all intents and purposes a Redemptorist and the others, except Hewit, were in sympathy with him. If his vocation differed from theirs, he would have to follow it. But after the decree and Barnabò's advice, it was inconceivable that Hecker would strike out on his own.[2]

On May 10, he arrived in New York to find the fathers still living on Rutgers Street while finishing a mission at St. Bridget's church. He was in high spirits, though friends thought he had aged a bit and noted the first appearance of gray hairs. He found his companions "full of courage on account of the decree and full of joy at my return." The day after his arrival, Hecker called on Archbishop Hughes, who invited him to stay for dinner and requested that the group make their headquarters in New York. Hecker had already decided on New York, but he told the bishop that this decision and others would be made when the fathers completed the mission. When it was over, they moved into temporary quarters on 13th Street, in the rented top floor of a "respectable boarding house," which Hecker later referred to as "the upper room."

The five men who gathered in May 1858 were in the prime of life, mature, talented and energetic. They were all converts, but familiar now with the Catholic community. Each brought distinctive gifts, and each was a strong, independent personality. Their commitment to the church, the priesthood and missionary work had been forged from that same situation of freedom and self-consciousness which shaped Hecker's vocation. There could be little doubt of the sincerity and finality of their Catholicism, but because it developed through difficult, personally painful choices, it had a unique quality of deliberation, a lack of taken-for-grantedness that set them apart from many other Catholics.

Walworth was the most assertive member of the group, very much in charge during Hecker's absence. He had taken the lead in organizing the movement toward an English house. While he did not oppose reasonable efforts to win conversions, he did not share Hecker's enthusiasm and worried that his ideas might weaken support among the bishops and clergy. Walworth seemed completely dedicated to the missions and to the disciplined life of the Religious, but he was also a strong, independent man who had chafed under the regimen of the German-dominated houses. He was very impatient with the secrecy and evasiveness which marked congregational government. Ambitious for the church, he felt a great need to have the mission band organized in such a way as to allow for rest, study and planning for aggressive expansion, all of which had been hampered by Redemptorist policy.

Like Baker and Hewit, Walworth was a product of the American Oxford movement. Indeed, he was at the heart of that movement. Born in 1820 of a distinguished Saratoga family, Walworth was the son of Reuben Walworth, the last Chancellor of the State of New York. In 1841 he converted to the Episcopal Church and entered General Theological Seminary in New York City at a time when it was stirred by the controversies arising from a high church movement in the United States, identified with Bishop Henry Hobart, and from the Tractarian movement in England. Together with two companions, Edgar Wadhams and Henry McVicker, he attempted to launch a monastic community in the Adirondacks. When the sympathetic Bishop William Onderdonk was suspended by the Episcopal convention, Walworth began taking instruction from Father Rumpler at the Redemptorist church in New York City. He was baptized in 1845 and joined Hecker and James McMaster, another defector from General Theological Seminary, in the Redemptorist novitiate.[3] A well-educated man of eclectic interest, Walworth later wrote important articles on science and social thought. He also became a leading temperance reformer. While hardly "the American Newman," as his college alumni paper called him years later, he was a man of fierce pride and sharp intelligence, never to be taken lightly.

Augustine F. Hewit was the least content with his Redemptorist vocation. Several times he had considered leaving the congregation to work as a secular priest and perhaps find a career in seminary education. An authentic Yankee of distinguished lineage, he was born in Fairfield, Connecticut in 1820. His father, Nathaniel, was a Congregationalist minister who served in Bridgeport for fifty years, winning renown as an orator and temperance reformer. Hewit's mother, Rebecca Hillhouse, was the daughter of James Hillhouse, who served Connecticut in the United States House and Senate. Young Nathaniel (he changed his name when he became a Catholic) had an excellent education at Philips Academy in Andover and at Amherst College. Bred in the "strictest Calvinistic doctrine," he later claimed he early felt a "spontaneous repugnance" to that "dreary system of religion."

Hewit studied for the ministry but could not overcome his intellectual and emotional problems with Congregationalism. Reading the Oxford writers, he came to see the Anglican Church as one of the three branches of the one Catholic Church, so he entered the Episcopal Church and began studying for its ministry at the home of Bishop William Wittingham in Baltimore. Ordained a deacon, he considered going to Constantinople as part of a mission to work for reunion with the Orthodox, until that project was scuttled by the convention. At Bishop Wittingham's home he met another candidate for the priesthood, Francis Baker; the two young men visited Catholic churches in the city and shared their concern for a revival of Catholic elements in their own communion. Hewit felt drawn to Catholicism's doctrines of the real presence and papal primacy. Confused and ill with tuberculosis, he went south to the home of a friend in North Carolina. There he prayed, studied and, on February 19, 1846, decided to become a Catholic although, as he recalled years later, he had "no acquaintance with Catholics or with Catholicity in the concrete."

To enter the church, Hewit went to Charleston, where Bishop Ignatius Reynolds placed him with a brilliant young priest, Patrick N. Lynch, for instruction. He was received into the church at Easter 1846 and ordained for the diocese in March 1847. For two years he lived in the household of Bishop Francis Kenrick in Philadelphia, editing and revising the works of Charleston's famous Bishop John England and assisting Kenrick, a noted scholar, with scriptural translations. During that period he was attracted to the active Redemptorist community in the city and, desiring a stricter, more religious life, he applied for admission and was received into the congregation in October 1848. After completing a novitiate under Father Rumpler, he joined the returning Hecker and Walworth on the English mission band.[4]

By the time of the crisis of 1857, Hewit felt alienated from the Redemptorists. A quiet, reserved man, he found himself unsuited to the missionary life; he remained only from "sentiments of duty and from obedience to external circumstances." He would have preferred to work in the formation and education of clergy, or in a pastoral role outside religious community.[5] He was a more conventional Catholic then Hecker, but, with his strong family bonds, he was more respectful of non-Catholic Christians and fully committed to the convert apostolate. When the time came, Hewit joined the others and brought some indispensable qualities to the new enterprise.

Hewit was an organizational man with a gift, though no love, for administration. He again and again would do the basic work needed to translate Isaac Hecker's ideals into action. He wrote the documents constantly needed to win Roman approval for the developing congregation; he supervised the life of the house, mediating disputes, soothing hurt feelings, keeping people together. While Hecker did the public relations work and won the trust of the Catholic public, Hewit attended to community affairs. When years later, Hecker launched the *Catholic World*, many of the editorial and publication details were left to Hewit. When recruits arrived, Hewit took charge of organizing a novitiate and seminary, supervising studies, evaluating candidates, arranging for their assignments. Most important, he was Hecker's confessor and spiritual director.

Hewit, a tall man, was kind but possessed of a dignity which kept people at a distance. He seems to have retained something of the fear of pride of his Puritan background, for he was known as a scholarly, not a passionate, preacher. Few knew him well. Yet the bond between Hewit and Hecker was powerful and permanent. It fell to him to listen to Hecker's religious experiences, to his ideas of the apostolate, to his developing consciousness of the presence of the Holy Spirit in his life. A man of tough New England common sense, he almost alone could call Hecker to account, confirming his basic spiritual experience but warning against excesses of enthusiasm, occasionally and crucially drawing him back to a sense of responsibility for the work of the community. Throughout, this highly intelligent, balanced, mature, seemingly most integrated man remained profoundly devoted to Hecker, completely convinced that Hecker had a call from God, and that he was in the end to be revered and followed.

Francis Baker was another convert from the Episcopal church. Born in Baltimore in 1820, his father was a prominent doctor and his mother the daughter of a Philadelphia Methodist minister. While a student at Princeton University, he entered the Episcopal Church and returned to Bishop Wittingham's house in Baltimore to study for the ministry. Ordained in 1846, he served as rector of St. Paul's Church in Baltimore for five years, pained by the split with Hewit caused by the latter's move to Catholicism. As a minister he was known for his care with liturgy and ceremonies. By 1849 the continuing controversies in his church produced doubts. Finally, in April 1853, he resigned from St. Paul's. It was a mark of his attractive character that his congregation gave him a warm farewell. He then went to the Redemptorist house in the city, where he was received by his old friend Hewit. He entered the Redemptorists, experienced his novitiate under Rumpler, and was ordained in 1856. As a junior member of the mission band, he was not part of the planning that went on prior to the crisis of 1857, but he thought the expulsion of Hecker demonstrated "a complete misapprehension of our motives and character . . . blindness to our necessities in this country." He quickly volunteered to share the fate of the other fathers.

Baker enjoyed a reputation as a splendid preacher; this was the major point emphasized whenever his name appeared in the press. His association with the new endeavor was highly valued; his departure caused enormous regret to the Redemptorists. A faithful and loyal member of the community, he was perhaps the greatest source of encouragement to Hecker personally, but he avoided disputes, rarely put in writing his view of the new community, and played a less visible role than the others in shaping its early history.[6]

George Deshon, the last of the original band, was from an old American family of French Huguenot stock, seven generations in America. Born in New London, Connecticut, in 1823, he was raised a Congregationalist. In 1839 Deshon entered West Point, where he was a classmate of William Rosecrans and Ulysses S. Grant. After several years of military service he entered the Catholic Church, aided by his friend Rosecrans. He also become acquainted with James McMaster, upon whose recommendation he entered the Redemptorist novitiate. Like the others, Deshon was devoted to the missions, where he often shared the daily instructions with Hecker, but he had little of the latter's enthusiasm for conversions. Later Deshon played an important role in negotiations between the American bishops and the federal government over Catholic Indian missions. The episode indicated something of Deshon's ability and his standing with the bishops. In community affairs he would prove equally able, but rather strict and unbending. Eventually he would succeed Hewit as superior and guide the community through the dangerous controversies that emerged after the death of their founder.[7]

This was the tiny, talented group which gathered in late May 1858 to lay the foundations for their future work. They were men of considerable ability, each had already attained a considerable reputation, and all shared a commitment to one another and to the visionary, mystical man who was unquestionably their leader. For his part, Hecker had great confidence in them; indeed they accounted in part for his belief that the work that lay before them could be of enormous, providential significance.

Little is known of the discussions that took place in "the upper room." However, three documents emerged, each of which suggests something of the debates that must have gone on. The first was the preliminary Rule and Constitution for the Congregation of the Missionary Priests of St. Paul the Apostle.[8] In this covenant they formed a congregation "under episcopal approbation" and agreed to pursue their own sanctification "by leading a life in all essential respects similar to that which is observed in a religious congregation." They would live "a life perfectly in common," in small rooms "furnished in accordance with the spirit of poverty," and adopt a manner of dress "plain and simple but neat and suitable for respectable priests." Each member was to make an eight-day retreat each year and a day of recollection at the beginning of each month. They were to perform two daily meditations of a half hour each, one in the morning at five, one in the evening, and an examination of conscience, with the litany of the Blessed Virgin before dinner and a general examination followed by night prayers at nine in the evening. Each member would in private do a half hour spiritual reading, visit the Blessed Sacrament, and say the rosary. Each week the community would hold a "chapter of faults" for mutual correction, and a theological conference. While no particular method of penance was prescribed, it was "permitted to everyone to take the discipline in private on Wednesday and Friday evenings, unless for particular reasons he is especially prohibited by the superior. Public penances and acts of humility will also be practiced in the refectory." Silence was to be observed during the afternoon and from the time of night prayer until morning meditation. Members were exhorted to practice a "continual recollection," a regular observance of spiritual exercises, and a "fervent and laborious zeal" in the duties of their ministry.

Until a permanent organization was arranged, with the approval of the pope, the congregation would be governed by a superior chosen for a three-year term, while the original members would constitute a provisional chapter to continue until the Rule was approved or until some other regulation was made. Any new house founded before the Rule was approved was to remain subject to the superior of the original foundation, with its superior appointed by him with the approval of a majority of the chapter. If the chapter decided, it could assign two consultors to assist the superior. On June 13 Hecker was elected superior. The provisional rule was signed by Hecker, Hewit, Deshon and Baker, and on July 7, 1858, it was approved by Archbishop Hughes.

Strikingly absent was the signature of Father Walworth. Walworth withdrew because he believed the fathers were departing too dramatically from the Rule of St. Alphonsus, particularly by the failure to provide for the taking of final vows. All but Walworth agreed to bind themselves by a promise to remain together until death. This arrangement, with the absence of permanent, binding vows beyond those of diocesan priests, was rather common in Europe, most notably associated with the Oratory of St. Philip Neri. None of the Paulists wished to disparage the vows; they had lived as Redemptorists, had not experienced the Rule itself as a burden, and had no intention of significantly altering their style of life. Hecker always insisted that a Paulist should be so deeply committed that he would be prepared to take solemn vows at any moment. But he preferred that, in a country marked by radical freedom, the members should be moved by inner conviction and the guidance of the spirit, not by external requirements. They would show, as Hecker put it years later, "that a body of free men who loved God with all their might and cling together, could conquer this modern world of ours." This was the only significant difference between the new Rule and that of the Redemptorists, but it was enough to cost the group the participation of Father Walworth.[9]

Walworth was sincerely convinced that "the voluntary principle" would prove "too weak to furnish the society with the necessary energy and unity." He told Brownson he also feared the spirit of innovation among his friends, but he tried to make his break as painless as possible. On their earlier mission travels, Walworth had been the outstanding preacher and had formed close relationships with many bishops. His withdrawal, therefore, was a real blow to the congregation. He himself felt it necessary to explain his actions to the many bishops with whom he had corresponded regarding Hecker's Roman efforts. They parted, he told them, on the "friendliest terms"; they should regard him "for all purposes of personal sympathy and friendship, as one of them." Walworth returned to his home diocese of Albany, placing himself at the disposal of Bishop McCloskey. Appointed pastor of St. Peter's in that city, he invited his colleagues to present a mission, which they did in July.[10]

The fathers seemed genuinely puzzled by Walworth's secession. Deshon felt that Walworth worried that the other fathers, by continuing to speak of doing other works "providence might offer," planned to reduce the importance of the missions, though they all denied it. While there had been differences over what aspects of the Redemptorist Rule should be eliminated or modified, disagreement had apparently been limited; all generally favored modifying fasting and eliminating the requirement of the discipline. The only substantial difference, the debate between Walworth's desire for perpetual vows and Hecker's desire to temporarily adopt the voluntary principle, was originally settled by a compromise of annual vows, together with a declaration of intention to remain for life by those entering the community. Archbishop Bayley told Walworth that such a solution was quite proper and all Walworth could expect. The others thought Walworth had accepted this and was ready to go forward on that basis.[11]

Hecker's contention that they had sincerely tried to meet Walworth's objections regarding vows was more than justified. On another crucial issue on which Hecker had strong views, acceptance of a parish, he had put his own feelings aside. The second document to emerge from the founding meetings was a formal agreement between Archbishop Hughes and the new Paulist fathers by which the priests agreed to take charge of a parish bounded by 52nd street on the south, 109th street to the north, Seventh Avenue on the east up to Central Park and Eighth Avenue above it, and the Hudson River on the West.[12] The Superior, Hecker, was to be the *ex officio* pastor, responsible to the archbishop for the fulfillment of parochial obligations. The church, with all its fixtures and grounds, was to be deeded to the archbishop. In return, the archbishop agreed to concede to the superior, duly elected and confirmed by him, "the ordinary jurisdiction of a superior in a religious family." He agreed to demand no other duties of them besides the care of the parish. Hughes also permitted them to retain title to their own religious house and the ground attached to it and granted them the use in perpetuity of the parish church.

At first glance this agreement to accept a parish seems surprising. Earlier, all the fathers agreed that the Redemptorists had jeopardized the missions by allowing themselves to be drawn into parish work among German immigrants. The prospect that some of their own number would be forced to work in English-speaking parishes outside the country had been the catalyst for their risky decision to send Hecker to Rome. Nevertheless, Hecker had also indicated from the start that they should settle in New York, as it was to be the "modern Rome," as he told Bernard Smith. Moreover, he was familiar with the city, had friends and family there, knew local sources of financial support, and enjoyed the personal confidence of the archbishop. Yet Hughes, like most bishops, demanded that religious communities in the diocese participate in parish work. All large dioceses still suffered from severe shortages of priests and churches; all were under continuing pressure from lay people to multiply parishes and provide more and more services. Hughes undoubtedly made it clear to Hecker and the others that they would be expected to maintain a parish. The other offers all had distinct disadvantages: Newark was under the direction of another convert in Bayley, and that might cause suspicion among Irish bishops and clergy. Cleveland was the only diocese which offered them a home without a parish, but the city was still outside the mainstream of national culture and somewhat removed from that "special class" to whom Hecker wanted to direct attention. Some of their best friends were to the south, but the growing sectional strife placed them on the wrong side for a religious community which sought to give missions to Catholics, almost all of whom lived in the north, and which wanted to identify with the rising nation.

The new band's leverage was limited, for they were, for the moment, secular priests who could not do as they pleased but must place themselves under the authority of a particular bishop. For all their problems with Hughes over the last year, they undoubtedly recognized that he was the most energetic and influential American bishop, seen as such in Rome and by many American clergy and bishops. Purcell, Lynch and Kenrick were all useful friends but none commanded truly national stature or marked respect in Rome. With Hughes on their side, their path toward formation of a religious community would be smooth; with his opposition they would have real trouble.

Hecker's reservations about parish work were well founded, for parish responsibilities would dominate the community in the early years and would eventually help change the character and direction of the Paulist vocation toward more conventional ministries than Hecker had anticipated. Equally important, neither in the agreement with Hughes nor in any of the other documents emerging from the founding meeting was mention made of convert work. Here, as so often happened in Hecker's life, the issue was not forced to a clear decision but sidestepped by vague language which allowed Hecker to pursue non-Catholics as he could while the congregation subordinated that work to other, more internal, projects. Hecker's later complaints that even his Paulist brothers did not recognize or accept his understanding of the community's vocation were more than a little unjust, for he never challenged the community to make this work an explicit goal.

This was even more evident in the third and in some ways most important document to emerge from these founding meetings, a circular letter from the "missionary Priests of St. Paul the Apostle, to their friends of the clergy and laity of the United States."[13] In this letter, which was printed in Catholic newspapers around the country, the Paulist fathers announced that they had organized themselves as a religious congregation for "the more vigorous prosecution of the missions and other works of apostolic ministry which, as a body, they have been engaged in for the last seven years." In order to establish the congregation, provide for novices and students, carry on the missions, offer "gentlemen of the clergy and laity accommodations for making private retreats" and fulfill other appropriate duties, they needed to raise forty to fifty thousands dollars for grounds and a house.

They emphasized that the house they proposed to establish would not be "a merely local institution" but was "intended to be the center of missions to be given in all parts of the country." They then listed the many missions given since April 1851, a total of seventeen in diocesan cathedrals and sixty-six in parish churches. What they had done in the past they thought "the best pledge of what we will do in the future." With no further mention of their parish responsibilities, they indicated they would devote themselves "as long as we live to this work" of missions. They asked readers to make known the content of this circular to others and to provide support by sending contributions to Isaac Hecker at 23 Rutgers Place in New York City, the address of George Hecker.

In a letter to Bernard Smith on July 20, Hecker summarized the steps they had taken. Ignoring the parish agreement, he told Smith they would "lead a strictly religious life in community" and devote themselves "chiefly to missions and other apostolic works." He quoted Hughes as saying that he "had found no word to alter, to add or improve." Later Hughes said that their undertaking was growing on him and he had no doubt that, in a short time, Rome would approve it. In addition, he had invited the priests to give the October mission for the young men of his St. Vincent De Paul Society, about five hundred of them, and expected the event would fill the cathedral with two thousand people. Hughes further showed his support by asking them to give a retreat for his seminarians. The new community also had a request for a mission in Hartford in September and more were promised.[14]

Hughes' general support held firm. This was particularly surprising because, of all the bishops in the United States, Hughes was perhaps most suspicious of converts; in 1856 he had publicly challenged the projects of those he regarded as a potentially American party within the church. He had expressed annoyance at writings and lectures aimed at proving that the Catholic religion and American constitution fit together "like a lock and key," that, without any great change among Americans, the Catholic religion could be presented in such a way as to win the admiration of the American people. In a report to Propaganda as recently as March 1858, he had said regarding converts that, while it was "very consoling and very agreeable to receive them into the church, they sometimes betray the absence of Catholic discipline." Hughes did not approve of the various literary organizations, libraries and lectures founded to propagate Catholicism among non-Catholics, whom the converts "professed to know by heart." Once, when he heard someone praise a priest for his good relations with non-Catholics, Hughes muttered that he "never liked those Protestant priests."[15]

Yet he always liked Hecker and in writing to Rome regularly praised his clerical spirit and loyalty to the church and the Holy See. Hecker was aware he had Hughes' good will, but he also knew his attitude toward converts and those he regarded as an American party. He had told George that the bishops would "unite against any Catholic American movement." Bedini, who had visited the country, had written in his report that the bishops were suspicious of any movement which had a national spirit. Thus there was little likelihood that the bishops or Hughes would back any society organized exclusively or even primarily for conversions.

Still, the grand step had been taken; Isaac Hecker had a new congregation, composed of native-born Americans dedicated to both church and country. They stood as witnesses to an affirmative answer to the question Brownson had stated was central to Hecker's mission to Rome: Could

Americans be Catholics without ceasing to be Americans? The Paulists, as they were soon universally called, were men who had already answered yes to that question. In parish work, on missions, in new ventures toward other Americans, they would make that yes the central theme of their community.

Still, despite Hecker's optimistic attitude, his wishes had been less than completely fulfilled. Under the jurisdiction of Archbishop Hughes, faced with the staggering prospect of launching a new parish in a still-remote section of the nation's largest city, with only four members, the first religious order for men established in the United States had immediate problems. The gap between Hecker's own transcending vision of converting the country and the meager resources at his disposal would plague him for the rest of his life. Furthermore, the American church, with almost three million members, was well on its way to becoming an important force in American life, but along lines different from those Hecker had anticipated. Crowded into the cities of the northeast and along the Great Lakes, for the most part immigrants, Catholics were determined to preserve their ancestral faith while taking advantage as best they could of the economic opportunities of the new nation. Building parishes and schools was one means of ordering their lives, strengthening their families and stabilizing their communities amid the confusing pluralism of the country. Their priests and bishops had all they could do to meet the demand for pastoral services arising from the crowded neighborhoods. The Paulists would soon find themselves in a similar situation. Organizing their parish and developing their own religious congregation would take time, money and energy, so that both missions to Catholics and work among non-Catholics would become more, not less, problematic.

Given all this, it was remarkable that the initial establishment of the new community in New York went as smoothly as it did. Nevertheless, the less-than-clear canonical basis of their undertaking was bound to cause problems. It did, almost before the Paulists got started. One of those to whom Walworth had written was Archbishop Francis Patrick Kenrick of Baltimore. By the time Walworth's letter reached him, Kenrick already had reservations about the new undertaking. He told several other bishops that he had not anticipated, and did not approve the missionaries' departure from the Redemptorists.[16] Shortly after the New York meetings ended, Baker, visiting Baltimore to raise money, heard rumors that Kenrick was condemning the new community. Baker went to see the archbishop, who told him that his earlier support had been based on the supposition that the pope had encouraged them to go on as a community giving missions, but nothing was said of that in the decree. Baker explained the pope's support, but Kenrick was not satisfied. He told Baker that he and his colleagues had "cast off their vows" and nothing good could be expected of a movement that began in "resistance to authority."

After Baker left, Kenrick wrote Hecker charging that the case "appears to me plainly one of manifest violation of the vow of obedience." Public announcement of the organization of the Paulists and their intention to erect a convent and receive novices seemed inconsistent with the refusal of the Holy See to give any formal sanction to the association. The most they could do, Kenrick argued, was to work together without assuming any public character until they had gained formal approval from Rome. More important, he insisted that, as they had been released from their vows, each priest was "subject to his own bishop and none could leave the diocese without his approbation." As a result, Kenrick said, he would recall Father Baker and deny faculties to any of their number who came to Baltimore.[17]

Alarmed, Hecker wrote Bernard Smith in Rome, pointing out that Kenrick had earlier written strongly on their behalf and even offered them a parish at Ellicott Mills, Maryland. Now, he was repeating charges made by the General. Hecker insisted that all they had done was "follow the advice of the Cardinal [Barnabò] in perfect submission to the authority of his Grace the Archbishop of New York." He told Smith he was particularly worried about Kenrick's claim upon Father Baker, saying that he understood from Cardinal Barnabò and Smith himself that they were free and might choose their own ecclesiastical superior.[18]

By this time Hughes had been informed of the problems and once again was extremely cautious. He told Smith that the priests had published a notice of their organization without his knowledge. It appeared that the Archbishop of Baltimore and the bishop of Charleston, who had ordained Hewit, had claims on some of the priests. Hughes denied any personal interest: "As I have not the slightest desire to retain these gentlemen in my diocese, and as I have and always had serious misgivings as to the ultimate success of their project, I have left them, so far as depends on me, entirely at liberty to return each to his own diocese, or, to remain as they are." In any event, he asked for the guidance of Propaganda.[19]

Unaware of Hughes' letter to Smith, Hecker wrote again in August 1858, describing the support they had received in response to their circular letter, and quoting Bishop Connolly that they must expect some opposition even from "good and learned men such as the Archbishop of Baltimore." Smith told Hecker in mid-September that Propaganda was still favorable, but that Kenrick's claim to Baker might be justified. Hecker responded that submission to Rome was "the sincerest and deepest desire of my heart and of my companions." Still, he pointed out, bishops like McCloskey, McFarland, and Fitzpatrick had indicated their support. Most telling was Hecker's quote from Hughes' response to their circular letter of August 17:

"The under signed has approved of the zealous project of Reverend Father Hecker and his reverend associates until the same shall have been submitted to the supreme head of the church and, as we hope, approved by him. The under signed only regrets that he can not contribute as he would but begs as an encouragement their acceptance of one hundred dollars."[20]

On September 20 the Congregation of Bishops and Regulars rendered a confusing judgment: as the decree did not limit the rights of bishops or assign any special privileges to the priests, it must be assumed that the position of the bishops was safeguarded and the Paulists must work under the direction of "the ordinaries of the place." Smith interpreted the decision as unfavorable to the Paulists. He wrote Hughes that the priests were obliged to return to their respective bishops. "This shows that Rome censures the conduct of Father Hecker and his companions," Smith wrote. "Still I must say that Propaganda, believing that they would do good for religion, desires their success and hopes the bishops will not put them down. This, my Lord, is the *opinion* and *mind* of Propaganda regarding the case of Father Hecker." In other words, the bishops, including Kenrick, should allow the work to proceed. The same day Smith wrote Hecker that the decision was unfavorable but not to worry; they need only get the permission of the bishops and go ahead. A few days, later Cardinal Barnabò sent Hecker a similar message, once again expressing his confidence that they would be allowed to continue. Earlier, by encouraging Hecker to go ahead in forming a new community for the work of missions, Barnabò had gone beyond the wording of the decree, which had simply released the priests from their Redemptorist vows, thus returning those ordained elsewhere to the jurisdiction of their bishops. His letter to Hecker was intended, therefore, to support the decision of the Congregation of Bishops and Regulars while affirming his support for Hecker and his work:

> In spite of this interpretation it does not follow that the work you and your companions have begun with the approval of the Archbishop of New York should be abandoned. Since it concerns a society which may do great service for the bishops of the sees of the United States, I doubt that it will be difficult to obtain the consent of the ordinaries to whom your companions are subject.

He told Hecker to ask Kenrick's permission for Baker's services in "a dignified and respectful style of writing" and he was sure it would be forthcoming.[21]

Before receiving the decision, Hecker had written to Smith that he was sorry the issue had been taken up officially; he had only submitted it so that both sides would be heard. Once again he insisted that he had interpreted Barnabò's advice to mean they should together seek approbation from the bishop under whom they located. All those Hecker had spoken to, including the holy father, had said they were free to go home and organize themselves. One proof of this was that before dispensing religious from their vows, Rome ordinarily sought permission of their ordinaries; Rome did not do so in their case. Hecker was becoming angry, and indicated that it was only personal spite against Hughes that was leading Kenrick to prevent Father Baker from pursuing his vocation, for Kenrick's diocese was well-provided with priests.[22]

By this time Bishop O'Connor of Pittsburgh had become involved. He told Smith he would speak to Kenrick and try to win his approval. To ease the way, Smith informed Kenrick of the decision of the congregation and told him Barnabò had written Hecker insisting on the necessity for "perfect obedience to the American prelates." The following day, Smith wrote again to Hecker, indicating that Cardinal Barnabò was still favorable but was concerned that they not go on without the cooperation of the bishops. He advised Hecker to avoid any action which would give rise to a fear that they were launching an American movement within the church: "if you would get some old Catholics to join you I think it would serve you."

What remained now was to adjudicate the status of Baker. O'Connor, visiting Hecker in New York, advised him to have Baker apply to Kenrick for permission to work with them; he was sure it would be granted. He found Hecker reluctant to run the risk of refusal. O'Connor told Kenrick that, while Baker should have gotten permission earlier, his withdrawal would be tantamount to the end of the work. In early November, when Hecker visited Pittsburgh, O'Connor again told him to have Baker seek Kenrick's permission. Hecker's hesitation was justified, for Kenrick still felt Baker should return to Baltimore and that they should give up the new enterprise. There was still difficulty as well from the Paulist side, for Hecker told Smith that he was willing to act in accord with the rights of bishops, but did not know for sure what those rights were. The whole problem would not have arisen, he wrote, if Rome had acted expressly in giving them the privileges to organize before dispensing them from their vows. He stated without great accuracy that they had never thought that the decree of the Congregation of Bishops and Regulars had authorized them to form a new congregation, only that they had received permission to choose their bishop, so they were surprised that a question of this kind had arisen.[23]

Two days later, however, Hecker told his colleagues that he was going to approach Kenrick himself, rather than risk a direct appeal from Baker. A week later he sent a respectful appeal to Kenrick, quoting Barnabò at length and asking permission for Baker to work with them. The same day Kenrick wrote to Cardinal Barnabò in a more flexible manner. He did not question the motives of Hecker and the other Paulists; he only feared that they would fall into difficulties because they were converts. He was disturbed that Baker refused to acknowledge his authority, that they had issued their announcement prematurely, and that they were raising money nationally though they only had the approval of the archbishop of New York. Nevertheless, he would place no obstacles in their way. Bishop Foley of Detroit visited Kenrick a short time later and wrote Hecker that he thought matters could be mended. The archbishop had rejected O'Connor's mediation and would undoubtedly respond to Hecker in the same way. All that was needed was what O'Connor had recommended, that Baker write to Kenrick, acknowledge his error, and ask release to work with the new community.[24]

Foley was right, for Kenrick wrote to Hecker that Barnabò's letter, informing him that they had adopted an ecclesiastical corporation with the proper title, removed his objections. He would still not allow a collection in his diocese, because he could not see that they would obtain permanent success. He was surprised, however, that Hecker had asked permission for Father Baker to work with them. He had indicated to the bishop of Pittsburgh that he would only recognize a letter from Baker himself. On the basis of this letter, Baker finally wrote to Kenrick, requesting the proper documents which would remove him from the authority of the archbishop of Baltimore and place him under that of New York. He further expressed his regret that any misunderstandings had arisen and begged pardon for anything that he might have done which gave Kenrick pain. Apparently the proper documents were forthcoming, because with this letter the issue seems to have ended, removing the last barrier to the Paulist work.[25]

Meanwhile, the organization of the new religious community proceeded. In a chapter held in September 1859, rules were laid down for the treatment of visitors and guests. In November the chapter defined a daily schedule. Provision was made in 1860 for the admission and supervision of lay brothers. Hecker was annually reelected superior while Deshon was superior of brothers and Hewit zelator and admonitor. The biggest problem was recruitment. In Pittsburgh Hecker met two local priests on a train, one of whom "had the appearance and pronunciation of an American." Hecker told the other fathers that this priest "has all the qualities we require," but held back from joining them because he was reluctant to bring the matter before Bishop O'Connor. More promising was Father George McCloskey, brother of the bishop of Albany and at the time a priest of the archdiocese of New York. He indicated his intention to apply to the Paulists in December 1858, and in January wrote Hughes of his desire to make up for his lack of zeal in the past by participating in the energetic apostolate of the new community. Hughes responded that such a step would be premature until the new community had been approved by Rome. Once this was done, he promised he would place no unreasonable obstacle in McCloskey's way.[26]

Perhaps upset at the prospect of losing one of his more prominent priests, Hughes wrote Hecker that the Paulists would not be able to receive new members into their society until they gained formal Roman recognition. At the same time, he reminded them that, as secular priests within his diocese, they could not take up a general collection, for it would not be fair to other struggling pastors. Hecker discussed the matter with Hughes and told him that the Holy See could not grant approval until he saw how the new order was going, especially in terms of its growth in numbers. Hughes responded that he should petition the Holy See, and Hecker did so. In a cover letter to Barnabò, Hecker described the work of the missions and explained that American bishops made the charge of a parish a requirement for religious communities. Parish income was their sole source of support. Once the church was ready, parish duties would require the services of at least two of their number. Given that Hughes and others also wanted them to continue the missions, he never dreamed that there would be any problem accepting new members. In April the Congregation of Bishops and Regulars granted a favorable decision, indicating that, subject to the jurisdiction of the archbishop, the Paulists did have permission to begin a "simple congregation of secular priests who are to be engaged in giving missions" and therefore, presumably, could indeed expand.[27]

To prepare for the reception of new members the community established a novitiate. It extended twelve months for new members, shortened to six to nine months for those who were already priests. In August 1861 the novitiate opened under Hewit's direction, with two novices and two brothers. The delay resulted from the lack of acceptable candidates, although in late October 1859 the first major accession to the community took place. Robert Tillotson was a member of Newman's Birmingham Oratory in England, but an American by birth. After visiting Hecker in early October 1858 he wrote that, if such a community had existed when he was making his vocational choice, he would have entered it. Hecker responded energetically, insisting that in the Paulists Tillotson would find a wider field for his talents, and sympathetic, familiar people. After a year's indecision, Tillotson decided to try the Paulists and received permission from Newman to do so.[28]

Another valuable recruit was Alfred Young, a convert, native of England, graduate of Princeton and former physician. After entering the church in 1850, Young became a priest of Bayley's Newark diocese. He met Hecker while on retreat at the Redemptorist house in New York in

1856. Bayley was reluctant to release him to the Paulists, but Young finally was granted the necessary papers and joined the community in 1861.

More relief of the manpower problem was found with the return of Father Walworth. On December 15, 1860, he asked if he could reenter the community. He had wanted to try parish life, but found himself "if not precisely a fish out of water . . . at least like a fish in a bottle. There is room enough to float, but not much to swim." The rule they had adopted was not what his soul craved when the "Redemptorist plank broke under me," but it had the great advantage of being made to fit the other four and he now thought he could "make myself to fit it." He yearned for the work of the missions, for regular hours and religious exercises and, besides, his heart and sympathies had always been with his old companions. "If you think the old horse can be of any service, I offer him," he concluded. Deshon expressed the reaction of the group when he told Hecker "you have my hearty concurrence in taking back the lost sheep." In the spring Walworth returned and, in a generous gesture, was ranked next to Hecker in order of seniority.[29]

Still, recruitment proved extremely difficult. The Paulists were selective, for their understanding of their mission required men of high caliber and great personal maturity, while external pressure was exerted to bring in men who were "born Catholics." That combination was difficult, given the fact that the immigrant church was not producing a vast number of educated laymen, and of the small number who considered the priesthood there was intense competition between dioceses and religious orders, some of which Hecker had himself experienced when he was considering his own vocation back in 1845.

The Paulists also had a string of misfortunes with those who did join. In 1859 Richard O'Brien applied for admission, was accepted and sent south for studies but left with the outbreak of the Civil War. A short time later Francis J. Haggerty was sent to St. Charles Seminary in Baltimore but was soon forced to withdraw because of ill health. Even more tragic was the case of Otto Mayer, an orphan adopted by the principal of the public high school in Pittsfield, Massachusetts. He and his stepfather were converted during a mission in that city in 1863 and that fall, after graduating from Seton Hall, he joined the Paulists. Considered one of the Paulist's most promising seminarians, he was stricken with typhoid and died while visiting his home in the summer of 1867. Eugene Kavanagh of Milwaukee, another Seton Hall graduate, entered the novitiate but died of consumption in the summer of 1870. Two English brothers, Alfred and Louis Brown, joined the community in the 1870s; both died within four years of their ordination. Still others who were ordained for the community left to take up parish work. Joshua Bodfish, a former naval officer ordained in 1866, left for the Boston diocese in 1875. Henry S. Lake, ordained in 1861, and William J. Dwyer, ordained a decade later, left for diocesan service. Francis Spencer, ordained in 1869, left for the Dominicans in 1871. James Kent Stone, former president of Hobart College, left after four years to join the Passionists in 1876; Benjamin Hill followed three years later.[30]

Not until 1872 did the Paulists ordain their first "born Catholics," Adrian Rosecrans, son of Deshon's West Point classmate William Rosecrans, and Walter Elliott, who would devote his life and considerable gifts to Hecker's ideals. Last born of nine children of a Detroit businessman and judge, Elliott attended Notre Dame, was admitted to the bar, and joined the Union army on the outbreak of hostilities. Both his brothers were killed in the war and Elliott himself was a prisoner of war. In 1868, back in Detroit, he attended a lecture by Hecker. Stirred to the depths, he wrote the Paulists and, before receiving a response, left for New York, where he presented himself and was admitted to the novitiate. More than any other Paulist, he was to be Hecker's disciple.[31]

The Paulists not only had to organize and develop their new congregation, they also had to establish a new parish, even while continuing the missions. The setting for the parish, named St. Paul's, was not very inviting. The bulk of New York City's population was still south of 34th Street. Above were scattered farms and estates, but movement was being accelerated by the building of Central Park, authorized by legislation in 1856. There were six Catholic churches north of 34th Street, with a total of eight priests. The new parish assigned to the Paulists was three and a half miles long by a half mile wide and included small farms, market gardens, and a few mansions. There were no street lights and only four houses between 57th and 61st streets. Across from the land the priests intended to purchase there was a truck garden, mostly occupied by goats. Nevertheless, Hecker's brother George, who had first seen the property in January and had held it for their use, believed that the building of Central Park would attract new commercial ventures and eventually new housing. Work had begun on the park in 1857, and by July 1858 fifteen hundred laborers were employed. Property owners on adjacent lots, which were appreciating, were being assessed to pay for improvements. Knowing prices would skyrocket, the priests acted quickly. For thirty-two lots facing Ninth Avenue between 59th and 60th streets, the Paulists paid ten thousand dollars in cash, assumed a twenty thousand dollar mortgage, and took a second mortgage for ten thousand dollars. The estimated cost of the first building was fifteen thousand dollars.[32]

With such a thinly populated parish, the Paulists had to depend initially on their own earnings from missions and on their fund-raising abilities. The Catholic press carried their appeal and each priest called on his friends, with Hecker being the most active. He combed the city with a small notebook, taking pledges and first payments. Father Baker wrote in some amusement to his friend Dwight Lyman: "Father Hecker has turned out a regular highway man, and challenges almost everyone he meets with 'your purse or your life.' "[33] A "practical friend," probably George Hecker, pledged two thousand dollars and two others gave five hundred dollars. In addition to a number of gifts of from one to two hundred dollars, they received twenty dollars from Isaac Hecker's mother and fifty dollars from Fernando Wood, the mayor of New York City.

Fundraising was suspended when the missions resumed in September 1859 in Providence, Rhode Island; they then returned to New York for a mission at St. Patrick's and the retreat for St. Vincent de Paul men. After that they went to Covington, Kentucky, for a mission, following which the rest of the fathers proceeded to Michigan while Hecker returned to New York to look after parish business and meet with an architect. When the missionaries returned, Deshon stayed with Isaac at George's house; Hewit boarded at St. Anne's parish; the others stayed with Father George McCloskey at Nativity Church. They agreed together to build a red brick convent and church combination, placed well back on 59th Street, leaving room for the later building of a permanent church. After ground was broken in February, Hewit left to take up collections in the south, soon sending along one thousand dollars from his home diocese of Charleston, South Carolina. Hughes allowed no general collection in New York, but several pastors invited individual Paulists to preach and take up collections. Hecker, preaching at St. Mary's in July, collected eleven hundred dollars. In the fall they again were on the missions, and when they returned, they rented a house on 60th Street between Eighth and Ninth Avenues. They continued collections in hopes of being able to pay for the building when it was finished and acquire no additional debt. On June 18, the archbishop laid the cornerstone before a group of some ten to twelve thousand people. He spoke warmly of the value of the new parish to the city and the value of the priests' labors around the country. The three-story building faced 59th Street; when the permanent church was built around the corner on Ninth Avenue, it would become the community residence. Newspapers estimated the cost at twenty thousand dollars and foresaw a great future for the parish as municipal transportation moved up Eighth and Ninth Avenue toward nearby Central Park.

Hecker wanted St. Paul's to become a model for other parishes in New York City. He wrote regularly and enthusiastically to Smith and Barnabò describing the growth of the parish. Only a few months after the blessing of the building, Hecker reported establishment of a St. Vincent de Paul society of twenty-two men and a sewing group of ladies who provided clothes for the poor. Hewit, with the help of several laymen, organized a Sunday school in 1861; three years later the parish added a lending library for children. Hecker wanted St. Paul's to be a parish of "perpetual mission," where the quality of preaching and liturgy would elevate the tone of Catholic life and draw the attention of non-Catholics. Once formally established, parishes often gave missions to draw in the wavering, excite the committed, and set the tone of parish life. The Paulists, who had helped so many parishes, did the same in their own. From December 18 to Christmas 1859 they filled their little church for morning Mass and instruction and evening mission sermons. Hecker happily reported that 725 adults and 95 children had taken part.

In April 1860 a New York paper described the "wonders" taking place at St. Paul's, where all seats were occupied and many people were left standing for Sunday services. So powerful and persuasive was the preaching that the saloons in the neighborhood were closing. The ceremonies of Holy Week had been particularly moving; according to a reporter some said they had never seen them done so well in this country. New York papers frequently printed letters from residents testifying to the work of the parish, the sinners converted, the people returning to the sacraments, the throngs in church and the influence on non-Catholics. The *Tablet* noted in May that in general the preaching in the city was poor, lacking not intelligence or good English so much as sincerity, faith, charity and burning zeal. In contrast, the paper praised the Paulists as preachers, noted the impact they had on their parishioners, and urged other priests to take preaching as seriously. A month later McMaster's *Freeman's Journal* reported on a particularly powerful sermon Hecker had preached in response to Hughes' request for support for the Holy Father during his time of trial in Rome.[34]

The parish, in fact, became known for the quality of sermons delivered there. While the American church had a few outstanding preachers like John Hughes, for the most part priests were uncomfortable in the pulpit, some because of the language barrier, others because of the absence of a rich English-language homiletic literature. The American Redemptorists enjoyed the popularity they did in part because they were often the first skilled preachers heard from a Catholic pulpit in the cities they visited. To broaden their influence, the Paulists published an annual collection of their sermons in 1861 and for several years thereafter. Hewit, Baker, Walworth, Deshon, Tillotson and Hecker spoke on a variety of themes, sometimes inspired by the gospel of the day, always by the desire to exhort their parishioners to a more intense spiritual life and more regular reception of the sacraments. Moral themes, emphasizing orderliness, sobriety, and self-discipline, predominated, as they did in other parishes, but these well-educated and energetic priests brought literary grace and oratorical ability to the service of moral exhortation.

Most notable was a generally optimistic understanding of human nature. While American Catholic piety at the time was increasingly negative, emphasizing human depravity and the temptations of the world, the Paulist sermons were characteristically positive, aiming at the sanctification of the souls of parishioners in the midst of everyday life. Hecker, of course, led the way, explaining in an 1863 sermon that everyone was called to holiness and modern society, by offering the opportunity to unite the pursuit of God with intelligence and liberty, provided a unique situation to respond to that call. In a New Year's sermon that same year Hecker denied that Christianity aimed only at an other-worldly happiness and regarded "the earth as hateful and the world nothing but sin." The Gospel was not one of "gloom and despair but of glad tidings and great joy." To be happy people had only to determine the end of their life, their destiny, then give all their energies to its pursuit. By practicing "those virtues which constantly lead the soul nearer to the end of its existence," and by using the means which the church made available, especially the sacraments, people could find not only salvation but earthly happiness as well. Comforting his listeners, he reminded them that all Christians fail occasionally to do their duty, but the only final sin was despair. Each could start again, on the New Year. Hecker's message to his parishioners was the same he offered to non-Catholics, to determine their destiny and commit themselves to its pursuit, all in the freedom which was their birthright:

> What would you say of a great artist who had designed a masterpiece, and ceased to work before he had given it the finishing touches? You would condemn him. You are that artist, your picture is the image of God in your soul, a few more strokes of self denial, a few more touches of humility and generosity, in God's service, and you would render its beauty complete.[35]

Another particular concern of the Paulists was the quality of church music. In September 1860 the chapter resolved to hire an organist at two hundred dollars a year, as well as a soprano and two additional paid singers. It also initiated an effort to train a volunteer choir. A year later the chapter hired an organist and choir master at a salary of one thousand dollars a year, no small sum in those days. When Father Young became active in the parish, he devoted particular attention to the music. By 1872 they had a renowned male choir of forty-two voices and had established a musical conservatory to offer instruction.

Efforts to lift the tone of Catholic life did not end with religious services. In 1864 a neighborhood Catholic Association began with its own hall on Eighth Avenue. The Association used the parish library and reading room, sponsored a baseball team and boating club, and began plans for a gymnasium. Reports of the Association's work brought inquiries from around the country, including one from Father John Ireland of St. Paul, Minnesota, a young priest who had achieved fame as a Civil War chaplain. All of this attracted the respectful attention of non-Catholics. In 1862 lectures for non-Catholics were offered after Sunday vespers; a similar series was offered on Sunday evenings during Lent.[36]

The missions, the parish, and the supervision of novices strained the community to the breaking point during the 1860s. Hecker and Tillotson, who was frequently ill, looked after the parish, while Hewit worked with the students. The situation worsened in 1865. In April Father Baker died tragically. The little community had hardly recovered when Father Walworth again withdrew. On July 15 he wrote Hecker that he could no longer live in New York and breathe the "malarial atmosphere" that surrounded the house. Despite his claims about illness and the prospect of a long convalescence, he soon accepted charge of the Albany Cathedral and, a few years later, took over a large parish in Troy. It must have been hard to avoid the conclusion that he had traded the insecurity of the Paulists and discomforts of religious life for the promising work as a leading figure in his home diocese and the comforts of his family's home at Saratoga Springs. With Walworth's loss, the Paulists were forced to suspend the missions.[37]

For all the success of their parish work and the demands for missions, the Paulists were still far from a secure position in the church. The tortuous process of obtaining official sanction as a religious community seemed never-ending. In April 1861, for example, Hecker called on Hughes and was informed that the Paulists should have their Rule ready for presentation to a provincial council in June; if the council approved, it would be forwarded to Rome. The war seems to have delayed the meeting of the provincial council, but a year later, in April 1862, Hecker reported to Cardinal Barnabò that he had been urged by the archbishop to take advantage of the visit of the bishop to Rome to present a petition for approbation. He included a letter of recommendation from Bishop Martin John Spalding of Louisville, Kentucky, who had become a strong Paulist friend. At about the same time he reported to Connolly that he was only seeking this recommendation from Rome as a result of being pushed by Bishop Hughes. The request for approbation was again delayed until the end of the Civil War. Barnabò indicated it was too early for such formal approval, but the pope would send his blessing, which he did.[38]

Formation of a new religious community, recruitment and training of candidates, organizing a new parish, all absorbed much of Hecker's energy.

For awhile, his dream of converting Americans was put aside. Still, the dream did not die, nor was Hecker's spiritual struggle over. A central tension had always existed in his life, one between contemplation and action, between the inner call for a deeper experience of God, to be achieved in solitude, and an equally compelling call to a life of apostolic endeavor on behalf of God and his church. For a time that tension was resolved, as it had always been, by a providential interpretation of his own history. He set it forth in a letter to a new friend, Adrian Rouquette, in November 1858. His "love for solitude and contemplation proved necessary only as a preparatory means of discipline for a more extensive and energetic action," he wrote. "It appears to me that the pressing wants of our time, and in a special manner, our own country, demand apostolic men . . . men like Sts. Peter and Paul who will face our modern Republic as they did the ancient one of Rome, with deathless resolves to conquer it." In earlier years, even when unable to study, and absorbed in contemplation, it had been Hecker's "most intimate conviction that God's providence was preparing me for a great work, the conversion of our countrymen." The work in which he was engaged, raising money, beginning a parish, launching the religious order, seeking to attract members, and attempting to respond to the request for missions, all was laying the basis for the active apostolic effort to bring about the conversion of America. "The conversion of the American people to the Catholic faith has ripened into a conviction with me which lies beyond the region of doubt," he wrote. "My life, my labors and my death is consecrated to it. No other aim outside of my own salvation and perfection can occupy my attention for a moment. But all other things in view of this, art, science, literature, etc., enter in as part of the means, and command my interest, and demand all the encouragement within my reach. In the union of Catholic faith and American civilization a birth awaits them all, and a future for the church brighter than any past. That is briefly my 'Credo.' "

For now, the community itself was the vehicle for uniting Catholicism and America; its witness would eventually lead to the work. "Individually, the faith has been identified with American life. Our effort is to identify Catholicity with American life in a religious association," he told Anna Ward, a New England convert Hecker had assisted in Rome. What had been heretofore an individual undertaking to convert the country now would become a collective one. The new institute was "the first attempt to identify the faith and American life in a religious association. Individually this has been accomplished and I am confident that when this is also accomplished in a community, our young men will flock around our standard and devote themselves to the conversion of the American people."[39]

But already the barriers which existed within the Roman communion to this kind of work were clear to him. He still believed that intelligence and truth were made for each other and intelligent people would embrace the truth when it was fairly seen. Unfortunately, Catholic truth had not yet been fairly presented to the American people; it was now "our work to do it." Of the results he had no doubt, for it was indeed "the mission of the church to convert the world." He saw many signs then and later that people were seeking solutions to the problems which were plaguing the country, solutions which could indeed be found within the Catholic Church. Unfortunately, there were problems within the church which continued to inhibit it from presenting those answers. "The world is governed too much is no less the truth in the ecclesiastical than the political world," he wrote. "The systems and customs and laws suitable to the infancy of society, are not only unsuitable, but barriers to the advancement of the youth or the manhood of society."[40] What was true in the civil realm he clearly believed was also true in the church, and many of those barriers were being placed before him as he sought to launch the work of the Paulist fathers. American Catholicism still remained in its "infancy"; Hecker was going to try to bring it to "manhood."

11

The Future Triumph of the Church

When Isaac Hecker first experienced the movement of the Spirit and set forth in quest of vital work, he left politics behind. He retained at least a casual interest in political affairs as late as the spring of 1845, when he dropped in on a neighborhood political meeting, but he paid little attention to politics while at Brook Farm and none after entering the seminary. He took little notice of the Know Nothings after his Roman article, which claimed the movement helped the church, and he hardly mentioned the raging issues of slavery and expansion. He was well aware of the nervousness among Roman officials at the apparent chaos of American public life, but he made light of it. In August 1860, in the midst of a bitter presidential campaign, he chided Bernard Smith about the turmoil in Italy arising from the seizure of the Papal States. "We Yankees thank Providence are not entangled with affairs the other side of the ocean," he wrote pleasantly. "Occasionally we have difficulties of our own concerning which we make a great noise, and end in general quiet." By February 1861, with secession underway, he seemed unworried, telling Smith "the country is in some trouble, but I guess we will come safely out of it." Father Baker was distressed at the crossfire in which his native Baltimore was caught, but Hecker remained optimistic; it would all end peacefully, he thought, even though the Paulists were forced to cancel a mission in Mobile. When war came, Hecker thought it tragic and predictably blamed "hot heads" and "fanatics" on both sides. Sadly, war now seemed "to have been inevitable." Before it ended, it was "likely to be a severe one."[1]

On the most profound of the issues dividing the nation, slavery,

Hecker's views were quite conventional. When he visited Jane Sedgwick, a convert and friend in Stockbridge, Massachusetts, in the spring of 1861, he must have defended the church, which had never condemned slavery, for she wrote him later of her sharp disagreement. She wondered how an argument, presumably his, which justified servitude under certain conditions, could be extended to the perpetual control of human beings and their descendants. Further, she wondered how American slavery could be justified at all, for the original claims on the slaves were based on "rapine and fraud." Finally, she challenged Hecker's argument that the church only opposed slavery when there were accidental abuses connected with it. How could such abuses be more widespread than they were in the United States, she asked, for in the South open violations of God's laws were almost universal, and yet there was no condemnation? She concluded by stating frankly that no Catholic citizen could support extension of slavery into territories which to that time had been free. There is no record of Hecker's response to Jane Sedgwick's excellent questions.[2]

Once the war came, Hecker told friends he had always been opposed to slavery; he even told Bishop Lynch of Charleston that he regarded the war as a punishment of the South for its evils. He particularly deplored the disruptive effects of involuntary servitude on marriage and family life. In September he wrote:

> The sentiment of loyal Americans whether Catholic or not is getting always and more strong and united every day against slavery and without any change of principle. We have always taken the ground that it is an evil and a disgrace which might be tolerated for a time, but ought to be gradually abolished. The Constitutional rights of the States forbade, however, any direct meddling and made it our duty to protect the institution of slavery against unjust aggression. Now, however, since slavery is so destructive of national prosperity, and the south by its rebellion has forfeited all claim to the forbearance of the north, we think the time will soon come to expel slavery from our entire country.[3]

The war itself posed the problem of whether to allow Paulists to serve as Chaplains. First Hughes and then Bishop McFarland of Connecticut made requests, and Hecker resisted, determined to hold his small band together. In the midst of a flurry of correspondence on this subject came news which brought the war home. G. W. Muse of New Orleans had applied for admission to the Paulists and was preparing to come to New York when he was summoned to military service. He wrote Hecker that he could not "bear the thought of killing anyone," but, he added, "I cannot conscientiously forsake my country in her time of need." Muse was killed in battle on July 18, 1861.[4]

Hecker was initially cautious in writing to Rome about the war, but in 1862, angered by the "shameful" confederate sympathies of the British and by their seizure of an American ship, Hecker became uncharacteristically jingoistic, writing to Simpson: "My inclination is to leave the points in dispute to the settlement of the iron noses of our gunboats. Let them butt it out."[5]

But most of the time Hecker avoided comments on controversial matters. Like so many other Catholic priests and bishops in the North, the Paulists chose to ignore the issues of slavery and secession. Hughes went to Europe to promote the Union cause, and Bishop Lynch of Charleston, a close friend, carried out a similar errand for the Confederacy. Hecker's old associate McMaster was a lively partisan of the Democrats and eventually was jailed for his outspoken "Copperhead sympathies." But Hecker and his associates had little to say publicly about the war until it was over, and even their private views had little in them of "politics."

Instead, pastoral and evangelical work absorbed their energy. When the first volume of sermons preached at St. Paul's appeared in 1861, Simpson's *Home and Foreign Review* noted that they made no reference to the "exciting topics of the day." The second volume impressed the *Tablet* with its moral tone, "striking at the roots of vicious habits and assailing the demon of worldliness in his most ancient strongholds." The *Tribune* spoke of "something startling, indeed almost terrible, in the homely honest energy of their speech," directed at making their hearers good Catholics but even more "good men."[6] But neither partisans of Lincoln nor Copperheads could have found ground for complaint with their sermons.

In April 1863 Hecker told Smith that "in New York you can detect no difference from the times of profound peace." But in July Irish opposition to conscription burst into bloody riots, with mobs roaming the city, beating blacks, burning their homes and threatening the lives and property of respectable citizens. Several outbursts took place in the vicinity of St. Paul's, still located on the outskirts of the city but near a railroad line on which rioters expected the arrival of federal troops from Albany. One group was ripping up track under banners condemning the draft when Hecker, Walworth and Hewit, recognizing parishioners among the crowd, confronted them and, according to a report sent to Rome by Louis Binsse, began snatching weapons from their hands. When Hewit attempted to seize one of the banners, he was knocked to the ground by a blow on the head. Shocked by the priest's fall, the rioters calmed down and listened to Hecker's plea that they disperse. Hewit was taken to the convent, where he was treated by a surgeon, but Hecker continued to roam the neighborhood seeking to ease the tension and disperse crowds. Reporting these events to a friend a few days later, Hecker recognized the unfairness of the draft and blamed the riots on politicians who had stirred up the men. The panic that gripped the city occasioned one of Hecker's characteristic affirmations of the democratic spirit. "It always pains me at such times to hear men express doubt concerning the safety of our institutions," he wrote. "As for me, I would rather suffer from the license of freedom than from the oppression of authority."[7]

Privately, Hecker saw the war, like other signs of the times, in providential terms. While avoiding public comment, his imagination overflowed with images of a Catholic America. In a sermon prepared, but not delivered, shortly after Fort Sumter, Hecker reflected on the lost unity of the country. Just as no person alone and unaided could fulfill the aspirations of nature or answer the questions of the soul, neither could a nation fulfill its historic destiny without God's help, without religion:

> The national mind needs to possess common religious principles and convictions, to which in time of violence and discord an appeal can be made which will be regarded, and bring forth from the bosom of the people a response that renders them forgetful of private interests and makes peace take the place of discord and violence. But only a religion which has its sanction from God, and produces in the hearts of its believers a profound conviction of its divine authority, is capable of uniting the hearts of a whole people whose minds are blinded by passion and whose actions are singed by appeals to selfishness. For it is Religion that strikes the deepest roots in the human heart, raises man above himself, and can excite his enthusiasm to the noblest actions and deeds of heroic sacrifice. As for us we have no such religion; we are a people who have no religion which characterizes us as a people![8]

And now what of the American religious situation? Protestant sectarianism had sown "the seeds of discord," so the "unity and conservative principles of Catholicism were better appreciated by the public." In 1862 Hecker told Simpson that the war was leading Americans "to see the necessity of a greater dependence on God" and opened eyes "to the fact that Protestantism, without a divine sanction, its national influence disintegrating, and its origin and character revolutionary" was "wholly unfit for any people, and above all for one whose form . . . of government is like ours." In Europe, Catholicism was in a "fossil state," but in the United States, Protestants were building Gothic churches, starting Vespers services and even showing interest in the Blessed Virgin Mary. As the war dragged on

Hecker's optimism about its long-range significance never flagged. In May 1864 he told Simpson that the war had accelerated "the downfall of Protestantism and made the wiser portions of the community feel the necessity of a real religion like the Catholic."[9]

So convinced was Hecker of this providential opportunity for the church that, despite the pressing problems of personnel which forced curtailment and eventual suspension of the missions, Hecker was spurred to energetic activity. He lectured throughout the country, laid plans for a series of publishing ventures and attempted to promote a sense of apostolic and missionary responsibility on the part of bishops, clergy and laymen.

Hecker had long ago concluded that Catholicism in the United States would have to develop an evangelical style, seeking to persuade people to change their minds about the church. To evangelize America, then, required a technique designed to reach that objective. Initially, as in Norfolk in 1857, Hecker wanted to try a week-long series of public lectures following a mission. Almost always the excitement stirred by the mission attracted attention throughout the community; perhaps curious seekers would attend a series of lectures after the mission ended. He renewed the experiment in October 1862 in Jersey City, where the pastor of St. Mary's parish was a friend. Walworth, Hewit, Deshon and Young delivered a mission and three days later Hecker began an eight-part lecture series. He adopted the style of his books, presuming that the work of the day was less to defend the church against heresy than to address fundamental questions of existence and make a straightforward exposition of Catholic answers to these questions.

The series was well-attended, so a second took place in New Haven in November. Here the talks were given in a public hall and no mission preceded them. The hall had a capacity of one thousand and people were turned away the first night, but it was estimated that only a quarter were non-Catholics. For the last lecture the site was changed to a music hall seating three thousand, and the papers reported several hundred were turned away. This series established Hecker's reputation as a lecturer and confirmed in his mind the benefits of using a public hall and advertising in the local press. The topics of the New Haven series were themes Hecker would emphasize in lectures over the next several years: "A Search for Rational Christianity," "Why Did I Become a Catholic?" (always the most popular talk), "The Necessity for an Unerring Guide," "Confession: Its Necessity and Objections Against It," "Invocation of Saints" and "What Shall I do to be Saved?" Buoyed by the New Haven success, he went west to Columbus, where he delivered the first two of the above addresses and then to Dayton for the entire series. In the latter city he abandoned clerical garb for the lectures, wishing to appear as the "earnest seeker," the upright

American whose Catholicism was the product of the same honest search he believed many of his listeners were engaged in. In Ohio he also added some additional lectures to his repertoire, one on Eucharist as an answer to the yearning for union with God, another on the communion of saints, and a third combining several others into "The Way to Salvation Consistent with Reason and the Bible."

Returning from this first western tour, Hecker was elated. He told Bernard Smith that if he had only a few more Paulists to join this work, they would have all they needed "to convert the world." To Archbishop Bayley he wrote an account of his tour, describing his approach in detail. The ideas formed as far back as his books of the fifties seemed finally to come to fruition:

> The method I follow is the same as is laid out in my two books. I begin by searching for the element in man's nature to which the doctrine or sacrament for the lectures addresses itself. This found, I analyze it, develop it, illustrate it, until I have the audience alive with its reality and importance. Then I go forth and seek for the Religion which recognizes this element and is responsive to it. In this way I first examine Protestantism, and by the authority of the premise in their own bosoms, I overthrow it and repudiate it. By the same authority I establish the Catholic religion and call on my audience to be true to their intelligence, the voice of conscience and the instincts implanted in their nature by the hand of God. The power and reach of this method is much greater than I ever dreamed of. It does away with opposition and silences objections. What can a man do, deny the deep necessities of his soul, and with no intention of satisfying them? I avoid by this plan entirely, the old system of controversy, and everything personal. I throw off everything professional, preach from the platform or stage in my secular dress, extempore. I tell them frankly I come among them not as an advocate of the Catholic church, but as a man who owes supreme allegiance to truth; if I advocate the Catholic Church, it is because I am convinced that she is the true church, and for no other reason.[10]

Hecker's candor with the bishop reflected their friendship, but also the enthusiasm stirred by the lectures. Though he spoke for an hour and a half, he told Bayley, there were complaints it was too short; never had audiences been more attentive. Several listeners requested instruction, but he did not anticipate immediate conversions: "Seed time and harvest do not come in the same season." The lectures would have to be prolonged to produce conversions and, at this point, he had in view only to "try the capacity of my guns." In November he delivered the series in St. Louis during a week between two missions. Arrangements were made by a committee of local laymen; tickets were printed and distributed free through local Protestant bookstores. The hall held nineteen hundred and was filled each night. Bishop Duggan of Chicago attended four of the talks and invited Hecker to present a series in his city. On November 17, the closing night, he addressed the largest crowd of his career, writing the next day that this had only been a "skirmish" before the "great battlefield of Boston" where "I feel is to be fought the decisive battle."[11]

Yet he was less certain than he sounded. He wrote Simpson in December that the work required a company of priests to go from city to city to work directly for conversions. The work would take years, perhaps even centuries. In January 1863, he wrote to Mrs. Ward that he would not repeat the experiment with the lectures; in fact, he delivered only one other complete series, in Manchester, New Hampshire, in October 1865. He told her, as he had Simpson, that the plan now would be to go to a place for a period to work until conversions were accomplished. "It's God's work for the country and our people," he concluded, "and I am interested in learning how he is preparing me to become his travelling agent in this business."[12]

In April 1865 Father Baker died, a great loss for the community and for Hecker personally. Tillotson, whose health was never strong, was often ill; he would pass away in 1868. The shortage of men forced suspension of the missions; Paulist efforts after 1865 concentrated on the parish and seminary. This, along with another bout of illness, probably had something to do with Hecker ending the lecture series. But he did continue to deliver individual lectures after the war. In 1867 he toured New England and upstate New York to raise money for his publishing ventures, and the following year he went west again, writing that one of his "earliest dreams" was realized, lecturing to non-Catholics and getting paid for it. In December 1868 he was in Detroit to speak at the Young Men's Hall for a thirty cent admission. By February 1869 Hecker had travelled forty-five hundred miles and lectured to over thirty thousand people, of whom twenty thousand were non-Catholics. In 1871 he again indicated he would spend a great deal of his time lecturing, even as his colleagues were resuming the missions. Before he went abroad in 1873, Hecker gave six series of eight lectures and eighty-nine single lectures, scattered across the country.[13]

Newspaper reports indicated that Hecker was now a polished, skilled orator. Usually referred to as a "plain, straightforward" speaker, he presented himself—and was received—primarily as an American citizen. The Hartford *Courant* gave a report of him after an 1869 lecture:

> Father Hecker appears to be perhaps fifty five years old. His head is full and well formed, his height perhaps five foot ten and his form indicates vigor. His voice is pitched on rather too high a key, as it shows sometimes by breaking slightly when he grows animated. His delivery is good but both in language and manner of speaking, he is devoid of pretence, aiming first to convey his ideas clearly and in an interesting and logical sequence.

The editor of the Ohio *Statesman* reported that the Columbus series "was attended by an immense concourse, so large that many could not obtain seats or hardly effect an entrance." "His personality was all," a Paulist recalled years later, while a New York priest who heard Hecker described him as "a tall, pale, wiry man, with most expressive eyes, not an orator, but a very interesting speaker, full of earnestness." Sometimes his attempts at humor caused problems; he was accused by a Jackson, Michigan, newspaper of bad taste when he said that anyone who claimed that Martin Luther changed his position because of a bull of Pope Leo X was putting the cart before the horse, or rather, bull. Nor was Hecker's optimism about audience reaction fully justified. An undated newspaper clipping in a Syracuse, New York, scrapbook favorably reported a Hecker lecture, but allowed that his argument that Catholicism was the only religion which did not "antagonize the fundamental principles of self-government" would shock Protestants and might be refuted by them. Nevertheless, the reporter was pleased that a Catholic priest would say such things; if "the great and growing mass of our people who constitute the Catholic Church would listen to and even act upon the principles and emotions in such lectures, we would have no cause to regret their frequent repetition."

At the other extreme, not all Catholics received his addresses in the spirit in which they were intended. When Hecker was invited to Detroit to speak in a public hall in 1868, one Catholic told the bishop "every Catholic in the city should attend if for no other reason than Martin Luther is to be skinned by a Catholic priest, not simply at the invitation of a Protestant society, but better still, at their expense." As Hecker told Simpson, "Catholic truth suffers more in many instances, and conversions are often hindered by the bitterness, lust for dominion, and ignorance of its advocates than from the prejudice of its enemies." But the lectures must have had some of their intended impact, for local papers often reported that local Protestant preachers were addressing the issues Hecker had raised on the Sunday following his lecture in a city.[14]

For all the success of his lectures, Hecker was frustrated. For real success, local Catholics had to follow up his talk with missionary work among non-Catholics, but bishops and priests seemed uninterested and lay people had little sense of their missionary responsibilities. The Paulists did not have enough men to continue the missions, while those around the country who did appreciate what could be done were unorganized and unable to act. Yet never had the prospects for Catholic progress or the receptivity of those outside the church been more obvious, at least as Hecker saw it. When his sense of apostolic possibilities expanded beyond his resources, Hecker often became ill, depressed in spirit and weak in body, uncertain how to proceed, but determined to wait upon the guidance of the Holy Spirit.

Since launching the Paulists, Hecker had enjoyed good health, but in the spring of 1864 he complained of headaches. By April he was in bed with "an incipient congestion of the brain, with blistering, belching." In May he visited the mineral bath at Saratoga but experienced only slight relief, reporting to a friend in June that he had been ill and depressed for eight days. As so often happened in his life, Hecker's illness coincided with frustration in his work. "The obstacles in the way of furthering my plans are greater than at first they seemed" he wrote one of his converts, Mrs. Jane King. "New tests have shown that efforts, as things are, are hopeless. I wait and hope in God. This has been my attitude for some time past."[15]

With the few Paulists so heavily invested in the parish and the new seminary, Hecker had little to work with for missions and conversions. His lectures were successful, but they could reach no more than a limited audience. Depressed, Hecker searched his soul and external events for a way to respond. The answer was the press. During his youth in New York he had read the penny press produced by the Locofoco Democrats, and he had worked for a time in the offices of the Methodist publications, which by mid century had become the nation's largest and most successful religious publishing enterprise. Indeed, the Protestant community dealt creatively with its missionary tasks by establishing powerful ecumenical agencies to produce and distribute papers, magazines, books, bibles and tracts. In Europe, Catholics were turning to the press as an effective vehicle to build Catholic solidarity in the face of hostile governments and to counter anticlerical propaganda.

Catholic leaders in the United States had long recognized the crucial role played by the popular press.[16] The two best-known Catholic publications at the time were Brownson's *Quarterly Review* and McMaster's *Freeman's Journal*. Both were criticized by bishops for their independence, and despite the fact that his brother had assisted both, Hecker found them unsatisfactory. He had long felt that Brownson's combative style and emphasis on a historical apologetic provided an inadequate foundation for an evangelistic counterattack designed to persuade non-Catholic Americans that the church was the surest guarantee of American democracy. He felt McMaster's Democratic partisanship on public issues and contentiousness with the bishops limited his effectiveness in broadening the audience for Catholic literature within the church and winning a hearing without. Hecker concluded that he would have to meet the need for a vigorous Catholic press himself. He worked out a plan that involved launching a new periodical of broad appeal, establishing a publication society to produce and distribute inexpensive pamphlets and tracts, and mobilizing the Catholic middle class to support these endeavors.

By January 1865, with George's financial support, Hecker had completed plans for a monthly "eclectic magazine of general literature and science" to be called the *Catholic World.* John R.G. Hassard, twenty-eight years old and a former associate of George Ripley and Charles Dana at the New York *Tribune*, agreed to serve as managing editor, while Lawrence Kehoe handled the business side of the journal. The blessing of the archbishop was secured and the first number appeared in April. Early issues included essays from the *Dublin Review*, *The Month*, *Civiltà Cattolica*, *Der Katholik* and *Le Correspondent*, fiction, historical essays, poems and items of contemporary interest, along with a section of "miscellany," which included short notices, book reviews and news items, many on scientific subjects. Hecker translated Italian articles, Brownson some of the French, while the latter also wrote some literary notices. The first article in the first issue, interestingly, discussed "The Progress of the Church in the United States," as seen from France. The author traced the impressive increases in population, clergy and conversions, attributing it all to the "more active and regular habits of life, sustained morality, respect for the marriage tie and regard for domestic obligations" of Catholics. The author thought future prospects most promising, for Catholic growth was taking place amid the decay of Protestant intellectual life and taste; even more, Catholic energy contrasted with the "serious and rapid degeneracy of the Anglo-American race."[17]

In October Hecker dropped the word "eclectic" from the subtitle and, a few months later, original articles, all unsigned, began to appear. Hecker solicited works from abroad, including the fiction of English novelist Georgiana Fullerton, poems of Aubrey de Vere, and Newman's "Dream of Gerontius." Brownson and Hewit began writing regularly on theology, philosophy and contemporary church affairs. In the early stages of the journal's history Hecker gave it a great deal of attention, despite the fact that he was again depressed in the summer of 1865. Working in the paper's offices, he insisted on an early response to every submission and proved an excellent editor. Not only did he get well-known Catholics to contribute, he also located and helped along new talent such as poet George Miles and women writers like Louise Imogene Guiney, Mary Agnes Tincker and Agnes Repplier, whose first essay, on John Ruskin, appeared in the journal. He was constantly on the lookout for new ideas, new writers, new art work, while at the same time seeking to improve the appearance and format.

Throughout the early months Hecker attempted to avoid internal church controversy. Returning a story, he told a woman writer he could not print anything that featured an Irish character, for he had been loudly criticized for a pamphlet he had printed which featured a debate between a Yankee and an Irish Catholic: "I made up my mind after that never to bring an Irishman on the scene again, or let him speak as one."[18] When Walworth submitted a tract on temperance, Hecker rejected it as "too much for an infant organization." On the other hand, the journal was surprisingly open in its treatment of some important problems emerging from modern science. In one of the earliest issues an article from the French journal *Etudes* discussed evolution. It was "useless to mix up theology and science," the author wrote, for the Bible was "not intended to instruct us on the secrets of the natural order." As for the new biology, it was "advisable to show great tolerance toward sciences which are still in their infancy," and must be "free to make a false step from time to time." In later years the paper regularly examined scientific issues, often under the guidance of Walworth and Paulist George S. Searle.

A journal of this sort could not avoid all controversy and Hecker did not wish to do so, especially when anti-Catholic attacks reappeared after the war. Hecker asked Brownson to use the pages of the *Catholic World* to answer some charges against the church made in *Harper's Weekly*. Such controversial writing increased as the years went on. While muted and civil for the most part, the controversial style departed from Hecker's normal apologetic; arguments became more historical and a caustic, defensive tone crept in. As early as the first issue an item from the *Dublin Review* charged that "outside the church . . . there has never existed any Christian art at all." Triumphalism, castigation of the motives of opponents, and belittling of non-Catholics, none of which were common in Hecker's own writing and all of which he thought counterproductive, occasionally marred the pages of his magazine. One reason, of course, was that the paper was in fact addressed largely to Catholics. The *Catholic World* fit less into Hecker's plan of direct evangelization than into his effort to awaken priests and laity to more zealous and intelligent concern for their own religion. "Only think of it," he wrote Mrs. King. "Here we have four million Catholics in this country, more or less. Our colleges and convent schools sending out a stream of young men and women and what have they to read, that is readable, as Catholics? Scarcely anything. We must supply this need, if we wish to keep our faith in our young people and the generation to come."[19]

The missions, reviving and strengthening Catholic faith, and the Paulist parish, serving a rapidly growing neighborhood in the city, were intended to provide a base for the larger work of evangelization. Intended to win support from Catholics concerned largely with internal problems, both always tended to distract attention from or postpone indefinitely Hecker's larger evangelical project. Something similar happened with the *Catholic World* and Hecker's later publishing ventures; the need for episcopal backing, clerical support and lay purchases forced Hecker to emphasize that they were intended to provide "intellectual food" for Catholics, to "constitute and make the people Catholic" by giving them a more intelligent appreciation of their faith, and to supply forums for answering attacks and sustaining Catholic morale.

Circulation grew only slowly; though Hecker believed it should reach fifty thousand, it never came close. More modestly, he told Purcell they needed six thousand subscribers to break even, but by April 1866 he had only four thousand. The five dollars subscription fee, payable in advance in cash, was quite high for the day, but the journal also paid its contributors well and refused to pirate popular material from abroad. From time to time Hecker would complain of the lack of support, but he thought the success of the *Catholic World* depended in large part on the fate of his other projects launched at almost the same time.[20]

No sooner was the *Catholic World* underway than Hecker took steps to establish a Catholic publication society. "It will be similar to the American Tract Society," he told Bernard Smith, referring to a Protestant venture begun in 1825 which had distributed literally millions of small tracts through an army of agents throughout the country. These inexpensive paperbound pamphlets, usually of four pages, were designed to reach a mass audience. In Hecker's view Catholic tracts would give ordinary Catholics ammunition to defend themselves against attack while also enabling them to set Catholic truth before the non-Catholic mind. Success required good pamphlets, written by competent authorities, produced in large numbers, and available for free distribution to poor people. Thus there had to be considerable financial backing, and there had to be an organization capable of disseminating these materials across the country. This led to the second model, publication societies established under official auspices throughout Europe, including Rome itself. In 1856 Pius IX had established a publication society, placing it in Jesuit hands, for the purpose of countering the "spirit of the times," which "through pestilential books, pamphlets, and especially journals, filled with every pernicious error and evil doctrine, and written with most bitter and altogether diabolical fury, hatred of our holy religion is spread far and wide."[21]

John Hughes had planned a tract society while still a priest in Philadelphia in 1827, and the American hierarchy called for establishment of such a society in 1829, but nothing substantial happened. Catholic publishers existed, but their support was sporadic; it seemed difficult to sustain a market for Catholic books or papers. Hecker believed that, as in Europe, a successful publishing enterprise would require the united efforts of the entire church, a mobilization of resources led by the hierarchy and backed by well-to-do laity. He first approached Archbishop Martin John Spalding of Baltimore in January 1866. Spalding had broached a similar idea for a "Catholic institute" headed by the convert layman Levi Silliman Ives for the publication of "books and tracts" as early as 1854. He jumped at Hecker's idea, responding that he would cooperate and suggesting a form of organization in which all bishops would be honorary members, clergy and laity would be invited to become life members for fifty dollars or annual members for five dollars, and publication would be in New York, subject to the authority of the archbishop there. Hecker next won the backing of Archbishop McCloskey, who had recently succeeded Hughes.

A prospectus following Spalding's outline appeared in the April 1866 issue of the *Catholic World*. Donations came in rapidly. Spalding wrote the first tract and arranged for Hecker to present the plan to the Second Plenary Council of Baltimore, scheduled for later that year. Spalding also suggested that a priest be appointed in every diocese, perhaps in every city and town, with responsibility to "look after the interests of the Society," a suggestion which Hecker elaborated in writing to other bishops. He asked Purcell, for example, to appoint a priest to be the society's agent in Cincinnati and told him that the pamphlets would be available at a price well below cost; they should be sold at the same price everywhere, hopefully to priests who would distribute them free.[22]

The publication project was aimed at the instruction of Catholics, especially the poor. If Catholics did not undertake the "education of our people" with methods suited to "their capacity and convenience," others would. Protestant tracts "were flying all over the country like leaves before an autumn wind." But the publications would also aim at the supposedly numerous and growing class of religionless non-Catholics. Ostensibly designed to insulate Catholics against Protestant proselytization, an objective endorsed by the bishops, Hecker's publication society had an additional missionary and evangelical purpose which would prove harder to pursue.

All of this required wide support, and that in turn required a clearer sense among Catholics of their evangelical responsibilities. The mission of the church, Hecker reminded the Catholic public, was "to convert the world to God." In the wake of the war prejudice was declining and the church had a better chance than ever before to gain a fair hearing. Now it must show that its teachings rested on sound reason and make them better known. So, while "it is chiefly among Catholics themselves that we predict the greatest success for this association," they in turn would learn to give an account of their faith before the world and, with the help of inexpensive works of good theology, make a profound missionary impact. For the work to be a success, however, it needed money, organization, coextensive with the church itself, and priests to take charge in every diocese.[23]

By this time the Civil War had ended, leaving Hecker excited about the future. The war had "shoved ahead our religion one generation," he told Simpson in May 1865. It "opened the eyes of the sober and conservative men and women of the country to the real character" of Catholicism, so that the church now "stood in a different attitude before the people and in a most favorable light in contrast with Protestantism." In short, "the war has worked wonders for the faith" and the "work before Catholics" was "colossal," he told Mrs. Elizabeth Cullen. "The whole welfare of the country and religion depends on our actions. The country's destiny in ten years will be in the hands of the Catholic body."[24] Convinced that Catholic foundations had been laid, that the church now was fully organized and available to all who needed her ministry, Hecker was more determined than ever to point his fellow Catholics toward the work that lay ahead of them. They should work to bring about the unity of the nation with Catholicism, in the process fulfilling the deepest hopes and aspirations of all Americans. Never would he have a better opportunity to make his case than when he answered Spalding's invitation to address the whole United States hierarchy at the Second Plenary Council Meeting in Baltimore in 1866.

On October 16 Hecker stood before the bishops and religious superiors of the United States in the lovely Baltimore Cathedral. It was the climax of his public career to date. Less than a decade had passed since his return from Europe to found the Paulists. The parish was progressing steadily and a handful of talented young men were studying for the Paulist priesthood, holding out the prospect of resuming the missions and finally implementing the Paulist vocation to engage America and convert Americans. The *Catholic World* was well-begun, with an appreciative audience, and the nascent Catholic Publication Society enjoyed support from the highest ranks of the American church and stood a good chance of winning endorsement by the council. Hecker himself, after some bouts of illness and depression, was in good health and high spirits. He attended the council as head of a recognized American religious community. Appointed to the committee on publications and the press, he was working with apparent success to win support for his publishing ventures. Now he was to address the entire council, a singular honor.

The bishops had called the council to reaffirm the bonds of unity strained by the war. Many Protestant denominations had split apart over the slavery issue during the tumultuous years following the war with Mexico. The American bishops had maintained their solidarity, partly by avoiding the slavery question when they assembled in 1854. During the war they supported their respective governments, but with a strong dose of pragmatism, speaking in measured tones of the duty to obey properly constituted authorities but generally resisting any effort to escalate the war into a crusade for either slavery or freedom. There had been a few extreme voices on both sides. Bishop Martin of Natchitoches, Louisiana, issued a pastoral enthusiastically defending slavery. That document was sent to Rome for examination; Rome delayed until the course of the war was clear and then roundly reprimanded the Louisiana bishop. In Cincinnati the *Catholic Telegraph* strongly supported the Republicans; it was thought that this partisanship arose from the fact that the auxiliary bishop was the brother of Deshon's old friend, William Rosecrans, now a famous Civil War general. Most northern bishops deplored the Cincinnati position; Martin John Spalding of Louisville wrote strongly to Rome demanding action against the Cincinnati bishops, whom he charged with breaking the carefully constructed unity of the American episcopate. Spalding and others were less than happy with Hughes's European mission, especially as they disliked the Republicans and knew of Hughes's friendship with the Secretary of State.[25]

Still, the bishops kept in close touch with one another, generally avoided political involvement or unseemly enthusiasm for the war, and moved quickly once the war was over to reestablish themselves as a national body. Summoned by Spalding, who had succeeded Kenrick as Baltimore archbishop and titular head of the hierarchy, forty-six bishops and archbishops gathered in Baltimore in October. The opening ceremonies, with bishops parading through the streets of Baltimore before crowds estimated at forty thousand, provided an impressive demonstration of Catholic growth, progress and unity. Observing events with rising excitement, Hecker thought it "the grandest day for all concerned"; he was sure much would be done for the wants of the church at a time of "crisis in our country."[26]

When he rose to deliver his own address, the images of the opening ceremonies stirred Hecker's imagination. He said those ceremonies "appeared to me like a vision of the day of Pentecost, the day when the Holy Church first sprung unto life, Christ's Kingdom on earth began." Not resting on the scene, his "vision was cast forward to a day even more glorious," when the council would joyfully conclude its work. The two days "typify two epochs in the history of God's church: the beginning of God's kingdom on earth . . . and the day of the Church's triumph." It was on that triumph that he chose to speak, choosing for his text the words of Isaiah: "Arise, be enlightened, Jerusalem, for thy light is come, and the glory of the Lord is risen upon you."

The day of the church's glory remained unknown, Hecker admitted, but "if it be allowed to interpret the signs of the times, its harbingers have already appeared." Convinced that the Catholic Church was "the center at which all aspirations meet, the answer to all the wants of the human heart," Hecker saw everywhere signs of great opportunity for "the conversion of the entire world." The whole movement of history, technology, science, transportation, the decline of Protestantism, the encounter with non-Christian religion—one after another Hecker read events as signals of missionary possibility. Most enticing of all was the United States:

> Nowhere is there a promise of a brighter future for the Church than in our own country. Here, thanks to our American Constitution, the Church is free to do her divine work. Here, she finds a civilization in harmony with her divine teachings. Here, Christianity is promised a reception from an intelligent and free people, that will bring forth a development of unprecedented glory. For religion is never so beautiful as when in connection with knowledge and freedom.

God had done "wonders" for his church in the United States "within twenty, nay these last ten or fifteen years," Hecker wrote. Hecker issued the challenge: "Now, God calls upon us to do our part, for they will have the country who will do most for it." The episcopate must take the initiative and guide and direct the "great enterprise" of converting the nation. They should call upon the clergy to "advance the standard of the Cross in this land." The laity could help overcome error and, through "love for souls," bring "our erring brethren" to the fold of Christ so that there might be "One body and one spirit . . . one lord, one faith, one baptism." He sent forth the call to action that he had been trying to sound since returning from seminary:

> Let us, therefore, arise and open our eyes to the bright future that is before us! Let us labor with a lively faith, a firm hope, and a charity that knows no bounds, by every good work and good example, for the reign of God's kingdom on earth![27]

This was vintage Hecker, the enthusiastic portrait of the opportunities open to the church, the positive emphasis on the comprehensiveness and depth of Catholic Christianity, the conviction that other forms of Christianity were on the verge of collapse, and the call for evangelical action to win all people to the church and in the process contribute to fulfilling the promise of American life. All could be won to the church if all members of the church, bishops, clergy, religious, laity, would simply become strong, confident, active and apostolic. For all Hecker's love of freedom and respect for conscience, he was a triumphalistic Catholic, thoroughly convinced that the church was the agency for bringing about the Kingdom of God, sure as well that in the long run the nation, and ultimately the world, required one religion if there was to be one people.

But other things were evident as well in Hecker's response to the Civil War and in his apostolic activities. On the surface he was playing the role of mediator between the church and American society. Among Americans, there no doubt was a growing respect for the church and its conservative role in the community, especially because it had avoided divisions, concentrated on pastoral work and at least publicly did not encourage commentary on divisive issues like emancipation and unconditional surrender. The courageous nursing work of religious women, both near the battlefield and in urban areas struck with disease, transformed the image of sisters in the public mind. Similarly, concern for unity behind the war effort worked to moderate, even suppress, interreligious conflict, while the participation of Catholics in the military gave the lie to doubts of Catholic patriotism. These same factors, of course, undoubtedly worried Protestant leaders, accounting for the rapid reappearance of anti-Catholic polemics after the war. Furthermore, the participation of younger Catholics, including priests, left some with an enhanced spirit of national identity, embarrassment at the church's lack of courage in facing the slavery issue, and a desire to play a more active public role in their own community and in the nation. A similar development was evident among some lay Catholics, especially those few who enjoyed rising economic and social status.

On the other hand, Hecker's response to the Civil War indicated that he had something more in mind than improving the image of the church, something more even than winning individual conversions or promoting greater public spiritedness among Catholics. He sincerely wanted to make America Catholic. If he had little in common with the self-centered righteousness of churchmen like his friend Spalding, who told Rome that the war was to be understood as the triumph of a radical republicanism at odds with the church, neither did he share the desire to achieve the comfortable denominational status that informed the Americanism of more progressive

Catholics. Rather, he was convinced by the war that his basic vision was being realized, that the Providence of God was guiding the nation toward a time when it would recognize, collectively, the need for a single religion, a true religion, Catholicism.

"The future triumph of the church" was not as simple as winning converts or increasing Catholic population and prestige, nor was it a matter of bringing the church, as it was, to a dominant role in American society, though both were important. It was an eschatological vision of a future Catholic Christian commonwealth, when, converted, all Americans would acknowledge the presence of God in their own hearts, in the church, and in history. If non-Catholics needed to be converted to understand Catholic truth, so did Catholics, who had to become aware of their missionary responsibilities. It was not enough simply to draw people to the church, important as that was for those persons, even more than for the church; the goal was to make America a truly Christian nation.

Learning how to respond to God's will meant learning how to make Americans one people, and enabling that people to play its providential role in the world, as well as learning that one should go to church. Already, in his spiritual direction with converts, Hecker was claiming that all the works of the church, including her sacraments, were aids to the soul to achieve union with God, not ends in themselves. The converted soul responded to God's will in all of life, not simply in church. The future triumph of the church, then, would come not when enough people went to church or accepted the authority of the pope, but when enough people, through the church, came to such an intimate relationship with God the Holy Spirit, dwelling in the human heart, that they would unselfconsciously worship, praise and serve God in every area of their lives, spontaneously, without surrender of their human aspirations, without the loss of integrity, without a segmentation of life into church and world, religion and society, piety and politics. It was a radical vision, one that implicitly at least called Catholic and non-Catholic alike to conversion.

Unfortunately, while Hecker said all this, few heard. Instead, the message that came through was either sectarian, that this engaging, attractive man gave the church new ammunition for the battle with other churches and an increasingly pagan world, or denominational, that he offered a path over which people could travel to be successful Americans while remaining loyal Catholics. Both responses were less than Hecker wanted, or thought the Holy Spirit would provide. Behind the facade of energy, enthusiasm and activity of Hecker at this point of rising expectations were dreams that would eventually marginalize him in the process of doing him honor.

12

Steam Priest

At the Baltimore Council in 1866 Isaac Hecker was at the peak of his career. Less than a decade after returning from Rome he had taken two giant steps toward his goal of evangelizing America. First, he had established himself as the best-known and most-respected Catholic spokesman before the American public. The wisdom of the New York location was evident in the publicity his own projects and the Paulists' work received in the New York press. With McMaster damaged by his Civil War partisanship, Brownson marginalized by the suspension of his *Review*, and Hughes gone, Hecker was the most visible American Catholic in the public eye. Second, Hecker had taken an even more important step by establishing his reputation within the church. Here Hecker had been fortunate. When Hughes died in 1866, his place was filled by Hecker's mentor and friend, the mild John McCloskey. In Baltimore another friend, Martin John Spalding, who shared Hecker's concern for the intellectual vitality of the church, became archbishop in 1864. When he died he was succeeded by still another Hecker admirer, James Roosevelt Bayley, the convert who had offered the fathers a home during their troubles with Rome.

In the complex world of Catholic politics Hecker had avoided the twin dangers of excessive nationalism and Catholic chauvinism. When Hughes blasted the convert editors who wanted to "take the engineering of the American church into their hands" in the 1850s, Hecker, the guiding spirit of the convert group, escaped untouched. Hecker never publicly criticized Irish or German ethno-centrism, thus avoiding the wrath of their often testy clerical and lay leaders. Nor did he arouse non-Catholics; as convinced as Hughes or Brownson of the superiority of Catholic claims, he never became the focal point of nativist or anti-Catholic attacks. At the same time, his ideas and his work convinced intelligent Catholics that he was at least the equal of others in defending the church. In short, Hecker enjoyed the respect of Catholic leaders of all schools. If some thought him rather unrealistic, they kept their doubts to themselves. As a result, Hecker had a strong personal base within the church. It was an indication of his unique position that his vision of the "future triumph of the church" enchanted Catholics while, strangely, it seemed not to offend non-Catholics. So far, at least, Hecker's career had been a remarkable success.

A special correspondent for the New York *Tribune* at the Baltimore Council provided a good description of Hecker. Of all those attending the meeting, the reporter thought, Hecker was the individual "who exercises the greatest influence over the public at large, if not the clerical body."

> He is a tall, well-formed, vigorous, hearty-looking man, 47 years of age, with light hair and a long sandy beard; keen, but rather humorous eyes peering through spectacles; a resolute mouth, round, which plays at most times a kindly and infectious smile; prominent features, a quick, decided step, and a ringing earnest voice.

The great aim of his Paulists, the reporter continued, was "to work with all their might for the conversion of America." They believed that "the old religious orders, useful as they may have been for their day and generation, are unsuitable for the evangelization of the present age." Hecker travelled around the country, preaching with remarkable success; he never was without "some great project in hand," like beginning a magazine or tract society. "A thorough-going American, he is full of plans for the benefit of his own countrymen; and though a most devout and obedient son of the Church, he is not afraid of progress in the path of improvement and liberality in all things allowable." Hecker was "the very personification of industry" and there was "an electrical energy about him which sets everybody in motion with whom he comes in contact." The reporter recalled that when "busy, bustling" Bishop John England visited Rome, "slow ecclesiastics" there called him "the steam Bishop"; Hecker, he thought, "might very well be called 'the steam priest.' "

James Parton offered a similar sketch in the *Atlantic Monthly* in May of 1868. Describing the New York parish, the *Catholic World* and the tracts of the Catholic Publication Society, Parton told his readers the Catholics were "adopting, one after another, all our Protestant plans and expedients." Under the direction of the "excellent and gifted" Father Hecker, the

Paulists were "putting American machinery into the ancient ark, and getting ready to run her by steam." He then recounted the tale of Hecker's own life, concluding with an admiring portrait of a Catholic priest Parton clearly thought was also a model citizen. Hecker was delighted, for Parton presented him to the public precisely as he wished to appear:

> Here, for once, is a happy man—happy in his faith and in his work—*sure* that in spreading a broad knowledge of the true Catholic doctrine he is doing the best thing possible for his native land.[1]

The "steam priest" could be dreamy at times, and less sanguine observers might have wondered at his claims for the Catholic church, but at this stage of his life Hecker's hesitation was gone and he was indeed filled with plans and projects, not just for the Paulists but for the church. After all, evangelization was a work for the whole church—bishops, priests, religious and lay people. Missions, lectures, publications and tracts could only do so much; the inspiration to convert the nation had to be translated into effective organization to forward that goal. It was necessary to educate and organize Catholics to engage the problems of their age and nation while carrying on the engagement with every available means. By the time Hecker received the recognition of addressing the council in 1866, he had a program to do all this. It included expansion of the press, organized support for the Catholic Publication Society, parish societies and libraries, and the introduction of a national Catholic Congress that would bring all sectors of the church together to mobilize its resources for mission.

First and more pressing was the publication society. Appointed to a council committee on books and periodicals, Hecker presented his appeal. The need for a tract society was obvious, Hecker argued. As always, the benefits for Catholics came first. There were thousands of Catholics in prisons, hospitals, armies and otherwise beyond the reach of regular church services who needed "instructive and edifying reading material." People in out-of-the-way areas infrequently reached by priests would also benefit by their distribution. One priest in a western diocese had already agreed to purchase sixty thousand tracts during the first year. In addition, Catholic children needed Sunday school papers and parishes needed good libraries; the society would publish educational materials and low-cost books for these purposes. Equally important, short explanations of the faith and "solid books of controversy," inexpensive and easily available, could reach "a large class of non-Catholics" at a moment more "favorable to the propagation of our faith" than any before. There was an urgent need, therefore, to provide every possible means for the "instruction of the faithful" and "to spread Catholic doctrine among the American people."

Previous attempts had failed because of their "sectional character," Hecker believed. A new effort required the cooperation of the bishops and clergy, which, in turn, would insure the cooperation of the laity. Protestants had many societies of this kind; the American Tract Society in the last year had distributed 54,387,840 pages of publications, supported by gifts of $64,633 and receipts of $162,573. There were now five million Catholics in the United States, ready to do their duty and rise to the needs of the time. Already subscriptions of twenty thousand dollars had been received, but more was needed, perhaps as much as one hundred thousand to purchase steam presses and type and establish a bindery and a store. Once established, the society should be self-sustaining. It remained for the clergy and bishops to lend their support to make success sure. Collections should be taken in the principal churches, a general agent should be appointed in each diocese to supervise collection and distribution, and parish societies should be organized to distribute tracts. Parish committees were crucial, for bookstores were limited in number, very insecure economically, and demanded too great a profit. St. Paul's had already launched a model parish "Christian Doctrine Society," which donated three hundred dollars to the Society and raised an additional hundred to purchase tracts for local distribution.[2]

Hecker was overjoyed with the warm endorsement of the Catholic Publication Society in the pastoral letter issued at the end of the council. He immediately prepared a persuasive circular containing the council's endorsement and explaining the project. In April 1867 the *Catholic World* reported that a half million tracts had been distributed during the first year and the Society planned to open its own publishing house, with equipment to print at great speed and minimal cost. Once established, it would produce not only tracts but Sunday School books and a "cheap and attractive Sunday school paper." Hecker was busily at work lecturing, soliciting funds, enlisting support from bishops, and supervising the purchase of publishing equipment. Nevertheless, costs quickly outran receipts. Hecker told Bishop Spalding in May 1869 that he had borrowed forty thousand dollars on his own responsibility. Much of the money came from George, who eventually invested two hundred thousand dollars. Despite financial problems, the Catholic Publication Society expanded rapidly. In 1869 it added a very successful *Illustrated Catholic Family Almanac* to its list of publications. Five thousand copies were published the first year, twenty-five thousand the next and fifty thousand in 1871. Prayer books and books on church history, spirituality and apologetics multiplied, and texts for Catholic schools were added to the Society's list.

One item Hecker considered of immense importance, as it was with the Protestant houses, was a Sunday School paper. In March 1869 he invited Brownson's daughter, Sara, to help with the editorial work, but a short time later Josephine Hecker, George's wife, accepted editorial responsibility, assisted by Anna Carey of Boston. Both were new to such work, as were many of the writers. Hecker was an encouraging, affirming leader. He pleaded with his female writers at the *Catholic World* to write "funny" "heroic" stories. When one hesitated, Hecker told her: "You can't do it? It must be done! You are sick? It must be done! You are dead? Who cares for that? It must be done!" A variety of problems hampered production, but the first copy of *The Young Catholic* finally appeared in October 1870. Later, Hecker began writing a popular series of "Uncle Ned" letters, emphasizing love for church and country. The paper was an immediate success.[3]

By 1870 the Catholic Publication Society was doing almost all that Hecker had hoped. According to John Hassard, however, it enjoyed only limited support from the laity. The rich had their own libraries and rarely bought Catholic books, Hassard wrote. Colleges, seminaries and female academies graduated a thousand students a year, but they seemed to have little literary interest. Like all publishers, the CPS could make money only on school books and papers and prayer books, generally sold to poor people. The grandeur of the enterprise and the poverty of results was frustrating. Another *Catholic World* contributor, J. G. McGee, urged establishment of parish libraries where good reading could be available to the poor, who were "practically cut off . . . from good books." There were at least twenty-five hundred urban centers where parish libraries could be established in schools or church basements and half as many more, mainly in the west, where smaller libraries could serve. Hecker loved this idea; St. Paul's had a library, but few other parishes did. As Archbishop Spalding wrote in 1871, "Alas, our Catholics are not a reading people."[4]

The monthly review, tracts and books did not exhaust Hecker's ambitions for the Catholic press. Hecker also hoped to see a Catholic weekly or even daily newspaper started in New York. He was involved with several efforts to start such a paper between 1868 and 1871, but nothing came of them.[5]

Hecker had been optimistic that the Catholic people would cooperate in these ventures, and he refused to accept defeat. He was pleased with the quality of the *Catholic World* and of the materials published by the new society, and he was convinced both should be growing more rapidly. The reason they were not, he thought, was that clergy and laity did not have a clear understanding of the missionary character of the church and were not sufficiently organized for projects larger than those of the parish. The need, then, was to mobilize Catholic resources behind an evangelical vision of the future triumph of the church. The idea of organizing the church more comprehensively, with special attention to the educated middle class, had been circulating around New York for some time. Hecker may well have learned from earlier experience the need to work closely with the bishops and the dangers of independent action, but the program was more or less his, including the formation of "Catholic Clubs."[6] He believed that the splendid opportunities before the church in the wake of the Civil War called for organized action to improve intellectual and cultural standards, to awaken missionary enthusiasm and to guide it into constructive channels. This, in turn, required unity, cooperation and organization of the whole church in the United States. As he wrote Archbishop Spalding on the eve of the 1866 council:

> Allow me to express to you a thought that has occupied my mind for some time back. It is deplorable that the interest in our holy religion in this country has not enlisted in its behalf more exertion on the part of the laity. In Germany, France and Belgium a great deal has been done in this direction by the Congresses held in these countries. How many important matters laymen might consider, discuss, cooperate with the hierarchy in promoting: Architecture, Painting, Statuary, Music, Catholic Literature, books, magazines, tracts, newspaper publication, Sunday School books, societies, etc. Reformatories, and other charitable institutions. Men interested, intelligent, and filled with Catholic faith and spirit in these matters are scattered all over our land. Would it not be apropos to the plenary council to call them together in Baltimore at its close, or at the same time? It would certainly add eclat. The effect too on the pubic would be striking, and dispelling the idea that lay Catholics had nothing to do in their religion.[7]

Beginning in Germany in 1848 European Catholics had held a series of Catholic congresses, bringing together priests, laity and bishops to discuss matters of common interest and, it was hoped, develop a sense of solidarity that would enable the church to defend its interests and make its influence felt in society at large. In Germany the congresses were lay-led and concentrated on art, literature, the press and charity, while in Belgium the hierarchy took a stronger role. As Hecker saw it, these congresses were ideally suited to strengthen the church's independent basis for positive action at a time when the church was too often simply reacting to events. The *Catholic World* was excited by the congresses. There were thousands of laypeople competent to cooperate with the clergy "in every branch of religion, science, art, and charity. If they would add their minds to their money and put their own individual energies to the wheel, a power would at once be created in the church in the United States irresistible to its enemies and a certain guarantee of the glory and triumph of our holy faith." All over the country one met Catholics "in the forefront of life" but unacquainted with one another. What they and the church needed was "union, opportunity and mutual acquaintance and support," through which they "could exert enormous influence and inspire respect for the church and the faith." What could be more effective than a national congress?[8]

A European-wide congress was scheduled to be held at Malines in Belgium in the fall of 1867, and Hecker was named one of its vice-presidents. Assisted by a gift of three thousand dollars from parishioners and friends, he left on July 24 for Dublin and London. He planned to attend to business for the Catholic Publication Society, then attend the congress "in hope of one for our country." Hewit travelled with him on the early stages of the journey, assisting in securing English and Irish writers for the *Catholic World* and European agents for CPS publications. They visited Newman at Birmingham, Manning in London, and many prominent Irish and English Catholics, soliciting writers and subscriptions and filling themselves with news of the church abroad. Newman found Hecker "fluent, clever, just the man to propagate Catholic truth among the Yankees." In Paris in August Hecker visited with a number of his French acquaintances and paid a call on the famous lay leader, Charles de Montalembert. Moved by the story of Hecker's conversion, Montalembert was taken with the American, writing in his diary that he had "never met anyone who impressed me so much."[9]

In Malines, Hecker's "Report on the Present Religious Condition of the United States" sounded the familiar themes: the decline of Protestantism, widespread public immorality, the increasing power and influence of Catholicism. In his most triumphalist mood, Hecker, discussing divorce and "Free-Love-ism," charged that "Protestantism appears to have had a strange tendency to polygamy even from the first." One result of such Protestant failures was a decreasing birth rate, especially among those of "the best stock." Hecker presented a statistical table which dramatically illustrated the rising number of Catholics and declining numbers of Protestants. He then argued that Catholics, in addition to their startling numerical increase, were receiving greater respect for their beliefs, which steadily were coming to appear the only possible support for free institutions. Even "Know Nothingism" had proven a blessing by forcing the fair-minded to look hard at the Catholic church; such investigations brought a better understanding of the church and its positive relation to American institutions.

The political machinations of the Protestant clergy, evident among Know Nothings and radical abolitionists, stood in marked contrast to the moderation of the Catholic clergy, who devoted "their attention to spiritual duties" and abstained "from all party and sectional disputes." Many Americans now believed that if the United States had enjoyed the unity of the Catholic faith the terrible Civil War might have been avoided. To sustain the work of the past and prepare to meet the wants of the future, the church needed far more priests, publication societies, libraries, schools, protectories, orphanages and charitable institutions. To meet these needs and accept the opportunities before it, he told his listeners, the church in the United States urgently needs "a great Catholic Congress such as you gentlemen have conducted here in Europe."[10]

Hecker's words about American Catholic progress encouraged the liberal Catholic cause in Europe, a cause which was in retreat before the mounting pressures of conservative reaction. An unsigned article in the *Catholic World* made light of these conflicts. Noting press charges in Europe that the Congress had been biased towards the liberals, a charge based on the delegates' enthusiastic reception for Montalembert and other liberal Catholics, the writer argued that there had been full unity in support of "complete liberty for the Catholic Church from the tyranny both of governments and revolutions."[11]

Hecker paid little attention to the conflicts stirring the European church, however, for he was caught up in promoting his many projects, with a national congress now high on the agenda. Among the "important matters" he thought a congress should consider were united action "to get public support for our schools," to build support for "free Sunday Schools," especially outside the major cities, and to unify the work of parish St. Vincent de Paul Societies. As in Europe, much could be done through a Congress to improve Catholic music by establishing training schools, conservatories, contests and prizes for talent and originality. Disorder in the liturgy could be reduced by bringing artists, musicians and scholars into contact with one another. Priests and laity might be persuaded to support provision of libraries and reading rooms. There were Catholic millionaires willing to donate for a Catholic university; many agreed it was needed, but there was "no united, powerful body of Catholics to undertake it." The congress would provide all this, not directly, but by exposing Catholic leaders to a vision of the future and giving them a sense of what could be accomplished if they worked together. A congress would give unity and effectiveness to the laity; it would please the clergy, "who are anxious to keep up their own tone of respectability;" and at the same time, it would "influence by unanimity the great work of the conversion of the whole United States to Catholicity."[12]

Unfortunately, no Catholic congress was held until after Hecker's death, and then it was far more limited than he had outlined. There is no evidence of a response from the bishops to Hecker's proposals, and no sign that support came in from priests or lay people. The bishops may still have been concerned about lay independence, for the trustee controversy had agitated the church only a few decades before. Perhaps more important, American priests had subscribed in large numbers to petitions for greater canon law guarantees, unsuccessfully submitted these to the 1866 council and, finally, asked Rome to intervene to limit the bishops' arbitrary authority. Add to that the fact that many regarded the European congresses as political in purpose, and therefore sure to arouse the suspicion of non-Catholics, and the hierarchy's lack of interest in Hecker's proposals is understandable.

The period following the Civil War was the climax, in many ways, of Hecker's career. His long held views of American destiny and the responsibility of the American church were deepened and strengthened by the Civil War. With national pride broken by the tragedy of war and the inherent weaknesses of Protestantism exposed, the whole nation had become an "earnest seeker" face to face with fundamental questions of national meaning, unity, purpose and destiny. All that was needed was to broadcast the Catholic answer by proclaiming it in the press and witnessing to it in an alert, progressive, unified, organized Catholic community. The *Catholic World* and the Catholic Publication Society were the fruits of that vision.

Like all Hecker's projects, however, the ventures in the press were plagued by a fundamental ambivalence built into contemporary American Catholicism. He hoped the publication society and its auxiliary organization of agents would become zealous in persuading non-Catholics to look more closely at the claims of the church; he hoped that the *Catholic World* would bring a Catholic voice to public debates on religious, cultural and political questions, winning respect for the church and eventually conversions among that "special class" of educated Americans. But the tract society was presented to bishops and priests as a means of instructing Catholics; its most successful ventures, like the family almanac and the Sunday School paper, were mainly of service to Catholics themselves, and lay missioners did not appear. Conversion efforts were viewed with skepticism by most Catholics, but efforts to educate and instruct Catholics or defend Catholic teachings and interests were most welcome. Even the *Catholic World*, launched with such creativity, was soon bristling with hostility toward the rising tide of anti-Catholicism, picking up every gauntlet thrown down by the enemy. McMaster, many bishops, and even Brownson believed that what the church needed was writing that would sharpen the boundaries between Catholics and non-Catholics, clarify the superiority of Catholicism to all alternatives, and enhance the morale and solidarity of the Catholic minority. It was hard to resist that demand, especially if one wanted, or needed, to maintain a leading role within the church.

By 1870 it was clear that the hopes Hecker had invested in the publishing apostolate would be realized slowly, if at all. Placed against the political and literary press of the country, almost all of which was in Protestant hands, Catholic publishing counted for little. The Methodists produced two thousand volumes and one thousand tracts a year and millions of pages of Sunday school papers, and other denominations had smaller but still impressive publishing programs. *Harper's Weekly* had a circulation of one hundred thousand while only the *Pilot* of Boston, edited by John Boyle O'Reilly, had over ten thousand paying subscribers. Because of such modest support, Brownson's *Review* had died and only the *Catholic World* and four or five other magazines survived. Though it had the biggest subscription list, the *Catholic World* was barely able to meet expenses.[13] The *Catholic World* had become a journal of real quality; the Catholic Publication Society was producing useful and in some cases distinguished books and intelligent, if somewhat elementary, pamphlets. But the longed-for mechanism for distribution had not appeared and there were few enthusiastic agents to spread the materials throughout the country.

Nor were the bishops showing interest in mobilizing their clergy and laity for missionary enterprises or a Catholic congress. One clue to the problem could be found in the Second Plenary Council in Baltimore, which had served as a launching platform for Hecker's projects and had provided him with an occasion to set his vision before the leaders of the church. When the decrees of the council were published in 1868, Hecker tried to get Bishop Lynch of Charleston to comment on them for the *Catholic World*. When Lynch declined, Hecker wrote himself. He explained that the Council of Trent had ordered provincial councils of bishops to meet every three years, but many rulers had prohibited the practice in Europe. The American bishops were credited with reviving such councils in 1829. Since that time they had held seven provincial councils and, in 1866, their second plenary council, a national meeting bringing together bishops from all the provinces of the country. Ordinarily Rome did not approve of such national gatherings for, "enlightened by wisdom from above and rich with the experience of the ages," Rome "looks on a tendency to nationalism in the church as one of the greatest dangers that can arise, almost, indeed, as the forerunner of heresy." However, for the sake of uniformity of doctrine and discipline in a mission country, these councils were held "to look after the wants of the whole American church and do for it what a provincial council does for a province."

Hecker explained that the problem was to apply the general laws of the church to the United States where "the whole social fabric is different from that of Europe." Taking counsel among themselves, the bishops adapted the law to national conditions. Now, approved by Rome, the council's decrees were binding on American Catholics, and the young American church took its place among the best-organized of the Western world, well-prepared to face a new era, one filled with opportunities to bring about "the future triumph of the Church."

Yet the decrees of the council evidenced a rather different tone from that of Hecker's commentary, or his address at the council. They began by insisting on the need to enter the church in order to be saved, excepting only those who sincerely remained in "invincible ignorance" while fulfilling the commandments. The bishops attacked "indifferentism" and condemned Unitarianism for rejecting the divinity of Christ, universalism for denying eternal punishment, and pantheism and transcendentalism for destroying the personality of God. As for the vogue of spiritualism, they saw in it the presence of the devil, unsurprising, they thought, in a society in which so many remained unbaptized.

At other points in the decrees they mentioned the attacks on the church by the various sects, the unjust control of wayward Catholic youths by courts and Protestant agencies, and the dangers of the public schools where indifferentism reigned supreme and vicious companions endangered Catholic young people. Internally, the council reemphasized the need for episcopal control of church property, subordination of Religious to episcopal authority, and avoidance of the dangers of secret societies and other associations with non-Catholics.[14]

In short, the council evidenced the growth and improved organization of a church cautious in the face of external hostility, determined to unify and regularize the life of its own community and supply it with needed services, all under the almost exclusive authority of the bishops, avoiding even the degree of clerical and lay participation required by ordinary canon law procedures. The bishops showed little interest in the conversion of the erring brethren through any method other than the uncompromising assertion of Catholic truth.

Hecker recognized, in practice if not in theory, the importance of building Catholic strength by a vigorous defense of Catholic ideals and interests. Yet that defense, clearly aimed more at a Catholic than a non-Catholic audience, was never for Hecker simply a matter of enhancing Catholic self-confidence, but of supplying Catholics with the information and motivation to convert others and, equally important, to bear the public responsibilities which would necessarily be theirs in due time. His enthusiasm was as strong in 1871 as it had been eight years earlier:

> The mind of the American people was never so much turned to the consideration of the Catholic Church as it is at present. Since my visit to Baltimore, I have lectured extensively in the East and West. Everywhere an unusual attention of the most intelligent and educated classes of our American people is engaged on Catholic questions. Our numbers and consequently our power is compelling the attention of thoughtful minds. Fifteen years from the present date, at most twenty, the New England states will be under the control of Catholic votes. Some towns we are already in the majority as to souls. In others where I have enquired about the births, I have found that where we are only one ninth the population, half of the births are of Catholic parentage. The soil is rapidly transferred also into our hands. It is by the aid of the press we can give to our people that direction which will enable them to use aright the influence and power which they ought and will inherit.[15]

The bishops, bent upon maintaining the faith of the immigrants and achieving a secure place in American society, were preoccupied with spelling out the boundaries of the Catholic subculture and emphasizing the differences that existed between Catholics and other Americans. This emphasis on differences helped clarify Catholic identity, motivate dedication to organizing parishes and schools, and persuade Catholics to support their church. Like Hughes in the last generation, most bishops found it useful as well as necessary to slay the church's enemies, for it was the presence of enemies, far more than the promise of a Catholic future, which seemed best to raise morale and solidify the Catholic ranks. Catholic immigrants, anxious to preserve the faith and customs they had brought with them, find meaning in their poverty, and lay the groundwork of a better future for their children, seemed far more attracted to a religious rationale that stressed Catholic distinctiveness and treated those outside the church as energetically seeking their destruction rather than as earnest, if misguided, seekers.

Yet Hecker hardly noticed. Undiscouraged by the slowness of Catholic response to his many projects, undeterred by the pressure upon the Paulists to service their parish and evangelize among Catholics, he remained convinced that the church was moving forward and must assume responsibility for the religious future of the nation. He recognized and accepted the discipline of a more organized church. To take a small example, Archbishop Purcell, a long time supporter, complained in 1868 that Hecker and another Paulist, Father Young, disregarded the council's "prohibition of beards" for priests. A few months later Bishop William McCloskey of Louisville told Purcell that Hecker's beard had "gone by the board."[16] His loyalty and priestly demeanor won him great respect, but he had not yet succeeded in persuading the bishops to mobilize the Catholic body. He still discerned many signs that the Holy Spirit, who had inspired the vision of the church's future triumph inside him, was also signalling the confirmation of these messages in the larger church and the world beyond. The providential movement of history, guiding America to the forefront of human progress, must eventually bring the whole church to a realization of its enormous responsibility for the new era that was rapidly approaching.

In 1869 another signal came from Rome. The pope summoned the bishops and leaders of religious orders to Rome for an ecumenical council. Hecker was overjoyed, convinced that the Holy Spirit was intervening to guide God's church. He determined to be present and find in the church, gathered in council, the confirmation of his hopes and dreams.

Part Three: The Crisis of Modern Catholicism

13

Vatican I

Isaac Hecker's concern for the American church was rarely narrow, seldom provincial, never nationalistic in an exclusive sense. Indeed, his enthusiasm about its prospects arose precisely from his convictions regarding the providential role of the United States in universal history. After all, the same Holy Spirit shaping American history guided European and universal history as well, so there was much to be learned from the contemporary European church and much to be hoped for in the awakening of its energy, its new independence, and its strengthened organization.

So Hecker was extremely excited when Pope Pius IX announced that he was summoning an ecumenical council. A council, meeting at the call and under the leadership of the pope, was the most complete expression of the church. Guided by the Holy Spirit, informed by the living experience of churches in every part of the globe, representative of Catholics of varying convictions, the council would be the universal church in miniature, collectively deliberating on the course it should follow in responding to modern history. This could not fail to stir Hecker's imagination, schooled as he was in reflection on the signs of the times. If, as he believed, his life was ordered toward some profound divine purpose, and if that purpose was to be fulfilled within the church, the living presence of Christ in the world, then his own life and that of the church must converge around this magnificent historic event. He knew he had to be present.

In March 1869, however, Cardinal Barnabò told Hecker that he was not listed among the abbots and superiors general eligible to assist at the council. He immediately wrote Archbishop Spalding with the news, adding that a number of European Catholic leaders had "expressed a warm desire" that he be present. Hecker must have tried some other avenues, for a month later he wrote Spalding that he had now heard that bishops would not take theologians with them. A few days later Hecker learned that bishops who could not attend the council could have a "procurator" go in their place; friends promised to be on the lookout for such a bishop. Although Bishop Connolly wrote him that bishops could in fact take theologians, Hecker told Father Gabriel Chatard, rector of the North American College and a friend in Rome, that the only way he would be able to attend was as a procurator. Somehow, perhaps through Deshon, Hecker secured an invitation to serve as procurator for Bishop Rosecrans of Columbus. On October 20 he left on the steamship *Russia* in the company of several bishops. Brownson, with whom Hecker had recently clashed, had written to his son Frank that Hecker was "growing less radical and will no doubt return from Rome as conservative as I am."[1]

Brownson's remark reflected the increasingly bitter debates surrounding the council. Ultramontane Catholics anticipated and liberal Catholics feared that the Council would complete the conservative, centralizing movement of the nineteenth-century church. Many European Catholics seemed to think that the council should simply define the infallibility of the pope and endorse the condemnations of modern life summarized in the *Syllabus of Errors*. This prospect, together with the more disciplined organization of the church in many European countries, led some governments to fear that the council would divide the population, undermine liberal reforms and strengthen royalist political parties.

Among churchmen the issue that dominated preconciliar discussion was papal infallibility. While all agreed that the church was ultimately protected against error, there was less unanimity about whether that power of infallibility was located in the church as a whole; in the body of bishops united with the pope, as most American bishops and theologians believed; or in the pope himself. The latter view had spread rapidly in the nineteenth century, first among liberal Catholics anxious to secure the independence of the church from kings and aristocrats, later among conservatives anxious to strengthen the church's ability to reject religious error and resist liberal, anti-clerical governments.

Pius IX, shocked by his treatment at the hands of revolutionaries in 1848, had become increasingly conservative, regularly condemning modern liberties, affirming triumphalist, exclusive views of the church, and taking to himself the full power of ecclesiastical government. Ultramontane bishops saw themselves as delegates of the pope rather than as participants in a college of bishops; weaned from nationalist traditions, they had come to see their own jurisdiction as deriving from the universal jurisdiction over the whole church given by the Lord to Peter and, by extension, to the holder of the office of bishop of Rome. In 1854, after a show of consulting with the bishops, Pius IX declared on his own authority the doctrine of the Immaculate Conception, a step toward the infallibility he quite clearly believed was his own.[2]

Thus the council was an international event of considerable significance. As for Hecker, he, as always, wished to avoid divisive internal controversies. He had no doubt at all of the infallibility of the church; in July 1845 he had written in his diary:

> The doctrine of the infallibility of the Catholic Church is the only ground upon which there can possibly be any settledness and security in our faith. If the Church may err, as undoubtedly individuals do, then we have no surety of our faith, and consequently of our salvation.

On the other hand, Hecker shared with American bishops of his acquaintance a general feeling that the pope should exercise his teaching authority in concert with the bishops. Aware of the divisions which existed, he doubted the issue would be decided by the bishops, at least not without extended debate.

Before departing, Hecker preached a farewell sermon on the council; it reflected this moderation. Just as the Pharisees constantly tried to trap Jesus, he said, modern enemies tried to force the church to choose between faith and reason, grace and nature, liberty and authority. Hecker assured his parishioners that, rather than choose one side and lay herself open to attack from the other, the church would consistently "embrace and reconcile them all, giving to each one of them all that is justly due to it."[3] The council, however it acted, would be under the guidance of the Holy Spirit so it could be trusted to express the will of God.

Hecker was well-informed about European controversies and on his way to Rome he visited with leading churchmen, almost all moderates and liberals. He travelled with Bishop Connolly and Archbishop Peter Kenrick of St. Louis, both strong opponents of papal infallibility. In England Richard Simpson read Hecker sections of Cardinal Manning's strongly ultramontane pastoral letter on the council, in which Manning defined the pope's personal infallibility in terms which seemed to separate it from the broad infallibility of the church. Such views were countered by historical arguments of papal heresy, with which Simpson also made Hecker familiar. Extreme pro-infallibility arguments like Manning's were calling forth equally strong opposition. Hecker was told, for example, that the cardinal archbishop of Prague had said that neither he nor any of his suffragan bishops would dare publish the decree if it were defined as its supporters hoped it would be, for it would create "a storm of opposition" to the church. Sensitive now to how divisive the issue had become, Hecker warned Hewit back in New York to "keep by all means the question out of the columns of the *Catholic World*."[4]

Some leading anti-infallibility leaders thought the American hierarchy would play a key role at the council and that Hecker had impressive influence with them. In England Hecker called on John Henry Newman, who gave him a copy of an address to the German bishops of a number of French bishops opposed to infallibility; Hecker thought their argument "very logical," Newman reported. Newman also wrote a friend that the American bishops were "likely to play an independent part" and that the best way to reach them was through "Hecker and the Paulists." Simpson gave Hecker a letter of introduction to Lord Acton, who was in Rome lobbying against infallibility. After dining with Hecker and Archbishop Connolly in London, Simpson assured Acton that Hecker was a kindred spirit who thought it "impossible to believe against evidence and not only impossible but wicked to attempt it." Accordingly he was wholeheartedly opposed to "the Jesuit school whose triumph he thinks would be the greatest of calamities." Simpson assured his friend that the Paulist, who had "great influence with the episcopate in the United States and Canada," thought the American hierarchy would "go the right way and would stand to the last against any innovation." Simpson also advised Acton that the English and Irish bishops should be approached through the Americans, "who are perfectly misunderstood at Rome. They have the art of hiding uncompromising resistance under the show of the most hearty loyalty and so they are more listened to than we are."[5]

Hecker's apparent alliance with the anti-infallibility party extended as he proceeded to Rome. On November 22 the German historian Ignaz von Dollinger reported to Acton that "Father Hecker from New York" had spent a couple of hours with him the day before, telling him about conditions in America. Hecker assured Dollinger that the American bishops all opposed the proposed definition but were personally very devoted to the pope. Dollinger indicated that Hecker had a letter of introduction from Simpson and it would be advisable to cultivate his friendship: "He seemed deeply convinced that the triumph of ultramontanism would be a most pernicious thing for the church in America."[6]

A short time later Hecker arrived in Rome where he dined regularly with Connolly and saw McCloskey almost daily. He visited with George Ripley, who was writing for the *New York Tribune*, dined with Jane Sedgwick, the Massachusetts woman who had challenged him on slavery, and had a "wonderful interview" with Cardinal Barnabò. He found excellent rooms, entertained regularly, and made some new acquaintances, including Jesuit Henri Ramiere, leader of the Apostleship of Prayer, and Mrs. Pauline Craven, whose book had been published by his Catholic Publication Society. He sat for a bust (which George Hecker eventually paid for) by the artist George P.A. Healy. His first project was to persuade someone to write about the council for the *Catholic World*; he finally secured the services of Bishop Lynch on condition that only Hewit and Hecker know who wrote the unsigned articles. Hecker also visited the Vatican to get permission to say Mass. Cardinal Patrizzi, the official in charge, gave him a warm reception.[7]

Hecker was thrilled by an audience with the pope. When Hecker asked for his blessing that he might become a great apostle in his country, the pope placed his hands on Hecker's head and answered, "Yes, and may you obtain the grace of perseverance and sanctify your own soul." A few days later Hecker visited some catacombs, saying Mass at a temporary altar decorated with flowers and lighted candles. "The peace, the silence and the whole scene made the most solemn impression on everyone present," he reported. During the Mass he prayed that an association of women would arise to join the Paulists in the work of conversion. He preached at the end of Mass, referring to St. Agnes who had overcome physical persecution; today Catholics faced intellectual and social opposition, but, with just a few women and girls like St. Agnes, the Church could "conquer the nineteenth century."[8]

Hecker was impressed, even a bit overwhelmed, by the universality of the gathering of bishops and cardinals, but Rome again made him feel more American. On December 19 he wrote: "there is no place like home and, the further from the United States, the more intense this feeling." However friendly Barnabò, Patrizzi, and even the pope, Hecker once again, as in 1857, found Roman officials difficult to deal with. Worried, he was awaiting a decision whether procurators would be admitted to the council, but the issue was being dealt with in the Italian fashion: "First, never do today what you can do tomorrow. Second, avoid giving a decision by all means. Third, if a decision is inevitable, let it be a compromise."[9]

In his first weeks in Rome, Hecker worked actively in the anti-infallibility cause. An international committee of opposition was formed to contest the pro-infallibility prelates, led by Manning. Hecker appears to have served as a liaison between English- and German-speaking opponents, at one point delivering a list of American and Canadian bishops to be included among candidates for election to a key conciliar committee. However, Manning's list was elected, and only one-fourth of the prelates signed a petition against placing infallibility on the council's agenda. Spalding, a strong supporter of Hecker's projects at home and his sponsor in Rome, was elected to the major coordinating committee of the council. At first opposed to a definition on practical grounds, he shifted to support a compromise which would state the infallibility of the church and papal primacy, leaving the pope's infallible role implicit but unmentioned. This failed and Spalding eventually voted in favor of infallibility.

Hecker, while clearly associated with the minority, was not a theologian, nor was he convinced by the historical arguments of Acton and Dollinger. Rather, he was concerned about the autonomy and collegiality of the bishops, and disturbed by the tendency of the more extreme proponents to separate the pope's personal exercise of infallibility from the generally accepted infallibility of the church, expressed both in episcopal participation in the church's teaching office and reception of the teaching by the church at large. He was even more worried by the tendency of Manning and others to extend the scope of infallible authority over ideas at a far remove from dogma, like those contained in the *Syllabus.* Father James Corcoran, in Rome to assist in preparations for the council, spoke of a "mania" for definitions. Hecker found the same atmosphere, and it worried him.[10]

Back home, Bishop Rosecrans complained that Hecker was not keeping him informed, but Hecker had finally learned that procurators would not be allowed to participate in the council. He therefore settled for an appointment as theologian to Archbishop Spalding, a position that allowed him to see the council documents and participate in meetings of the American bishops. Earlier he had hoped that, given the divisions which existed, the question of papal infallibility might be dropped. Once in Rome he recognized that the question was certain to come before the council. Privately he was appalled by the tone of the debate going on outside the council halls. On checking sources quoted by both sides, he often found they were being misused. He still thought most of the Americans and perhaps one-fourth of the assembled bishops would vote against the declaration on practical grounds, but he was growing less certain and more cautious. "The rule of faith is in the authority of the church and to dispute that is not to be Catholic," he wrote George. "To go into any details on my position would not be prudent, and I fear do no practical good."[11]

Acton remained confident that Hecker was with the anti-infallibility party. He wrote Dollinger that the Americans could be counted on to oppose the doctrine and "Hecker is active in the same direction." Acton worried, however, about the depths of American conviction; a few days later he reported to Dollinger that many bishops were wavering "despite Hecker's assurances." On January 22 Acton reported Hecker's statement that the view of American Catholic bishops "is universally the sound one"; not more than five had signed the address urging the pope to bring the infallibility question before the council. So confident was Acton that he was considering bringing Hecker into communication with the English bishops. Further evidence of Hecker's involvement is found in a comment of Bishop Martin of Louisiana, a supporter of infallibility, as late as April 18: "I am ashamed of the French episcopate, ashamed also of our own, of which 25 or more let themselves be taken in tow by two factious Archbishops [Kenrick and Connolly] and the celebrated ex-Redemptorist, Father Hecker."[12]

Although Hecker told his sister-in-law he felt "a great repugnance to preach in Rome," he did so in January before two congregations, including several bishops. He used the Epiphany to sketch a vision of Christ and Christianity fulfilling human hopes and contributing to human happiness in this life. It was Hecker at his humanistic optimistic best, two sermons of joy aimed at American bishops who, amid the gloom and conflict of the council, might forget their national promise and the evangelical mission of the church. Still, the whole atmosphere of the council bothered him, as the central work of mission was ignored. Catholic life "everywhere" increasingly "appears to be drawn not directly from the primary truths of divine faith, but from the secondary," he told George. "Instead of placing the primary truths in a newer light, others are proposed to be added," which brought "decadence and deterioration" or at least made evangelism far more difficult.[13]

Hecker had long admired Archbishop Peter Kenrick of St. Louis, now one of the strongest and most consistent opponents of infallibility. In January Kenrick told Acton he had handed in a blank ballot in elections, as he felt the maneuvers of Vatican leadership had deprived the council of its freedom. In March he wrote that "the Council appears to have been convoked for the special purpose of defining the Papal infallibility and enacting the propositions of the Syllabus as general laws of the church," both purposes he regarded as "inexpedient and dangerous."[14]

Kenrick and several other American bishops persisted in their opposition. Hecker shared many of their concerns. He wondered whether an *ex cathedra* decision by the pope required the consent of the bishops before, during or after it was given in order to make it unerring. In any case, the principle of infallibility was reduced in terms of actual power, as the need for episcopal consent severely confined the authority of the pope. On the other hand, if an *ex cathedra* decision was made without reference to reception by the episcopate, "you have an *absolute* monarchy." He went further, arguing to himself that if the bishops could define infallibility, it must be because they "by divine right" are able to judge what is of faith. And if so, "how can the pope be declared to be alone unerring?" It was possible that the party favoring the definition, if they succeeded, would ignore these problems, push on to some other points "of their own," then adjourn, leaving "the great practical matters for some future meeting" or to the "wisdom and judgment and direction by the Holy See." Hecker's anxiety was evident in his comment: "my fears run in this direction."[15]

These remarks were made privately in a notebook he had been using since arriving in Rome. There Hecker reflected regularly on the significance of the events going on around him. He had hoped the council would provide some confirming signals from the Holy Spirit for his own vision of a missionary church responding to the signs of the times. Instead, the domination of conciliar proceedings by proponents of a policy of resistance to the modern world forced Hecker to face some real challenges to his optimistic vision of the church's triumph. In doing so he tried to locate what he saw within his providential understanding of history and to examine more concretely the differences between the United States and Europe, and between the American church and the church abroad.

One theme that emerged was the difference between the Italians and other Latin races, and those to the north, defined by Hecker as "Saxons." "The Italians are eminently a people conservative and stationary," Hecker wrote. "It is providential that the *depositum fidei* was given for safe keeping to such a nation." On the other hand, among "Western and Saxon people" there is a "predominance of the critical faculty." They "analyze everything" and "submit even divine truth to the mortar and pestle, pound it to powder, throw the strongest acid on it, subject it to the action of fire, then inspect the remains by the most powerful microscope!" The Italians, he feared, would have infallibility declared without looking at its consequences or even examining points of history. Others would "examine it critically in all its bearings and present perplexing doubts and difficulties." He worried that the two parties were dividing so dramatically that each would be tempted to push matters to the extreme. He hoped the council would proceed slowly, perhaps taking years to complete its work.[16]

Hecker's considerable uncertainty regarding the issue of infallibility convinced him that it would be unwise for the *Catholic World*, or the Paulists, or he himself, to become strongly identified with either party. The *Catholic World*, with Brownson and Hewit writing regularly, had always taken a strongly pro-papal position. For example, one article backed the North American College in Rome, where young Americans, who would have to "labor in a country like ours, filled with every form of religious error," could learn "true devotion to the Holy See, which is the surest test of orthodoxy." The magazine was evenhanded in its reports on preparations for the council but Hewit despite Hecker's warnings made clear his own sympathies with the ultramontane view. On November 15 he reported to Hecker plans for a sermon in which he would "establish the truths proposed by the *Syllabus* [*of Errors*]" in its condemnation of liberalism. As for the council, Hewit clearly came down on the pro-infallibility side. In an article on Cardinal Manning, Hewit argued that "the ultramontane doctrine has been almost universally held and taught in the Catholic Church in the United States." While trusting the free discussion of the council would bring forth the truth, Hewit was convinced that continued toleration of dissent on infallibility and denial of the need for submission to the holy see, was dangerous. The clergy and laity of the United States, he claimed, would welcome a pro-infallibility decision "with the greatest joy."[17]

When news of this article reached Hecker in Rome, he was very upset. He wrote Hewit in considerable irritation that the *Catholic World* should print no more articles on the subject. "I hope and pray what the *Catholic World* has already said may do no harm," Hecker wrote. "It is contrary to the almost unanimous opinion of the hierarchy of the United States." He told Hewit that of the forty-eight archbishops and bishops from the United States, not ten, perhaps not six, thought it opportune to define papal infallibility. As for Hecker himself, he asked only that "the Holy Ghost may inspire a definition which will embrace the whole truth of papal infallibility and authority, condemn every error on the subject and give peace to men of good will everywhere." Until then "public journals must keep silence on matters before the Council." No wonder Hewit wrote Brownson urging him to "keep up the fire" in favor of infallibility as he was now "somewhat restricted on these things."[18]

Hecker's caution was echoed in the series of articles Bishop Lynch wrote for the *Catholic World.* Lynch all but ignored the bitter controversies and instead offered glowing descriptions of the wisdom, piety, zeal and learning of the bishops. Only in the May article did Lynch refer to the question of papal infallibility. He simply took note of the political opposition that had been mobilized against the declaration, arguing that it constituted another attempt on the part of the church's enemies to convict Catholicism of opposition to progress, enlightenment and liberty. In fact, Lynch wrote, Americans should welcome the fact that the church stood forth as "a solid rock of truth providing an infallible guide to the truths of divine revelation and insuring that nothing contrary to those truths would be admitted as anything else than error."[19]

While Lynch put a happy face on the council and safe words in the *Catholic World*, Hecker remained preoccupied with the significance of the debates. He still hoped for patience and moderation; "nothing could be more regrettable than hasty decisions in matters pertaining to the faith and the great interests of the Church." Most important, the council presented a unique opportunity for the rulers of the church "to learn the condition of things elsewhere by the mouths of those who have actual experience."[20] The more the council moved away from this practical work, the more Hecker felt compelled to review his work in the United States. Whatever the outcome of the great infallibility debate, he would return to his labors with renewed conviction that his efforts were "directed to the best interests of the well being of men in the future and to the greatest glory of God." Europe, "unless destined to follow Africa and Asia," had no choice but to examine the path "pointed out by the light of our [American] experience religiously and politically." In March he wrote George: "My present experience in one way and another seems to have prepared me to lay a foundation for action that will suit centuries. . . . I shall return with the resolution to continue [my work] with more confidence, more zeal, more energy."

In February and March 1870 Hecker, emphasizing the providential role of America in Europe, expanded his vision of the Paulists. The problems infallibility was supposed to solve, the divisions and weakness of the church, had another solution, evident at home. "The work that divine providence has called us as a religious community to do in our own country, were its spirit extended throughout all Europe, it would be the focus and element of its regeneration," Hecker wrote in his journal. "For our country has a providential mission in view of Europe and our baptizing and efforts to Catholicize and sanctify it gives it an importance and a religious aspect of a most interesting and significant character. Were there a sufficient number of Paulists, I should like to see a community established in every center of Europe, in London, Paris, Vienna, Madrid, Berlin, Florence, Rome. They would be an element of reconciliation of the past and the future and of reconstruction."[21]

"Europe may find not only her political regeneration in the civilization on the other side of the Atlantic, but also the renewal of Catholicity," he wrote in his journal in January. "Europe needs men who, from a fresh view and contemplation of truth, and a deeper love springing there from, should consecrate themselves to the propagation of the faith and the good of humanity, men who are, from this higher view of truth, free from all parties, schools or prejudices, who are neither ultramontanes nor Gallicans, ontologists or psychologists, ancient regime or '89, conservative or radical."

In a letter to George, Hecker wrote that the people of Europe demanded a larger share in the political government of their countries and that this was a reasonable demand, and also inevitable, for either greater political power would be extended to the people or there would be revolution. At the same time, what religion required for its renewal was "withdrawal from its dependence on and support from the state" and reliance once more "on its true foundation, personal conviction and personal sacrifices." The only alternative to this type of renewal of religion was "apostasy." American civilization showed that both greater political participation and the resting of religion on personal conviction were practicable; indeed religion flourished on that basis. The conclusion was clear: the "complete regeneration of Europe . . . is to come from the light of the new civilization on the other side of the Atlantic, from the shores of the United States."

For Hecker this vision of the future was linked to his constant belief in the Holy Spirit. "My hope has been and is, that the divine element for the renewal of the world would spring from the light of the Holy Ghost and the Council; but the human element on and with which it can alone work, will be furnished by the civilization of our Republic." If the civilization of the United States was to play such an important part in the future of the world, the position of the Paulists, the first religious community based on American principles, was crucial and the work before them had a "character and extent not easy to exaggerate." If the community had a sufficient number of priests to send "to England, France, Germany and Italy" they could effect momentous change. He closed by asking his brother not to read this note to others.[22]

The ideas set forth in his personal notes and in his letters to his brother had become sufficiently clear at the end of January that Hecker was anxious to put them in print, but his way of doing so was round about. In late January he composed a long letter to Brownson, suggesting that he write an article for the *Catholic World* based upon these ideas. He sent a draft to Brownson through Father Hewit, urging Hewit to write the article himself if for any reason Brownson was unable to undertake it. In the covering letter he told Hewit that, in his opinion, the only road by which Europe could escape revolution and widespread apostasy was the one he pointed out in the article, namely through more democratic political participation and church efforts to convert the masses to a more personal and interior faith. Church officials who were in favor of dealing with royal courts were not apt to like his approach, he said, but all who sought the true interests of religion should support the developments he outlined.

Although Hecker asked Brownson to write the article because important leaders like Mermillod, Deschamps and Manning wanted to know all they could about the condition of religion in the United States, the draft he enclosed was entitled "The Present Condition of the Church and State in Europe—1870." In the letter Hecker told Brownson that Europe and the church were passing through what he called "a crisis of transition." The success of the experiment in "political self government" in the United States was exerting great influence on the people of Europe, who were now demanding a larger share in the direction of their own countries. This demand would have to be satisfied. England had already granted an enlarged suffrage, Napoleon III had made concessions to preserve his crown, and the other nations of Europe would have to follow suit. It was the "dictate of political wisdom" to prevent revolution by conceding political responsibility to the people, and it was the work of the church to prepare the people for the use of these concessions so they would advance the general well being of the community.

The extension of political liberty was not in any way hostile to the interests of religion; on the contrary, the more such responsibility was shared and rightly exercised, the greater the glory of God and the merit of the individual. "Intelligence and liberty are necessary to every act of virtue," Hecker argued. "If kings derive their right to govern through the people, why should not the people exercise their rights in proportion to their ability to govern themselves?" Such an extension would call forth "fresh energy of the church in instructing people to fulfill properly their new duties." This would give the church wider influence, excite gratitude for her services and show the necessity of religion, "for as countries become less dependent on the authority of kings in directing their destiny, the more the people have need of virtue and personal direction from on high. It is the office of religion to supply this."

Hecker went on to argue that it was "no less evident that a change in relations between the church and the state" was becoming inevitable in Europe. The union of the past was no longer possible. Concordats were already modifying historic relations, and these were appropriate as long as governments were in the hands of kings or a few individuals. The question, however, was no longer the opinion of the king but "public opinion, the vote of the people." Separation of church and state was "inevitable, whatever may be our opinion about its necessity, or desirableness." By this change the church would be called upon to "assume her independence and look for her chief support to the voluntary offerings of her faithful children." Clearly such a change would bring "no little difficulty and great sacrifices." It would require on the part of priests and bishops "a closer following of the apostolic example of living, a more earnest and direct manner of preaching the gospel, and a closer union of the priesthood and people." Separation could bring other benefits, including greater freedom for people to follow the authority of the church and keep the laws the church regarded as necessary for salvation. Most important, it would place religion "in the position of the early times of Christianity, in the conviction of each individual soul."

The American example was particularly important, for in the United States, where the independence of the church was recognized and complete, in the midst of many "opposing sects" the church was making conquests which "vie with the conquests of the church in the early ages of Christianity." Similarly, in Ireland and England, as oppressive laws were abolished, the church had a good chance to recover her position by the "zeal and voluntary offerings of the faithful." Hecker summarized his argument: "By opening the doors to a larger share of political power to the people, by accepting the changes of the relations of the church and state, two of the greatest evils which can befall the state and the church, revolution and apostasy, will be avoided, and a new career, and a brighter future will be opened up to the state and to religion."

Still, for all his commitment to American institutions, Hecker did not consider himself a liberal as the term was then understood. He reassured Hewit that he did not make the mistake of Europeans like Montalembert of treating separation as final, complete or desirable in an ultimate sense. He told Brownson that no one who had made a serious study of the subject could "pretend that separation of church and state can be maintained as the normal or more perfect condition of society." After all, "religious dogmas are the basis of political principles, whether we recognize the fact or not, and sooner or later an intelligent people will see they harmonize and seek a union." Europe, for Hecker, was now in an act of "temporary separation" from an inherited form of union. "This partial separation is necessary to a transition to a more perfect union."[23]

In additional notes appended to his copy of this article Hecker compared conditions in Europe in the nineteenth century with those in the sixteenth, when discoveries in printing and navigation had created a desire for change which led to division and heresy. In the nineteenth century, steam, railroads, electricity, education and the press were causing a new desire for reform in matters political and religious, and this time the church was in a better position to face them. Unfortunately, the Vatican Council was not in fact meeting these emergencies, and Hecker's confidence in the council was shaken, though his belief that the voice of the council was that of the Holy Spirit never wavered. He noted on April 21 that "some of the transactions of the Council" suggested that "instead of being a free and deliberative assembly of independent and thinking men . . . it is nothing more than a big caucus meeting." This remark may have been sparked by the depressing deterioration of public disputes, the so-called "pamphlet war." Two prelates he admired, Kenrick and Spalding, were now on opposite sides, and the former had publicly challenged the motives of the Baltimore archbishop. Hecker's loyalty to Spalding, who had championed his projects and was his sponsor at Rome, prevented him from siding publicly with the opposition, despite the fact that his theological doubts were far from resolved.[24]

By March Hecker's health predictably began to deteriorate; in April he decided to leave for home, though the council was entering its most important phase. On April 27, the day before infallibility came on the council floor, Hecker began a leisurely tour through northern Italy. He said Mass at the tomb of St. Francis. Shortly after he was in Genoa, noting that St. Catherine of Genoa was a model for the modern church, for she "knew how to reconcile fidelity to the interior direction of the Holy Ghost and perfect obedience to the divine external authority of the Church." His friends kept him informed of events in Rome. The freedom with which opponents of infallibility wrote him suggests that Hecker's private views were far more hostile to the declaration than he let on.

Bishop Connolly, for example, wrote in early May that there were probably a hundred negative votes left, despite considerable intimidation and pressure. Kenrick had gone to Naples to have a pamphlet printed questioning the ecumenicity of the council, but Sherwood Healy, an American seminarian, wrote in June that there was gloom in the ranks of the opponents. The final decision to take up infallibility was made before Kenrick got to speak, so he refused to attend sessions until he could vote *non placet*. According to Healy, Kenrick, who believed there was not one text of Scripture to support the doctrine, was regarded with suspicion; there was even talk of his losing his faith. Nevertheless, proponents were reluctant to pass the decree with a hundred bishops in opposition, so negotiations continued. The vicar general of Rome, who had laughed with Hecker in December, told the holy father he should be "crowned" with infallibility. In reply, Pius IX divided the bishops into three groups, the enlightened, the vacillating and the ignorant; he wished enlightenment for the ignorant, courage for the vacillating and perseverance for the enlightened.[25] Connolly, writing Hecker later from Halifax, assured him that he was perfectly "tranquil" about his actions in Rome. Now he was prepared to accept the decision of the council. "I have gone as far as I ever intend to go," he wrote. "Schism under any guise or form or for any reason whatever is indefensible in my mind; once the definition was made I bowed and now bow."[26]

Any doubts Hecker himself may have felt were not evident in a sermon preached at St. Paul's on his return from Rome. He noted the contrast between the weakness of the papacy only a few years before, when Garibaldi occupied Rome, and the attention excited by the council. That attention, even among hostile governments, could only benefit the church, as interest in religious questions would lead to examination of Catholic truth which "need only be known to gain the assent of sincere men." Always alert for silver linings, Hecker told Chatard that the widespread interest in infallibility demonstrated how "the question of the Catholic Church" was "latent in all Christians." Furthermore, he told the people of St. Paul's, the range of nationalities, experiences and talent in the body of bishops assembled in Rome, together with the intense theological and historical research occasioned by the questions before the council, were sparking an intellectual renaissance by which the church would not only "catch up" to "the active intellect of this age" but would "captivate it again and lead it into the certain paths of true progress." Finally, the apparent conflicts and divisions provided evidence of the humanity of the church. Far from disturbing the faithful, the arguments should excite the most intense interest, for the "trial of our faith will strengthen it and impart to the church fresh zeal and increased energy." The truth was safe, he was certain, because entrusted to men "who feel above all human considerations, and are ready to give up all things for honest and intelligent convictions. The Vatican Council has for its mission to call heroes in the Church and it has done it."[27]

Nor were Isaac Hecker's personal reservations clear in the pages of the *Catholic World*. The final report from Rome was written by Chatard, not Lynch, and presented with considerable candor the issues that had been at stake. The council's teaching was now the teaching of the church, Chatard wrote. The judgments of the pope were infallible; in setting them forth he lay down "the tenets of faith for the whole church." All were bound to obey him, "no power could be set up against him, the bishops depended on him, received their jurisdiction from him and could exercise it only at his word."[28] In August 1871 Hewit presented a long defense of papal infallibility, concluding that "there was never a time when the continuous and immediate exercise of the supreme teaching authority of the vicar of Christ was so necessary." Six months later, in an article entitled "Popular Objections to Papal Infallibility," an unsigned writer argued against Protestant criticism that "a divinely instituted authority that is infallible in faith and morals" was the only guarantee of liberty. It alone could tell the state "how far it may go and where it must stop." In its absence the door was open to "civil absolutism." Acton was upset by these articles, but claimed they did not represent Hecker's views; Hewit told Brownson they caused "surprise and chagrin" among "liberal" Catholics who had counted on the support of the *Catholic World*.[29]

Despite the *Catholic World*'s strong defense of the Council, Hecker clearly was disappointed, less with the decision itself than with the internal preoccupations of so many church leaders, their lack of confidence in the Holy Spirit, and the continuing tendency of ultramontanes to spread the cloak of dogma, and with it infallibility, over a widening body of ideas, traditions and opinions. He wrote Simpson, as the latter reported to Acton, that he was more upset with "adding things" to the body of belief than with infallibility itself; he would "like to make a clean sweep and have nothing binding but the Apostolic Creed." This was undoubtedly written at a moment of excitement, for by the time he returned from Rome Hecker had worked out an interpretation which allowed him to retain his optimism about the future while submitting to the definition. Distinguishing between the external forms of the church and its interior spirit, he argued that the council had completed the external forms, securing the faith and order of the church. It was now time to release the Spirit.

Protestantism had attacked the external authority of the church, which spent three centuries defending itself by developing its "doctrine of authority." While this helped preserve the church, it had the unfortunate effect of producing among the faithful a "habit of looking outside the soul for guidance, instead of to the Holy Ghost within." With the foundations of orthodoxy now secure, the church was in a position to seek a revival of its interior life. "The Holy Ghost will be shed more abundantly in consequence in the hearts of the faithful, and the whole face of the church will be revealed." The council definition thus made a return to emphasis on the interior life of the spirit possible, and that path would lead to the freedom and eventual triumph of the church.[30] Thus, slowly, Hecker incorporated the council into his providential vision of church history.

The Vatican Council thus turned out to be a major turning point in Hecker's career, but in ways different from those he had anticipated when he left for Rome. Then he had expected that the storm over infallibility would be diminished by the wisdom of the assembled council fathers, who would instead concentrate their attention on the need for greater apostolic exertion to defend the church and promote the faith at a time of dramatic transition in European history. It was this concern for positive action rather than negative condemnations which led him to associate with liberal Catholics, who for their part had shown affirmative interest in his ideas and his work since he first met Simpson while awaiting ordination in England in the 1850s. At Malines he had met with many progressive Catholics and was impressed with their positive attitude toward the age, as they were with his. Like so many of his new European friends, Hecker was less concerned with the truth of the string of condemnations summarized in the *Syllabus of Errors*, or with the doctrinal orthodoxy of a particular definition of infallibility, than with the attitudes which lay behind passionate calls for authoritative condemnations. He wanted such problems to be put aside, so that the church would turn its face outward toward the world and ahead toward the promised Kingdom of God.

Troubled by events in Rome, he thought long and hard about his own ideas, his vocation, and the prospects for the church. Far from reducing his commitment to an evangelization premised on freedom and church state separation, he reaffirmed it in fuller and wider terms than ever before, now anticipating that the reconciliation of Catholicism with the age could take place in Europe as well as in the United States. The role of the American church was as crucial as ever, but now he was convinced that the conversion of the world must go on in Europe and America simultaneously. The providential movement of history was leading to a correspondence between the goals of the church and the needs of society. The same demand for freedom stirred political revolutions and produced religious apostasy; the church therefore had to address the consciences of persons, awaken their hearts to the voice of the indwelling Holy Spirit, just as the state had to entrust the citizenry with responsibility and accept larger measures of democracy.

What held both church and state back from trusting the people was fear that authority would be undermined and institutions overthrown by the awakened passions of the masses. This fear could be overcome by realization that the same Holy Spirit who spoke in the human heart spoke also through the church, so that the extension of the faith through evangelical action aimed at individual conversion would extend as well the influence of the church, which in turn would render stable and fruitful the quest for liberty in civil society. This position stood in sharp contrast to that of the party that continued to oppose infallibility. At the same time, Hecker's position distanced him from those who welcomed the doctrine of infallibility as one more symbol to enhance Catholic self-confidence and to attack those outside the church. Infallibility, in short, provided an even firmer foundation for evangelical action; in fact, zeal for conversion of people and the world alone could validate and justify the completion of the church's "external authority."

Thus Hecker returned from Rome more determined than ever to pursue his life goal of evangelization, now not only in America, but Europe. He was more convinced than ever that the Paulists must turn their attention to conversions, that the American church must reach out to non-Catholics, and that he himself should assume a more international role in pointing toward the future and away from the conflicts of the past. Once again, however, the way to do all this was far less clear, and the resources and support were even less than they seemed in the past. Not surprisingly, then, Hecker was almost immediately beset by ill health, entering one of those recurrent periods of depression and illness that always came when his vision was clear but his practical alternatives uncertain. All this was taking place at a time, too, when his relations with his Paulist brothers were strained, and when his life-long friendship with Orestes Brownson reached the breaking point.

14

Hecker and Brownson

Hecker returned from the Vatican Council still convinced that the church needed an offensive strategy to comply with the demands of Providence. Hecker now had a unique interpretation of modern history he thought could reconcile contending parties and make infallibility the foundation for more positive engagement with contemporary culture. The basic elements of Hecker's vision, acceptance of personal and political liberty, reliance upon the indwelling Holy Spirit, and a sense of the providential role of Americans and the American church had shaped his Catholic life from the start. Recent experience had confirmed his earlier intuitions, but located the church, the Paulists, and his own vocation in a larger, more universal setting. The most significant change, however, was that his evangelizing zeal was now also directed inward, toward Catholics. If they could be persuaded of the providential opportunity that lay before their church, its triumph would be assured.

Perhaps the best evidence of the uniqueness of Hecker's ideas was his relationship with other converts. He and McMaster were no longer close. In the 1870s McMaster, alarmed by labor radicalism at home and anticlericalism abroad, became a passionate advocate of Roman authority and American Catholic separatism. Among the Paulists, Baker was gone, Deshon had never had much interest in the non-Catholic apostolate, and Hewit, though still concerned with conversions and with raising the cultural standards of Catholics, differed with Hecker over infallibility and evangelical strategy. Most important were his differences with his oldest Catholic friend, Orestes Brownson. Their break had begun years earlier, but reached the point now where Brownson was openly critical of Hecker and of the *Catholic World*, identifying both with a liberalism which, dangerous before the council, was all but tantamount to heresy thereafter. In the divergence of their paths lay hints of the disappointments that lay ahead for the Paulist leader.

When Hecker returned from Europe as a Redemptorist in 1851, he had formed a clear idea of his special vocation and the manner in which he should carry it out. As he wrote his two books in the 1850s, Brownson was moving in a different direction as became clear in the latter's criticism of *Aspirations of Nature*. The key to understanding this division was found in several articles Hecker wrote about Brownson years after the latter's death. Although the articles demonstrated that Hecker's memory had become shaky, they presented an accurate description of the issues that first drove the two friends apart. Their differences did not arise from the shifting tides of church politics, but from their sharply different understanding of Catholicism's role in the modern world.

In Hecker's opinion Brownson came to the church by "a philosophical road." His "passion for truth" made him "an uncomfortable man for a coward to know" and "a dangerous man to have for a friend if you were not ready when the time came to make the sacrifice of all things for the love of truth." Brownson found his way to Catholicism by a "new path," Hecker argued. The big issue, one which they pursued together, was to establish the reality of human consciousness itself; it was "the first and by all odds the greatest of the struggles of Brownson's life." With no solid ground for objective truth, the "earnest seekers" of the age would be left entirely on their own. Many people, non-Catholics and Catholics alike, in fact doubted the reality and the reliability of their inner experience of God. Brownson was persuaded ("and so am I," Hecker wrote) "that the greatest fault of men generally is that they deem the life of their souls, thoughts, judgements, and convictions, yearnings, aspirations and longings, to be too subject to illusion to be worthy of their attentive study and manly fidelity; that even multitudes of Catholics greatly undervalue the divine reality of their inner life, whether in the natural or supernatural order." The most common error was to interpret these realities, "the aspirations and unappeased desires of the soul toward the infinite, as the renderings of the sentimental imagination; they are mere projections into activity of feelings entirely subjective." If so, there was no real object for the mystical, or even the religious, impulse among human beings.

Hecker remembered trying to provide foundations for his own religious experience by reading the French and German philosophers Brownson recommended. He all but gave up after reading Hegel: "my wits were in such a tangle and snarl that there was no such thing as getting them straight again till I shook him off." But Brownson discovered in Pierre Leroux the idea of the necessary element of objectivity in every act of a subject. On this basis he established a "sound realism," which put him and Hecker on the way "to truth, right conduct, peace of mind, and finally to boundless, triumphant and permanent joy." "What consciousness or apprehension attests must be certain," Hecker wrote. "The immediate source of human life is the intercourse between the human intelligence and reality. Reality conditions life. Life is real. Life cannot be otherwise than real." Any other view of life opened the door to "imbecility." Perhaps this seemed commonplace to many, Hecker admitted, but it brought joy to them at the time. It enabled them to preserve the transcendentalist faith in human subjectivity, render it intelligible, and ground a reasonable search for religious truths confirming and corresponding with interior religious experience. Both men "were led to the Church more by having sound views on this question than by any other means."[1]

So far the two had traveled together. The tragedy, as Hecker saw it, was that Brownson, once in the church, turned away from the very theory that led him there. As Brownson described the process in his book *The Convert* he found that Bishop Fitzpatrick, to whom he went for instruction, either did not understand or rejected Leroux's philosophical doctrine of communion. So clear was this that Brownson neglected even to discuss it with the bishop, adopting instead the more standard historical and logical apologetic current in Catholic circles. Brownson by then found such Catholic ideas convincing, but long afterward admitted they would not have led him to the church, not because they were unsound or untrue, but because they would not have sparked the needed subjective response. Worst of all, Brownson's shift of ground stunned his many admirers who had been closely following his development and might have been prepared to respond positively to his explanation of his conversion. Instead, when they first heard him speak as a Catholic, they could not, in Brownson's own words, "perceive any logical or intellectual connection between my last utterances before entering the church and my first utterances afterwards." They thus incorrectly looked upon his conversion as "a sudden caprice or rash act taken from a momentary impulse, or a fit of intellectual despair, for which I had no good reason to offer."

Hecker always believed Brownson was wrong to yield to the bishop's influence. His previous views, while fully orthodox, were also coincident with the best American thought. From his own experience "he was providentially fitted to open a movement toward the true religion among the leading minds in America." Instead, the bishop forced him to enter "the traditional line of controversy against Protestantism at a time when the best minds of New England had long given up belief in the distinctive errors of that heresy." Brownson himself acknowledged that his arguments were better suited "to strengthen the convictions of those in the church than to attract others to her fold," and indeed these were precisely their purpose, as leaders like Fitzpatrick were far more concerned with preserving the faith than with winning converts.

Hecker, who wrote few harsh words about anyone, nourished something of a grudge against the Boston bishop. He recalled that when he visited Fitzpatrick in 1844, the bishop, suspicious of the young man's background, questioned him to determine if he held any erroneous views on private property. Hecker had already settled these matters on "Catholic principles," but he told the story to "illustrate Bishop Fitzpatrick's character." When he met Fitzpatrick in later years, the bishop criticized him "in a bantering manner but, I thought, half in earnest too." As Hecker saw it, Fitzpatrick had "probably never experienced even the most shadowy doubts concerning the truths of religion." His Catholic ties were taken-for-granted, "like an heirloom of an ancient family, or like the old homestead, not simply valued for its intrinsic qualities, but also [made] sacred by ties of blood and family." Boston Catholics "had the opportunities of becoming the representative Catholics of America," but were instead given Fitzpatrick's peculiar "ultra conservative stamp." With uncharacteristic bitterness, reflecting the disappointments of his long career, Hecker recalled the Boston bishop as "a type of mind common then and not uncommon now—the embodiment of a purpose to refute error, and to refute it by condemnation direct, authoritative even if argumentative." He became "the hierarchical exponent of all that was traditional and commonplace in Catholic public life."[2]

Returning to Brownson, Hecker noted that, at the time of their conversion, people were interested in "the great problems of human destiny, problems which cannot be avoided, without accepting the mission of Christ and availing yourself of the aid of the Catholic Church." That indeed was the result of Brownson's long struggle. Protestantism, by making "individual consciousness" rather than "the concrete and objective revelation of God" the criterion of truth, left truth to the subjective disposition of individuals, or "his race traits or the tendencies of the age in which he lived." Hecker, who had no religious affiliation, investigated all the Protestant churches and found the Episcopalians ready to tolerate anything, the Calvinists filled with pessimism, and the Methodists dependent on a purely emotional conversion "with the notorious exclusion of the intellect." Brownson provided him the philosophical preparation for Catholic truth, and what Brownson did for Hecker, he might have done for others. He should have been called after his conversion to explain the two "providential theses of his life," the objective reality of the facts of human consciousness and the fact that human destiny could not be solved in accord with reason without Catholic teachings and direction.

> If he had made it his life task to refute the errors which he had successively embraced and abandoned, if he had taken up and developed the truths which had led himself into the fold of the Catholic Church, how many might have followed him! I do not mean to say that he did not do much good. Such a man would do good wherever placed. But if he did the good which Bishop John pointed out to him, he left undone, or nearly undone, the work which his providential mission called him to do, and which is still left to be done.[3]

Instead, Hecker himself took up the work, at first with the older man's warm support, but Brownson's ill-timed critical review of *Aspirations of Nature* dealt a fatal blow to their intimacy. He would never enjoy Hecker's full confidence again. It was not the substance of his argument that bothered Hecker, for Brownson had warned him several times about his tendency to "mysticism" and his overemphasis on the ideal of communion. But now he worried that Brownson's motives were not entirely disinterested. Clarence Walworth believed Brownson had "cast off his former ideas of the mission of America" in order to gain a more secure place among Catholics. To be sure, Brownson had his problems during the 1850s. He was charged with disloyalty for criticism of the Irish, which their leaders thought played into Know Nothing hands. Bishop Hughes never liked Brownson's independence. The two men clashed openly, and thereafter Brownson took pains to allay any suspicion of Americanism.

Yet Brownson was never a lackey for the hierarchy. He had little sympathy with the desire of the pope to regain control of the papal states. Secretly reported to the Vatican by unknown bishops, Brownson registered his submission, but he was furious. His disgust deepened during the Civil War when Rome's neutrality, the silence of most American bishops and the copperhead attitudes of many Catholics seemed tantamount to support for the Confederacy. "The great body of our Bishops and clergy have grieved and disgusted me and the mass of Catholics have justified the charge of disloyalty brought by Know Nothings against them," he wrote a friend. "The Holy Father ordered them to take no part on either side, which they appear to have understood to mean, take the side of the rebels."[4]

In the 1860s Brownson had a resurgence of liberalism. In 1861 Hecker told him Richard Simpson hoped he would contribute to his new review, and it was an indication of how aroused Brownson was that he wrote cordially to the pugnacious English editor. Brownson's conservative apologetic had little in common with Simpson's, nor did his pessimistic view of human nature square with Simpson's controversial ideas about the Fall. But now, irritated by the "imbecile tyrannical temporal government of the Pope," he was ready to fight the "obstinant obscurantis." "Unless we can have manliness and freedom within the church, it is idle to hope for any considerable extension without," he wrote. Not only must church and state be separated, but the "old machine that has driven nearly the whole world into schism, heresy and infidelity must be broken up."[5] But, burned by his problems with church authorities, Brownson kept these views private. He announced in 1863 that his review would no longer discuss Catholic affairs. Instead, he turned his attention to political questions, leading to publication of his last major work, *The American Republic*. In 1865 he suspended publication of the *Review*. Assisted by an annuity raised by Hecker and other friends, he wrote regularly for the *Tablet* and for Hecker's new *Catholic World*. By now he was a political conservative and after his short flirtation with liberalism, he once again made the traditional Catholic apologetic his own. In 1867 he told his son that his views and Hecker's did not harmonize, but they were able "to jog on together without much mutual snarling and growling." Brownson visited the Paulist house occasionally, where he would see his confessor, Father Hewit, and then engage in heated discussions with Hewit, Hecker and other Paulists; at times the awe-struck seminarians feared they would come to blows.[6]

It was not easy for the strong-minded Brownson to accept the editorial direction of others at the *Catholic World*. In January 1868, for example, he told Hecker he had "worried much" and even developed a "fit of gout" over an article on original sin he had submitted. It was a subject on which he and Hecker had never agreed, Brownson wrote, while Hewit's position on the question, in Brownson's view, "denied original sin entirely." If his article were rejected "on account of its doctrine" he would have to give up "writing on the philosophy of religion for the C.W., which I should be sorry to do." Hecker and Hewit did reject the article and Brownson must have been upset when they met, for he wrote a few days later, "I did not mean to convey the impression that you had grieved or pained me." He agreed that an editor always should be "an autocrat," but, having been his own editor for thirty years, he found "difficulty in making my mind work freely, if while I am writing, I am in doubt whether what I write will be accepted or not." A short time later Brownson told his son that he had had a "fight" with Hecker that grew out of Hecker's rejecting one article and "mutilating another" because his views on original sin conflicted with those of Father Hewit. He concluded with satisfaction that "Father Hecker was sick for a week from the scolding I gave him." At the same time, however, he was writing Hecker, in response to what must have been an appeasing letter from his friend, that the gout was bothering him but he did not "murmur against providence." His illness had not made him "feel more kindly to you, but your letter did, while it pained me to hear that you had been suffering." A few weeks later Brownson told his son "Hecker and I have made up friends. He can't do without me."[7]

Yet, Brownson was unhappy. In March he told Hecker that he was afraid to propose articles; his mind was active, but "not in your direction." He admitted he was growing more conservative. "The truth is I am beginning to be once more an *oscuranti* and can hardly be said to belong to the Catholic Movement," he wrote. He had "become a convert" to the "Syllabus of Errors" and, to make matters worse, he had begun "to despair of the American experiment." Hecker, as always, was unwilling to accept all this as permanent. "You cannot be very far gone into oscurantism [sic] or you would not be willing to confess the fact," he responded. As for the problems of the Reconstruction and resurgent anti-Catholicism, which so upset his friend, Hecker was characteristically positive. "God is calling on our nation to exert its national conscience and it will do it," he wrote. "This is his way of educating us *as a people*." Their differences over "the fall" and "the best policy" were not so great that they could not work together. Brownson would have none of it, accusing Hecker of refusing to allow him "to war on the modern spirit, or spirit of the age, which I hold is the spirit of Satan, false and mischievous in its essence and not merely an abuse or misapplication of a truly Christian tendency."[8]

A few months later, writing in another Catholic paper, Brownson attempted to defend Hecker against an attack levelled at the Paulist as a result of a Hecker lecture entitled "The Church and the Republic," but he could not help including some criticism. Hecker had argued, as always, that Catholic doctrines were the only basis on which human beings could be regarded as capable of self-government, an argument Brownson did not find very useful. For one thing, it seemed to suggest that, if church teaching should prove incompatible with democracy, it was the church which should give way. Brownson preferred to emphasize the superiority of the church to all political systems. Hecker argued that Catholicism maintained man's reason and goodness against the doctrine of total depravity, but "democracy assumed not only the essential goodness of human nature since the fall, but the probity and rectitude of all [human] instincts, passions, propensities and affections, which no Catholic can concede." After all, man had fallen, Brownson reminded his readers, so he was inclined to sin and "left to himself he runs into all manner of iniquities." People did not have the "rectitude and purity of nature" necessary to make them capable of self-government "as democracy supposes and as Father Hecker seems to concede." Neither democracy nor any other form of government, "by nature alone," is capable of "answering the end of good government" without the infusion of grace and "the inculcation of those principles which the church and she alone . . . asserts and maintains." Hecker quite naturally wondered how such remarks defended him against criticism. When he met John Sadlier, publisher of the *Tablet*, in which Brownson's article had appeared, he complained. Sadlier reported the conversation to Brownson, remarking of Hecker: "Unless you see everything 'through his spectacles' he is not pleased."

Sadlier thought Brownson gave Hecker too much notice, and the writer agreed that he did "not wish to bring Father Hecker prominently before the public." His own views differed from Hecker's, Brownson continued, and "every day I find myself less and less in sympathy with his movements." In Brownson's view, "Father Hecker is not sound in his theology; he inclines too much to rationalism and socialism and is too disposed to adopt and appropriate the machinery of the sects," an apparent reference to the Catholic Publication Society. A few days later he wrote his son Henry that he was diverging more and more from Hecker's "liberalism" and "virtual rationalism." He doubted they would be able to get on together much longer.[9]

In early August 1868 Brownson went after Hewit, again over the problem of the Fall. Brownson distinguished two schools of thought regarding original sin: one which saw human nature losing something positive; the other arguing that human beings retained their original integrity, and lost only additional graces and benefits available in the state of creation. Brownson pointed out that the schools led to different attitudes toward politics, the latter favorable to democracy and self-government, the former understanding the need for grace, and therefore the church, to fit people for civilization and society. The "facts of human nature" demonstrated to Brownson's satisfaction that no form of government could work well founded on nature alone. The church was the medium for "those supernatural graces and virtues which elevate man above nature and supply through religion to democracy the support . . . without which it cannot subsist and prove a good government." This point was of particular importance to "those Catholics who forget that our work is to Catholicize America, not to Americanize Christianity." Brownson also attacked those who adopted a conciliating tone in controversy, "smoothing down those features that are most offensive to non-Catholics. They do not mean to be untruthful, disingenuous, or to disguise the real doctrine of the church," Brownson conceded, "but simply to adopt the course most likely to draw those without within the fold." Not only did Brownson doubt that the approach would work, but he now agreed with Hughes's old argument that it would damage the church. Those within the church needed to be cared for, that should be the first priority, he argued. Conciliationists should consider the effect arguments that reduced the differences between Catholics and non-Catholics would have on "partially instructed and weak minded Catholics who find themselves isolated among non-Catholics."

The heart of the matter was the doctrine of exclusive salvation. It sounded liberal to say that there was no reason to doubt the salvation of "rigid old New England Puritans," Brownson wrote, but "what is the use of saying so when everybody knows that it is a Catholic dogma that without the Catholic faith it is impossible to be saved?" All false systems contained some truth, to be sure, but to avail for salvation those truths must be held in unity with the Catholic church. If this were not true, what was the aim of trying to bring some in or keep others from going out? Difficult as it was, "uncompromising Catholicity is simply Catholicity." Believing, as he did, that human nature was left "disordered" by original sin, that social problems could only be solved by "conversion to God and real submission to his laws," and that salvation could only be achieved in communion with the church, Brownson had become an uncompromising ultramontane. Such triumphalism, combined with his concern for the maintenance of the Catholic subculture, rather than the missionary extension of Catholic influence, was bound to complete his separation from his oldest and dearest Catholic friend.[10]

After the articles attacking Hewit appeared, Brownson reported to his family that he and Hecker had again quarreled, but at Hecker's request he continued writing for the *Catholic World*. A few months later he complained that he was getting the higher rate of pay but fewer pages to write, while Hecker, his "dearest friend" had "so many women at work for him" on the *Catholic World* "that a gentleman stands little chance." This last remark anticipated problems with an article he had written on women's suffrage. While Hecker was "seemingly less conservative" than himself, he could not believe that the *Catholic World* would not oppose the suffrage movement, which Brownson called "the most dangerous [question] that has ever been attempted in our country" and, a week later, "the ugliest and most dangerous question that possibly could be raised." Hecker did not rise to the bait but accepted the article, all the while working hard to encourage women writers and accepting articles on the subject more restrained than Brownson's almost hysterical attacks. Brownson remained fearful that all his articles would "jar on the mild and conciliatory tone" of the *Catholic World*, which they did.[11]

The two old friends regularly patched up their differences, though Brownson kept hoping that Hecker would come to his Catholic senses. In 1869, for example, the Paulist befriended a well-known French preacher,

Père Hyacinthe, who had a particularly strong commitment to better relations with Protestants and was in serious trouble with church authorities. In November he announced he was leaving the priesthood. Hecker wrote sadly of the incident to friends, but Brownson saw some affinity between Hecker's optimism and the French priest's idea that Catholics and Protestants "all belong to the same brotherhood of faith." His defection had "frightened" Hecker, Brownson thought, and his friend was now becoming more conservative, "almost if not quite a papist," as he told his son.[12]

Brownson publicly described Hecker as "an earnest, zealous Catholic priest, loyal to his church" but belonging to "a different school of theology." As neither school had been condemned, their differences did not "break the bond of charity" between them. "We are probably more conservative than he, and have less confidence in the value of copying the machinery in use by non-Catholics," Brownson wrote. "We are old fashioned Medieval Catholics in our habits and convictions. Father Hecker is more of a nineteenth century man than we are, and believes more in the intelligence and good faith of the people than we do." Tolerate Hecker he might, but he could not approve. He had "never been among those who looked for a speedy conversion of the American people to the Church," in part because the church demanded obedience and Americans regarded all authority as despotism. Wives were insulted by the wedding service injunction to obey their husbands; children grew up without any sense of the obligation to their parents. "Family government, family discipline has fallen into disrepute," while government was regarded simply as "a machine constituted for each one of us to use for his own private advantage." As a result, all the "habits, dispositions and principles" which provided the natural basis for missionary work were missing. Despairing of direct appeals to non-Catholics, Brownson tried to serve the Catholic cause by defending Catholics against their enemies and laboring to make them better Catholics and citizens. The best way to promote the conversion of the country, it seemed, was to "increase the moral and religious weight of the Catholic population."

On this score he was more hopeful. Despite their revivals, organizations and money, Protestant churches were losing their hold over their people. The result was an "intense hatred, mingled with fear" obvious in the Protestant press. The progress of Catholics religiously and socially, the obvious fact that despite their poverty they "introduce and sustain a higher order of civilization, greater refinement of manners, and purity of morals," was leading to a substantial number of conversions among the "more educated and enlightened class of non-Catholics," Brownson stated. Operating freely, following its own laws, the church in the end would draw the whole population into her fold.[13]

That this did not mean Brownson agreed with Hecker was evident in an exchange resulting from a long review of Henry Ward Beecher's *Norwood*, published in the *Catholic World* in December 1869. In it Brownson praised the Puritan founders of New England. For all its faults, Brownson contended, the sturdy Puritanism of the past was far preferable to Beecher's liberal religion. In response to a Baptist's comment on this review, Brownson sharply distinguished the writer of the *Catholic World* article (himself) from the magazine generally, charging that the *Catholic World* often forgot "that there is no salvation outside the Church." The *Catholic World*'s Catholicity was "not of a sufficiently uncompromising sort to suit us," he wrote, once again making dangerous charges:

> Its concessions to the Liberalism and sentimentalism of the age are, it seems to us, such as Pius IX, gloriously reigning, has taken several occasions to warn against. The danger that besets Catholics is Latitudinarianism; and we can have little motive to labor for the conversion of our non-Catholic neighbors, and little success in converting them, unless it is unequivocally true that they can be saved only by becoming Catholics.

He professed not to know the proper theological qualifications of the doctrine of no salvation beyond the church, but he denied that those qualifications could affect anyone who read the *Catholic World*. To insist on qualifications, he argued, had "the practical effect of spreading a latitudinarian mode of thinking among Catholics and to lull non-Catholics to sleep in a false security. It is never well to make concessions to the prejudices of the age."[14]

When Brownson again associated the *Catholic World* with liberalism in the *Tablet* in January 1870, while Hecker was in Rome, Hewit finally responded. He noted that all of the men at the Paulist house had been hurt by Brownson's remarks. He believed he had tried as hard as Brownson to be faithful to the doctrines and teachings of the church. Brownson answered that he, Hecker and Hewit had serious doctrinal quarrels. In the *Tablet* Brownson apologized for being unable to find the citation on which his earlier criticism was based, but he still charged that the *Catholic World* defined exclusive salvation "a little too loosely." He claimed he had never accused the paper of "any sympathy with the false liberalism of the age, or country." Still, he worried because the paper did not attack liberalism, but "labors to direct and correct it." By appearing to merely correct it, "we in fact mislead the minds of many Catholics and approach the very evil we wish to cure." Brownson preferred a "more open, manly, and, in our judgement, more prudent" method, "to attack more directly the error," a method which, he added, was, "as well, more in accord with the syllabus [of errors]." Nevertheless, after all this, he called the *Catholic World* "the ablest magazine of the day."[15]

Hewit and Hecker undoubtedly bristled at Brownson's articles, coming as they did during the Vatican Council, when the taint of liberalism could be especially damaging. Hecker, however, must have felt a special isolation, for Brownson and Hewit both favored the declaration of infallibility and both agreed with the conservative doctrines summarized in the "Syllabus of Errors." Like the pope, Brownson measured political systems by their degree of hostility to the church. The American system, for all its faults, was acceptable because it made allowance for the freedom and independence of the church. Unlike Protestants, Catholics were intolerant, claiming that the church and it alone represented Christ on earth and offered the means to salvation. They need not demand that the state practice a similar intolerance, though ideally the state should simply be the political expression of a single Catholic people and thus should recognize the superiority of the church, subordinate itself to the church's teaching, and administer those laws of which the church was the custodian and interpreter. For the moment, at least, Brownson argued that the American system was not transferable to Europe, for there religious liberty was only a grant of the state, subject to its removal. The church did make concordats, to gain what independence it could, but there was little to be gained by recognizing liberal claims about religious liberty or the secular state, because both were simply revivals of pagan absolutism, now in the name of the people, or, as Brownson called it, "democratic caesarism."

From this Brownson drew a number of conclusions which stood in sharp opposition to Hecker. The church should not attempt to conform itself to the age but to conform the age to itself. It should avoid accommodation to secularization, because the end result was to leave society, economics and politics beyond the reach of the church's moral authority, and thus of morality itself. Religion thus ended up confined to "private and domestic life, to the personal and domestic virtues" with "nothing to say in public affairs." The church must resist the world, Brownson argued; the very teachings most offensive to the present age were precisely those the age most needed for its protection and safety: reliable, authoritative norms regarding marriage, sex, women and the other problems of the day.[16]

Among the articles in which he set forth these views was ironically, the one on church and state Hecker had solicited from Rome. Hewit, at least, was pleased with the article, praising Brownson for making it "so conservative in tone, reserved in language and explicit in avowing the principles of the 'Syllabus.' " He thought it a mistake to predict, as Hecker did, the "triumph of the revolution." Hewit was confident the papacy would know "what instructions to give to Europe when a new emergency arises." Although fully loyal to the American Constitution and government "because it is legitimate and the only one possible for us," Hewit told Brownson he would not "share in the enthusiasm for popular sovereignty." He supposed Hecker would be satisfied with Brownson's "modest recommendation of American principles," though he might wish they had gone further.[17]

Hewit and Brownson, therefore, shared a body of ideas which were in sharp opposition to Hecker's, a fact which must have made him feel deeply isolated. Hewit's article on infallibility, which had so upset Hecker when he read it in Rome, and Brownson's article on church and state, provided convincing evidence that his two closest friends and collaborators were in full agreement with the conservative drift of the church climaxing at the council. Brownson regularly reminded his friend of their differences. In August 1870 he told Hecker that they had little in common in their views of democracy:

> Catholicity is theologically compatible with democracy, as you and I would explain democracy, but practically there is, in my judgement, no compatibility between them. According to Catholicity, all power comes from above and descends from high to low; according to democracy, all power is infused, is from below, and ascends from low to high. This is democracy in the practical sense, as politicians and people do and will understand it. Catholicity and it are mutually antagonistic, as the spirit and the flesh, the church and the world. . . . I have heretofore wished to affect a harmony of the American and Catholic ideas, but I believe such harmony impractical except by sacrificing the Catholic view to the national.

In the 1850s Brownson had argued that Americans were easily governed when approached as free men, but by the 1870s he was convinced that Americans had translated freedom into license. Not one in twenty would believe the decree on papal infallibility, he thought; not one in a thousand would approve the ideas embodied in the "Syllabus of Errors." Americans, Catholics and non-Catholics alike, would listen to the voice of authority only when it corresponded to the wishes of the people. As a result, Brownson had reached conclusions entirely contrary to those he and Hecker had once held together:

> These considerations make me feel that the whole influence of democratic ideas and tendencies is directly antagonistic to Cath-

> olicity. I think the Church has never encountered a social and political order so hostile to her, and that the conversion of our Republic will be a far greater victory than the conversion of the Roman Empire. You must see how this conviction must modify many of the views which we formerly held in common. . . . I hate [democracy] under any form it can assume in practice, as I do Satan.[18]

In the following months Brownson, still dissatisfied with his relations with the *Catholic World*, considered reviving his own *Review*. Hewit urged Brownson to continue writing and Hecker did the same when he returned from Europe. For the moment Brownson was satisfied and continued to drop by the Paulist home, but their views were no closer. In November he wrote his son Frank that Hecker's confidence that democracy was favorable to the church was "worse than foolish."

> Democracy rests on popular opinion and never looks beyond and no people that makes popular opinion its criterion of right and wrong is or can be Catholic. Catholicity spreads among a people only in proportion as they habitually act from the law of God, which is above kings and peoples alike, above popular opinion and the pleasure of the prince.[19]

A few months later he told Frank that Hecker needed his articles for the credit of the *Catholic World* and his problem, oddly, was not Hecker, but Hewit: "The only trouble I have grows out of the fact Father Hewit is not sound on the question of original sin and doesn't believe it is necessary to be in communion with the Church in order to be saved." Hewit thought Protestants could gain salvation through invincible ignorance, and original sin was sin only in the sense of the sin of Adam. Hecker agreed with Hewit on these points and was "in fact semi-pelagian without knowing it." So Brownson felt himself "restrained from bringing out what I regard as the orthodox doctrine of original sin and of exclusive salvation" though now "in all other respects I feel unrestrained."[20] At heart almost all the problems which arose had to do with the independence and freedom of the individual. So fearful were Catholics of subjectivism, making faith, knowledge or political action dependent on free consent, that they could spy out even the most submerged tendencies toward such evils. Thus Hecker and Hewit seemed pelagian to Brownson, who even charged that Newman, in his understanding that belief in God rested, in part at least, on evidences acceptable to reason, tended toward subjectivism: "We become our own centre and standpoint, our own ultimate judge, a light and law to ourselves, really subsisting in an intellectual independence of God," thus ceding to the rationalists all the ground that they needed.

The final break came in 1872. In December 1871 Brownson submitted two articles he thought would give Hewit a "Migraine." He was right. A long correspondence followed, with Hewit contending that Brownson came dangerously close to upholding an immediate intuition of God and Brownson charging in return that Hewit's views were contrary to explicit church teaching. In January he decided to withdraw from the *Catholic World* and concentrate on preparing a book and writing in the *Tablet*. Brownson told Hecker that the ontology dispute was the occasion, not the cause of the break, and his daughter reported that her father was "inclined to think Fr. Hecker wanted to get rid of him." Hecker told a friend that "the old man and I have had a fight, the fiftieth, I suppose." It would probably last a month or two, but it was a "peaceable one." Brownson remained upset, telling his son that an article published by Hewit in 1872 was aimed at him; he disliked its "dogmatic and arrogant tone" and regarded Hewit as "no philosopher and an indifferent theologian." He briefly revived his *Review*, explaining to Archbishop McCloskey that he did not ask permission as he did not want to embarrass the archbishop with the Paulists.[21]

He had no contact with Hecker during the latter's European travels. When Hecker returned, he solicited Brownson to write again for the *Catholic World* and he agreed, over his daughter's vigorous objections. A few months later Brownson died. The Paulists honored the philosopher with a service at St. Paul's, and Hecker wrote a touching letter to his children:

> I owe much, and more, perhaps to your father than to any other man in my early life. My friendship and sense of gratitude to him has never been affected by any event during forty years. No man has done more disinterestedly what he considered to be his duty.[22]

The Brownson-Hecker friendship provides one of the great stories of American Catholic history. Americans, "to the manor born," converts, strong defenders of the church, ardent advocates of American independence and nationality, these two men seemed to embody the heart of the American Catholic experience, the struggle to reconcile religious faith and American identity. Yet, more than most have recognized, they became very different kinds of Catholics. While both ended their lives disappointed, and while both found the church of their day uncongenial to their deepest aspirations, the one, Brownson, was in the end a great churchman, who found in the church what he could no longer find in human life. When the crucial moment came during the discussion of papal infallibility in 1870, Brownson had the following note inserted in the New York *Tablet*:

> In consequence of some misunderstanding with regard to his position in relation to the Papal infallibility and so-called Liberal Catholicity, Dr. Brownson wishes us to say for him, that he firmly believes and always has believed since he became a Catholic, that the Pope, as the successor of Peter, is the Supreme Pastor and Leader of the Universal Church, and that when declaring the faith or condemning errors opposed to it, he is by the assistance of the Holy Ghost infallible, and his definitions are irreformible. As to so-called Liberal Catholicity, if for a brief moment some years ago he seemed to yield too much to his Liberal Catholic friends, he has never knowingly made or sought to make any concession to the revolutionary or so-called Liberal spirit of the age, and that he regards what is called Liberal Catholicity as a mixture of Heathenism pure and simple. He has always refused to subordinate the Church to nationality or to any particular form of government, and holds that he can as a Catholic defend no nationality and no political order not in conformity with the law of God, as interpreted and declared by supreme authority of the Catholic Church. He is a republican for his own country, because republicanism in his own country is the legal and the only practicable form of Government, and while it is so, his Church demands him to be loyal to it. He defends civil and religious liberty in their Catholic sense; because the Church is the basis and support, here and everywhere, of all true liberty; but he has never understood liberty in the sense of modern infidels, non-Catholics, or even Liberal Catholics. He wishes to be regarded as the defender of Liberty by authority, not of liberty against authority.[23]

So different in many ways from Pope Pius IX, Brownson was at one with him in the conviction that there was no salvation, or at least very little, outside the church, that modern history was notable only for its multiple violations of church teachings, that little could be done other than to hold on to the Catholics who remained, fling down the gauntlet at the pretensions of a flawed humanity, and wait for the advent of a Kingdom of God which would be a massive Catholic Church built on ultramontane foundations. In the end he became an apologist for the anti-democratic Catholicism which could find no truth or wisdom outside of itself. Led to the church by the search for a ground for the truths of religious experience, he came to confine that experience to church and to belittle the promptings of spirit, if not conscience. The pressure of his new found friends in the church confirmed the predictions of his older friends in New England; the old lion's claws were pulled and he was fully domesticated in the household of faith. He reserved what anger he had for the violations of the church so evident in the world outside and became a watchdog over the citadels of a fortress church, whose continuing cries had far more to do with the morale of the inhabitants than with the crimes, or the needs, of those at whom they were directed. None would shatter the walls; neither would any be invited to enter, save under the flag of unconditional surrender. His old friend Hecker, who wanted to dismantle the walls altogether, inviting the outsiders in and sending the insiders out, seemed less a traitor than a fool. Ironically, though, both friends were left alone, the one to wonder why none could share his so different version of events, the other to suffer the loneliness of a powerful guardian, useful in defense but never fully trusted not to turn his strength against the inhabitants. Both stood as prophetic countersigns to the drift of the church they loved.

15

Crisis

Following his return from the council, Hecker's health rapidly deteriorated. In July 1871 he told a friend that his "head had given out"; even a week at Lake George, "with pure air and unsurpassed scenery," brought no improvement. During the following winter the Paulists resumed the missions, and Hecker was hard at work on *The Catholic World*, the Catholic Publication Society and, especially, the *Young Catholic*. He thought the latter was "doing more for the future of religion than any other work" with which he was engaged. Its circulation was increasing during its second year of publication, an "unheard of thing." His hopes had never been higher, at least on the surface, but his health plagued him. In January 1872 he reported that his body had been weak for several months; in June he spent two weeks at his brother's because he felt "wretched." That summer he returned to Lake George, where some land had been donated to the Paulists. When he arrived, he had an attack of diarrhea and was looked after by neighbors.[1]

That fall he returned to New York, feeling no better. Doctors advised travel south for the winter. As he explained to Bishop Lynch, "my nervous system has run down, and repose and nourishment, with less rigorous climate" would make things right. By January he was in Baltimore arranging to travel to Florida with his old friend Archbishop Bayley. The two men did go to Florida, where they visited Bishop Verot, whom Hecker had met in Rome, but Bayley left Hecker behind when he returned to Baltimore in February. The next month one of Bayley's Florida friends, Julia Beers, wrote the archbishop that "poor Father Hecker is here—a broken down man." Throughout this trip Hecker remained in close touch with Hewit, who was left in charge of community affairs. He urged Hecker to return. If unable to live with the Paulist house, he could stay at his brother's home in New Jersey. He also suggested that if no improvement took place, Hecker should consider a trip to Europe. In mid-April, Hecker arrived at his brother's home; after consulting with George, Hewit and the doctors, he decided to go abroad, accompanied by Deshon and later to be joined by George and his family. At the same time Hewit wrote to Father Chatard in Rome that Hecker had been sick for over a year, and there seemed little hope of recovery.[2]

It was, and remained, unclear to everyone whether the source of Hecker's illness was physical, spiritual or both. Physically, he suffered from "habitual exhaustion," headaches, loss of appetite, digestive troubles and severe nervousness. Yet his inner anxiety was also intense, and Hecker himself frequently associated his physical ills with the "light" from God which filled his mind and heart at times of physical weakness. From Baltimore in April 1873 he wrote Hewit that along with physical illness, he had experienced a complete detachment from his work. "My past self seemed to my present like a perfect stranger," he wrote. His present life sprang from "new and fresh sources" making his previous "views and occupations," not "incorrect or mistaken," but simply less important. Slowly, he reported, his mind was opening more clearly to "the mission of the church, the philosophy of her history, and the ultimate aims of Christianity."

He claimed that his spiritual experience had clarified "the providential work and meaning" of the Paulists, the reasons why the church was "everywhere in conflict and oppressed," and how her "future victory" could be secured. At the same time he was seeking to be perfectly resigned to God's will, and prepared to set aside his "duties and responsibilities" if that was what God required of him.[3]

This seemed to suggest that he should turn away from the activities in New York and await direction from the Lord. As in his earlier illness, his vision had far outgrown available resources. Hecker had ambitious plans for the conversion of Europe, with Paulists in all the world's great cities, and this led him to be increasingly critical of his colleagues, absorbed as they were in parish and mission work. Reality was the struggling life of the Catholic Publication Society, the modest success of its Sunday School paper, the tiny improvement in Paulist affairs evidenced by the resumption of the missions, and the growth of the parish, where Deshon and Young were trying to find the money to build a scaled down version of the "basilica" Hecker had planned earlier. Brownson and Hewit were uninterested in his ideas. There seemed no one in America, save his brother perhaps, who even understood, much less supported them. He was, in fact, alone.

If there was tension between his hopes for the Paulists and the work in which they were engaged, there was even deeper tension between the lessons learned from his spiritual experience and the apparent direction of the church universal. While he had been more than willing to abide by the decision of the council, he had been troubled by the political maneuvering in Rome and the tendency of many to place under the newly established authority of infallibility ideas and attitudes far removed from dogma. He had already sketched an interpretation of the council as a providential event providing the basis for renewal, and he once again confirmed this interpretation by a reading of his own experience. As he wrote to one of the people to whom he provided spiritual direction:

> God has pleased to teach me in the same school of interior guidance of the Holy Spirit. . . . The Holy Spirit can do for all and everyone what he has done for our souls . . . [the Church] will recover her strength and regain her place in the world by a greater reliance on the power of the indwelling Holy Spirit to her honor and teaching her children that same reliance on the immediate guidance of their souls. For the measure of the strength of the Christian character is the measure of the soul's immediate reliance on the guidance of the indwelling Holy Spirit.[4]

While these ideas expanded his earlier intuitions, one important shift had taken place. He no longer was as convinced as he had been that the evangelical proclamation of Catholic truth alone would convert the country or the world. The center of God's providential action had subtly shifted from the world to the church, from the non-Catholic community being prepared for conversion to Catholics themselves, who were being opened to a new life in the Holy Spirit.

> I hope for pentecostal days for the Church by directing the attention of her children primarily to the interior direction of the Holy Spirit. The divine external authority of the church being now defined and fixed, the day for the interior divine authority is coming. The two are one—the external is the criterion and the internal is the immediate means of Christian perfection. In this short sentence and in its application in preaching and practice the whole future of the Church lies.

In Rome Hecker had avoided identification with a party and, like Newman in England, he had a distaste for internal conflict within the church and a vision which transcended the problems of the moment. These problems arose from pre-occupation with the past, reading the signs of the times from the perspective of old trials rather than from that of the perennial promise of God's Kingdom, the triumph of the church. "My face is turned toward a rising sun, and I catch gleams of a promise of a brighter future for the church and humanity," he wrote. "While in Europe men's faces are turned toward a setting sun. We are looking in opposite directions."[5]

Hecker may still have had his New World eyes on the promised land, but, for the moment at least, he was confined to the interior life, and in this state he set off on his journey to Europe. In July 1873 he was in London while Deshon toured Ireland; he wrote Chatard that the doctors diagnosed his problem as "defective nervous nutrition." He was headed for Paris, then the Alps, where he would rest. In the fall, if all went well, he would take a "trip up the Nile and spend Easter in Jerusalem." In August he arrived with Deshon at Ragatz, a resort in Switzerland popular with Americans. Two weeks later people said he looked better but, after another week of improvement, he was ill again. On September 6 he left to visit friends in a number of Swiss and German cities.[6]

Back home, his colleagues seemed to be growing impatient. Hecker was particularly disturbed by a letter from Hewit prudently advising him to recognize that he was becoming older and must settle himself on the work of the next ten or fifteen years. "There is enough for you to do, to get the congregation in that state that you can hand it over to the younger members," Hewit wrote. "You can do this quietly, without attempting any more than moderate labors, and living a tranquil life at home in the house, and as for the other things let God and those [to whom] he commits them take care of them." Having read this letter, Hecker wrote George that the community's anxiety for his return hampered his physical recovery. "The truth is that it is only by my entire oblivion of everything, and complete resignation to the guidance of divine providence, that I can find repose and improvement of health," he wrote. As for Hewit, he brushed aside his concerns. He was perfectly confident in Hewit's discretion and not anxious about the direction and prosperity of the community. He reminded Hewit of his last words to the community, that whatever they decided was best would have his full approval. He asked only that they try as much as possible to act together.[7]

As he traveled across Europe, learning of continued conflicts between church and state, he became more convinced than ever that "politics and religion" were "secondary," as he told his brother; "the renewal of religion in the souls of men must first take place." But, if the church continued to expand her external organization, prospects would be "fearfully depressive." Torn by conflicts between his hopes and his fears, he headed for "the land of the crocodiles," on his own "flight into Egypt."[8]

From Cairo in December he described preparations for the river journey. He and his traveling companions had to arrange for a boat and people to staff it, and purchase supplies. To McCloskey he wrote a description of Cairo itself:

> Specimens of every civilized nation, of every outlandish, and even barbarous tribe, costumes of infinite variety, some most gorgeous and then others contenting themselves with a sheet or a nightshirt, jostle you as you walk the streets of Cairo. Your ears are greeted with all the languages and strange sounds that were started on Babel.

On the evening of December 8, dressed in cassock and stole, he blessed the boat with holy water, christening it the "Sitti Miriam"; on the following day they set forth.[9]

During the journey up the Nile and back, Hecker kept a diary, recording sunrise and sunset and describing the scenery. Despite his extensive reading on Egypt before coming to Europe, Hecker's observations seemed peculiarly innocent. He was struck, for example, by the unselfconscious semi-nakedness of the sailors and people along the shore. He was impressed as well by the manner in which religion filled their lives. Regularly people stopped work, the men went to the water and made their ablutions, turned their heads toward Mecca, prostrated themselves and prayed. In the whole process there was an indifference to others and outward things. "The Arabs have a gift for prayer," he wrote. "We Christians might learn from them a lesson on this point and not a small one either. For prayer is the beginning of all other graces." There was a real challenge here to the assurance of Western Christians:

> In the morning early I open my cabin window, breathe the balmy air, watch the shore as we pass now and then a village—a line of mud huts and palm trees—listen to the birds chirping, and some singing, now the noisy cock crows; all invites repose, quiet and silence. Unless it be our sailors who have to change the sail, and even they do it while singing a prayer in Arabic: "Oh Lord we hail thee." For these Arabs whom we have learned to despise pray at all times, in whatever they do, whether in the shops, or on the vessel, or in the streets, or on the banks of the river, anywhere and at all times you will see them kneel down, rise, prostrate their

> foreheads against the earth or floor, sit on their heels with their arms resting on their knees and their faces turned toward Mecca and their eyes up to heaven. The very picture of abstraction and interior recollection of a saint! These Moslem Arabs have a gift of vocal prayer! Let those explain it who can![10]

Along the way he saw the churches of Coptic Christians and, in each, a Franciscan friar. On Christmas day he said Mass at a small church "a couple of centuries old, open in the roof, birds go in and out, chirping and singing during service, quite in harmony with service." The Gregorian chant of the few men and boys at the Mass blended into the chanting heard from the Muslims, not far away. Once again, he noted that "the whole life and every one of his actions with the Muslim who is faithful to his religion is interwoven with and connected by different acts of devotion and consecrated by prayer." He contrasted "the oriental and western mind," the "one habituated to the region of the spirit, the other fastened on the material world, the one that looks naturally upward as the other does downward. The former is at home when occupied with acts of devotion, religion, and at a loss in worldly things; the other is at home in what is called modern progress—steam, machinery, firearms, printing press, comforts of this life, while at a loss, and betrays his feelings of strangeness . . . in acts of religion and workings of God." He began reading the Koran and found many things held in common with Catholicism. This reading also helped him understand the Christian desert fathers, their fastings, devotions, prayers and simple dress.[11]

On December 30 they reached Karnak and viewed the ruins of an ancient civilization. For "massiveness, colossal grandeur, and incredible extent, there is nothing in the world that can be compared with the ruins of the hundred gated Thebes," he wrote. The sight was full reward "for all the inconveniences, trouble and expense of coming to Egypt." On New Year's Day he saw a slave market and commented on the appearances of the slaves, but said nothing more. Delighted with the trip, he noted in his diary that, if given the choice of any one trip for his whole life, this was the one he would take.[12]

Musing over the ruins he had seen, Hecker noted that the experience of Egypt changed one's chronology. Time moved backward so far that the birth of Christ became modern. This new sense of time produced "a revolution in one's thought, reflections, and forces one to reconstruct entirely his intellectual apparatus." Caught up now in a moving spiritual adventure he could hardly think of things back home. In early February he wrote his brother that Paulist affairs "must be left in the hands of others for some time and if they do not go on as I should wish, under the present conditions of my health I could not do much." Only freedom "from past cares and repose" would restore his strength. Again, a few weeks later, he wrote that "thought of the past disturbs my mind" and, later, "anxiety" about old problems brought on the return of his "nervous depression." In contrast the peaceful trip up the Nile, far removed from such anxieties, had a beneficial impact on his health. It had been "almost like an inspiration, such have been its beneficial effects both to my mind and body." He felt "like one who had been in solitude for three or four months," and he enjoyed it.[13]

On March 30, 1874, they were back in Cairo. Pleased with the trip, he thought it had provided "the richest four months of my whole life . . . intellectually and religiously as well as physically." But awaiting Hecker in Cairo was a letter from Hewit, written in January, requesting his return. He hoped that Hecker himself would want to come home after Easter "to the charge of your community," no matter what his friends might advise. His New York doctor had said from the very beginning that Hecker could return in the spring, for he would by then have received all the benefit possible from travel. Hewit shrewdly argued that there was a crisis in the community, which he did not explain in detail; he also promised "to be more docile and obedient than I have been, to take the greatest care not to worry you by opposition or tiresome argumentations, and to second your plans and efforts according to the time and strength I may have." Because of a mix-up in mail service, Hecker did not receive Hewit's "kind letter" until early April, but he had been warned of it in a letter from George, who told him Hewit, feeling the unwelcome weight of responsibility, had written on a sudden impulse, without consulting the other fathers.[14]

Thus forewarned, Hecker answered Hewit quickly explaining that his "actual experience," whatever the doctor's opinion, was that only a fortnight at home, even with few responsibilities, would lead him to "break down and become a burden to others." Despite good weather, he had taken only two meals in the last five days, and those in bed, this despite "the quiet and repose" of the Nile trip. "I am like one walking on thin ice, sufficient to bear me if I walk lightly, but with one heavy tred I break through," he wrote. Once again he attributed his physical condition at least in part to his spiritual state. The new "light" he had received had separated him entirely from his past in order to free him to live fully in resignation:

> There is nothing left to me to do but to wait on the will of Divine Providence. Perhaps all this was intended for my purification, and he will open in due season, the way for my return to my labors. There is only one desire in my heart, one aim in my life, and that is to do God's will, purely and simply, and in whatever

> way that may be. It is only in keeping this fixedly and nothing else before my mind, that I can find peace and repose . . . remaining away, considering all these things . . . is a necessity, as well as best for you all, as well as for me.

He went on to argue that he understood the difficulties before Hewit and the community. If his absence was "voluntary on my part," he would be "guilty of a great dereliction of duty and of sin." But it was a trial, the hand of God was in it, the community was "God's own work" and they would all have to trust more in God.[15] Hewit responded quickly, assuring Hecker that he was now convinced it would not be prudent for him to return as yet and expressing confidence that Hecker would return when he could. His spiritual state seemed comparable to "the obscure night of the spirit" described by St. John of the Cross, he added encouragingly.[16]

Back in New York the work of the community proceeded. At a chapter meeting in April, a permanent rule was adopted for presentation to Rome and plans were finally begun to build the new church and convent. Father Young wrote Hecker that the parish was bursting at the seams, with more than two thousand communions distributed each week. Father Augustine Brady was teaching fifteen hundred children in Sunday school. "Father Elliott is a man, a religious and a preacher after your own heart," Young wrote. "If God spares him, he will be a strong pillar for the community." Even more touching was a letter from Father Rosecrans, expressing his love and devotion and describing the work of the two mission bands. In addition to a full schedule, he and Elliott were trying to put into practice Hecker's plan of a lecture series for Protestants following the missions. The warmth and affection of these and other letters from community members seemed to confirm George's judgment that Hecker would find on his return "a great change in the views of most of the Fathers, that is there will be more willingness to cooperate in your work and less opposition." The crisis to which Hewit referred was not evident on the surface, though problems had come up with the church building, and Hewit himself disliked supervising the others.[17]

From Egypt, Hecker's party traveled to Palestine, where they visited Jaffa and Jerusalem. Deeply moved by the Holy Places, Hecker said Mass over the site where Jesus was taken down from the cross. Later he wrote his mother that it would take a lifetime to exhaust all the Holy Land had to offer. For the moment the visit had the effect of deepening his awareness of God and making his religion more "personal." By the time this letter reached home, his family had suffered a great loss. When Hecker came to Europe, he expected George, Josephine and their children to join him. However, the reunion was postponed when George separated from the family business and entered into a lawsuit with his brother John, a step which naturally caused him considerable anguish. Then John died suddenly on May 7, 1874. On receiving the news, Isaac wrote his mother a letter of consolation, recalling John's devotion to the family. To George, he wrote of his concern for his mother, who had now become their responsibility. This made the family conflict arising from the lawsuit even more difficult. Isaac wrote George several times, assuring him that he was doing what he thought best, and suggesting that, if he was troubled, he should pray and be more attentive to charities. John's death also occasioned a letter from Hecker's 78-year-old mother, who had been cared for by John for many years. She compared herself to Mrs. Wesley, mother of the founder of Methodism; when asked if she would give up her son for a good cause, she had responded, "Yes, if she had a dozen." But Isaac still puzzled her and her words echoed those of thirty years before: "Isaac, tell me what ails you, and what your complaint is." As then, she recommended to him a trust in God which was now the comfort of her own life: "I cannot help you, but you know where to go. The Lord is all sufficient. He is the only Doctor I have now."[18]

Hecker spent the early summer of 1874 in Paris, traveling occasionally to visit friends and attend a Catholic congress at Mayence. Visiting in Malines, he met some German Catholic leaders and engaged Monsignor Mermillod, editor of one of the leading Catholic papers in that country, to write for the *Catholic World* on the conflict between the church and Bismarck's Imperial government.

He was not entirely adverse to Paulist business, it seemed, for in early June he sent home some architectural plans for the new church and some detailed comments of his own, adding that they were intended simply to advise the fathers, as he had complete faith in their judgment. He urged Hewit to send him copies of the new Rule and later received instructions about delivering the final documents in Rome. Josephine wrote of her work with the *Young Catholic*; when copies arrived, Hecker began writing her regular advice. He solicited materials and photography from Europeans and sent short items for the paper, which became known as the Uncle Ned Letters. In the fall he visited Fribourg, where he found a religious community of young women who lived together and published several newspapers and journals, an arrangement close to his dreams of a supportive community for the *Catholic World* and the publishing society.

In June, before leaving for the Mayence Congress, he noted that, in his conversations with leading continental Catholic leaders, he was struck once again by the sharp racial and cultural divisions in the church. It was as difficult to get the "Celtic mind" to appreciate the internal character of the church as to get the "Teutonic mind" to appreciate "her divine external constitution" and the importance of authority, discipline and liturgy. The weakness of the former and the persecutions being visited on the latter, particularly in Germany, were teaching "practical lessons" to both sides. Divine Providence, it seemed, was shaping them toward a new "synthesis," a process hidden from "ordinary observation" but nonetheless "certain" and "beautiful." He remained far more confident than his spiritual state suggested: "Underneath all the persecutions, the oppression, the false action, the whole outwardly critical condition of the Church and society, there is an overpowering, counteracting, divine current leading to an all embracing, most complete and triumphant unity in the Church."[19]

By July he was back in Ragatz for the summer, taking the baths, beset once again by physical and spiritual depression. While the waters were a "tonic," he was confined to bed for several days in August; any exercise caused pain in his chest. The doctors would only say that "it comes from nervous weakness." Late in the month he moved on to St. Moritz, where he spent much of each day in bed, rising for long walks. He was making tentative plans to travel through Italy in the fall, then again to the eastern Mediterranean, and then perhaps to Russia, as the doctor advised him to travel, not staying too long in any one place. But in early September he was deeply depressed, with nothing but "darkness" before him and "desolation and bitterness" within. "Cut off from all that formerly interested me, banished as it were from home and country, isolated from everything, the doors of heaven shut," he felt "overwhelmed with misery and crushed to atoms." A few days later he wrote that he had some relief from his "interior trials" and some revival of physical health, but each new cycle of this sort left him "more quiet and tranquil."[20]

His belief in an expanded vocation was unshaken. In October Hecker wrote from Geneva, after meeting with several leading church figures, that "Divine Providence is employing me in a larger field and a more important one than in the past." A few days later he thought three alternatives possible. One was to be "put on the shelf completely because of my broken down health." At times this seemed probable, but more commonly his recovery seemed likely, in which case there seemed to be two other possibilities: reestablishing himself in his former work, "with some necessary changes," or "entrance upon a new, wider, more important field of work." The choices were much like those he faced before his conversion, to return home "with necessary changes" or to find a larger field, more appropriate to his religious experience. He said he was prepared to leave the choice to God's grace, but it was clear his preference was not his work back in New York.[21]

When he wrote a particularly discouraged letter to Hewit, one in which he spoke of death, Hewit responded that he was sure Hecker was "in no danger of dying for a long time." The desire for death was a "sentiment in the soul, not a symptom of bodily disease." As Hewit saw it, Hecker seemed occasionally to be "a little thrown off balance" but no more than would be expected, considering his "temperament and the circumstances," from "any invalid who is nervous, who is alone, in the company of invalids and tired of inaction." He praised Hecker's patience and urged him to remain quiet until God chose "to bring you back at the right time." When God's will for Hecker's return to the community became clear, Hewit was sure his friend would obey as if it were "a command from the Lord himself."

By the time Hewit's letter arrived, Hecker had begun to explore means of setting his ideas about the state of the church, so far confined to letters and conversations, before a larger public. Ready to renounce "all relation" to his "past labors and position," he decided to prepare "a full programme" and submit it to "competent judges at Rome," as he had done in 1857. If "it was approved," it would give "security and strength" to his own future actions, and "satisfy [his] former companions."[22]

In November 1874 he began writing his program still convinced that the large events of contemporary history were also signs revealing the meaning of his life and pointing toward his future vocation:

> What else has been my exile from home, etc., for, unless to prepare my soul to make my life-experience applicable to the general condition of the Church and the world in its present crisis? The past was for the United States, the future for the world. To this end all particular attachments to persons, places, labors, had to be cut off, not to give a bias to the judgement, and not to interfere with my action. . . . I now see why I called myself "An International Catholic."[23]

Hecker's program was a larger project than his 1857 report. Then he had been primarily concerned to set his personal history within the signs of the times in the United States. Now he thought he discerned the meaning of contemporary history for the universal church. As he wrote George and Josephine, and later Hewit, the church was nothing less than "God acting directly on the human race, directing it to its true destiny." If this were true, one should avoid a merely "external," superficial interpretation of the council, of Bismarck or Cavour's persecution of the church, and of the defensiveness and shortsightedness of church leaders. Instead, one should try to discern what God was trying to do through these events. Hecker's program was nothing less than an essay in metahistorical interpretation, written, as he said later, while he was "having many lights" from the Holy Spirit. As he summarized its arguments to George and Josephine:

> If I be not mistaken, it contains an interpretation of the past, an explanation of the present and perspective of the future which will give light to a great many minds, relief to a large class of persons, and direction to all who seek it. It is nothing else than a general outline of a movement from without to within, as that of the sixteenth century was a movement within to without. This was occasioned by the nature of the attack of Protestantism. The Church having protected what was assaulted . . . can return to her normal course.

If she would do so, trusting in the interior work of the Holy Spirit, the church could attract the increasingly dominant Saxon races and pave the way for its own triumph, once again understood as the triumph of God, directing the human race to its true destiny and setting it on the road of "all true progress."[24]

His original title was *The Church and Europe, with a Glance at the Future,* but later he changed it to *An Exposition of the Church in View of Recent Difficulties and Controversies and the Present Needs of the Church.* In the English edition, eventually published in London, Hecker inserted on the title page two quotations from Pope Pius IX. The first read: "These are not times to sit with folded arms, while the enemies of God are occupied in overthrowing everything worthy of respect." The second: "Yes, this change, this triumph will come. I know not whether it will come during my life . . . but that it must come I know. The resurrection will take place and we shall see the end of all impiety." These two quotations sounded the themes of the pamphlet: a defense of the church against its enemies, and a confident expectation of an early victory for the church.

Hecker began with an outline of his providential interpretation of history, built on his newfound sense of the mission of various races. The importance given by Latin and Celtic races to the external constitution, or what Hecker called the "accidentals" of the church, eventually excited the animosity of the Saxon elements and brought about the Reformation. In contrast, rationality, energetic individuality, and a great practical activity in the material order predominated among the Anglo-Saxon peoples. They often lacked full appreciation of the church's external organization, they accused the church of formalism, and they opposed the increase of external devotions, minute disciplinary regulations, and papal authority.

Catholicism, of course, could not prosper among a people if it impaired their natural instincts, attacked their national development, or was incompatible with their particular genius. That was true in the sixteenth century; it remained true in the nineteenth. Opposition to papal infallibility, such as that of Dollinger's "Old Catholics," and attacks on the church as incompatible with national unity, such as Bismarck's *Kulturkampf*, suggested to Hecker that Catholicism must adapt itself to the German character and the new needs created by the German empire. It was not a matter of making concessions, as conservatives feared, but of presenting divine truths in such a way as to enable the German people to recognize that they would find in the church a life which affirmed their legitimate instincts. For the Holy Spirit placed nations as well as souls in relationship to God and helped them attain in this world as in the next their highest development, happiness and glory.

Hecker noted that in many countries Catholics constituted the majority of the population, but governments were controlled by hostile minorities. The roots of this situation could be found in the Reformation, which exaggerated personal independence against the authority of the church. By a "fixed law," the denial of one truth in the church required its vigorous defense and greater development. In this case, undue emphasis on personal independence caused the church, under the guidance of divine providence, to give ever-increasing emphasis, and finally dogmatic definition, to its own authority. For three hundred years the church's main concern had been to develop, strengthen and express its authority over its own members. The Jesuits had been particularly important agents in strengthening the discipline of the church and preparing the way for the doctrine of papal infallibility. It was to their work that the distinguishing mark of modern Catholics, their special devotion to the Holy See, was due. Unfortunately, this development also favored the restriction of personal initiative. "The defense of the Church and the salvation of the soul were ordinarily secured at the expense, necessarily, of those virtues which make up the strength of Christian manhood," Hecker argued. As a result, emphasis on externals had the temporary disadvantage of reducing the energy of the church, accounting for the fact that Protestants and unbelievers were able to politically overwhelm larger numbers of Catholics.

Hecker then asked the question "Is there a way out?" and examined a number of proposals presently before the church, rejecting each as impractical or only partial. Returning to earlier arguments, he said that any real solution must be both radical and practical. Solution of the problem of human destiny lay in religion, the basis of every true human interest. In "civilized" nations, religion meant Christianity and, properly understood, that meant the Catholic Church. The church was, in fact, God acting directly upon the human community through a visible organism, the church, and, through its members, upon society. The church provided the answer to all problems; it was through the church, then, that the restoration of religion and the solution of modern problems could be found.

At this point Hecker turned to a detailed examination of the Holy Spirit. The church was animated by the Holy Spirit, and the Holy Spirit's action through the history of the church was the source of all true human progress. At the personal level as well, the actual, habitual direction of souls by the Holy Spirit was the essential principle of Christian life. The object of God's revelation was to establish the Kingdom of God in human souls and, through them, in the rest of the world. The church taught that the Holy Spirit's gifts were infused into the soul at baptism. Christians were instructed to cultivate virtues which aided in the practice of holiness, such as spiritual reading, reception of the sacraments and good works. In the modern era the church required people capable of living fully in the new atmosphere of liberty and progress, people whose intimate union with the Holy Spirit gave them intelligence, courage, full liberty and untiring energy. With the authority of the church now fully established in the papacy, the faithful were free to follow the inspiration of the Holy Spirit with greater confidence and freedom. Like the fulcrum of a new lever, infallibility could lift religion higher and reconstruct society. The suffering of the faithful under persecution, therefore, was but a first step to a greater future for the church. By the loss of power and material strength, Catholics were purified, and must turn to their spiritual sources; from them would come a new strength and a rich outpouring of the Holy Spirit.

Hecker attempted to clarify the twofold action of the Holy Spirit in order to quiet the fear that spurring the faithful to vigorous action would damage the unity and integrity of the church. Certainly if the proper role of external authority were not recognized, such dangers would be real. Yet an exclusive regard for the church's authority, without a clear concept of the nature and function of the Holy Spirit within the individual soul, would render devotion formal, obedience servile, and the church weak and sterile. The operation of the Holy Spirit, therefore, in the visible church and invisibly in the soul, formed an inseparable synthesis. In the external authority of the church the Spirit acted as infallible interpreter of revelation; in the soul, it was a source of life and holiness. The same Spirit that taught divine truth through the church disposed the soul to grasp that truth. There could be no contradiction between them, for there was only one Spirit working in different ways toward the same goal, the regeneration and sanctification of the soul, and the fulfillment of human destiny. The sign of a true Christian, therefore, was unhesitating obedience. The Holy Spirit was "the immediate guide of the soul in the way of salvation and sanctification; and the sign that the soul may be guided by the Holy Spirit is its prompt obedience to the church's voice in each and every dubious matter."

Following such a path avoided dangers and enabled the soul to proceed with complete security and perfect freedom:

> The definition of the Vatican Council, having rendered the supreme authority of the Church, which is the unerring interpreter and criterion of divinely revealed truth, more explicit and complete, has prepared the way for the faithful to follow, with greater safety and liberty, the inspirations of the Holy Spirit. The dogmatic papal definition of the Vatican Council is therefore the axis on which turns the new course of the Church, the renewal of religion, and the entire restoration of society.

Perfected now on the external side, the divine institution of the church was free to attend more diligently to the internal side by development of deeper personal faith and a more vigorous spirituality. Explanations of the spiritual life of the church, of the intelligible side of its mysteries, and of the intrinsic reasons which confirmed revealed truths, combined with the external note of infallibility, would produce in the faithful a more vigorous conviction of Christianity's divine truth, stimulate their missionary energy and thus encourage the return to the church of those who had left it. Increased attention to the action of the Holy Spirit and closer cooperation among all the faithful could bring about a new era for both church and society.

Hecker then traced the movement of universal history toward the North and toward the Saxon races, which were now providing the dynamic element in world history; the church, as in the past, should reach out to convert them. In England and in the United States, composed of "mixed Saxons," there was a strong, surprising movement toward the church among the more cultured and influential classes, Hecker argued. In Latin countries, on the other hand, there was an opposite movement flowing from the revolutionary forces unleashed against society because of the loss of cultural dominance by the church. Threatened with violence to the north and desertion to the south, the church was in painful combat, the outcome of which could be fatal to the faith, especially if the church demanded the sacrifice of human nature and the legitimate tendencies of nations. But this need not be so. The principles proclaimed by the church provided answers to all these difficulties. What was needed was full knowledge of Catholic principles and their application to the present time, for God was the author of nature as well as grace, of reason as well as faith, so that, properly understood, God's revelation, and God's church, could meet the legitimate aspirations of all.

Looking toward the future, Hecker argued once again that the completion given the church's external organization should allow her to escape her past conservatism. In the earlier era the external defense required by the times was repressive and unpopular; the new work of evangelization, in contrast, would be expansive and popular. Human activity would be stimulated by a divine inspiration which would render it fruitful and glorious. The races with which Northern Europe and the United States were populated, by recovering their understanding of the divine character of the church and using their skills and their immense means, would become the providential instruments through which the light of faith would be diffused throughout the world. The predictions of the prophets, the promises of Christ, and the constant aspirations of noble souls would be fulfilled. This was what the age called for and, in Hecker's opinion, it was all possible.[25]

The *Exposition* added little to the ideas Hecker had been developing since the Vatican Council. He had been cautious in expressing them publicly; there had been a large gap between his public and private views of the council. Now he was sure that his "light" was from God, so he was anxious to set his ideas before the Catholic public. Arriving in Rome, Hecker arranged for the printing of his program. He reassured George and Hewit that he had obtained the permission of ecclesiastical authorities, the printing would be done at the Propaganda Press, and he had been advised by the editor of *Civiltà Cattolica* to present a copy to the pope. He sent one copy to the *Catholic World* for publication, telling Hewit that it was meeting approval from all sides in Rome; he was having no trouble arranging the *imprimatur*. A few days later, however, he wrote Hewit of the disapproval of two Roman theologians, one of whom was his old advisor, Bernard Smith, so publication had to be delayed.

Privately he noted that the type had already been set when word came to stop. His own doubts were evident in his notes:

1. One may think he is right and be mistaken.
2. One may be right and premature.
3. One may be right but not hit on the right way.
4. One may be right, but requiring opposition etc. to keep him on the right path.
5. One may be right, and by contradiction and condemnation open the way to the success of truth.

Earlier he had been expelled from the Redemptorists but "God did make use of me for his designs." Now, he wrote, "my views are condemned as inexpedient; may it be only preliminary to a future work."[26]

After thinking about the matter for two weeks, Hecker acted decisively and sent the manuscript to England for printing. He did not ask advice from Roman authorities as he did not want to "implicate them indirectly." He had already sent proofs to influential persons. Cardinal Manning wrote of his general agreement, especially with the argument that the "low state of mind in respect to the Office of the Holy Ghost in the Church has caused most of our modern errors" and had led Catholics to become "unspiritual and merely natural." He was less certain there would be an outpouring of the Spirit. Some of Hecker's European friends had other reservations. Peter Rossi, a Lazarist he had met in Genoa, worried because Hecker had failed to call attention to the threat posed by an increasingly irreligious working class, while Edward Dufresne thought his comments on the Jesuits unduly harsh. In contrast, Dufresne's son Xavier, who was becoming a Hecker disciple, told Hecker his essay "simplifies theology by reducing it to a simple principle of unity, just as the theory of universal gravitation of Newton simplified astronomy." But Hecker's acquaintance, Cardinal Deschamps of Malines, while he found the pamphlet useful for "controversy against Protestants," thought Hecker underestimated the dangers of the age and overstated the church's stress on authority. Some liberals thought Hecker had not gone far enough. Joseph Burone, for example, thought Hecker's emphasis on the Holy Spirit too "vague"; he wanted a sharper criticism of the Jesuits and of their overemphasis on authority, which threatened to bring greater "suspicions, fears, repressions, a spirit of lies and falsehoods," all in the name of service to the Church.[27]

Perhaps the most interesting response came from John Henry Newman. He found the pamphlet "clear, interesting and winning" and sufficiently reserved to "avoid giving offense to the Master of the Sacred Palace." He wished he could agree with its "beautiful," hopeful views, and he admitted that the proverb "man's necessity is God's opportunity" was in Hecker's favor. But that was a maxim of faith and the pamphlet was an argument about history. "Whereas you infer 'we are so bad we are sure to get better,' " Newman wrote, "I feel there is another inference conceivable and possible in fact: 'we are so bad off, that we are likely to get worse.' " In fact, "the main point" on which the pope insisted, was not the "effusion of Divine Influences" but "the maintenance of the Temporal Power," making Hecker's forecast less likely. Newman closed with a comment that must have bothered Hecker: "I am grieved to observe the line that the *Catholic World* has taken for some years." Hecker told Hewit that Newman "appears a little soured."[28]

Despite the reservations of many he admired, Hecker was pleased with the response to the *Exposition*. For him the church always was an ideal, struggling to take shape amid the baggage of each particular historical period. At every step of his Catholic life he was reminded that the process was far from complete. Yet he was not naive and fully understood that people would misread his ideas and oppose his projects. He told George and Josephine that he anticipated charges of "mysticism, illuminism, millenarianism, Americanism, Protestantism, etc." from Catholics who "see things almost exclusively from the outside." But, stripped of "outward honors and dignities" the church could turn the future into "channels of success and increased glory." What she needed were "men who will have that universal synthesis of truth which will solve the problems, eliminate the antagonisms and meet the great needs of the age; men who will turn all the aspirations of the age, in socialism, in politics, in religion . . . which are now perverted against the church, into means of her defense and universal triumph." This sounded like Paulists, at least as Hecker envisioned them.[29]

Hecker knew that those who saw "things almost exclusively from the outside" were in charge. Yet he had the courage to urge the church to criticize itself and risk adopting entirely new strategies for the age. As he told his brother:

> We are clearly in a fix—But have we not been brought into it as much by our own fault and mismanagement as by the fatal course of events? Has there not been much of needless boasting, of empty claims, of narrow opposition to what might have been dealt with in a larger and friendly spirit? And to the abyss that, from the nature of the case, separates the spirit of the Church from that of the Age, have we not added another of our own making?
>
> The wisdom of God freely imparted to his children can remedy all,—of course it can. But that wisdom He gives to his Church only in a limited way—sometimes sparingly. Hence although deserving unlimited trust in Her dogmatic utterance, she is not entitled to the same in her practical guidance. 1st because in the latter she is not infallible. 2nd, because the inferior agencies through which she acts are not a *sure* expression of her real wisdom. 3rd, because even these are tortured into all manner of shapes by those who find it pleasant to throw them in other people's faces.
>
> In fact authority is so much *abused* at the present day, that it requires a thorough belief in it as a thing divine, not to conceive a hearty dislike to everything that comes under *its flag*![30]

Faced with all this, Hecker nevertheless searched for signs of the movement his pamphlet anticipated. He took hope from news that his old mentor and friend Archbishop McCloskey was to be made a cardinal, the first from the United States. Hecker joined other Americans in Rome to celebrate the event. He told his oldest Catholic guide that his elevation was "a cheering sign" that the church represented all nations, making "its universality more complete." McCloskey did not come to Rome; instead Americans in Rome held a dinner to honor the Roman emissaries going to New York to install the new cardinal. McCloskey's elevation was for Hecker only one of a series of moves by authority in the same direction. The new appointment, if it foreshadowed a dozen different nationalities sharing direction of the church, would mean that God was "denationalizing the church," making it more truly universal and opening the door to the fullest expression of its spirituality.[31]

A cardinal's appointment, though, had more to do with "externals" than with spiritual awakening. Still Hecker looked hopefully for signs of the in-breaking of the Holy Spirit, for the emergence of a more spiritual, personal, energetic Christianity within Catholicism. He was to be disappointed, more disappointed than in any of his previous crises. Others, understandably, were Catholics in their way, many of them churchmen who felt a powerful personal responsibility for the well-being of the institutional church, the church as they knew it in the here and now. Placed in charge of parishes, dioceses, schools and religious orders, their vocations were grounded in specific, immediate problems. Like Hecker, they saw the dangers which threatened the church, its doctrines, discipline, membership and organization. Many, like Cardinal Manning, even shared his faith in the Holy Spirit and in the eventual triumph of God's church. But, in the meantime, they had innumerable daily decisions to make about this parish, this school, this diocese. Hecker had faced such decisions in organizing the Paulists, launching the parish, winning support for his publications, but now, as in the earlier times of crisis in his life, he had turned his back on such responsibilities, opened himself to the interior life of the Spirit and come back with plans for action grounded in fact in no particular responsibility. Even his warmest supporters received his ideas in the setting of specific commitments within the organized Catholic subculture, so that Hecker's call to evangelization was ignored as a nice but distracting idea or, even worse, was welcomed as one more arrow in the quiver of Catholic self-righteousness. Even among Hecker's friends, Hecker's ideas, and even Hecker himself, became all too easily a triumphal means of defeating Protestants, winning members for the church and increasing the participation of Catholics in the organized sacramental life.

Hecker remained in Rome through the winter, having a pleasant audience with the pope in February. No mention was made of his new ideas. Instead, he presented the holy father with several gifts, including a painting which included several donkeys. The pope asked if they grew that large in Hecker's country, and he responded, "Asses nowadays grow larger everywhere," which brought a laugh from the holy father, who then gave his blessing and an indulgence for all who contributed to the new Paulist church in New York.

Yet these were not happy days for the American evangelist. Energetic work on the pamphlet did not end Hecker's spiritual anxieties. He noted in his journal that his "fretting" disturbed his health and reduced his strength. Julia Beers, Archbishop Bayley's niece with whom Hecker had stayed in Florida three years before, was in Rome that winter and once again found Hecker "a broken down man." He lunched with her almost daily for two months and Beers reported that "he is more care than *ten* babies would be—he is incapable of deciding anything for himself, wants constant distraction to turn his mind from his own sufferings, which seem, after all, to be more mental than physical." She had planned to join him and others on a trip to the Holy Land, but several had been forced to withdraw, so they abandoned their plans. She sent Bayley a copy of the *Exposition*, noting its history and the decision of Propaganda to stop publication. That decision stung Hecker, she responded; "its being disapproved of here was quite a blow to him."[32]

Nevertheless, Hecker continued to promote the pamphlet. Mrs. Pauline Craven was translating it into French and Joseph Burone was arranging for its publication in Italian. By June Hecker was back in Switzerland, where young Dufresne found him in better health than the fall. In fact, however, Hecker's health remained poor. He wrote George and Josephine that he awoke at 7:00 each morning but did not rise until 10:00 or later, and then had to nap in the afternoon. He did not have the strength for much exercise and was sleeping longer than at any time in his life. He was still sure he could not return home; he would find no rest with community affairs, in which his "intellectual interest . . . has ceased." He would have to remain in Europe, alone and obscure, he wrote in a tone of self-pity. Yet there were rewards in his spiritual life: "In an oblivion of all created things, without any solicitude about one's physical health or one's future, the soul finds itself in the immediate presence of God, and divinely exercised. What beyond this can we ask? What more can it desire?"[33]

While Hecker contemplated his future, his fate was being decided. By July 1875 the Community's patience was exhausted. The first indication came from Father Young. "As we have had considerable changes in our parish projects, and I might even add in our parish politics also, for I think we will all turn Republicans, I think it my duty to write you," he began a letter on July 7. First, the plans for the new church sent to New York by a Lyon architect at Hecker's request "might do for the mausoleum of some old heathen jurisconsult, but most certainly would never be mistaken for a Catholic Church." They had been returned, but the architect was now demanding payment. Deshon hoped Hecker had not promised a payment unless the design was accepted, but nevertheless he would leave the matter for Hecker to settle. Second, a company had obtained a charter to erect a huge cattle yard and slaughter house in the neighborhood; despite protest meetings, petitions and Deshon's three weeks of lobbying in Albany, they had failed to stop it. Worse, an elevated railroad was creeping up Ninth Avenue and would be in front of the proposed church by October, while the company was negotiating the purchase of the adjacent block for a locomotive and car depot. In addition, there was a national economic crisis which convinced Deshon that the elaborate plans for the church would have to be drastically reduced. They would have to look elsewhere for a place to build their convent and house of studies and settle for a church no larger than the present one. Finally, need for a house was now critical. Hewit had told Young to lay these problems before Hecker and he did so reluctantly, adding some cheering notes. Everyone saw the Paulists as the leaders of the church in New York, they had more requests for missions than they could fill, and the community had assumed a position before the public that was all Hecker could wish for. Still, they badly needed his "guidance and leadership."[34]

While Young was writing this troubling letter from 59th Street, Hewit was at the Lake with the novices, writing another. His self-control, his desire to avoid burdening Hecker, and his restraint at his leader's wanderings gave way before the pressure of work and the multiplying problems of the Congregation. Noting the changes in the neighborhood, Hewit stated that he had the novices at the Lake but had no place to take them in the fall. Hewit himself felt the pressure of working with the students, while the *Catholic World* and Catholic Publication Society desperately needed looking after. The Rule provided that a superior should have been elected the previous September, but that had been postponed. Hewit noted that Louis Binsse, an old lay supporter, had inquired why Hecker had not gone to Lourdes to pray for a cure. Hewit was annoyed, for he found it hard to answer that often asked question, especially when the Paulists had promoted that devotion "and it seems to the world that you cast a discredit, or at least show a want of sympathy with the Catholic sentiment." But the real issue was Hecker's return, and his spiritual director spared no words in telling him to come home:

> The whole future of our Congregation is at this moment depending on your action and your fidelity to the call of God's providence. If you falter and fail, the temptation which had been threat-

> ening its disruption ever since you went away, will return again, viz. that the whole idea and enterprise was an illusion from the beginning, and a merely human undertaking, not inspired or destined to be blessed by God. I do not wish to have on me the responsibility of the success or failure of your work, or of having changed or marred it. If it is necessary you ought to make willingly the sacrifice of your life in order to fulfill your duty to God, and act up to the sentiments you have expressed and inculcated of heroism and devotion.[35]

Hewit's devotion and love were unquestionable, then and later. It must have been very difficult for him to write Hecker in this tone, using Hecker's own favorite themes of Providence and heroism. A retiring, scholarly man, Hewit disliked the leadership role he had been forced to assume, and he felt all his life that the Paulists were Hecker's responsibility, a responsibility to which he had been specially called by God. Yet, as his spiritual director, he also knew of Hecker's weaknesses, his doubts and hesitations, his lapses into self-pity, and his occasional indifference, even to his own most cherished projects.

The letter must have worried Hewit, for four days later he wrote another, beginning by softening the demand, but ending by reaffirming it more strongly than ever. They need not hold the Chapter in September; indeed, given the problem of locating the students and the fact that some of the fathers were scheduled for a mission in Minnesota, December would be more convenient, so Hecker could delay his return into the fall. He did not insist that Hecker come to live with the community, either. He could spend some time with George, recovering from the voyage; by then he expected they would have a house for the students in some "pleasant part of town above 58th Street" where he could have "a comfortable and quiet place." Hecker would not "be troubled with the details of governing the community at St. Paul's, which F. Young can manage passably well." After these compassionate suggestions, Hewit reiterated the decisions that needed to be made. Would they proceed with plans for a grand church and convent at the old site or accept Father Young's proposal of a parochial establishment there with the principal house and perhaps a studentate elsewhere? Furthermore, Hewit wrote, if forced to choose someone other than Hecker for superior, the members would be satisfied with no one but himself, yet that position was clearly incompatible with that of director of the students. Thus "our affairs are in a sort of deadlock," which "can only be opened by yourself and your presence." Hecker could hardly expect further benefits from travel beyond those already received. Besides, the work of superior which would devolve upon Hecker would be only "about one fifth part of the work you used to do." In conclusion, it seemed to Hewit that it was Hecker's duty, and the will of God, that he return "whatever the state of your health may be" and leave the outcome and the "wants of the future" to Providence and "to those of your brethren who have the right to determine what your duty is."[36]

As each of these letters arrived, Hecker responded quickly but without a clear decision. To Young he wrote expressing grave concern about the building plans. Insisting that his was only advice, subject to the will of the community, he urged delay, hoping that things would be clearer in a year or two. He had doubts about the quality of the uptown property suggested by Young and concern that the problems at 59th Street would be repeated there with the rapid expansion of the city. A separate establishment for the community and students would be a great expense; if it turned out to be necessary, he suggested going further out to the country or into New Jersey for the right property. Recognizing the dangers, particularly if the railroad company did succeed in building a car lot next door, he nevertheless argued against hasty decisions. To George, he wrote more critically that the community had gotten into a building frenzy. Responding to Hewit's first letter, he repeated his counsel of caution regarding the property. As for Lourdes, he responded: "who is to judge whether I should ask God for a miracle?" Regarding the chapter, the *Catholic World* and the necessity of his being present in September, he wrote defensively: "The past has not given any reasonable grounds for suspicion of my willingness to sacrifice myself for the good of the community, and as for the present, it is in its hand." Despite the fact that Hewit had said he had the backing of the consultors, Hecker insisted that the members deliberate again. If they decided on his immediate return, they should send him a telegram and "it will find me indifferent to my health or what physicians may say." At the bottom of this letter he wrote that, having reread Hewit's letter, he found it so strong as to require him to send a telegram containing his appeal for community deliberation. His "state of health" did not allow him to enter into all the points raised by Hewit further than to say that, up to this period, he and his fellow Paulists always acted out of a "supreme sense of duty and with fidelity to the grace of our vocation, let us not swerve from this first principle. In this sense, I am now as I have always been by the grace of God, indifferent to 'the world.' "[37]

Hewit's second letter arrived two days after Hecker had dispatched his telegram. In response, Hecker explained that he had asked for a community decision because Hewit had given no intimation he had consulted anyone and because he wanted to avoid acting from "a sudden impulse." Hewit's argument that Hecker's health could not benefit from prolonging his stay was a judgment which "requires data not in your possession." It seemed to Hecker that "medical men" would be the best judges but, even if they should be against his return, Hewit might be right "in view of higher and greater reasons." He wished only to know the divine will and therefore awaited their telegram. He took up the points Hewit had raised. As the Rule would probably be delayed in Rome, it would be best to postpone the Chapter to December, as Hewit had suggested. Father Byrne should be assigned to relieve Hewit of some of his work and some promising students sent for higher studies to prepare for seminary teaching. Finally, he felt nothing should be done with the 59th Street property until they were "*certain*" what disposition would be best.[38]

Calm and apparently undisturbed as his letters seemed, Hecker was in turmoil, for the now irresistible demand for his return conflicted directly with his emerging sense of mission in the universal church. The work of the Paulists, good and admirable as it was, remained enclosed within another vision, opening up few new possibilities. As always, Hecker wanted to turn toward the future, while circumstances and concrete loyalties and responsibilities tugged toward the past. "Is it not wiser and better to give one's thought and energy to prepare the way for the future success and triumph of religion, than to labor to continue the present which must be and is being supplanted?" he asked himself. "Such an attitude may not be understood or [it may be] misinterpreted . . . still it is the only one that can be consistent with one's sense of duty."

> There is an approaching conflict between the society of the nineteenth century and the Church—which has already begun—it is more threatening than that of the sixteenth century—This requires a reawakening of the spirit of Christianity, recurrence to the renewing Holy Spirit—new aims, new adaptations. Where are the men sensible of this? Preparing for it? My whole soul is alive to this great work. My conviction of its necessity is complete and irresistible. My intimate conviction that the voice of God calls me to labor in this direction is equally complete and irresistible.[39]

Before he could mail his second response to Hewit, a telegram confirmed the community's urgent request for Hecker's return. He scrawled across the top: "As soon as I engage passage I will let you know the date—likely I shall take passage to arrive before 1st of Nov." On the same day he wrote George that he had no real objections to returning. The work before him was growing clearer and he was confident the Lord would arrange affairs so that he could do it. The pamphlet, he wrote optimistically, was providing a common ground on which many different parties could meet and agree. If things could be arranged in such a way as to overcome "the interior conflict from which I have suffered," his duties in the United States and "the work before me in Europe" could be reconciled and the major cause of his "feebleness" would be removed. "While engaged in this interior struggle there was no possibility of regaining my health," he wrote. "You who know me perfectly can easily recall what past conflicts have cost me, and can easily interpret the present." In any event, he said, his soul was now quiet and tranquil, open to God's will.[40]

Nevertheless, Hecker was still not completely resigned to his return. On August 9 he wrote Hewit that he had booked passage for October 2, and would spend the first half of September in Paris, the second half in London. He added that, as the result of the urging of friends, he had consulted a physician and enclosed the doctor's opinion that his health was such that all "active occupation" would be dangerous. He was affected with a general weakness requiring "distraction from all intellectual work and all moral preoccupation." The doctor advised "an absolute abstention from all preoccupation with the affairs of his past life, during a year at least, and a stay at one of the Spas of Europe next year." To George, Hecker wrote that he could not do much of anything and was forced to resist all attempts to burden him with cares, however slight. Nevertheless, he said, he was resigned to God's will.

When Hewit received the doctor's certificate, his patience snapped and he wrote Hecker the strongest letter he would ever receive. The community could judge whether the doctor's report was strictly correct when Hecker returned. If he was indeed unable to bear the responsibilities of superior, he of course would not be required to do so. "In that case," Hewit wrote sharply, "it is necessary that you live under the obedience of a superior who is elected to take your place, and whoever he may be, he will not require you to do any work whatever or fail to give you rest and every indulgence compatible with your state, and which anyone who is disabled has a right to expect." Indeed, if he was as feeble as the doctor indicated, Hewit argued, it was not safe for him to remain abroad. As Hecker's spiritual director and friend, Hewit noted that a longer stay would be dangerous for his spiritual welfare and public reputation. He reminded him that he was a religious, subject to obedience and to the vow of poverty:

> After such a long absence and such extraordinary measures for renewing your health which no other father can ever expect in a similar case, it would be contrary to the spirit of a religious state to prolong such an enjoyment of privileges which only rich men can afford. If you cannot actively serve the community you can passively serve it by giving an example of obedience, patience,

> and resignation, and leave it to God to restore you to health or prepare you for heaven as he sees fit.[41]

Hecker responded both mildly and defensively. "Let us keep our minds free from all agitations, looking upward to the Divine Will alone, as we have always aimed and striven to do," he wrote. He was prepared to "lay bare to any scrutiny" every step he had taken in Europe. He clearly resented the imputation of comfortable selfishness in Hewit's letter:

> All the sufferings of my past life appear as nothing compared with those which it has pleased God to lay upon me these three years. They have taught me to love suffering until the moment of my leaving the body. It appears to me that this prayer is His Will, and it will be accomplished.[42]

Resigned now to returning, Hecker noted privately that his return would bring him "face to face with the difficulties" which had been present "since the beginning of the movement of the Paulists." In a revealing passage, Hecker set forth the heart of the matter:

> The conception of a movement of the Paulists was one which had preoccupied my mind a long while. It was one in which the elements of self-control, conscience, and internal guidance of the Holy Spirit, should take the lead over the control of discipline, Rules, and external authority. How far such a conception could be practically realized in our time, and with individuals of different characteristics, and form a community, was a question of actual experiment and experience. During the years of the formation of the Paulists, all my companions were more and more inclined to increase the discipline, fixed rules, and external authority, than I was. This necessarily produced in my interior a conflict—a struggle between my own attrait and idea, my type of Christian perfection in St. Phillip Neri, and theirs, St. Ignatius.[43]

He believed now that this struggle had caused his physical breakdown. It was a conflict in Hecker "as it must have been in them, between their idea, conscience, and the attrait of grace, and the means in harmony with their realization." As soon as his health required him to leave the direction of the community in other hands, "the increase and expansion in the direction which they desired became at once manifest, in the community, parish church, and etc." At the same time there was "in my interior a change in the opposite direction beyond expression." Now his companions were anxious for his return either to resume direction of the community, if his strength allowed, or, if not, to remain and live with them. If he resumed the direction, considering the turn they had given to the development of the community and the direction which his own "interior" had taken, "past difficulties would only be greatly increased, and either I should soon break down again in the effort to reconcile the different views, or fail to give them the satisfaction which they naturally would require." Obviously there was trouble ahead. "To live in the community would be to stifle my own convictions—a thing impossible morally and physically, and a slow consuming martyrdom," he wrote. "It would be impossible to avoid this, and what strength remains in my body would soon be consumed, and it would be impossible that there should not be those who would discover this, and it would probably lead to trouble." As always, however, Hecker reached an optimistic conclusion, for there seemed to him to be "a course which appears to reconcile both sides," the extension of the Paulists to Europe:

> What is the fundamental idea of the Paulists? It is the idea of organizing the practical side of the church in view of the needs of the age and the triumph of Religion, for the greatest expansion of the ideal Christian life possible. What is the ideal Christian life? It is human nature in its entire force, sanctified and transformed by Christianity. This is the idea which underlies the Paulist movement and which idea needs to be practically organized in Europe in harmony with the instincts and dispositions of its different races, nationalities and needs, in order to prepare the way for the triumph of the church. Whatever light, grace, strength, impulse God may have [given] and does give me, all turns to this point.[44]

What this appeared to mean was that he would lead the Paulists in New York, if he could, back to what he regarded as their foundation ideals, while at the same time working to extend those ideals, and the Paulists themselves, to Europe. The vision which had informed his view of the Paulists was more solidly rooted in Hecker's personal convictions than it had been in 1858. As he put it in his private notes on September 4, 1875:

> What else is the church in all her activities than the means instituted by God to place all souls in more direct and complete communication with himself, and of rendering them participators in His substance—Divine Expansion. The whole practical side of the Church in the present needs to be recast in view of future expansion, the same as it was recast three centuries ago, on account of then threatening dangers, in view of repression. Not by

> repressing or diminishing authority, discipline or the external notes of the Church, but by accentuating, developing and fortifying the internal action of the Holy Spirit in the soul, developing the internal notes, and stimulating personal initiative and courage.[45]

As he told his friend Richard Simpson, "If my instincts don't deceive me, you will find me stirring up folks this side of the water some day."[46]

Hecker was indeed to "stir up" Europe and European Catholics, but not in his own lifetime. When he left for home at the end of September 1875, he had thirteen more years to live, but he would not see Europe again. His worries about the Paulists proved justified, his health remained poor, and the course of events in the American church and church universal frustrated his plans for Paulist overseas expansion. Yet his career was far from over. He would work and write; his ideas would continue to inspire a minority of energetic Catholic leaders; and his witness to those ideas would command respect, even reverence, from almost everyone with whom he came in contact. But for Hecker that respect would be tinged with sadness, for things could not yet be what he hoped, either in the church or in the larger world whose destiny was his deepest concern. In the confusing and difficult years to come, Hecker's life would be dominated by the inner experience of God and the adventure of the spirit, while his public life would be marked by a series of disappointments. The long stay abroad, the quest for restored physical health, and the patient waiting upon God would bear fruit in a deeper and richer experience of the Spirit; their ultimate result would not be known even a century after his death.

16

Making America Catholic

In October 1875 Hecker was back at his brother's house, suffering from headaches. Hewit, sending his welcome from Lake George, told Hecker to rest with his family until he felt strong enough to rejoin the community. Deshon was less patient, writing from St. Paul, Minnesota, where he was giving a mission, that Hecker should take up the pressing problem of finding land and buildings for the Paulists. Hewit had no "genius" for such matters, Deshon complained, while Young, the superior of the New York house, needed help to "straighten his ideas." Hewit, writing again, agreed that Hecker should assume leadership, even though he had returned against his own inclinations. In December the long delayed chapter meeting was held, Hecker was unanimously reelected superior general, and the Rule and Statutes were put in final form for resubmission to Rome. Hecker, still living most of the time with his brother, took an active role in chapter deliberations and intervened to give direction on a number of Paulist problems.[1]

One of the most pressing difficulties was *Catholic World*, which had fallen on financial hard times. Under Hewit's direction, and perhaps still influenced by Brownson's acerbic style and pessimistic outlook, the journal had grown cranky and defensive, blasting away at critics of the church and holding forth a somewhat triumphalistic vision, attitudes which undoubtedly influenced Newman's comments that he was disheartened by its direction. Hecker, though often confined to his bed, took charge after his return. To assist, he hired John McCarthy, a newspaperman formerly with the *New York Tribune*. McCarthy was friendly with Brownson and told him

Hecker felt keenly the need for a change: "The idea is to make it bristle with the living questions of the day, most especially those immediately around us." For the next few years the *Catholic World* would be the only vehicle available to Hecker to propagate his ideas.[2]

Back in the United States with no immediate means of remaining involved in European church affairs, Hecker narrowed his gaze for the moment to the old project of making America Catholic. He had become far more aware of the barriers that stood in the way. Religious, social and cultural differences still separated Catholics and non-Catholics. Prejudice and misunderstandings were regularly reinforced by clashes over public policy matters like education and charities. Catholic writers still needed to defend the church against attack, if only to secure their credentials among Catholics. At the same time, Hecker was acutely aware that few Catholics shared his sense of the movement of divine providence or his desire to reach out to others. Both sets of problems, external hostility and internal self-centeredness, were more severe than ever. Yet Hecker entered the battle again.

Both during his lifetime and later, there was considerable confusion about Hecker's approach to non-Catholics. Some of his admirers thought his greatest contribution was to help make Catholics American. By his own example, by his reasonable, sensitive style of presenting the faith to the American public, by his evident love for the country, its institutions and ideals, and by his concern with broad religious and civic problems, he made credible the possibility that Catholics could, after all, be good Americans. Moreover, he promoted modern forms of organization, communication and apostolic action; he was the "steam priest," changing the image of the American church from that of a backward, archaic, reactionary faith associated with unlettered and somewhat disorderly immigrants to that of a legitimately conservative institution which disciplined its members while gradually making its own the best techniques of modern civilization. For middle-class Catholics who wanted to be good Catholics and successful, respectable Americans—without worrying over much about the relationship of the two—Hecker became a convenient symbol; he was what they hoped to be, a man of the church and a man of his age, with few rough edges to upset other Catholics or other Americans.

This picture of Hecker as a comfortably denominational American Catholic could not be further from the truth. The nineteenth-century church's preoccupation with orthodoxy, unity and loyalty was in retrospect a sectarian strategy designed to insure its survival. In Europe, as Hecker had found, Catholic alienation from modern society made isolation into a virtue. Many identified the church with supposedly authentic national traditions and placed it in a posture of an establishment in exile, patiently waiting for the collapse of the rebellion against God to return to restore order, authority and unity. In America, where personal freedom, political democracy and economic progress exerted a powerful attraction upon the Catholic minority, conservative religion settled gradually into denominationalism, where the church used its freedom to maintain its historic claims over its own members, while at the same time affirming American institutions, encouraging its members to seek a better life and to participate in political affairs, and avoiding even the appearance of that yearning for power so characteristic of European ultramontanism. Thus the militant Catholicism of John Hughes and Orestes Brownson had far more to do with enhancing Catholic morale and clarifying the boundaries between Catholics and non-Catholics than with mobilizing Catholics to take charge of American society. They helped to build a Catholic subculture whose denunciations of Protestantism and, with growing force, secularism, obscured the fact that Catholics and their church were enjoying considerable success and settling quite comfortably into the contours of a pluralistic religious culture marked by toleration, civility and goodwill. Most Catholics had no passionate desire to defeat or to convert non-Catholics; they wished only to be loyal Catholics and loyal Americans.

Hecker never accepted denominational status as a permanent condition. He was deeply convinced that the church was not intended to be a minority but to embrace all men and women. Someday, in the providence of God, America really should and would become Catholic and, after America, the world. This expectation of the future triumph of the church was the deepest conviction of Hecker's public career. In his vision that triumph would come about when the church expressed the "spontaneous conviction of the mass of mankind."

He wanted more than anything else to invite non-Catholics to enter the church, but Hecker's evangelical zeal went deeper than individual conversion. Evangelization was not primarily a matter of membership, but of bringing all human life, art and science, politics and culture, to their fullest realization. It meant inviting people to be part of a church which itself was part of the redemptive work of Christ.

Of course Hecker was forced to deal with the realities of a sectarian church and a denominational society. In later years he spent more time on the defense of Catholic interests and less on promotion of Catholic answer to common problems. And, of course, there were flaws in his vision and his arguments, all of which reflected his special experience as an American, a convert and a mystic. But no aspect of Hecker's life makes sense outside the context of his deep conviction that the long-range goal was to make peoples, cultures, societies and nations Catholic. He was polite, civil and tolerant; he was also completely convinced that Catholicism was *the* church, "a divine institution commissioned by her founder to conduct men to their divine destination."[3] He thought that the very best of good news.

This conclusion, that Catholicism was catholic, embracing every person and every aspect of life, was at the very heart of Hecker's understanding of the church. In 1866 Hecker wrote that the great work "to which all things in this world are subordinated is that of man's redemption." This was the purpose for which God had become man in Christ; his redemptive work continued through the church, which was "the real center of the world." Accordingly, "the conversion of the world" was "the great work of the church." The reason to desire a greater integration of the church into American society was to bring about such a conquest. For the church, as Hecker saw it, "to work for the conversion of the people of the country is a necessity of her being—it is her life and existence; and as we live her life, sympathize with her aims, identify our interests with hers, it becomes our work, our life and existence." To be a member of the church was "to labor in whatever position God has placed us for the conversion of our people."

To bring that about Catholics should "seek the truth amidst the error, establish its existence, applaud it and endeavor to make it a basis for further truth and a fulcrum for the overthrow of the error connected with it." This was what Hecker tried to do in *Questions of the Soul* and *Aspirations of Nature*, which were aimed at those who had escaped Puritanism's "sour image of all that is beautiful in nature" and, like Thoreau and Emerson, had "a lively sense of the dignity of the soul." Those pillars of transcendentalism had "a living view of religion"; their thoughts often coincided with those of the great Catholic spiritual writers. Their passion for truth and personal integrity could not be sustained for long without lapsing into infidelity. If one assumed, then, that a universal religious hunger existed, and that it could not be filled by pessimistic Calvinism, emotional evangelicalism or cold rationalism, then indeed the time was ripe to present Catholicism's message to a starved generation.[4]

For years Hecker all but ignored devout Protestants and instead courted open-minded rationalists and moderate Christians dissatisfied with the churches. During the Civil War, for example, he carried on an occasional correspondence with Catherine Beecher, who was trying to develop a "common sense" theology that would spell out the common ground among Christians and overcome sectarian divisions. Hecker found her demonstration of the truths of natural religion a "necessary preamble to revealed religion" and "the common method of Catholics." Beecher was friendly but unresponsive. Other New Englanders retained much of the tolerant skepticism Hecker had found among his friends after his own conversion. When Hecker sent the old New England poet and essayist

Oliver Wendell Holmes a copy of the Paulist *Sermons* for 1863, Holmes was amused, responding that Hecker should not hope to make a Catholic out of him; it would take a miracle.[5]

In fact, Hecker made few converts. There is no way of knowing how many may have been led to the church by his lectures and writing. Those in whose conversion he was personally involved were few, the best known a group of expatriate Americans he met in Rome during the fateful winter of 1857–58. The artist George Brown was one. Anna B. Ward, wife of a prominent New England lawyer and close friend of Emerson, was another; later, the Paulists in New York would also receive her sister into the church. Another Roman convert was Jane Sedgwick, daughter of an old New England family whose conversion led to a lonely isolation from relatives and friends in her hometown of Stockbridge, Massachusetts. She hoped to work in some apostolic service but, like many others, her health prevented her from doing so. There were others, but the list of those converted by Hecker's zeal was short, testimony less to the weakness of his arguments than to the complexity of the situation he confronted. Hecker was neither surprised nor discouraged, for he knew the conversion of the nation would await the providence of God and might take centuries. Even the public presentations following missions were designed to lessen prejudice and awaken interest in the church; local follow-through in the form of lay and clerical evangelism, instruction classes and deliberate, continued effort at conversion was needed.[6]

Hecker's conviction that it was from the unchurched, especially those tending toward rationalism, that the most significant converts would come, did not rest on empirical evidence. In fact, his fellow Paulists and many of their converts came from devout Protestant families and were themselves inclined toward "high church" ideals rather than toward Unitarianism or infidelity. Hecker's preoccupation with the latter, however, reflected his desire to make the whole nation Catholic rather than to simply expand the membership of the church. He did not see the problem as one of competitive churches alone, so he did not give attention early in his career to seeking common ground with Protestants. Rather, he viewed it as a Christian problem, bringing the full message of Christ into harmony with all of life. Accordingly, the strategy should be one of rebuilding the Christian (read Catholic) church from the ground up, touching the consciences of all persons, rather than simply reuniting those who already accepted Christianity. Even if the outcome of declining Protestantism was not a generation of earnest seekers but a rise in paganism, as Brownson argued, that would be no argument for turning back to the Christian minority alone, but an even more demanding reason to evangelize on the basis of what all human beings held in common. Hecker came to see even materialism and hedonism as expressions of a fundamental hunger which in the end could only be fed by God. The efforts of traditional Catholicism and orthodox Protestantism to find common ground partook of rearranging the organization of a church which had lost its faith in its ultimate destiny of union with God. Rather than focus on the controversies of the past, which had divided the Christian churches, or on the short-term differences of the present, rooted as they were in cultures and ways of life that were passing, one's sight should be fixed on the promised land, the Christian commonwealth, that lay in the future, calling all Christians to reach out to their fellow human beings in order to fulfill God's will for the human race, beginning in the United States.

Hecker's sense that Protestant decline was Catholic opportunity arose once again from his experience. He saw himself as an earnest, honest seeker after truth, who began his religious quest with no prejudices against Catholicism, indeed with no preferences for any particular denomination. He "had never been a member of any denomination," he wrote in 1878; the creed he had recited for Bishop McCloskey was his "first adhesion to any form of religion."[7] He had been led to Catholicism by the promptings of the Holy Spirit within, touching his emotions and rendering him almost helpless at times, drawing him toward God. Reason had been important, guiding his quest, confirming his rejection of some proposed answers to his religious questions, supporting and endorsing those answers he accepted. He was concerned with the human person as a whole. The aspirations of human nature, articulated through reason, and the questions of the soul arising from "instinct," were expressions of a single human nature. Catholicism, that form of Christianity established by Christ to continue the fact of the Incarnation, provided a complete, integral response to both inner spiritual needs and reasonable, logical questions. It provided both love and truth.

Hecker believed that there were many other Americans whose experience was similar to his own, who were emancipated from historical prejudice, open to the arguments of contending groups, ready to respond to the truth and to the reality of love where they found it. No longer Protestant, neither were they pagan. Hecker saw his American as Hawthorne saw Melville: "He can neither believe, nor be comfortable in his unbelief." Where others saw indifference and failure to attend church as signs of decadence threatening the social order, Hecker thought he spied beneath the unravelling of popular Protestantism a deeper piety waiting to be awakened. He would have appreciated Hawthorne's statement of his own failure to attend services: "Doubts may flit around me, or seem to close their evil wings [but] never can my soul have lost the instinct of its faith. . . . Though my form be absent, my inner man goes constantly to church." Indeed, there was reason to be optimistic, for Christianity was both dead and alive, in that half-begun and half-ended state which always seems to mark its history. As John Updike wrote of Hawthorne: "A very vivid ghost of Christianity stares out at us from his prose, alarming and odd in not being evenly dead, but alive in some limbs, and amputated in others, blurred in some aspects, basilisk-keen in others, even in part upside down."[8]

One reason for the growth of such uncertainty was the decline of the traditional and prescriptive power of the Protestant churches. In the midst of religious pluralism, the taken-for-grantedness of conventional Protestantism declined, factions multiplied, each offering only partial truths, each rendered unstable by the principles of private judgment secured by American pluralism. The task of Catholics, as Hecker saw it, was to present the fullness of Catholic truth; it must be full in order to demonstrate its comprehensiveness in the face of Protestant partiality. But it must also be only essential truths, stripped of those cultural accretions that had been sources of prejudice and had erected barriers to a response.

In this vision Protestantism was seen as relatively passive. Hecker, unlike Hewit, had experienced little enthusiastic Protestant evangelization in his own youth; at least as he described them later, those Protestant divines with whom he had spoken seemed rather uninterested in his soul. Unitarians and transcendentalists were so individualistic they seemed to have all but abandoned the church. Hecker rejected the Episcopal Church because it "tolerated" every belief. Although his mother's Methodism left many traces on Hecker's piety, he brushed off that church and most other evangelicals because they were emotional and "had no intellectual basis." At mid-century a large majority of American Protestants were Baptists and Methodists and those churches were swept by perfectionist enthusiasm. Hecker saw such movements as the natural outburst of unmet religious needs, which could never be fully or permanently satisfied by revivalism, which swung uneasily between an overt anti-intellectualism that could not satisfy the aspirations of nature and a comfortable affirmation of conventionality, which could not touch the depths of the soul.[9]

Necessarily, in view of all this, Hecker was uncomfortable with normal religious controversy. The combative apologetics of Archbishop Hughes or the logical polemics of Brownson did not serve the cause of Catholic evangelization, Hecker believed, because they almost always focused not on the common ground which united Catholics with rationalists or lukewarm Christians, but on the differences which separated them. Hecker found that common ground in the basic elements of human nature. Convinced of the truth of Catholicity, Hecker wished to show how the needs and aspirations all people experienced were most comprehensively answered by the Catholic form of Christianity. To make this argument he had to uphold the native goodness and intelligence of persons, limiting the effects of original sin and risking Brownson's charge of being "semi-Pelagian." Later critics would argue that he minimized doctrines of sin and watered down Catholic teaching; that is, he overemphasized human goodness in order to win converts. In fact, the truth was the reverse; because he trusted human nature and thought people basically good, he tried to convert them.

Hecker's original Paulist colleagues were less optimistic than Hecker. Having come to the church through high-church Episcopalianism, they naturally aimed their apologetic at Protestants seeking a secure foundation for Christian belief. They were more respectful of Protestantism than Hecker, even at times ecumenical. Paulist work was shared, and Hecker's views never were fully embodied in the community's activities. Hewit played a strong role in the *Catholic World*, and his views on religious controversy were as prominent in its pages as Hecker's, at least until after Hecker's return from Europe in 1875.

Christians should seek common ground and only then move to the discussion of differences, Hewit believed. There was true faith and holiness outside the visible communion of the church and Catholics, for their part, were "bound to cultivate the spirit of Christian charity toward those who profess allegiance to our common Lord." In addition, there were many goals they could seek in cooperation: to defend Scripture, solve the difficulties posed to Christianity by modern science, counteract tendencies toward apathy and indifference, protect Christian marriage from divorce, "suppress intemperance, licentiousness and immoralities destructive to the well-being of society," protect the liberty of all religious societies and the property they devoted to religious, charitable and educational purposes.

Hewit, of course, remained confident that the quest for the unity desired by all would eventually lead to Catholicism. Catholic dogma and discipline contained all that was positive in all Christian bodies and would eventually assimilate and integrate American Christianity, but Catholics made no arrogant demand for submission. They only wished to make a start by explaining their own beliefs in order to promote better understanding, reduce prejudice and open up the question of the need for a visible authoritative church, all in a spirit of respect and charity. Hewit's eyes were fixed not on Hecker's "earnest seekers" but on the "good Protestants" seen in the image of his Congregationalist family and the genteel culture of the nineteenth century. For Catholicism to exercise its power successfully, it would have to "master that element."[10]

The evangelical project was even more complicated than the question of defining the primary object of proselytization. The *Catholic World* was designed to simultaneously rebut Protestant and secular attacks, carry on intelligent dialogue with non-Catholics of goodwill, offer reasonable Catholic commentary on religion and public affairs, and improve the intellectual quality and cultural tone of American Catholic life. It was a complex assignment, arising from the unique situation of the American church, internally composed of immigrants, for the most part poor and badly educated and connected to an increasingly conservative, highly visible European church, while externally confronting the twin enemies of a hostile Protestantism and equally hostile liberalism. Reasonable discourse in such a situation was extremely difficult, particularly because the church and the rest of American society seemed to be drawing further apart, less over specifically religious questions than over fundamental judgments about human nature. Ironically Hecker, who had brushed off Protestantism as a religion unsuited for Americans because, in his view, it held to a pessimistic, Calvinist view of human nature, found similar pessimism growing within the Catholic Church, while the Protestants, guided by the Beechers among others, were developing a liberal theology premised on humanity's essential goodness. It was an absolutely critical problem because, if Brownson was right and people were mainly sinful, the most important thing about the church was that it offered a way to overcome sin by directing one away from a sinful world. In that case, Hecker's whole project, not just of conversions but of reconciliation of the church with the hopeful aspirations of modern men and women, would become all the more difficult.

Even before the Vatican Council, interreligious antagonism, dormant during the Civil War, had revived, challenging Hecker predictions of Protestant decline and Hewit's hopes for cooperation with respectable Christians angered by the assaults of anti-Catholic publicists like *Harper's Weekly* cartoonist Thomas Nast. Catholics demanded a vigorous counterattack, and Brownson and Hewit gave it to them. In 1868 Hewit wrote to John Henry Newman that "the controversy with Protestants is waxing hot and fierce here." He happily reported that Protestant churches were divided, few attended services and "the mass of the people are becoming more irreligious and immoral everyday." A *Catholic World* writer charged that Protestants had "lost the church, lost practically the Bible, lost faith, lost doctrine, lost charity, lost spirituality, fallen into a sickly sentimentalism, and was plunging into gross sensuality."[11]

Hecker, of course, had always professed to dislike such polemics, but he was no ecumenist. "Protestantism is the spirit of individualism, antagonistic selfishness," he wrote in his diary shortly after his conversion. It fostered a civilization based on "the competitive spirit," which led to "wretchedness, crime and selfishness." Wherever Catholic and Protestant cultures came into contact, "they must generate war"; the two Christian religions could "never agree in the same community."[12]

Never was Hecker's attitude toward Protestantism more clear than in a lecture on the religious condition of the country delivered in Boston's Music Hall in April 1869. The tendency of the age, he argued, was toward Catholicism or infidelity, and "the great issues between truth and error [would] be decided, not on the banks of the Thames, the Rhine or the Tiber, but on those of the Hudson, the Mississippi and the shores of our great lakes." Protestantism was no longer relevant; it had "lost all grasp on the fundamental truths of Christian revelation." Beginning in an "exaggerated supernaturalism," which exalted God and despised nature, Protestantism had followed Channing's "noble work" of rebelling against such negations only to end in the opposite extreme of an "exaggerated naturalism": "Formerly Christ was all and man was nothing; now Christ is nothing and man is all." Protestant theology, with its emphasis on private judgment, and Protestant philosophy, with "its exaggeration of the interior authority of the soul," could have no other outcome. The conclusion was drastic and, to Protestants, insulting:

> I define, then, Protestantism from this point of view, to have been the emancipation of the human passions from the restraints of Christian law, tending to dismember families, and bring on the ruin of the State and the destruction of the human race. . . . The religious development of Protestantism . . . ends in Rationalism; the philosophical development of Protestantism ends in atheism and the moral development of Protestantism ends in the destruction of the human race.

Catholicism, of course, spoke with the authority of God, whose revealed truths were to be tested and accepted by reasonable men and women. The church upheld the moral law, respected informed conscience, defended the state and contributed to authentic social and cultural progress. In the contentions of the day over public policy, Catholics asked only for liberty and justice—"fair play"—the same fairness they would show when they became the majority of the country. "Treat us fairly, and when our turn comes we will treat you fairly," Hecker told his Protestant listeners. "I know we shall [for] no people love our institutions better; no people would sacrifice more for our liberties, than our Catholics, and because they are Catholics." While Hecker's mild manner won admirers, his message, belittling Protestants and assuming future Catholic power, could not but arouse Protestant animosity and liberal fears.[13]

While Hecker was abroad, first for the Vatican Council, later in search of physical and spiritual repose, he saw the prospects of the Catholic Church on a larger historical stage. In Europe the contemporary struggle of the church was no longer with Protestantism; as Hecker saw it, that three-century period of post-Reformation conflict had concluded with Vatican I. In the next period of history the battle would be fought between Catholicism and irreligion. When he returned to the United States in 1875, he found the climate even more highly charged than when he left. The Republican party was increasingly adopting an anti-Catholic stance, particularly by supporting proposals for a national system of public education. The Free Religion Association was vigorously attacking the church while promoting the secularization of educational and charitable services. The Evangelical Alliance regularly denounced Catholic power and opposed access by priests to public hospitals, prisons and asylums. In New York continuing fights over political corruption, vice and social services were further embittered by Catholic anger at Protestant proselytization—Paulist George Searle called it "bribery"—in urban neighborhoods, all of which were discussed with passionate intensity in the pages of the *Catholic World.*[14]

Nevertheless, when Hecker resumed direction of the magazine in 1875, he was less sure of the prospects of dialogue with liberals, more convinced than he had been earlier that the church should reach out its hand to non-Catholic Christians. While in Europe, especially during his trip to the East, he had given the matter considerable thought. One idea was to distinguish sharply between the weakness of Protestant theology and the sincerity of Protestants themselves:

> It is for us Catholics who possess the divine truth in its fulness and in security against all error with a conviction which excludes all doubt, that should give an example in kindness, charity and Catholic spirit towards those who are groping in darkness after the light. . . . If we regard all non-Catholics as formal heretics and infidels, and in return they are left to look upon us as bigots and superstitious, the present lines of separation will only be made broader and we who ought to know better and break through these lines with the light of truth, and do not, will make ourselves guilty of their error.

The fault for Protestant-Catholic hostility did not all lie on the Protestant side:

> If Protestants are guilty of the sin of ignorance in regarding Catholics as idolators and superstitious, are Catholics free from the same sin when they look upon them as personally guilty of schism and heresy?

The conclusion was clear: "In our intercourse with Protestants, were we to dwell more on the truths which they hold in common with us, and less on those in which they differ from us, we should open the way for the more speedy return of many of them to the fold of the church." The more open, dialogic approach was confirmed for Hecker by the new Pope, Leo XIII, who succeeded Pius IX in 1876. In place of Pius IX's condemnation of "the evil tendencies of the age," Hecker argued, Leo "has been given, let us hope, the more consoling mission of pointing out to the world the good tendencies of the age, interpreting its truths and virtues in that light which will make the way clear to society of a loftier, and better future.[15]

In this spirit, Hecker set out to improve the quality of the *Catholic World*. By 1880 the magazine had a new format and typeface and, in Hecker's opinion, was ready to advance to meet the new opportunities of the age. In an editorial that resounded with optimism, Hecker noted a worldwide movement away from the narrow and parochial preoccupation of "sects." The editorial promised to avoid negative cries of breakdown and decay and look for the power of the spirit, opening hearts and minds: "There is a longing to know God, which can never be stilled, a thirst for divine truth, a desire for light on the destiny of man, a restless search for satisfying answers to those questions of the soul which spring up unbidden always and everywhere, for solutions of problems which are forever presenting themselves before the human mind."

Catholics possessed "those universal, certain and most needful principles for determining truth and making knowledge practically applicable to the great needs of the human mind and heart" and the temporal welfare of the human community. There was a "colossal" work to be done to educate themselves, and to address the problems of the day. The objects of the *Catholic World*, therefore, were hardly parochial: "the diffusion of Catholic knowledge, the dissipation of popular errors, the general promotion of religion, virtue, intellectual, moral, social and political well-being by the inculcation of Catholic principles."[16]

Yet the *Catholic World* remained a Catholic journal, its support dependent on the favor of Catholics, and most Catholics and non-Catholics had their eyes fixed not on the promised land of the future but on each other. Less than a year after the above editorial appeared, there was another, signed by Hecker, rejoicing in new subscriptions but ignoring the positive themes of the earlier statement. Instead, the editor emphasized the defense of Catholic truth and the refutation of errors:

> It is plain in these times to everyone that there is no truth, however sacred or essential, whether of divine revelation or human reason, which is not unblushingly attacked or flatly denied. To

> every one of these attacks must be posed a triumphant refutation, and in the face of every one of these denials there must be affirmed, in the light of God's presence and in the accents of sincerest conviction, its opposite truth. This is what is incumbent upon Catholics of our age, especially those who conduct the Catholic press.[17]

The reason for the change in tone was the continuing conflict between Catholics and other Americans, conflict which was eroding Hecker's confidence in the sincerity of other Americans.

In June 1881, for example, Hecker wrote in response to the Protestant charge that the Catholic church repudiated the authority of reason and discouraged its exercise. So false was this charge that Hecker found it hard to maintain his moral assumption of the goodwill of those who made it. Abandoning the style of his previous apologetic efforts, he felt compelled to answer these "railing accusations." Catholicism and reason were "inseparably united," Hecker contended; the church "appeals with entire trust and unswerving steadfastness to the decisions of reason for her defense and support." In addressing outsiders the church insisted that "the exercise of reason goes before faith"; indeed, without the knowledge reason provided, no faith was possible. According to Catholicism, the "light of human reason is the light of God shining in the soul"; "the value of human reason is absolute and its knowledge of first principles and the truths that flow immediately from them is accompanied with unerring certitude." After a lifetime of making this argument, Hecker was no longer convinced of non-Catholic goodwill. When would his fellow citizens overcome bigotry "and have the intellectual independence and fairness to examine the just claims which the Catholic Church makes on their intelligence and conscience?" he asked. He was no longer sure there were very many "earnest seekers" waiting to hear the message.[18]

In October 1883 Hecker began another all-out assault on Protestantism. He argued that Protestant understanding of the church as a voluntary association contained the seeds of its own destruction. All agreed that "the only way of becoming a Christian was by a personal communication from Christ," but Protestants had no answer to the question of how Christ communicated with human beings. Some answered the Bible, but they could not escape the dilemma of private interpretation. Others experienced Christ's communication directly, but again they had no criteria for distinguishing between true and false communication, between passion and the inspiration of the Holy Spirit. The falling off of church membership, lack of candidates for the ministry, and growing impiety were all evidence that the "divine right to bolt" left people free "to push forward their protest against all Christian truths, whether intellectual or ethical, as though chaos were the garden of paradise." Catholics, in contrast, believed that the church made Christians, not Christians the church. Christ "designed his church," chose its "first officers . . . conferred on them special powers, instituted the sacraments, laid down the principles of her discipline, and formed the main features of her worship." Fortunately, people whose intelligence controlled the formation of their religious beliefs were turning away from Protestantism "as being as destitute of an intellectual as it is of a moral basis." "Sound and healthy minds" sought Christ and "a closer fellowship with God." Nothing less could satisfy the inner hungers of the soul.[19]

Hecker's assault continued in November 1883 when he celebrated the four hundredth anniversary of the Diet of Worms with scathing denunciation of Luther and Protestantism generally. Having substituted "Luther's imagination" for "the authority of Christ's Church as the divinely authorized interpreter of revealed truth," Protestantism had introduced the "spirit of free individualism," which "breeds dissensions . . . lives in insurrection and rejoices in revolution." From their denial of the authority of the church followed "denial of the divinity of Christ," which in turn led to denial of the Trinity, agnosticism and atheism. "Protestantism in its logical outcome is a protest against all religion," he argued.[20]

By the 1880s, then, Hecker was far less optimistic than he had been after the Civil War that the conversion of America was impending. For Hecker the war proved the inadequacy of Protestantism and enhanced the prestige of Catholicism; perhaps for those very reasons a non-Catholic counterattack upon the church quickly followed Appomattox. Hecker had long believed that lukewarm or disillusioned Protestants would be open and honest in examining Catholic claims, particularly if Catholics presented their case simply, avoided identifying the faith with particular European customs or traditions, and treated other Americans with respect. He had long ago learned that Protestant ministers became irrational and hostile when faced with the Catholic challenge, but he believed such passionate attacks played into the hands of the reasonable, respectable Catholic evangelist. After his resumption of the *Catholic World*, however, he made a point of attacking Protestant doctrine and even Protestant leaders, whose persistent attacks evidenced, to his mind, their lack of Christian charity and goodwill.

The chasm between Hecker's desire for dialogue and his anti-Protestant passion reflected an older and deeper problem. Hecker's apologetic method made many Catholics uneasy. Catholicism defined as a universal response to universal human needs made sense if one was truly seeking to establish the church as a universal church; it was less helpful if one was trying to secure the church as a minority within a non-Catholic society. Brownson understood more clearly than many others that Hecker's apologetic, like the optimistic anthropology on which it rested, could loosen the bonds and weaken the discipline of the Catholic Church by blurring the boundaries between Catholics and others. Hecker himself, as he became more Catholic, a priest, founder of a religious order, pastor of a growing parish, active promoter of reform within the church, found that such concerns became more and more his own. To the degree that he became a responsible Catholic leader rather than a semi-independent commentator, he was forced to justify his position and demonstrate his loyalty to and solidarity with the bishops, the pope, the increasingly organized and militant American Catholic subculture. To the extent that Protestants were militantly anti-Catholic and liberals passionately hostile to Catholic interests, that need to be more clearly and explicitly Catholic, as the nineteenth-century church was defining the term, became more pressing, not simply because it was demanded by his superiors or by the interests of his community, but because external hostility weakened his arguments about the prospects of a post-Protestant age.

During the revival of anti-Catholicism after the Civil War, at a time when Hecker's optimism was at its height, he had sharpened his arguments on the inadequacy of Protestantism and rationalism. After 1875, his hopeful vision endangered by intense interreligious conflict, he was compelled to add a strong defense to his positive strategy. This was easier than it appeared at first glance; his evaluation of other Christian churches had progressed little beyond the contemptuous dismissal which marked his letters to his mother from the seminary thirty years earlier. If he was right in charging that many Protestants showed an evident lack of charity and goodwill in assessing Catholicism, they could not be blamed if they noticed the same qualities in Hecker's remarks about Protestantism. Hecker believed that the Christian commonwealth was the destiny of all of God's people, but he also believed that there was only one Christian road to approach the Kingdom, the way of the Catholic Church. As he wrote in an article rejoicing at Leo XIII's new opening toward the modern world, Catholicism and human destiny were one and the same:

> If an exposition of the Catholic religion were made . . . in the light of [which] the prejudices against the Catholic faith would disappear, its beauty would find unbidden entrance into the hearts of men, the religious revolution of the sixteenth century would be reversed, and humanity as one man would advance with rapid strides to bring down the kingdom of heaven upon earth and, in so doing, fit itself for its loftier and ampler destiny above.

At the end as at the beginning, Isaac Hecker's goal was the triumph of the church. Catholics, to be Catholic, must pursue the goal of a Catholic America and eventually a Catholic world, when the divisions among nations and the barriers between people would be overcome:

> Catholics are left no choice. They must either raise up their thoughts and courage to the height of the aims of Christianity as the absolute and universal religion destined to gain the entire world, or cease to be Catholics, and content themselves to take the ignoble part of one among the thousand of different religious sects, and with them finally disappear and be forgotten. . . . Our hearts are therefore lifted upward and our hopes are onward; for the great church which civilized and Christianized Europe, formed its people into nations, and into one great Christian family properly named Christendom, is fully competent to do the same work, and with greater ease considering modern facilities and appliances at her disposal, for the whole world.[21]

17

Not Yet the Promised Land

The last years of Hecker's life saw no slackening of his conviction that Catholicism was "the absolute and universal religion." But they did place a new set of problems in the way of his preferred method of promoting the Catholic cause. In the United States, winning respect for the church and eventual conversions to her ranks depended upon convincing honest inquirers, "earnest seekers," Protestants and post-Protestants alike, that the church not only presented no fundamental challenge to democratic values, but in fact provided a firm foundation for them. It depended as well upon the basic good will and honesty, on the "earnestness," of American citizens. Here too Hecker's optimism was sorely tested.

Hecker had always walked a tightrope in his effort to be an influential leader within the church and a respected spokesman for the church with other Americans. In the last decade of his life the question of education emerged as an issue around which interreligious hostilities converged. It forced religious controversy into the public arena and became the test case of pluralism. Catholic loyalty demanded all out support for Catholic education, but separate schools threatened to institutionalize Catholic defensiveness and postpone emergence of a missionary spirit. Hecker therefore saw the need to promote a public policy on education that would respect the rights of each religious group while at the same time meeting public needs. When he did so, other Americans proved unresponsive, even unfair, bringing further frustration.

Education was not the only problem which aroused doubts about the sincerity of the American people's commitment to religious liberty and their willingness to look at the Catholic church with an open mind. The declaration of papal infallibility rekindled non-Catholic suspicions about Catholicism's acceptance of freedom of conscience, leading Hecker to defend at length the church's balanced understanding of the internal and external action of the Holy Spirit. Yet he appreciated the honest concerns aroused by the Vatican Council, and his writings on infallibility were measured and respectful. Surprisingly, he was far more upset by the response of the American public to "the Roman question." In 1860, when the Kingdom of Italy seized the papal states outside Rome, Hecker was quiet, apparently agreeing with Simpson and Brownson that the pope's temporal jurisdiction was antiquated. In 1870 Italy completed the destruction of the temporal power by taking over the city of Rome itself. The pope refused to recognize the legitimacy of this action and closed himself off in the papal palaces. The Italian government proceeded to dismantle papal administration, while the pope forbade Italian Catholics to participate in the new order. The Vatican attempted to arouse international support for the restoration of the pope's temporal authority, claiming that his spiritual leadership could never be freely exercised or accepted unless his freedom was guaranteed by recognition of the papacy as an independent state. Like most Catholic leaders, Hecker regarded the Italian government as a "robber state" whose only claim to Rome was force. More important, he believed the government's treatment of the church showed a tyrannical determination to establish a godless secularism and limit, if not destroy, the freedom of the church.

Hecker all but ignored the problem in the *Exposition*, and he clearly disliked the emphasis many churchmen placed on the Roman question. He was far more upset, however, by American non-Catholic reaction. According to Hecker, Catholics, in supporting the pope, were defending religious freedom, and they expected the support of other Americans who professed devotion to that principle. Instead, the public press was filled with praise for the new Kingdom of Italy and attacks on the papacy, which enraged Hecker. Not only did it appear hypocritical, but it called into question his lifelong argument that Catholics should trust the native fairness and decency of their fellow Americans. Writing in the *Catholic World* for April 1882, he charged that the press had taken the side of the church's oppressors. "The force of recent events compels us to say, with unfeigned regret, that whatever credit of good faith Catholics were disposed to concede to those who differ from them in their religious belief, that this has been dissipated, for one generation at least, beyond hope of recovery," he wrote with uncharacteristic finality. Hecker issued a stern warning to anyone who defended Italian assaults on the pope: American Catholics had "the common right and common duty to raise our voices and in unmistakable tones of sincerity to warn him—beware!"[1]

By far the more important question modifying Hecker's views of the public role of the church, however, was the school question. Hecker himself had attended a public school until he was 12 years old. That school, however, was not part of a common school system but one of a series of charitable schools conducted by the philanthropic, Protestant-controlled Public School Society, which annually received a share of the school funds collected from taxes by the New York Common Council. In 1841 John Hughes had challenged this group's control of the city's eduction. New York Catholics petitioned the city for a share of school funds, charging that the charity schools forced Catholic children to read the Protestant Bible and use insulting texts. Receiving no redress from the common council, Catholics moved to the state level, demanding either a share of school funds or, failing that, the extension of the state's common school system to the city. In the 1841 elections Hughes put muscle into the demand by sponsoring an independent slate of candidates from the New York Assembly, a tactic that brought about the defeat of some unsympathetic legislators and led the following year to legislation which placed the city under the common school system.

The episode hardened nativist sentiment and polarized Catholics and non-Catholics, but it had the effect as well of uniting church members behind Hughes, who used the opportunity to build support for parish schools. For the rest of his career Hughes worked hard to provide schools for Catholic children, often insisting that the school be built before the church. New York led the nation in support for parochial schools, which also found backing among German immigrants wherever they settled. Yet by no means was the entire American church united on the issue. In some places Catholics attended public schools quite happily; in others arrangements were made between local authorities and the church to allow priests and sisters to teach, while offering religious instruction after school hours. Support for independent Catholic schools developed slowly through the 1870s when, under pressure from concerned Americans, Rome instructed the American bishops to avoid the public schools and attempt to provide schools organized under church authority. In 1884 this was ratified by the Third Plenary Council of Baltimore, which legislated that within two years there should be a school in every parish. This unrealistic goal was never reached, and the school controversy burst into the open again in the 1890s; only at the turn of the century were parochial schools universally accepted as a basic commitment of the American church.[2]

Throughout the century the school question disturbed Catholic relations with other Americans. The bitter conflict in New York was followed by a series of disputes around the country over the reading of the King James Bible in classrooms. When church authorities attempted to win approval of plans to exempt Catholics from these exercises, opponents translated this into an attack on the Bible and trouble began, leading in Philadelphia to street riots which left several churches burned and a score of people dead. In the 1850s the Know Nothing Party made the growth of parochial schools one of the themes of its anti-immigrant, anti-Catholic campaign. After the Civil War more and more Americans came to believe that the common schools were the most important instruments the nation possessed to overcome ethnic, class and religious conflicts, bring stability and order to local communities, provide some common values and make Americans one people. Protestants eased their control of curriculum and texts in favor of efforts to make public education universal and uniform, so that the schools now seemed to many Catholics not Protestant but, equally dangerous, "godless" and "secular."

The battle lines became even more sharply defined by federal efforts to bring about educational reform. In 1871 Senator Henry Wilson proposed a "new departure" for the Republican Party that included development of a national system of public education. The controversy aroused by his plan continued into the 1880s, when Senator Henry W. Blair of New Hampshire sponsored a bill to provide federal funds to the states for education. Both plans drew passionate Catholic opposition. For one thing, the funds available to public schools would make it harder for Catholic schools to compete, while federal control would make the public system more difficult to influence. Catholics were heavily concentrated in the cities of the North, where they constituted a substantial portion of the population and had higher levels of political influence than they did nationally.

The school question was the classic convergent issue of America's religious pluralism. By the 1880s, most Americans, at least in the North, regarded elementary education as a public responsibility and thought access to such education a basic American right. The haphazard collection of private, semi-public and public schools characteristic of the United States in the 1840s was giving way to a more organized public school system. Most agreed that the goal of common education went beyond basic skills to encompass at least a general moral education. Protestants had come to accept the need to offer such moral education on a non-denominational basis, expressing common Christian teachings while leaving it to the home and the Sunday school to instill specific denominational tenets. But to Catholics the fact that this moral instruction was generally Christian did not help. As reformer Elihu Burritt, not a Catholic, put it in a letter to the New York *Tribune*:

> Ninety nine common school teachers in one hundred in all the Northern states are Protestant . . . the literature in all our reading books and the atmosphere of our schools and even our out-door sports are Protestant in their influence. . . . We ask and require [Catholics] to yield some of their scruples in sending their children to schools which are effectively Protestant and which they have considerable reason to think will influence their young minds.[3]

Protestant-sponsored charity schools had threatened to wean children from the church, while in the common school the child might learn that denominational differences were incidental and that the common morality of the community was sufficient to living a decent life. They might be encouraged to neglect their duty to contribute to the support of the church, which depended entirely on the voluntary donations of its members. Worst of all, the public school encouraged the promiscuous mixing of boys and girls of all faiths, who as a result might marry outside the church, the surest route to disaffiliation, if not apostasy. To this was added the immigrant concern that in the public school children learned nothing of the language, history and culture of the homeland; they might absorb values and attitudes which would lead them to look down upon their parents and disdain those things their parents thought important. German immigrants strongly identified preservation of their language with the preservation of the faith. Irish immigrants were split on the school issue, but Poles and other Eastern European immigrants, coming when the uniform and standardized public school system, under an ideology of Americanization, was expanding, tended to support the German position and thus lend a mass base to the hierarchy's growing concern to preserve and strengthen the church by erecting a Catholic subculture, with the parochial school at its center, which would monopolize as much as possible the private side of its members' lives.

The school question could not be solved in the private sector, for education had come to be seen as a public responsibility. Catholics had to pay taxes to support public schools; they had to demonstrate that their own system met public standards; they had to convince others that their schools, while inculcating distinctive religious tenets, also fulfilled the community's interest in securing a literate, patriotic and disciplined citizenry. In short, public policy decisions had to be made and all groups had a stake in those decisions; the school question played a convergent role, crystalizing dormant anxieties, focusing generalized distrust and giving form to conflicts which were deeper and broader than education.

Hecker's involvement in the school question reflected these developments. He showed little interest early in his career. As far back as the 1850s, when he ignored Simpson's comments on *Aspirations of Nature*, he had avoided taking sides in internal disputes within the American church. However strong his private views, he knew it was dangerous for a convert, especially one regarded as something of an enthusiast, to become embroiled in arguments with bishops or other priests. Indeed, he thought Brownson's lust for combat sharply limited his influence. Later, as an editor, lecturer and writer, regarded by many as the most influential intermediary between Catholicism and American society, he could hardly avoid being drawn into the school question, and it posed some painful problems for him.

His entire approach to his ministry had been premised on some fundamental assumptions about American society and the American people. He believed the constitutional system respected Catholic rights and left the church perfectly free to be the church. He argued that Americans were fair-minded and would do justice to Catholics when issues were clearly presented to them. He believed that Christian faith was strongest and the church most itself when grounded in the free and intelligent commitment of its members, so he could hardly defend with enthusiasm any policy which sought to cut people off from controversy and protect a conventional faith and habitual religious practice. On the other hand, he regularly argued that Catholicism was the great custodian of art, science and all forms of human knowledge. He admired the work done by religious orders, especially among the poor, and he pointed to Catholic schools as an expression of the church's social concern and its respect for community well-being. Accordingly, Hecker had to define a position which would avoid the twin dangers of isolating Catholics by justifying separatism and, at the other extreme, avoid undercutting pastoral necessities by arguing for assimilation into a uniform, colorless American mainstream. He would have to show that the Catholic position was one which would also be the proper one for all Americans.

This could be done by limiting the role of the state and upholding a denominational school system. The *Catholic World* took such a position from the very beginning, questioning the right of the state to educate, placing primary responsibility with the family, denouncing secular education as godless, and calling for a system of denominational schools, subject to state regulation. If Protestants found the public schools satisfactory, they were welcome to use them, but Catholics thought the segregation of religion from other elements of education unwise for the community. The charge that such schools were divisive was superficial, for unity should not be achieved at the cost of religion and morality. Catholics were willing to accept reasonable public standards, enforced by public inspectors, and there was no evidence that the quality of education was less than that available in the public schools.[4]

By the end of the 1860s *Catholic World* contributors had presented a solid, reasonable case of Catholic education. They clearly expressed their reservations regarding a secular system of education and offered an alternative of denominational-based schools, such as those available in Canada, England and several continental European countries. However, as public debate heated up around the Wilson proposal for a "New Departure," the tone of the *Catholic World*'s contribution deteriorated.[5]

When Hecker returned from Europe in 1875, though a sick man, he immediately took note of the school issue, which he told Bernard Smith was "agitating the public mind." Worried by the bitter tone of public debate, he still thought that, if Catholics put forward their claims with "patience, prudence and forebearance," they would not only obtain justice but produce "great benefits for the church." He was soon corresponding with an old acquaintance, Bernard McQuaid, the bishop of Rochester and one of the most skillful champions of Catholic education. Hecker told McQuaid in early February 1876 that public policy on education was still an open question. Parents, the church and the state all had a stake in the educational enterprise. Catholics should ask only for recognition of their rights and for an arrangement which did not exclude them. "Let the state demand and exact its standards of knowledge and leave the communication of this knowledge to those to whom it rightly belongs, the parents," he wrote. If a tax was needed, let it be distributed fairly to all who would choose to educate. "Our watchword is 'Free Trade in Education,' " he concluded.[6]

Unfortunately, there was mounting evidence that the freedom of Catholics was not respected and their interests were not taken seriously. On the contrary, they felt under assault, forced to pay taxes for a system of which they could not approve. For Hecker, it had become a test question. As he wrote in 1881:

> The American people may rest assured that whenever a question arises involving fundamental principles, Catholics will always be found, as a body, on the side of liberty, fair play, and equal rights. Such an issue happens now to take shape in the public-school question; and it is a test question of the sincerity of the American people in their profession of liberty of conscience in religious matters. That is what the school question means.

To make a fair test, Hecker had to explain the Catholic position as fully and carefully as possible. He began by attempting to correct the misunderstanding that Catholics were "unfriendly" to the public schools. Catholics had done nothing to weaken the public schools or to prevent anyone from attending them. Catholics held firmly that knowledge of Christian truths and the practice of Christian virtue were essential for true happiness and for the welfare of society. Religious instruction, in and out of school, was thus of paramount importance.

Still, "having no wish to force or impose their convictions upon others," Catholics respected parental rights and said in all honesty: "Send, if you choose, your children to the public schools; let them grow up, if you prefer it, under the instructions and influences they there receive; and may they grow up to be a credit to you and an honor to the land." So sacred did Catholics hold parental rights, he continued, that they paid their share of the general tax while supporting their own schools at their own expense. They regarded this "double cost" as an imposition, but believed that once understood by "fair-minded Americans," it would be corrected. For the moment they chose to "suffer patiently this wrong" rather than be robbed of their parental rights over the proper education of their children. Their position was a matter of conscientious conviction; they asked only that their religious freedom to follow their conscience be respected. Catholic Austria and Protestant England did justice to religious minorities by providing public assistance to separate schools; America should do the same. He was emphatic: Catholics would fight for their rights. "Catholics, in this land of freedom, be it known, if it is not yet known to everybody, have the same rights as Protestants."[7]

Despite his willingness to respect parental choice for the public school, Hecker took pains to argue that the question was broader than Catholic rights, for the spread of secular education posed grave danger to the nation as a whole. Secular education "produces men and women fitted only for those forms of worldly activity which require little or no moral discernment," he wrote. "The ambitious, unscrupulous adventurer is the legitimate product of such an education; and of such characters the world has never known a dearth." Ironically, the system established to "decatholicize the children of Catholics," had instead loosened the hold of Protestantism and was "peopling the country" with "skeptics, infidels, if not atheists." Everywhere people were complaining about the loss of membership and the lethargy in the churches. Catholics had foreseen such results and taken steps to guard against them, building schools or, if that was impossible, providing solid programs to guard the faith until the school could be built. Now he noted the growing concern of Protestant leaders; Hecker was convinced that, left to themselves, most Americans would prefer religious schools. Agreement about the need for Christian education was emerging, and Hecker had the solution: Let secular and religious schools stand equal before the state; let the state meet the cost of the instruction needed to make students "intelligent voters and good citizens." Public schools would continue and receive their fair share, side by side, with denominational schools. Religious instruction would be left to the individual churches.

To the argument that the common schools led to the unification of divergent peoples, Hecker responded that the "genius of our republic" favors "the cultivation of individual greatness, not the creation of a powerful nation at the expense of the manhood of its citizens." The spread of indifference and infidelity was a danger to which all religious people and all Americans should be alert, and the solution was available. Hecker ended with a question, filled with uncharacteristic ecumenical spirit:

> Catholics and Protestants both agree that, in view of their parental responsibilities, they cannot send their children to other than positive Christian schools. But it is admitted by all that a state such as ours cannot teach or pay for teaching religion. Therefore, the defects of our public-school organization must be remedied by amending it according to parental rights and consistently with American ideas of religious liberty. Will Protestants join in this issue against the common enemy of Christianity, save the Christian faith of their children, and secure the future of our Republic?[8]

Only such a system could honestly express the nation's religious differences. Catholics and some Protestants regarded the church as divinely established to preserve and teach the doctrines of revelation and accomplish Christ's work in the world, while other Christians placed their reliance on Scriptures and grace and saw the church as a voluntary association. These two groups differed enormously over the nature of Christian education. Education, furthermore, was defined as fitting a person for the fulfillment of his or her destiny, and religions differed sharply over the nature of that destiny and the means to achieve it. "There is no denying the fact that the religious problem sums up all other problems," Hecker wrote, "and in the last analysis it is religion which shapes, and by right ought to shape, among intelligent men, all institutions, and none more so than the education of youth." The school issue, therefore, went to the very heart of religious differences; it could not be solved, compromised or dealt with by the surrender by either side of principles they held as essential. It could only be solved by an agreement which respected those clear religious differences.[9]

Hecker returned to the battle a few months later to repeat his argument against defenders of the common school, and he was growing impatient. Now he described the schools as both "unChristian" and "unAmerican," not "common schools" but "schools of the worst sect of all—the sect of secularism." Protestants were seeing the problem, but they were not acting, continuing instead to accept spurious arguments about the democratic and unifying effects of public schools. "How long will an intelligent Christian people continue the suicidal policy of paying their enemies to dig the grave of their religion?" he asked. He seemed to be growing doubtful of the answer; non-Catholics were not passing the test.[10]

As the school question demonstrated, the anticipated movement of a post-Protestant generation toward the church was not taking place. Hecker's fellow citizens adopted unreasonable and unfair positions on the Roman question and public education. If it turned out that there were few earnest seekers, and if even the most fair-minded non-Catholics ignored Catholic pleas for justice, then the prospect of a Catholic America would recede even further into the future and Hecker would find himself in the position of many of his former critics, defending Catholic rights and Catholic interests and defining Catholic progress in terms of Catholic growth and Catholic power.

One reason for the dilemma might be the lack of intelligent, skillful Catholic leadership. According to Hecker in the *Exposition*, Catholic majorities in Europe suffered under the tyranny of non-Catholic minorities because they failed to mobilize their resources and develop a coherent, positive strategy. In the United States, as well, Catholics had to learn that they could not gain justice or refute slanders "by the means we are now employing." Instead, they would have to adopt an approach appropriate to the age. In the *Catholic World* for May 1880 Hecker set out an agenda for the church in face of the intellectual needs of the age. The diffusion of education and the growth of science had increased the need for a reasonable case for Christianity, but most Protestant churches had abandoned their original creed and were promoting secular education. So it was left to Catholics "to answer satisfactorily the intellectual demands of the age." As the "fever of controversy passed away," there was "reason to hope that if the Catholic religion is presented . . . without exaggerations, and in the light of its real character" it would attract "the more impartial and intelligent minds." The largest barrier was the impression held by many non-Catholics that Catholicism was based exclusively on "external authority," which finds "absolute expression in the commands of the pope; and if obedience is not the sole virtue of a good Catholic, it is at least the one above all others put in practice by the Catholic system." Hecker agreed that the words and actions of many of the church's defenders seemed to confirm this view, some arguing that authority was the essence of Catholicism. Catholics who made that case were concerned about the rebellion against authority made in the past and the improper love of liberty all too present in the nineteenth century.

Granting the worthy motives of those who gave a one-sided emphasis to authority and obedience in their defense of the church, Hecker believed they were deeply mistaken. "The essence of Christianity is the elevation of rational creatures, by the power of the Holy Spirit, to a union with God." Religion communicates the indwelling Holy Spirit, which makes a person "a participator in the divine nature and . . . transforms him . . . into a child of God." Authority is always subservient to a larger end, "the promotion and safeguarding of the action of the indwelling Holy Spirit by which the soul is united with God." This being the case, it is an "axiom" that "the outward authority of the church effaces itself in a direct ratio to the action of the Holy Spirit within the soul." Furthermore, to surrender one's intellect and free will would be to deny that which constitutes man as man, a surrender neither "possible or desirable." Christianity "violates no law of our being, asks no surrender of our faculties, and is in perfect harmony with all the genuine instincts of our nature," Hecker concluded, and it was this idea which should inform the invitation the church issued to "the men of this age." In short, "he who would gain the men of this generation must address their intelligence, acknowledge their liberty, and respect their dignity." Catholic intellectual renewal, therefore, turned upon faith in the truth, universality, and reasonableness of Catholic teaching.[11]

For all the defensive polemics which marked his writing in the 1880s, Hecker's long struggle to communicate Catholicism to the American public ended where it began, in a plea for honest examination of the most fundamental questions of life. In an essay on Emerson and Matthew Arnold published shortly before his death, Hecker once again posed the religious question: What is the destiny of man? He still believed this was the fundamental question, and he still was sure that reason offered no final answer. Emerson had seemed to admit as much, at times of grief acknowledging his inability to make sense of tragedy. Without religion, Hecker still believed, no one could know his or her destiny in its fullness or know it with certainty. Those who relied on human wisdom alone necessarily became "minimizers of Christ and maximizers of themselves." Only supernatural revelation could make clear and certain that each person did have a destiny and what that destiny was, a sharing in divine life and union with God. Alone and unaided, even the best of humans, Emerson and Arnold among them, took a path downward away from the sublime and the good into the mire of atheism, amorality and despair. Almost angrily, Hecker lambasted these "apostles of skepticism," who offered nothing but treated those who responded to divine revelation "as sickly children holding onto the skirts of their mother," as Thoreau had cracked so many years before.[12]

In the end there was a fundamental ambivalence in the approach to the church characteristic of the Paulists and their founder. On the one hand, as converts, they had themselves experienced a personal quest for faith and for a church which secured that faith. They took for granted, and affirmed, the first principle of religious liberty: that each person could by right seek and claim a religion for himself or herself. In addressing the non-Catholic community, they explained their own road to Rome and refuted the slanders directed at Catholicism. In doing so, they necessarily accommodated themselves to religious voluntarism. Facing their own church, they recognized that educated, English-speaking, middle-class Catholics would in fact decide for themselves the character of their commitment to the church. They needed to be persuaded to make greater sacrifices to support the church and the projects of the Paulists. They needed to be aroused from their lethargy to become apostles in secular culture; they needed to be exhorted to take seriously their lay responsibilities.

Yet in the missions, and in their parish work, the Paulists—and Hecker himself—never challenged the tendency of pastoral practice to insulate the church's people against the corrosive effects of modern society, particularly its voluntary principles. Indeed, they felt a certain nostalgic and sentimental attraction to the vision of a secure, peasant faith held within the uniform symbols and routines of supposedly Catholic ages and countries. They wanted a more intelligent approach to religious education so that lay people would be more alert to their responsibilities and would be able to give an account of themselves before the public, but by no means did they agree that Catholics should be encouraged to go through the same process of searching and choosing that they had. For, in the end, the church was not a voluntary society but the living organism of God's presence in the world, larger than and independent of the decisions of individuals. It was a visible body prior to the invisible soul. It was united under the papacy as a divinely established organization through which the truths revealed by Jesus Christ were preserved, the intuitions of religious experience were confirmed or corrected, and through which, alone, union with God was possible.

Thus, according to Hewit, each bishop and priest was "the mouthpiece of the whole Catholic church" and from any one of them a child could learn "all needed for salvation." Much as they desired a more vigorous intellectual life, their understanding of the church did not stimulate such activity. Those outside the church had to search for the true church and "when found, receive its teaching with docile faith" while Catholics "have a certain and complete religion," a "genuine and integral Christianity" and had "no need to . . . restore unity and reconstruct the church." While Hewit would undoubtedly modify these statements in concrete situations, there was an assurance and confidence that contributed to, rather than challenged, the drift toward a Catholic subculture and an articulation of faith which would sustain it and define its boundaries. The limits on Paulist apostolic endeavor were not imposed from without but grew from seeds already planted within.[13]

On this, as on other matters, Hecker might argue that his Paulist brothers had departed from his teaching. Yet as his polemical articles made clear, he had no reservations on Catholic doctrine and the intellectual encounter of the church with modern culture was, in all essentials, one way. Catholics had much to learn *about* American society and the modern era if they were to convert it; they even had much to learn *from* that world about such matters as organization, motivation, technique, style. But Catholics and Catholicism could only teach, not learn, on the essential matters of human destiny and human nature, freedom and salvation.

For all the conflicts of the period, Hecker's initial confidence held firm. If once he had felt the only problem was to present Catholicism clearly to disinterested minds, he had learned that the church itself had to overcome some barriers to make evangelization effective. He remained convinced, of course, that Catholicism was true and the only sure source of faith and of unity among people. He also remained hopeful, though less certain, that the church could triumph by trusting in the fairness and decency of other Americans. In one of his last published articles he welcomed a Protestant journal's statement that Protestants should put aside their crusade against Catholics and emphasize the many things on which they agreed. Hecker attributed this approach to the yearning for unity he thought one of the most remarkable signs of the age. Until recently "trained up in a condemnatory frame of mind," Protestants were now, for the most part, sincerely seeking the truth.[14] He could say this still even after the doubts and disillusionment which had come with the controversies of the last decade.

If Protestants were seeking unity, Hecker argued, Catholics were exploring the deeper meaning of freedom and intelligence. While there were Catholics "who are neither very free nor very intelligent," all possessed "a knowledge and a certain knowledge of the essential truths of Christianity." They did not, should not question that unity could only be brought about through the teachings and discipline of the church, divinely instituted by Christ. If one took any point of agreement between Catholics and Protestants and traced it out, Hecker was sure one would learn that Catholicism alone offered the full expression of that doctrine and its surest guarantee. This meant that doctrine, already clear, must be expressed in terms comprehensible by the American people. The new Catholic University established in 1886 meant a major effort in that direction was being made.

> The work of the new University, planted in the political center of this free and intelligent people, will tend to shape the expression of doctrines in such wise as to assimilate them to American intelligence—not to minimize but to assimilate. To develop the mind there is never need to minimize the truth; but there is great need of knowing how to assimilate the truth to different minds. The work of the Catholic University is to precede the conversion of the country. For if we wish to attract Americans, we must present Catholicity to them as affirming in super abundance those qualities of our character which are distinctly American—affirming them in an aspect which reveals their universality.[15]

Thus Hecker ended in a Christian spirit, welcoming the fact that both Protestants and Catholics were increasingly willing to explore Christian truths in a humble, reasonable, civil manner. Fools may misinterpret this, Hecker added, prophetically, but the reconciliation of obedient faith and intelligent liberty was a problem for both parties to help solve. So he urged all to cultivate the "things that make for unity" and understand that there was no reason unity should not come about in the nineteenth century, just as disunity came about in the sixteenth.

Hecker had not resolved the ecumenical problem. He could denounce Protestantism in the strongest and most offensive terms, and then urge Protestants and Catholics to work together to achieve unity. He was fully convinced that the Catholic Church was absolute and universal and that the Kingdom of God would be Catholic. He was equally convinced that Christianity was strongest and most authentic when united with liberty and intelligence, so that the Kingdom must come through freedom, and must express the "spontaneous convictions" of humanity.

Hecker had no doubt that the Catholic Church as an institution was the presence of Christ in history, so that persons should be invited to its communion. At the same time he recognized the shortcomings of Catholics and the real barriers the church presented to that invitation. He was loyal to his church and its people and could defend them against slander and injustice; he was also loyal to his country and wanted to find solutions to common problems which had to be solved in a world still marked by religious differences. If he was at times torn between his Catholic faith and commitment, his confidence in God's presence in the midst of history, and the voice of his own conscience, he was not alone. He struggled, with more success than most, to preserve his integrity and fulfill what he took to be his vocation and divinely-bestowed responsibilities in a church and an age which had not yet reached the promised land of his youth.

Part Four: In Spirit and in Truth

18

Public Catholicism

Isaac Hecker's promised land was something more than a gigantic cathedral. The future triumph of the church would take place not when the existing Catholic Church persuaded everyone to join it, but when all men and women, freely and spontaneously, responded to the spirit and lived in peace, justice and harmony with God and one another. Conversion was required of Catholics and non-Catholics alike, and it embraced the institutions and culture within which they lived. When converted men and women united in the church of Christ, lived wholly Christian and human lives, politics, society, art, science, literature, economics, in fact all areas of human life, would be informed by the truth of Christianity and ordered toward the end of human existence, union with God.

The religious question came first, for the individual and for society at large. America's social problems would be fully solved only when America became Catholic. Americans would become Catholic only when they found Catholicism credible. Catholics, therefore, had to be model citizens as well as models of holiness. The church's engagement with society and politics, at its best, would bear witness to its conviction that, through its teaching and ministry, solutions to human problems could be found, solutions compatible, even identical, with the deepest hopes and aspirations of the American people. It was a noble vision, located far beyond the narrow parochialism of the contemporary church.

Hecker's political ideas arose from and were confirmed by his personal experience. As a young man he posted handbills, worked on political campaigns, and even, at the age of fifteen, proposed to a ward meeting a set of resolutions on the money question. In this setting he met Brownson, then the leading champion of radical social democracy in the country. There was little religion in their politics, Hecker recalled, but they often referred to a generalized Christianity: "Christ was the big Democrat and the Gospel was the true Democratic platform." Hecker's memory often played tricks on him. In fact, his youthful participation in his brother's reform activities continued only sporadically after his powerful religious experience led him to embark on his search for a new direction for his life. Still, it is significant that later, when he searched his own experience for evidence of God's intentions for him, he interpreted his life as a progression from political reform to social reform, then to a consideration of first principles, which in turn led to religion. "I had gone through the different heresies of Protestantism and the different social and political theories which assume to take the place of religion," he recalled with understandable exaggeration. "Oh! How long did I try to make politics serve for my religion!"[1]

At Brook Farm, it became clear to Hecker that social evils were "not so much social as personal, and it would not be by a social reform that they would be remedied, but by a personal one." In his diary in 1843 he expressed this schematically in a triangle with the three sides labelled personal reform, social reform and political reform. Within the triangle appeared the words, "Unity, Church, Religion." Preoccupied in those years with his own loneliness, he regretted the manner in which American society separated individuals from one another. What could bind them together into one nation and inspire self-discipline, community and mutuality? Only religion, and only a religion universally recognized as true. One key to such a religion he found in the crucial passage from the Catechism of the Council of Trent:

> Every true Christian possesses nothing which he should not consider common to all others with himself, and should, therefore, be prepared promptly to relieve an indigent fellow creature: for he that is blessed with worldly goods, and sees his brother in want, and will not assist him is at once convicted of not having the love of God within him.[2]

In Catholicism he thought he found a religion which addressed the moral issues rooted in the human heart, brought people into a solidarity that transcended barriers of wealth and class, and called forth that loving sacrifice which alone could provide the foundation of a free, just and peaceful social order. "Certainly Christianity in attacking sinners, goes to the root of all our evils, which, while social and political, had their origin in personal evil," Hecker wrote. "Make men sincere Christians and society will be regenerated, reform accomplished, and the halls of legislatures purified." He united that conviction with the Catholic argument that the church, given authority to teach in God's name and itself providing a model of freedom, justice and equality, alone could inspire the social reforms needed in modern society.

The combination was unusual in the United States. The Christian perfectionism of Methodist and holiness movements often spilled over into a determined commitment to do God's will by driving sin from the land, but Hecker, while concerned about human suffering, rarely moralized in that fashion. On the other hand, neither did he share the restorationism which plagued so much of nineteenth-century Catholic social thought. He agreed with conservative European Catholics that Protestantism was the source, not of modern progress, but of modern evils. Nevertheless, unlike many European advocates of the social question, Hecker looked forward and not back. "The eyes of the Church are set on a divine vision of things that the world has [not] yet ever witnessed," Hecker wrote. "This is not in the past but in the future, and it consists in the reign of perfect justice, truth, reason and love."[3]

Hecker never fully internalized the radical separation of the church and the modern world, characteristic of nineteenth-century Catholicism. Unlike liberal Christians, he never accepted a subordination of religion to culture which would make of the church simply one agency of goodness among many. Unlike some evangelical Protestants, he could not accept a sense of social obligation and responsibility that was purely personal. Redeemed persons could not make a just or happy world by themselves; they needed an organized body, the church, for the security of their faith and for the full realization of their shared humanity. Conversion to Catholicism, for Hecker, was a reconciliation of persons with God and with themselves, a reconciliation that would ultimately bring about both a united, universal church and a fully human culture. Only when all were attuned to the voice of the Holy Spirit within and to the presence of the Holy Spirit in the church would true democracy be possible. "If democracy is a virtue, then the church is the school in which it was born," Hecker wrote in his diary in the spring of 1844.[4]

Although he never gave extended attention to the social question, as the new class system was called, Hecker fully recognized that industrial society brought with it the contrast between progress and poverty which so disturbed reformers. "While wealth increases under the modern industrial, commercial and competitive systems of enterprise," he wrote, poverty and pauperism increased at a greater pace. Socialism was no remedy, he thought simplistically, because it would overthrow religion and morality. Nor could the state solve the problem, for its programs were expensive, inefficient and ultimately encouraged rather than relieved dependency.

Religious orders, on the other hand, composed of dedicated people, assisted by lay organizations like the parish-based St. Vincent de Paul Society, motivated by love and a belief in the dignity of every person, could relieve poverty in a way which would be inexpensive and ennobling in its effect upon both donor and recipient. As Hecker wrote at the end of the Civil War, "poverty, wretchedness and vice" were "evils of the modern system of selfishness, Protestantism in commerce." What was needed was "an association of individuals" to work among the poor "without any other reward than the love of God and of their fellowmen." Only the church could inspire people "to knock at the doors of our state prisons, poor-houses, etc., to take care of the inmates, for no other pay than the love of God."[5]

Before a Boston audience he compared the cost and ineffectiveness of New York's public charities with the inexpensive, loving and highly effective work of the Little Sisters of the Poor, concluding that "the practical and enterprising American people" would someday turn to such religious communities to care for the needy, and then "socialism and anarchism will threaten us in vain."[6]

In fact, local and state governments provided funds to some Catholic institutions to support indigent persons, particularly orphans and delinquents who had become public charges. Catholic immigrants, beset by the problems which always plagued migrating communities, provided a disproportionate share of criminals, alcoholics and paupers. This fact led a growing number of non-Catholics to charge that the church devoted too little attention to social problems and did not make a serious effort to overcome vice and dependency among its own people. Such accusations aroused indignation among Catholics, a response Hecker shared. For example, when *The Independent* called on Hecker to lead a crusade against the crime and vice it thought rampant among the Irish Catholic poor, the *Catholic World* blasted the magazine, blaming the poverty of Catholics on the English penal laws and continuing racial and religious discrimination. Moreover, the degrading, paternalistic missions of the Protestants compared unfavorably with the massive educational, charitable and social programs conducted at St. James parish in New York's poverty-stricken fourth ward. *Catholic World* contributors delighted in the contrast between busy parishes like St. James and the abandoned or nearly empty Protestant churches in working-class neighborhoods. Turning the charges against Catholics around, they accused Protestants of abandoning the city, leaving their own poor to lapse into ignorance and infidelity, risking the formation of an undisciplined, lawless mob, all in sharp contrast to the pacifying and uplifting effects of Catholic pastoral work.[7]

Hecker rarely wrote on such issues himself. As an editor, he sought out well-informed writers who offered a compassionate, though relatively conservative, response to most social questions, Hewit, in particular, wanted to appeal to the generosity and idealism of middle-class Catholics. In 1872 he wrote a series of six articles on the duties of the rich in Christian society. "No careful reader of the magazine could believe its editors would encourage any movement hostile to the just rights and reasonable privileges of the wealthy class," Hewit wrote. "We cherish a deep respect for all the hierarchical institutions of the political and social order, as well as for their more sacred and elevated counterparts in the ecclesiastical system." Anything that would "check our ultra-democratic tendencies, infuse a conservative spirit into our public opinion, give dignity, decorum, and stability to our institutions, elevate and refine our social tone, and add a becoming splendor to our civilization" would enjoy the *Catholic World*'s support and approbation.

The condition of the poor was always hard, Hewit believed; it "was a great and an arduous thing which is required of them to submit patiently to the supremacy of the higher classes." Religion alone would make their situation bearable, and then only if the poor believed that rich people acted on Christian principles and are "zealous laborers" for the good of all. The Catholic rich, in particular, had the responsibility to do what they could to aid the poor. They should avoid ostentation, cultivate refined tastes and pursue honorable, useful ends, while practicing a true poverty of spirit. They should serve the church by aiding charitable work, supporting the building of churches and schools, and uniting their resources with those of the priests through "voluntary associations under the sanction and direction of the hierarchy."[8]

Hewit's views reflected the social stance of the *Catholic World* and of the Paulists. Aware of suffering, aroused by injustice, and disturbed by indifference, all of which they blamed on non-Catholics, they were nevertheless Catholic evangelicals, combining appeals to individual conscience with Catholic conservatism, paternalism and solidarity.

Isaac Hecker agreed with much of this, but with one important modification. Nurtured on the equal rights idealism of the Workingman's party of the age of Jacksonian democracy, Hecker was more democratic in his instincts than Hewit and most of the *Catholic World*'s writers. Early in his career he had concluded that charity was less significant than self-help in alleviating the plight of the needy. "Is it not better to teach those who depend upon charity for their subsistence to live so as to be independent of alms than to be charitable?" he asked in 1844.[9] But he never explored the barriers to economic independence, nor did he notice the changes which came with the more class-conscious industrialism of the post-Civil War period. He shared with Hewit a desire to make Catholic businessmen and public officials honest and responsible, and he remained convinced that the surest road to social reform ran through converted individuals. But he never expressed the conservative paternalism that led Hewit to justify economic and social hierarchy and celebrate the pacifying influence of Catholicism on the restless working class.

In fact, one key to Hecker's life was the positive, optimistic view of human nature which formed his democratic temperament. He saw the spark of the divine in the people he met:

> Man is not aware of his Godlike capabilities. . . . Man thou has thy creation in thy own hands. . . . Men are not fully awakened to the responsibility that rests upon them, to the deep, eternal importance of every act of life, every word, and thought. . . . Man gives being to that which has no being. He creates something where there was nothing. He is a Creator. A God in God. Every man I meet is an unconscious prophecy to me. I would awaken him to the wonder of his being.[10]

Hecker thought a political society, or a church, was best where composed of people who had made intelligent decisions. Freedom, he seemed to believe, was the essential condition of authentic human life, a position far in advance of his church:

> The more a civilization solicits the exercise of man's intelligence and enlarges the field for the action of his own will, the broader will be the basis it offers for sanctity. Ignorance and weakness are the negatives of life; they are either sinful or the consequence of sin, and to remedy these common evils is the aim of the Christian religion. Enlightened intelligence and true liberty of the will are the essential conditions of all moral action and means of merit.[11]

Isaac Hecker trusted people, individually and collectively. He was prepared to work in the context of freedom, to deal openly and affirmatively with people as he found them. This attitude informed his evangelism, his understanding of the Paulists, his image of the United States and of modern society, and it led him to develop a distinctive spirituality. It also made him appear to some naive, even heretical. Hecker, of course, understood the dogmatic authority of the church, but his own experience led him to the conviction that people could be persuaded to accept Catholicity only from within, that their adherence to "the law of God," in principle above them, must be voluntary. This did not disturb him because Hecker believed so deeply that God's law was in fact conducive to personal happiness and social well-being. The disillusioned Brownson bombarded the public with news of its failures, hoping, but not expecting, that people would recognize their need for the church's authority and submit to it. Hecker, in contrast, persisted in his confidence in human nature, accepted the reality of voluntarism and celebrated it as indeed the best context for the church because it alone assured that adherence to Christ was free, honest and deeply rooted.

As for society as a whole, this led him to conclusions which differed in spirit, if not in content, from those of most Catholics of the time. If religion could be restored to its position of primacy in the human heart, if men and women would listen to the Spirit speaking through the voice of conscience, then religion could direct the tendencies of the age into their proper channels. "There is no denying the fact that the religious problem sums up all the problems," he wrote in 1881. "In the last analysis it is religion which shapes, and by right ought to shape, among intelligent men, all institutions."

Why didn't it? Just as he and Brownson had determined that the crucial religious problem of the 1840s was to insure the reality of the objects of human knowledge, so Hecker believed a quarter century later that "the secret cause of dishonesty in public life and frivolity in personal conduct in the case of men and women of good natural qualities is their hesitation and uncertainty concerning the reality of the objects of their higher aspirations." Such people were easily tempted to be "untrue" to themselves when they doubted the "reality and therefore the authority of the facts of consciousness." Accordingly, Catholic conversion was the road to social reform, conversion of persons to the truth of their aspirations, truths only made sure and certain by the Catholic Church.[12]

Given his awareness of freedom, his preoccupation with the integrating and unifying qualities of Catholicism, and his confidence in the indwelling Holy Spirit, Hecker's approach was inevitably evangelical, appealing to conscience. Such a message might have limited appeal to working class Catholics but it seemed an appropriate way of appealing to the two groups Hecker thought the particular objects of Paulist attention: non-Catholics and the emerging Catholic middle class.

To hopeful and aspiring Catholics, Hecker and other writers in the *Catholic World* offered a sense of the social question in which they and their church could provide examples of social responsibility and public service. Particularly after he resumed active control of the *Catholic World* in 1875, the magazine devoted more and more attention to social problems.

Reviewing John Lancaster Spalding's book *The Religious Mission of the Irish People and Catholic Colonization*, one anonymous author echoed Hecker's optimism in the face of the grinding poverty of so many immigrants. Providence had opened up the "illimitable spaces" of the continent "to relieve an exhausted world." Efforts to reach the West may have been unwise when "the church was still in a state of formation," but now a massive colonization effort such as that proposed by Spalding would "lift the veil that has hung for years over Catholic eyes, awaken a new Catholic energy of vast public benefit and usefulness, and give a new and needed turn to Catholic thought and Catholic activity."[13]

Another contributor, John Talbot Smith, offered frequent analysis of social problems, insisting that these problems be examined without "ideological blinders." He called for the abolition of child labor, strict regulation of tenement house construction, formation of "block societies to rightly manage them," and support for moderate trade unions, which were "not doing a communistic work enforcing a rise in wages to such a mark that a father can support a family decently."[14]

Even more remarkable was a series on the "Negro Problem," written by the pioneering Josephite missionary John R. Slattery. Presuming general ignorance among Catholics of the condition of freemen, Slattery presented statistics and descriptions of the increasing numbers and importance of the Black population. He defended strenuously the equality of all people before God, the special responsibility of the church toward the unfortunate, and the unique opportunity presented to the church by this large, religiously uncommitted population, many of whom had strong, clear ideas of Christianity but no definite church affiliation.[15]

Hecker hoped that intelligent Catholic lay persons would respond to such problems. One implication of his evangelical approach was that social and political action must be the work of the laity. The church could teach, and exercise authority on secular matters of moral significance, but it could only act through its members. More than any other prominent Catholic of the period, in Europe or America, Hecker respected the independence of the laity and saw the layperson's work in society, in family, neighborhood, factory, counting house and government hall, as religiously significant and central to the mission of the church.

In a sermon in 1863 Hecker noted that each age had its characteristic forms of spirituality and sanctity: martyrs in the early days of the church, the hermits and desert fathers in a time of cultural collapse, the cloistered life in the age of faith, the militant vigor of Ignatius Loyola and the Jesuits during the counter-reformation. "Each class of men did in their day what their age required," he wrote. What should characterize Christian presence in the nineteenth century? The age claimed to be one of "advanced civilization to be marked by unprecedented diffusion of intelligence and liberty." In such a civilization, the ideal of sanctification would be "the union of religion with a fully enlightened intelligence and an entire liberty of will, directed wholly to the realization of the great end of our being." In this setting, he pointed to the example of St. Joseph, who found God and spiritual perfection in the midst of daily life:

> He was in the world, and found God where he was. He sanctified his work by carrying God with him into the workshop. St. Joseph was no flower of the desert, or plant of the cloister; he found the means of perfection in the world, and consecrated it to God by making its cares and duties subservient to divine purposes.

Similarly, contemporary Christians should pursue holiness in the midst of daily life:

> Our age is not an age of martyrdom, nor an age of hermits, nor a monastic age. Although it has its martyrs, its recluses, and its monastic communities, these are not, and are not likely to be, its prevailing types of Christian perfection. Our age lives in its busy marts, in counting rooms, in workshops, in homes, and in the varied relations that form human society, and it is in these that sanctity is to be introduced. . . . This, then, is the field of conquest for the heroic Christian of our day. Out of the cares, toils, duties, afflictions, and responsibilities of daily life are to be built the pillars of sanctity . . . of our age. This is the coming form of triumph of Christian virtue.[16]

As this sermon made clear, Hecker's appeal to the laity and his arguments for lay spirituality were firmly anchored in his program of conversion. The active, engaged and holy Catholic was working for the long-range goal of a Catholic America. "Every Catholic, whatever may be his station in life, is called to cooperate in the work" of evangelization, Hecker told a lay audience in St. Louis. "Wherever you see a Catholic true to his religion, where you see a Catholic setting his face against the reigning vices of his time, there you will find a missionary." The signs of the times, visible in private immorality and public corruption, required a religious response, aimed at producing good Christians who would both resolve social problems and win converts for the church. "Honest men in commerce, unbribed legislators, upright lawyers, just judges, honest mechanics and servants, these are the apostles of the laity here and now."[17]

For Hecker, religion and human civilization, for the good of both, must eventually be integrated and that goal must inform all the work of the church. While in Rome in 1857 he noted that he was "for accepting the American civilization with its usage and customs" because, "leaving aside other reasons, it is the only way by which Catholicity can become the religion of our people." The mind set of those European and immigrant leaders who wished only to enable the church to survive in a hostile world seemed always, to Hecker, a fearful withdrawal from the essential task of reconciling religion and human culture, for religion was nothing more than one side of the entire human experience. Openness to American life was more than a tactic for expansion, it was an indispensable attitude if the church was to fulfill its mission of meeting the needs of persons and affirming and grounding human destiny. He believed that "the character and spirit of our people and their institutions must find themselves at home in Religion in the way those of other nations have, and it is on this basis that the Catholic Religion alone can make progress in our country."

Here again, his convictions ran up against the realities of American life. The reappearance in the 1880s of bitter interreligious disputes forced him to confront Protestant charges directly, even using some of the historical apologetics he had so disliked in the writing of others. The school question also raised doubts about the security of the church and the motives of non-Catholics, and compelled him to present the Catholic case for Catholic schools in the strongest language. In New York Catholics were fighting to gain access to public institutions and to defend the long-accepted practice of providing public funds for children in Catholic juvenile and protective institutions. These disputes were part of the ongoing process of accommodation among religious groups and between religious bodies and government. In that process the presence of organized, self-conscious Catholic voting blocs had far more to do with the church's success than did the persuasiveness of their arguments. Furthermore, the fact that Catholics were predominantly working class while educational reformers came from the middle class raised questions about economic and political power which Hecker never explored.

The fact was that the United States of 1880 was a far different country from the open, fluid world of 1840. Then the radical changes of the revolution gradually undermined the authority of most institutions, while the rapid expansion westward and the heady experiences of social and political democratization created a culture in which many, at least among the middle class, knew that they could choose a life for themselves. But immigration and nativism, sectionalism, slavery, civil war and the rise of a more brutal form of industrialization brought many changes, including the reappearance of strong institutions and the division of society into more sharply defined classes. At the same time, ultramontanism abroad and the requirements of an immigrant church at home sharpened the boundaries of Catholicism and added to the tension with non-Catholics. Earnest seekers were more scarce, disinterested explanations of Catholic ideals harder to uphold.

Hecker rarely dealt with these matters in depth. He was himself closely associated with a wealthy family, his brothers had been benevolent employers, and he never really focused his own attention upon the plight of urban working class Catholics. His was a liberal, progressive view of the social question, for always he perceived progress beneath the surface of conflict, emerging harmony beneath the appearance of discord. Most of all, he believed that men and women who had opened themselves to the Holy Spirit would be drawn to one another in love and would attempt to express that love in their social and working lives.

On a few occasions, Hecker bristled at Protestant use of government power to discriminate against Catholics, but on the whole neither in the church nor in society did he ever explore the problem of power and its use. This was clearly evident in a series of notes to himself concerning the career of Father Edward McGlynn.

Born in New York, McGlynn attended public schools and entered the seminary to study for the New York priesthood. Bright and articulate, he was sent to the Urban College of the Propaganda in Rome, where he was ordained. Returning to New York he became the pastor of St. Stephen's, a sprawling parish in the heart of the city. Soon he was one of the city's most popular preachers, attracting many of New York's finest families to hear his sermons. At the same time, he developed a variety of social services for his poor parishioners and refused to build a parochial school for fear it would distort the pastoral priorities of the parish. A brilliant, inquiring man, he was oppressed by the spectacle of multiplying poor in a nation which gloried in its economic expansion. A strong supporter of the idealistic programs of the St. Vincent de Paul Society, he nevertheless believed that its combination of youthful idealism, personal involvement and practical assistance would always be no more than relief; he deeply wanted to understand and help remedy the underlying causes of social suffering, injustice and inequality.

He found the answer in Henry George's *Progress and Poverty*, published in 1879. George held that the private ownership of land was the source of the problem; it could be solved by a "single tax" imposed on unearned increment created by rising land values. His solution was less impressive than his dramatic portrait of want in the midst of plenty, and his book touched the consciences of thousands of Americans. In 1886 the New York City Central Labor Council brought George to New York to run for mayor on a reform slate, challenging both the Republicans and the dominant Tammany Hall. Father McGlynn spoke strongly on George's behalf. Archbishop Michael Augustine Corrigan, son of a wealthy grocer and intimate with the city's lay Catholic leadership, was horrified. He fought back in two ways, issuing a pastoral letter stating that George's views violated Catholic teaching on property rights, and forbidding McGlynn from participating actively in the campaign. When the priest refused, claiming that the archbishop had no power to control his actions as a citizen, Corrigan suspended him from his priestly office.[18] After the election McGlynn refused to go to Rome when ordered to do so and was formally excommunicated. He continued his lectures for the Anti-Poverty Society until he was readmitted to the church by the new Apostolic Delegate in 1894 after a commission of experts found his views compatible with church teaching. The McGlynn episode created a major controversy in the church, dividing the New York clergy and the American hierarchy, and a major public scandal as well.

Hecker had been acquainted with McGlynn for many years. In 1866 he had accepted the young priest's invitation to deliver the eulogy for McGlynn's pastor and friend, Father Thomas Farrell, a speech in which Hecker praised the controversial priest who had been among the few Catholic supporters of abolitionism and who left his money to found the city's first black parish. Later, McGlynn and a number of other younger priests, several Roman educated, founded the Accademia, a discussion group which considered a variety of theological and pastoral issues, many of them quite controversial. Hewit and Hecker were occasional visitors to the meetings; the members admired Hecker and thought him a forerunner of the new type of independent, progressive priest needed in the American Church. Yet Hecker was not intimate with the group, whose avant-garde thought, casual anti-Romanism and gossipy ecclesiastical politics were quite foreign to his intensely spiritual faith and deep ecclesial loyalty.

McGlynn's controversial views and tragic career troubled Hecker. His private notes set forth many objections to McGlynn's ideas and behavior, but always with a tone of uneasiness; he kept coming back to them, perhaps because he felt that his own answers were not quite adequate to the questions McGlynn raised. Clearly Hecker sympathized with McGlynn's plight, perhaps because he saw in McGlynn some of his own youthful idealism. Ideas and aspirations for McGlynn were realities, not abstractions, Hecker though. As with the transcendentalists, McGlynn's passionate idealism led to extremes, especially on the social question. McGlynn would alleviate the condition of the poor without the help of the rich, abolishing classes instead of bringing them into contact with one another. McGlynn even attacked the church, but Hecker hoped McGlynn's criticism of the ecclesiastical "machine" was the result of passion. McGlynn had challenged the authorities of the church in the name of his rights as a citizen, yet once assured of those rights, he used them to assail the church, becoming an "outside reformer" of ecclesiastical abuses. "Does McGlynn suppose that with a band of kickers against the Catholic authority he can regenerate society?" While McGlynn and his friends might feel they were only attacking the "human side of the Church," their words seemed "simply anti-Catholic to the average man and woman." Most annoying was the conflict within the church: by arousing the wrath of the bishops, McGlynn made friends of a "true adjustment of means and methods and policies to the modern state and the aspirations of nations" afraid to act.

Hecker's unsystematic assessment of the social and political dynamics at work in McGlynn's conflict with the church was even more disturbing. He attributed McGlynn's actions to a revulsion from the European spirit "so violent as to disturb his equilibrium." Fearing that Catholics were not regarded as good citizens, he had an "extravagant" desire to prove the contrary. Worst was McGlynn's implied suggestion, in denying the hierarchy's authority to questions his politics, that "in the makeup of the good citizen, religion is not of prime importance." For Hecker, nothing could be further from the truth. "They make a great mistake who imagine that the future greatness of America lies in a further divorce between religion and the state," Hecker wrote. "All free institutions stand in need of the support of religion, and the love of country needs for its support the love of God." So, in a broad sense, McGlynn was "un-American," with a view of citizenship more akin to the "French democracy of 1793" than "the American ideas of '76." Hecker admitted that the "grave mysterious" problem of church and state, a problem that reached "into taxation, into public charity, into foreign relations" and had produced the "most deadly wars," was hard to resolve. "The great point to be borne in mind is that American institutions are entitled to freedom of expression and development; and in this connection it is pleasing to think that the Catholic Church has never antagonized them, nor any other true national institution or aspiration," whatever McGlynn might think to the contrary.

As these random private reflections made clear, Hecker found it hard to place the McGlynn episode in his framework of providential history. McGlynn, product of all the best that the modern church had to offer, was living evidence of the failure of the external methods of discipline, characteristic of the post-Reformation Church, brought to fruition at Vatican I but no longer appropriate in an era of freedom and intelligence. Undoubtedly the energetic, forceful McGlynn, a cultured and sophisticated product of American schools and Roman universities, priest, respected citizen and eloquent preacher, must have seemed the very embodiment of Hecker's hopes for American Catholics. His conflict with church authorities, and his response that the church had no authority in politics, troubled Hecker so much because it represented yet another question mark after his vision of "the future triumph of the Church."[19]

The United States was not yet a Catholic country, so the claims of citizenship might conflict with the claims of the church as they did in the case of McGlynn. Hecker was scandalized by McGlynn's public denial of the archbishop's jurisdiction over his politics, but he also knew that quiet submission was no better solution. The church could only promote its ideals, and protect its interests, through persuasion. "The divine authority of the church . . . possesses no practical value . . . except what is voluntarily given to it on the part of the faithful," he told congregations. The church in former ages had conquered whole nations and civilizations. Its task now was "to captivate the intelligence of a civilized people with the light of divine truth and to bring a nation of free men to the liberty of the sons of God." Freedom was happily the inescapable context of missions:

> The Catholic religion seeks free men, for it is only a voluntary homage to truth that is meritorious and worthy of the dignity of Man. It is with intelligence and liberty completed that Catholicity looks forward to its fullest development and glory.

Many evils persisted which the church opposed, but she depended on the free support of her members. "She does not, and cannot force submission," Hecker said. "Forced submission can make slaves, but not Christians."[20]

Hecker praised the freedom allowed to the church by the first amendment, but he saw separation of church and state, unlike religious liberty, as temporary. The day would come when church and state would be cooperative expressions of a single, unified Catholic Christian consciousness. When those institutions expressed "the religious faith and political convictions of the entire community," and when each acted in its own distinct sphere "concordantly with the other" to help people attain their divine destiny, then "the Kingdom of God upon earth approaches its nearest fulfillment." Thus, Hecker wrote, "every well informed Catholic knows that the separation of church and state is a great calamity." Yet the Catholic also knew that the destruction of the liberty of the church and her subordination to the state was worse, "perhaps the greatest of calamities." Once the "old system between church and state was broken and its recovery hopeless," then it seemed imperative to embrace every opportunity to secure "independence and freedom of action" for the church.

Hecker, of course, had little interest in restoring that "old system," which too often subordinated religion to dynastic or political powers. He did not hesitate on this basis to recommend for Germany, in the wake of the *Kulturkampf*, a program which would insure the liberty of denominations, modelled explicitly on the United States. For, after all, the church had flourished in America for over one hundred years without the patronage of the state:

> The tree of Catholicity grows stronger and bears precious fruit when planted in the soil of liberty and intelligence. Would to God that the Catholic Church everywhere in Europe enjoyed liberty to preach her holy faith and exercise her salutary discipline, as she does in these United States! Religion reigns most worthily, in an age tempered like ours, when she rules by the voluntary force of the intelligent convictions of conscience, and finds in these alone her sufficient support.[21]

Hecker had long believed that if the Constitution were being adopted in his day, it would receive "the sincere and hearty approval of Catholics." Hecker was, therefore, delighted with a speech given by Baltimore's Cardinal Gibbons in Rome in 1887 as he took possession of his titular church after being named to the sacred college. It was a strong defense of American society and its church-state arrangements. He saw Gibbons as America's "high commissioner" to a suspicious Roman court. While the church tended to make its people loyal to any form of government, Hecker argued the American form was "more favorable than others to the practice of those virtues which are the necessary conditions of the development of the religious life of man." It left a larger margin of liberty of action, and, therefore, "for cooperation with the guidance of the Holy Spirit, than any other government under the sun." The church could flourish in America, Hecker believed, to the extent "that Catholics in their civil life keep to the lines of their republicanism."

American Catholics did not wish "to plant our American ideas in the soil of other nations," but they did wish to be rightly understood, and that was not easy. Gibbons had "expressed the American idea in such terms as not to be misunderstood." In Europe, rulers wished to control "things spiritual," an interference "that can never be imposed on the American people." Here the state left religion its full liberty; "that is precisely what Europeans cannot or will not understand." The state was not indifferent to religion and did not ignore the precepts of natural law, but it did not meddle with the church. Leaving the church free to do its work, allowing Catholicism an open field to contest for the allegiance of the American people, respecting the moral and religious values held by the diverse churches, "American institutions were more in harmony with the principles of religion," than were any in Europe.

Hecker at times suggested that American institutions, while appropriate to the United States, might not be suitable for export, but more often he believed they were providential signs to the whole church:

> He who does not see the hand of Divine Providence leading to the discovery of the western continent, and directing its settlement and subsequent events towards a more complete application to political society of the universal truths affirmed alike by human reason and Christianity, will fail to interpret rightly and adequately the history of the United States. It is also true that he who sees Heaven's hand in these events, and fails to see that Christ organized a body of men to guard and teach these universal truths to mankind, with the promise of His presence to the end of the world, will fail to interpret rightly and adequately the history of Christianity. He is like a man who sees the light but has his back turned to the sun which gives it. But the discerning mind will not fail to see that the republic and the Catholic Church are working together under the same divine guidance, forming the various races of men and nationalities into a homogeneous people, and by their united action giving a bright promise of a broader and higher development of man than has been heretofore accomplished.[22]

Rome did not understand American conditions, he had learned, and until it did, "blunders will be made and religion will suffer." In part the problem arose because many European Catholics were suspicious of the independent spirit of Americans. "They are afraid of democracy at Rome," Hecker told Walter Elliott in 1883. "One of the charges made against me in Rome was that I was trying to introduce democracy into the Catholic Church." Accordingly, Hecker welcomed the advent of Leo XIII, whose early endorsement of republican government indicated that at least the pope would allow the American arrangements a fair trial. Moreover, Leo's effort to restore sound philosophical studies would give a more enlarged view of Catholicism to the outside world, stimulate rational inquiry and affirm liberty in literature and in scientific pursuits. This new freedom would bring "ill omens for all whose thought has run more for theological schools than for Catholic truth." Leo's pontificate, like Gibbon's speech, confirmed some of the optimism Hecker had felt when he wrote *The Exposition*.[23]

It may have been too late to revive his European project, but Hecker could write, and in 1886 he brought his recent writings together in *The Church and the Age*. In this book Hecker summed up his views of Catholicism and American democracy in a way which marked his final rejection of Brownson's pessimism and foreshadowed the difficulties that arose regarding his ideas after his death. To *The Exposition* and his comments on Gibbon's Roman address, Hecker added several items that had appeared since his return from Europe. Together they constituted the strongest affirmation of democracy and human rights yet written by a Catholic American.

His passionate statement of the unity of Catholicism and democracy would echo through the underground of American Catholicism for a century, until brought to theological affirmation in the second half of the twentieth century.

> What a Catholic believes as a member of the Catholic Church he believes as a citizen of the republic. . . . What a Catholic believes as a citizen of the republic, he believes as a member of the Catholic Church; and as the natural supports and strengthens the supernatural, this accounts for the universally acknowledged fact that no Catholics are more sincere in their religious beliefs, more loyal to the authority of the Church, more generous in her support, than the Catholic republican citizens of the United States. Catholicity in religion sanctions republicanism in politics, and republicanism in politics favors Catholicity in religion.[24]

In politics as elsewhere, Hecker's work was not fulfilled. Hecker's approach to politics rested on the conviction that religion and politics work together, so that eventually Americans must become Catholic in order to become one people and fulfill the promise of freedom. He never examined what a Catholic America might look like; in particular he never took up the issue of how church teachings, in a Catholic country, are translated into public policy without destroying human freedom. Like the clash of Christian churches, the contentions of political parties seemed the result of human sinfulness, to give way to an orderly consensus once everyone heard the Holy Spirit speaking the same message of natural rights and natural laws in conscience, in the church and in historical events.

Until that conversion took place, there remained the messy realities of pluralism, with Catholics forced to contend for their rights and in the process become one more denomination and, in politics, one more interest group. Lacking a positive understanding of pluralism short of the Kingdom of God, Hecker could only argue for denominational schools and civility. In doing so, he helped Catholics become more comfortably American, though his consistent argument for denominational schools as a public goal was a more responsible stance than that of those Catholics who all but ignored the public interest in education. Hecker continued to insist that the coming Kingdom would be Catholic, avoiding thereby the lapse into a crude civil religion in which the nation, under the auspices of a non-denominational God, became itself the agent of God's purpose in history.

But there could be little question that, in the absence of a broad Catholic constituency which shared his vision, and lacking a mass movement toward the church, Hecker's ideas could be, and were, assimilated into the ideology of an increasingly sectarian Catholicism whose Catholic vision of universal reconciliation became, in spite of itself, an ideology for an increasingly successful church. Building that constituency was the challenge as Hecker saw it. The church had nothing to fear from the freedom of its own members, much to gain by appealing to the minds and hearts of Catholics and non-Catholics alike. Even though he had not persuaded his church to trust in "a freer and more instinctive cooperation with the Holy Spirit's interior illuminations," and though he had not convinced even his own community that they could conquer the modern world, his own Paulist convictions remained firm, his hopes remained high. He would, at least, leave behind a legacy of faith in Christ, in the Holy Spirit, in the church and in the limitless possibilities of the human enterprise. Humanity had a destiny, the fullness of truth still lay ahead.

19

The Indwelling Holy Spirit

A major characteristic of modern Western societies, at least for that portion of those societies who escape the immediate imperatives of providing each day for food, clothing and shelter, has been the presence of alternatives. One can, unusual in the long sweep of human experience, decide for oneself. For people like Isaac Hecker, who thought themselves responsible for the direction and purpose of their life, that freedom could be agonizing. At each stage, when choices had to be made, Hecker suffered. But he was not alone. In Concord and New York he had a loving family and warm friends. In Rome in 1857–58 he had the trusting support of his brother priests back home, the unequivocal backing of his brother and sister-in-law, the friendship of important Roman officials and the gratitude and affection of resident Americans he led to the church. In the 1860s a number of women to whom he provided spiritual direction affirmed his special calling, while new friends he met around the country believed in his publishing ventures. On his long journey of the 1870s he still had George and Josephine to confide in and the blessing of new admirers wherever he went.

Decisions after 1875 were far more difficult. He had lost touch with his New England friends years before. The women to whom he had provided spiritual direction were caught up in their own lives, emancipated from dependence on him, as he had hoped. Among the Paulists, few even of his original band had ever fully understood his work among non-Catholics, much less shared his inner experience of God. Hewit, preoccupied with community leadership, was sometimes patronizing, sometimes simply impatient. Father Walter Elliott was closest to him, yet sadly he did not enjoy Hecker's complete trust, at times even his respect. In short, Hecker was alone. The questions still came; answers, choices, were still needed. Hecker struggled to make those choices, but the world and the church were unreceptive, his personal resources had shrunk with illness, and there was no one to pick up the banner he struggled to set before them.

Some, including Brownson, faced isolation and chose to reconcile themselves to the church and to the Catholic subculture as it developed in the nineteenth century. Hecker could easily have accepted the requirements of historical necessity as they were being defined in Rome and by conservative Americans like Archbishop Corrigan. He could have resigned himself to the seemingly inevitable drift of the Paulists toward denominational service. He did not stand publicly against the drift, for that was not his style, but neither did he think that was what God asked of him. So he persevered, confident that the Holy Spirit would somehow, eventually, guide the church toward a new pentecost, that eventually, in God's time, the deepest yearning of America and of the modern era would be fulfilled by Catholic Christianity.

The source of that persistence lay in Hecker's interior experience of God. From the moment he left New York in search of a foundation for his faith and a direction for his work, he trusted that inner voice. He joined the Catholic church to strengthen and make certain that inner experience; at times of trouble and crisis he turned, not to the church's externals, as when he refused to visit Lourdes, but to the Holy Spirit he knew was within. He could not resist the declarations of papal infallibility because of his trust that the Holy Spirit spoke through the Vatican Council; but he could not accept it as Hewit and Brownson did because papal monarchy did not correspond to the promptings of conscience. Looking to the future, as always, he found a way to reconcile outer events and inner experience in the vision of a new outpouring of the spirit taking flesh in a missionary church preaching the good news of Christianity to free men and women, but that was a vision, not a policy or program, and it was a vision at considerable distance from the realities of both church and society, as Newman, another who knew isolation, recognized.

What Newman could not know was that the *Exposition* did not arise in the first instance from a careful reading of historical events, but from Hecker's profound spiritual experience. This was the most consistent strand of his life. He had pledged early in his spiritual journey to be faithful to the voice of God within his soul, and he was. It cost him much in terms of influence, power and respect within the church; it led him to dreams and ambitions doomed to disappointment. At times it also led him to less attractive outbursts of self-pity, to moodiness, even to occasional moments of cruelty. But it allowed him, perhaps unusual in that troubled era in church history, to preserve his integrity. Whatever else can be said of Isaac Hecker, he was a sincere, almost transparently sincere, Christian, whose faith, hope and love, flawed by his humanity but evident to all who knew him, were the fruits of a serious experience of God.

There was a remarkable consistency in Hecker's basic approach to the spiritual life. As far back as his seminary days, reflecting on his own experience, he had concluded that spiritual perfection, union with God, could be achieved through a two-fold purification. First it was necessary to overcome the "sensual part of the soul." Love must be focused on the Creator and not the creatures, so a painful process of repression must take place, aimed ultimately at perfect detachment. Only when that stage was reached, when the things which had been objects of love, and thus hindered spiritual growth, had been reduced to their proper place, could one embark on an active life or on a career.

The second process of purification aimed at the "rational or spiritual part of the soul." Faith purified the intellect by emptying the mind of all knowledge which did not serve the goal of union with God. It was this process that hindered his studies and so worried his superiors. Memory was purified by hope, which set in perspective those events of the past which weakened the passion for God. This process explained his optimism and his consistent affirmation of Catholic and Christian possibilities. Charity purified the will, detaching it "from every pleasure and affection which was not of God." It was this virtue that led him to resist partisanship, to transcend conflict and avoid personalizing disagreements. These supernatural virtues, elevating and enriching as well as disciplining the natural virtues, served as indispensable means for attaining union with God. This struggle for purification and self-discipline was never-ending, painful and progressive. At times the Christian might seem to lose all, as Hecker felt he had on so many occasions, but with an eye on God, one realized that he or she had lost nothing but gained all. "The loss is transient," he wrote, "the recovery is permanent."[1]

Hecker's basic assumption was that the purpose for which the soul was created was this union with God; all human faculties and gifts should be ordered toward that end. Spiritual development, then, was not a repression of human nature but its fulfillment, not a contradiction of the human, but its foundation. The true religion was also the most human "because its aim is to give to all that is human the development which its author intended," not to set aside human instincts, "but direct them aright." As far back as the summer following his conversion he had written in his journal: "The influence of the Catholic church is preeminently favorable to the full development of the highest elements of man's nature." The human was good, as was all God's creation. The fall had left that essential goodness intact, while the revelation of God in Christ made clear the dignity of the human person, the nearness of God, and the care of God's son. "In creation God made man like himself," Hecker said in an 1870 Christmas sermon. "In the Incarnation God made himself like man." As a result "Christ is our brother whom we can approach with feelings of confidence and affection."[2]

Hecker's humanism was romantic, but realistic. In his search for God he had admired the optimism so strong in New England, but he had refused to rely on his own natural goodness alone. From the very beginning he seemed conscious of the reality of sin and the need for divine assistance. Freedom was not easy. "Man possesses to a fearful extent the power of directing his own destiny," Hecker wrote during the winter following his reception into the church. His sense of sin, however, was balanced against an appreciation of human goodness. On the feast of Mary's Assumption in 1844, at a time when he was much preoccupied with his own weaknesses, he broke forth in testimony to the human beauty and possibility he saw around him:

> In many faces I see passing through the crowded streets a veiled beauty, an angel, quickening me with purer life as I pass by them in anxious haste. Do we not see the hidden worth, glory and beauty of men as our own becomes revealed to us? Would the son of God have been needed to ransom man if he were not of incomprehensible value?[3]

It was this conviction that Christianity was the way to achieve human destiny and fulfill the deepest hopes and aspirations of the human soul that distinguished Hecker most sharply from his contemporaries, and from those who came later. At his best he wanted, in a real sense, to convert Americans first of all to be themselves, to listen as he had to the voice of conscience calling them to live a purer and more integral life, and to respond, as he had, to the best that was in them. Those hungers of the human spirit, those questions of the soul and aspirations of nature, were the voice of the indwelling Holy Spirit. People should become Catholic so that those hungers could be fed. At times, especially when under attack, Hecker could sound righteous and triumphalist, but in his best moments the competitive style of denominationalism, the sectarian strategies of churchmen and the prideful self-assertion of an insecure church and priesthood were foreign to his nature. He was at home in his world; he thought that world and its people were good; he wished only to bring that goodness to life in a living church and a humane society. Those who spent their days preserving an

The first Paulists: George Deshon (**above left**), Augustine Hewit (**above right**), Francis Baker (**below left**) and Clarence Walworth (**below right**). Hewit succeeded Hecker as the community's second general; Deshon was the third.

Above: A construction scene, 1878–80, of St. Paul the Apostle Church on Columbus Avenue and 60th Street, New York. The earlier church, a frame building, is seen behind it. **Below left:** "Father Hecker reading Goethe," sketched by John LaFarge in 1866. **Below right:** The first issue of *The Catholic World* in 1865.

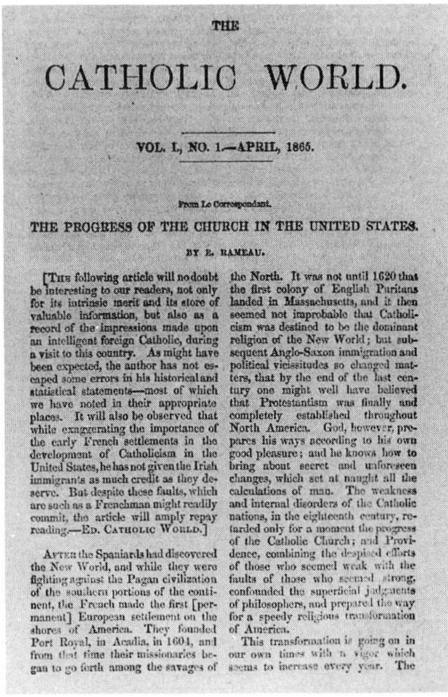

THE

CATHOLIC WORLD.

VOL. I, NO. 1.—APRIL, 1865.

From Le Correspondant.

THE PROGRESS OF THE CHURCH IN THE UNITED STATES.

BY E. RAMEAU.

[THE following article will no doubt be interesting to our readers, not only for its intrinsic merit and its store of valuable information, but also as a record of the impressions made upon an intelligent foreign Catholic, during a visit to this country. As might have been expected, the author has not escaped some errors in his historical and statistical statements—most of which we have noted in their appropriate places. It will also be observed that while exaggerating the importance of the early French settlements in the development of Catholicism in the United States, he has not given the Irish immigrants as much credit as they deserve. But despite these faults, which are such as a Frenchman might readily commit, the article will amply repay reading.—ED. CATHOLIC WORLD.]

AFTER the Spaniards had discovered the New World, and while they were fighting against the Pagan civilization of the southern portions of the continent, the French made the first [permanent] European settlement on the shores of America. They founded Port Royal, in Acadia, in 1604, and from that time their missionaries began to go forth among the savages of the North. It was not until 1620 that the first colony of English Puritans landed in Massachusetts, and it then seemed not improbable that Catholicism was destined to be the dominant religion of the New World; but subsequent Anglo-Saxon immigration and political vicissitudes so changed matters, that by the end of the last century one might well have believed that Protestantism was finally and completely established throughout North America. God, however, prepares his ways according to his own good pleasure; and he knows how to bring about secret and unforeseen changes, which set at naught all the calculations of man. The weakness and internal disorders of the Catholic nations, in the eighteenth century, retarded only for a moment the progress of the Catholic Church; and Providence, combining the despised efforts of those who seemed weak with the faults of those who seemed strong, confounded the superficial judgments of philosophers, and prepared the way for a speedy religious transformation of America.

This transformation is going on in our own times with a vigor which seems to increase every year. The

Above left: Brownson as an older man, painted by Paul Woods. *Courtesy University of Notre Dame Library.* **Above right:** Hecker during the 1880s. The two famous Catholic converts were estranged for a time in their later years. **Below:** Hecker, with helmet and cane, leans against a palm tree during a trip up the Nile in 1874. Behind him another American, Mrs. Donnelly, is seated on a donkey.

Left: Walter Elliott was Hecker's disciple and biographer. **Right:** Abbé Felix Klein in 1917. His preface to the French edition of Elliott's biography set off a dispute that led to the Vatican campaign against "Americanism."

unthinking faith, those who demanded unswerving loyalty and unquestioning obedience, those who identified the faith with buildings and institutions, even those, like his devoted disciple Elliott, who gave their lives to the defense of the church and an aggressive search for new members, all lived under a different inspiration and heard a different voice from the one that spoke to Isaac Hecker.

Hecker's Christian humanism undoubtedly was influenced by his family life, his experience in New England, and the sense of the autonomy of the self and the beneficence of history that permeated American culture as he experienced it. It was never shaken, however discouraging his own experience of people and events. Indeed, Hecker's work with converts and his spiritual direction confirmed his belief that the natural dispositions of individuals, who were cultural beings, must be reconciled with ecclesiastical obligations or there would be danger both for the church and for the individual. When ideas of religious duty held by a vigorous person conflicted with his or her personal "instincts or habits," or with their "national life," there was always the danger religion would give way. Converts, he had noticed, in the fervor of faith, at first loved sacraments, rituals and obedience to directors and superiors, but eventually "old habits and ideas reappear" and Hecker saw that "reassertion as also standing on a truth." In other words, the associations of family and friendship, the demands of vocation, the problems of earning a living and balancing one's time all were important, undeniable requirements of life. Conflicts must arise, for few were "so constituted as to set aside entirely [their] past life and take up an entire new one and live always peacefully in it." Thus, unless "a way for reconciliation is shown between faith and these needs," great dangers arose.[4]

It was, therefore, critically important to emphasize the positive relationship between natural and supernatural virtues, between the natural instincts of people and the demands of the spiritual life. In Hecker's own life these relationships went back to his original desire to respond completely to the call of the spirit and to find useful work; later they expressed themselves in his struggle to reconcile fidelity to the spirit and a life of strenuous apostolic action. This practical necessity, the personal corollary of the reconciliation of Catholicism and national life, was the ground for Hecker's humanism, quite as much as abstract doctrines of the Fall or philosophical understanding of nature and grace. A religious conversion which was only and finally *away* from the world, and a spiritual life lived only in church, simply would not and should not work in American and in modern society. In an era of freedom, external controls would stumble over personal autonomy, and automatic, unquestioning ritual practice would collapse with the dawning of consciousness. The dangers of personal egoism and material distractions, which so worried Brownson and conservative bishops, could be avoided only by persons of deep inner conviction.

The notion that grace builds on nature was a personal as well as a collective idea. Just as spiritual doctrines or ascetic theology must be shaped to culture, to particular peoples at particular moments in their history, so prayer should build upon, not repress or ignore, one's natural virtues and inclinations. In September 1851 Hecker advised Brownson that he should follow his "attrait" in prayer; if God gave him the gift of contemplation, he should not avoid it through "false fear." What he told his friend he repeated endlessly for almost half a century to brother Paulists and lay people alike:

> The best prayer for each one is that in which he succeeds best, from which one draws the most profit; it matters not what that sort of prayer may be called. There are some for whom the predominant influence is the external one . . . authority, example precept, and the like. Others in whose lives the internal action of the Holy Spirit predominates. In my own case, from my childhood God influenced me by an interior light and by the interior touch of His Holy Spirit.[5]

All of this led Hecker to offer those who sought it spiritual direction aimed primarily at building their confidence in God's presence in their own lives. The church's goal was to aid souls in their quest for union with God; spiritual direction should seek the same end. Accordingly, spiritual direction and pastoral action were works of liberation, freeing individuals from external supports so that the indwelling spirit could lead them to their destiny. Everything in the church was good, he told Jane Francis King, but people should keep in mind that the aim of all things was to bring the soul nearer to God and "into more perfect union with Him." People should realize that what helped their soul to achieve this goal was what they should be faithful to. Recognizing that his own love for "simplicity or sincerity in devotion" might be "too strict for many souls," he thought that individuals should study the ways in which the Holy Ghost attracted their soul, be faithful to those things and not take up other practices. "Fidelity to the solicitations of God's grace, recollection, in order to obtain this knowledge, and mortification, purity of heart, in order to remove whatever may hinder the operation of grace in the soul," these were everything in the spiritual life.[6]

In 1863 he told Mrs. King that the Holy Ghost was her primary spiritual director. In fact, he felt "more and more delicate" about giving spiritual advice to others, fearful that he might "interfere with the divine work of the Holy Ghost in their souls." He tried to confine himself to helping people "remove whatever hindrances may be in their souls to the direction of God's inspiration." "I feel jealous for the rights of God as the First and Supreme Director of Souls," he wrote. The soul should "rest in nothing—however good and holy—*outside of God* and employ nothing outside of God that does not bring it closer to him." Only the soul itself could tell what those things were which would bring it closer to God; the church supplied an abundance of aids, saying to each person that he or she should "choose and not abuse." Too little regard for these aids or too much dependence on them were "both hurtful." The convert, he argued, "like a starving man" was apt to become too dependent. Yet it was "a great breach of etiquette to give our attention or love to anything besides God, when He is present to the soul."[7]

Jane King was the widowed mother of two children. She once worked in the office of the *Atlantic Monthly*. In her letters, which are unavailable, Mrs. King must have sought strong direction, more than Hecker was willing to give, for again and again he emphasized that, while the desire for "more complete and explicit direction is natural," it was perhaps given to people in order to make them "turn more and more to Him, the Supreme Director." He emphasized that the union of the soul with God was "the true aim of Christian perfection" and that everything in the church should be ordered to this end:

> It sometimes happens that a soul is apt, in its admiration of the flowers of piety, to forget the Gardener. Our primary study is to bring ourselves under the influence of divine grace and the guidance of the Holy Ghost. All practices of piety, spiritual reading, and even the reception of the sacraments are important insofar as they conduce to this end. To profit by these, this end is always to be kept in view. If the reception of the Sacraments of Penance and the Holy Eucharist daily is conducive to this end, to some this has been so good. . . . The real question is, how far is the soul advanced in the ways of God—how closely is it united to Him? For this, and this alone, is the true aim of Christian perfection.[8]

Hecker admitted that he had a special reason for taking an interest in Mrs. King's spiritual life, for through her his conviction had been confirmed that American Christians required a distinctive approach to spiritual progress:

> Our American character is suitable for a certain type of spiritual perfection. Any attempt to bring out any other, or impose any

> other upon it, will be unsuccessful, if not fatal in many instances. Besides, our faith can make no great progress until we present the ideal of life as conceived by our best minds. To do this, requires the identification of our faith with what is good and true in our type of character. Our faith must take root in our national characteristics, and we must find ourselves entirely at home in it. My wish is to help my fellow country men and women in the work. I believe our civilization presents to Christianity a broader basis to rear a spiritual life upon, than any other form of civilization. I wish to see advantage taken of this, and prevent a narrow and repugnant form of spirituality from taking its place: one which we can not adopt and will not accept generally. It is my conviction that if there were everywhere souls presenting a type of Christian perfection consistent with our Faith, and its doctrines and teachings, and in harmony with our American character, this would go a great way in reconciling our religion to our people. I have the conviction that I can be all the better Catholic because I am an American: and all the better American because I am a Catholic. This shown, many obstacles in the way of the conversion of our people will be removed.

In a note written on this letter Hecker reaffirmed the point: "Every nation has its own peculiar character and ideal, which is only realized when it comes under the inspiration of common religion."[9]

In his advice to Mrs. King Hecker demonstrated that he had learned a great deal from those directors who had worked to moderate his own disposition toward penance and mortification years before. He regularly warned her against excessive penitential practices. She was too inexperienced for vigorous penances, which might injure her health or jeopardize her ability to fulfill her obligations to her family. Moreover, he sought to attain a balance between the spiritual hunger for God and acceptance of God's creation. "To love creatures aside from God is sinful," he told her in October 1863, but to "love creatures in God is lawful." Most important, she must understand, as he had learned, that "we are not exclusively spiritual. To postpone all our happiness to a state of being hereafter is unsatisfactory and cannot be part of God's plan. This life and this earth also is His. . . . Religion then must hold out to men a present happiness as well as a future hope of heaven." The separation of nature and grace, temporal and spiritual, this world and the next, all were part of the problem of the modern age, a problem Christianity could resolve.

The discipline of the spiritual life, ordering the quest for union with God, was not a way of escaping worldly responsibility or a means of overcoming a sinful bodiliness and humanity. Rather, in the end the soul's spiritual direction, and the destiny of the human race, meant the reconciliation of all things in God. The decisions of human life, guided by the spirit, should aim at this unity and integrity, and should seek to promote it in a larger world. There was a direct connection, then between Hecker's understanding of the work of evangelization and his spiritual direction, for "in spiritual matters, the same views and convictions actuate me."

> I aim to bring the Intellect and Will into complete union with Divine Truth and under its guidance will be brought about, in the individual, that which eventually will be developed in Society. Given the union of the soul with God, preserving at the same time all that is true and genuine in the American character, and you have the special object I aim at in personal direction. Now, where this identification of our religion with all that is genuine in our character is made, we shall have in such persons a model character, the type of what we may anticipate in the future, when our religion has become universal in our country. This type of character will be superior to any that can be produced by a false and incomplete form of Christianity, hence attractive, and the means of bringing the truth of our religion to bear on the minds of our countrymen. *Personal perfection* is a means of the conversion of our country.[10]

When Mrs. King became caught up in her own life, perhaps comfortable at last with reliance on the Holy Spirit, another woman, Elizabeth Cullen, became a regular recipient of Hecker's spiritual advice. Cullen was an intelligent, assertive woman, unusually so for her day. These qualities were always dangerous, Hecker thought, for there was "such a thing as an intellectual as well as moral prodigal." Perhaps he had a special problem when a woman displayed her learning and curiosity. Hecker compared the "inordinate" emphasis on the intellect to "a woman who puts on fine dresses rather to display them than to enhance her own personal beauty." The object of knowledge, as everything else, was to bring about an increase of love; where it failed to produce that result, it was pernicious, as with one "who eats too much food, the excess remains only to torment and weaken the stomach."

Yet, as with so many intelligent women, Cullen was plagued more by feelings of inadequacy than by intellectual pride. In addition, her life was complicated by the fact that her husband was not familiar with her religious activities, such as bringing her daughter for religious instruction at St. Paul's. Mrs. Cullen was also apt to overemphasize penance and mortification, but in her case, Hecker affirmed the value of such practices. "Exterior mortifications are aids to the interior life," he wrote in 1865. "What we take from the body we give to the spirit. If we will look at it closely, two thirds of our time is taken up with what shall we eat and where withal shall we be clothed. Two thirds of our life or more is animal, when you include sleep. I do not despise the animal in man, but go in for fair play for the soul. The better part should have the greater part."

Despite differences in age and situation, Hecker seemed to find in Mrs. Cullen a mirror of himself. Their long correspondence was filled with advice, eventually passing in both directions. For his part, he saw in her the dangerous and treacherous dialectic he had experienced between self-love and the attractiveness of divine beauty and grace. "All we do until he purifies us is all tainted with self-love and perverted by self-activity" he wrote. God wins the soul's attention, then exposes its "deformity, it's unworthiness, its perversity." At the same time God reveals Himself "with increased loveliness and beauty." The process continues in almost violent passion: "The battle of love between God and the soul will be waged until it is tried and made worthy to be His spouse." Even during the most intense sacrifices and mortifications, "self-love, self-activity, selfhood" creep in "like a cancer," only purged through a long, painful process, "the more subtle the more painful."[11]

For her part, Mrs. Cullen deeply valued Hecker's friendship and advice but, almost uniquely, she saw his faults and pointed them out. Once he told her, as he had said often in his diary twenty years before, that he would do almost anything to find a person with whom he could share his spiritual life and open his heart. She responded sometime later that he would be unable to do so until his heart was wrung pure by the suffering God sent him. She also spoke frankly of what she regarded as his lack of feeling for others. Intelligent, witty and strong-minded, she could one day beg to see Hecker, in desperate need of his help, and on another criticize him for his coldness, his refusal to bend to the weaknesses of others, and his too persistent advice to purge oneself of self-love. On several occasions, after visiting with him, she wrote of how hurt she felt by his critical insistence that her problems arose from the subtle workings of selfishness. After one visit, when she had felt in particular need of his sympathy and support, he had told her that her agony reflected the lingering effects of love of herself. She left him stricken and depressed until taken in and given some tea by a kind woman in the neighborhood.

She saw Hecker's frequent contradictions. His complaints of being misunderstood often seemed like self-pity, making her think of "a noble mastiff conscious of its own strength permitting the familiarities of a tiny kitten." A close observer of ecclesiastical life in the Boston area, she thought Hecker should aim his work at Catholics, whose conduct was often a scandal; besides, missions involving close contact with ordinary people might make him "bend a bit to the weaknesses of others." On another occasion, when he told her there was "no common basis for a priest and a woman to work together," she responded that there was nothing a priest would do for the love of God that she would not dare to try as well. When Hecker told her priests could not take advice or direction from women, Cullen challenged him, and she returned to the subject often, with considerable resentment. It seemed a strong, healthy friendship, one of the few in which Hecker met with critical comments. It may be significant that it was strongest during his most active and productive years following the Civil War.[12]

Still, Hecker's comment that priests could not receive spiritual direction from women was revealing, for he was well-aware that many great mystics and saints had done just that. In fact, Hecker was cutting Mrs. Cullen off, rejecting the intimacy she invited and he at times seemed to want. He had done that before with the women at Brook Farm, and it may have reflected a deep fear that he might in fact find a person to commune with. Isaac Hecker gave spiritual direction to others, but he rarely accepted that direction himself. Brownson, McCloskey and his superiors in the seminary all were held at a distance, and he remained on his own. Formally, Hewit was his director, but he seems never to have enjoyed Hecker's trust. Reaching out always to others, he could allow no one to touch him. In the end, he would find himself terribly alone, in a desert space to which he thought God had called him, but which was a space in part, at least, of his own making.

Despite Mrs. Cullen's criticism, Hecker was compassionate with people facing severe problems, particularly in his later years when he was himself experiencing frustration and disappointment as well as severe problems with his health. To a nun who had come to America to begin a contemplative community but found church authorities unsympathetic, he wrote that her lack of any "human prospects whatever" simply meant God had "taken your affairs in His own hands." What he was trying to do, he advised for her:

> Resignation, Patience and Fidelity to the Divine Will. Who knows but after all it may be the will of Divine Providence that when you have learned, by your present trials, the greatest of all lessons of the spiritual life, absolute dependence on God, utterly, regardless of all else whatsoever, you will find the intention and purpose for which you undertook your voyage is the one He has appointed for your first work in this country.[13]

A short time later he heard from Julia Beers, an old acquaintance who had cared for him in Florida and Rome. She reported that in severe illness she could not pray. At the same time Father Chatard wrote that Miss Beers had been stricken dumb, was threatened with "paralysis of the lungs" and had come to Rome to die. Hecker wrote praising her resignation and noting once again that the ready acceptance of God's will was the goal of all prayer and suffering. "Involuntary silence, voluntarily accepted, will lead the soul into that solitude in which God will speak to her words unutterable and give her to taste the eternal fountains of joy." If by her affliction she was forced to withdraw from "all commerce with creatures" and practice "passive acquiescence to His Divine Will," so that her soul would be prepared for union with Him, "wherein is your affliction?" he asked. As always he wanted her to see the work of God in the events of life. "God has the hook of his divine love entered deep into our soul, and he will not fail to accomplish His blessed purpose, to draw you near and transform you into him."[14]

Hecker's spirituality also guided his approach to the Paulists, who were to serve as living evidence of what all persons could become. They were to seek personal holiness and pursue apostolic works, to live in community freely, without vows, but with a commitment so deep that they would be prepared to take vows at any moment. "I do not think that the principal characteristic of our Fathers and of our life should be poverty or obedience or any of the special and secondary virtues, or even a cardinal virtue, but zeal for apostolic works," Hecker told them. Among those works were "the conversion of souls to the faith, of sinners to repentance, giving missions, defense of the Christian religion . . . and, in the interior, to propagate among men a higher and more spiritual life." That life they should model in their pursuit of perfection. In their pursuit of holiness they were to have few rules and great freedom. As the people he directed were advised to seek the aids which helped them, so the Paulists were to order their own lives in accord with their inner experience and their outward circumstances: "If one of our Congregation finds that poverty, or obedience, or contemplation, or liberty of spirit, or any other way, is the way that God leads him, he is free to enter by that door. Great fidelity in action with a great and large freedom of action, should be the spirit of our community."[15]

Models of such integral spirituality had existed in the past. One was St. Catherine of Genoa, whose life and work always fascinated Hecker. His 1873 preface to Mrs. Ripley's translation of the life of St. Catherine was a concise statement of Hecker's spiritual doctrine; it provides as full a measure of his anomalous position in the nineteenth century Roman Catholic Church as anything he ever wrote. Here, as so often, Hecker tried to "correct the misconceptions of many who honestly fancy that the Catholic church encourages a mechanical piety, fixes the attention of the soul almost, if not altogether, on outward observances," and demands "complete submission to her authority and discipline." The life of St. Catherine made it clear that "the reverse" was true; namely, that the immediate guide of every Christian Soul was the Holy Spirit. St. Catherine's "uncommon fidelity to the instructions of the Holy Spirit" made her worthy of being numbered among the church's greatest mystics.

Hecker argued that many people failed to see that "the indwelling Holy Spirit is the divine life of the church," and that the sacraments had for their goal to "convey the Holy Spirit to the soul." The many rules and regulations governing Catholic life guarded the soul "from being led astray from the paths of the Holy Spirit." God could have provided for the immediate communication of the Holy Spirit to human souls "independently of an external organization like the church," but that was not his plan. "He chose to establish a church as the extension of His Incarnate Son, Jesus Christ." Ministry, sacraments and government were provided to enable the church to serve God "as his body had," to complete by a visible means the work of human redemption. According to Hecker, it was "entirely false" to believe that the church was intended to be a substitute for the authority of Christ or for "the immediate guidance of the Holy Spirit in the Christian soul." On the contrary, the authority of the church was the authority of Christ, the sacraments nothing more than channels or visible means of "communicating the Holy Spirit to the soul," and it was this divine action in the church which gave "its external organization the principle reason for its existence."

Hecker argued that it was "absurd" to suppose that the Holy Spirit dwelling in the church and the same Holy Spirit inspiring the Christian soul should contradict each other. When conflict took place, it was not the work of the Holy Spirit but "the consequence of ignorance, error, or perversity on the part of the individual." The test of the sincerity of an individual Christian soul in following the inspiration of the Holy Spirit was "its prompt obedience to the voice of the Holy Church." Only when the soul went astray from the paths of the Holy Spirit did it find difficulty; "otherwise it is conscious of perfect liberty in the church of God." From this argument Hecker derived a practical rule which he used frequently in his apologetical talks and in his spiritual guidance: "The immediate guide of the soul to salvation and sanctification is the Holy Spirit, and the criterion or test that the soul is guided by the Holy Spirit is its ready obedience to the authority of the church." With this rule there was no danger of going astray and the soul could have absolute security in the pursuit of sanctity. This was, in fact, the basis for his argument that Vatican I's completion of ecclesiastical authority should usher in a New Pentecost.[16]

One reason he was attracted to St. Catherine was that her experience of God often took place outside the normal forms of church life, giving her a sturdy independence from the sometimes petty concerns of churchmen, to say nothing of her pushing beyond the boundaries usually set for women. Hecker had himself experienced the working of grace outside the usual means of the sacraments, an experience he thought God provided "to show me how much he can do and does do for others in the same way." Because his own experience had been so extraordinary, he was less inclined than most in his day to place emphasis on the supposedly normal channels of grace. While open-minded, he was skeptical that strict enforcement of rules and minute spiritual direction would prove useful in the modern age. "I think that Communion should be more frequent and Confession less insisted upon," he wrote. "I favor freedom in receiving the sacraments." There were souls who might receive communion daily and attend confession no more often than four times a year.[17]

Similar considerations informed Hecker's approach to the church. On the one hand, his doctrine of church identified it with God's presence in the world. As a result, even recognizing the indwelling Holy Spirit, he was still convinced that "there is no road open for man to approach the Redeemer except that of the Church." On the other hand, while the wisdom of God could surely solve all human problems, that wisdom was only in a limited way imparted to the church. He did not question that the church deserved unlimited submission in its dogmatic assertions, but he did not believe it deserved equally uncritical trust in its "parental guidance." In such matters it was not infallible. Too often even Christian truths were "tortured into all manner of shapes by those who find it pleasant to throw them in people's faces," he wrote. "In fact, authority is so much abused at the present day that it requires a thorough belief in it as a thing divine not to conceive a hearty dislike for everything that comes under its flag." In short, the anchor of faith rested not in the individual soul alone, nor in the church as an external authority, but in the spirit of God who lived in and through *both* the individual soul and the church; together, and only together, they constituted God's living presence in history.[18]

Isaac Hecker had not become a Catholic in order to abandon or reduce his interior search for union with God, but to follow in the path of the great mystics, to find the historic road to God through Christ, with assurance, support and loving correction. Still, he had never fully integrated the two until, he thought, his trip to Rome for the Vatican Council. Then, as he recalled years later, "the relation of the interior and exterior action of the

Holy Spirit as guidance and criterion came to mind." In fact, he had long believed that the interior guidance of the spirit was the means of Christian perfection; the authority of the church was the criterion by which one judged that interior guidance and found assurance or correction. In Rome, however, he clarified this relationship and anchored it within his providential sense of history. With external authority solidly grounded in the doctrine of infallibility, the time had come to return once again to an emphasis on the inner life. As he told Mrs. Cullen, "I hope for pentecostal days for the church by directing the attention of her children to the interior direction of the Holy Spirit." While in Rome, he thought about writing a book "on the foundations of the spiritual life" to show those who sought "Christian perfection" how they could attain it. The central theme would be the conviction that the "proximate means" of sanctification is the "operation of the Holy Spirit in the soul," while the criterion of the direction of the Holy Ghost in the soul is the divine authority of the church. He worked on that book for the rest of his life, producing a substantial set of notes and a lengthy manuscript, but it was never published.

After his death charges were made that Hecker exalted the active virtues associated with a vigorous apostolic life at the expense of the so-called passive virtues of resignation, meditation and docility before the power of God. His own experience, his diary, his reflections on Paulist life, his spiritual direction, all provide evidence that there was little truth to this accusation. He told his women followers and his Paulist brothers that the road to active apostolic work lay through the disciplines of the "passive" virtues. His notes on religious life, undoubtedly used for conferences with the Paulists, made contemplation and prayer the central themes of the pursuit of personal holiness. They were filled with calls for "greater simplicity," "to return more to our interior," to "forget" the "outer world" and "the world of memory" and concentrate on God, "who is in a special, singular and wonderful manner, the center of our being and the source of all true life." All "events and occasions" should be used "to get nearer to our creator" and "permit nothing to enter which does not tend directly to God."[19]

Still, Hecker believed as deeply as he believed anything, that there was no necessary conflict between a rich and vital spiritual life and vigorous activity in daily affairs, whether directly apostolic or not. Indeed, his dream of a religious community was precisely to provide a living witness to the combination of active and passive virtues, contemplation and action, and he always hoped to assist in founding a women's order toward the same end. Models of the compatibility, indeed the essential interdependence of prayer and work, such communities would demonstrate the necessity for religious seriousness and interiority to offset the dangers of materialism and pride so pervasive in the modern age. As he told one foundress of a new community of women, there were some who believed that "our age" and "our country" were antagonistic to the contemplative life. Given some forms in which the contemplative had expressed itself, there was an element of truth in the charge. But Hecker claimed it was his "most intimate conviction" that the gift of contemplation was necessary for both age and nation, and he was confident that God would bestow the necessary grace "on certain elect souls in our day, and precisely among us." Contemplation was "the only counterweight that can keep this headlong activity of our generation from ending in irreligion and its own entire destruction."[20]

If contemplation provided a needed counterweight to "headlong activity," respect for modern industrial culture provided a balance against the self-righteousness of the church and its tendency to denigrate the world, placing intolerable burdens on men and women necessarily called to live in the world. In 1859 Richard Simpson, embroiled with the English hierarchy, asked Hecker whether Christianity must "always be in that state of peevish antagonism to all development of modern thought in which people seem to like to keep it." Totally lacking in self-criticism, the Catholic newspapers of the day, in Simpson's view, acted as if Catholics were "the only immaculate lambs in creation." Hecker agreed. There was a considerable amount of "calvinism unrecognized by Catholics, which passes for piety and Catholic faith, not only in our papers, but in works on devotion, asceticism and in our pulpits," Hecker wrote. Insisting that people were sinful, many tried to engage the church in alliance with "old orders, on almost any terms." Instead, Hecker looked on the world more positively and thought pessimism crippled both healthy spirituality and vigorous apostolic action. There was no other way for the great mass of Christians to achieve holiness, after all, than through the manner in which they conducted themselves in the ordinary, routine affairs of life. "I think a larger playground may be given to the action of our natural faculties and instincts without displeasing their author," he wrote. "Faith does not demand the depression or mutilation of our nature, or its instincts. Religion gives completeness of character. The church asks for men, not cyphers or cripples.[21]

While the passive virtues, quiet, patient waiting on God, provided the foundation of all spiritual growth, Hecker clearly believed the times required vigorous activity and the virtues to support it. This led Hecker to stress a spirituality for the active life, best seen in the 1863 sermon on St. Joseph, with its affirmation of lay life, a sermon Hecker thought the "groundwork of all my thoughts, actions and plans." "Our country demands at present, not so much the passive, as the active apostolic virtues," he told Anna Ward in 1859. "The latter I know are the fruits of the former. It needs men who are filled with the apostolic spirit, attached to nothing but Christ, prepared for all things, poverty, contempt, suffering, and every kind of labor. A few such, working through our country would in a short period make some wonderful changes."[22]

Again and again in his life Hecker retired from activity to the practice of the passive virtues of patience, obedience, humility, even self-abnegation. He promoted the writing of the French Jesuits Lallement and Caussade, both of whom presented an attitude in the spiritual life summarized in Caussade's title *Abandonment to Divine Providence*. In the notebook kept during the trip up the Nile, he reflected that there were two types of "false action" in the world, one self-activity, characteristic of the West, the other self-passivity, characteristic of the East. Both were false and separated the soul from God. The "highest action" consisted of "cooperating with, and suffering, the divine action of the soul." In the eighties he was tested again. No answers came to the questions posed by his vision for the church. There was nothing, it seemed, that God wanted him to do. For Isaac Hecker, whose religious quest had begun with the vocational question burning in his breast, this was the most bitter pill to swallow. Yet he did so, accepting the signs that God provided, to return and stay at home and there turn his attention to that which was the end of the journey, the only real promised land, the God who had called him in the beginning.

Yet, as always, he could find larger historical meaning in his personal experience. He told Mrs. Cullen before leaving for Europe in 1873 that what God had been teaching him in his illness was to rely once again on "the interior guidance of the Holy Spirit" and in that direction "lies the renewal of the life of the children of the church." For "the measure of the strength of the Christian churches" was "the measure of the Soul's immediate reliance on the guidance of the indwelling Holy Spirit." He tried to spell out what that meant in the treatise on the spiritual life he left behind, unpublished. He did, however, sum up its spiritual ideas in a series of brief essays in the *Catholic World* in the last two years of his life.[23]

He began by dealing once again with the treacherous problem of natural and supernatural virtues. The goodness of nature was often indistinguishable from the holiness of the supernatural life, as the "impulses of the Holy Spirit first poured their flood into the channels of natural virtue, thus rendering them supernatural." Prudence, temperance, fortitude and justice were natural virtues creating a correct relationship with one's self, with Providence, and with created nature; enlivened by the spirit in faith, hope and love, they achieved a supernatural level and "placed the soul in its true and perfect relation with God—a state which is more than natural." Men and women, after all, had a role to play in their own sanctification. The natural virtues, so often passed over or ignored, were of themselves insufficient for salvation, but the continuity between a good natural life, with appetites subordinated to reason and natural virtues exercised, was the basis of an uninterrupted continuity of spiritual growth.

All people, Christians and non-Christians alike, searched for God outside the soul, ignoring the inner life, but God used the outer world for the sake of the inner. "There seems to be little danger nowadays of our losing sight of the divine authority and the divine action in the government of the church, and in the aids of religion conveyed through the external order of the sacraments," Hecker wrote. "Yet it is only after fully appreciating the life of God within us that we learn to praise fittingly the action of God in his external providence." If this doctrine were taken seriously, people would aim at more direct communion with God, "not merely for an external life in an external society, the church. They would seek the invisible God through the visible church, the body of Christ." The conclusion was clear, and for the time, for Catholicism, very radical:

> The Holy Spirit is thus the inspiration of the inner life of the regenerate man, and in that life is his Superior and Director. That his guidance may become more and more immediate in an interior life, and the soul's obedience more and more instinctive, is the object of the whole external order of the church, including the sacramental system.

A church, preoccupied with bringing its members to sacramental practice, broadening their relationships with each other in a variety of associations aimed at segregating them from others in the community, and deepening their loyalty to their priests and parishes, while instructing them in their responsibilities and in the law and doctrine of the church, could hardly be comfortable with that kind of piety.[24]

In these articles Hecker suggestively expanded on his treatment of the guidance of the Holy Spirit in the life of an individual. This took place in two ways, Hecker argued, one of which was the direct action of the Holy Ghost on the soul, of which he had often spoken in the past. The other was through God's providence in the circumstances of life, not just the circumstances of the larger society and church, but the concrete circumstances of an individual. By this he meant the daily situation of marriage, family, religious community, work, talent, wealth, income, neighborhood, all that complex web of personal realities and relationships that constituted the world of an individual's personal life. These, too, like national life and world history, were signs of God's providence, giving signals of his will. Given the complexity and diversity of individuals and their situations, minute, detailed spiritual direction was not only undesirable but impossible. The existence of both these forms of divine guidance, the inner, personal experience of God, and the external demands of life, meant that no person could guide another except to lead him or her to the true guide, the Holy Spirit.

The key to resolving many spiritual problems, Hecker concluded, was to recognize that the direct action of the Holy Spirit on the soul was in harmony with the spirit's external providences. Sanctity consisted in making them identical in every thought, word and action of life, and all sacraments and devotions should lead to that end. In short, a person had to harmonize as much as possible the inner voice of conscience and the outward conditions of life. As Hecker had done, persons had to make decisions about vocation, style of life, allocation to time, energy and talent, and do so in a way which gave life an integrity, a wholeness, which could be called sanctity. When there were outward circumstances which could not be changed, a sickness, as with Julia Beers, resistant authority, as with the contemplative sister, an insensitive husband, as with Elizabeth Cullen, then one had consciously to determine to accept those conditions with patience and resignation, as evidences of God's will. Thus the climax of Hecker's own career came when God finally did not provide the external circumstances through which he could respond to the inner voice of conscience. He had been shown the promised land and given no means to approach it.

As he told Mrs. Ward in 1881, he could "beat anybody in the score of weakness." Unable to act, there was "only one chance and that is the passive virtues." God was the "first mover" and "impresses on all things their first movements," which did not leave much room for egoism. Once he had cause to believe that the promised land could be approached through strenuous activity, appropriate and seductive in an age which valued energy and activity above all. Then he was the "steam priest," honored by many in and out of his church. Now, at the end, there was no steam, and he was left alone. The inner voice remained clear, and he remained faithful to it, but the outward circumstances had changed. He might have persuaded himself that those circumstances alone showed what God expected of him, as Brownson may have concluded. Hecker chose a different course, to remain true to his own inner voice, to accept the outward circumstances, even when they were most depressing, with grace, resignation and, when he was able, good humor.

Despite his occasional call for a theology appropriate to the age, and his announced intention to examine all aspects of the question, Hecker never developed a complete theology of the Holy Spirit. He did not systematically analyze the relationship between the three persons of the blessed trinity, the precise manner in which the Holy Spirit informed both the individual soul and the church, and the Holy Spirit's relationship to creation and history. Nevertheless, his basic insight into the presence of the Holy Spirit in the individual soul, in the church and in human history provided a practical and theologically justifiable resolution of some fundamental problems in the life of the modern church. Clearly he believed that in a democratic era marked by religious pluralism, reliance upon the indwelling Holy Spirit was a practical necessity as well as a providential requirement. At the same time, he had learned from experience and from observation of his New England friends that some external guide was needed, a guide he found in the church. Later he would be more precise in explaining that the internal light of the Holy Spirit was central to the life of the Christian church and that indeed the church existed to forward and strengthen the internal life of the Holy Spirit among its members. While his interpretation of Vatican I was overly optimistic, his argument that the authority of the church should allow the church to trust its members remains a central insight for those who seek to adjust Catholic Christianity to the demands of advanced industrial societies. There is a certain circularity to the argument, of course, for it is the church which checks the inward life of the spirit and the inward life of the spirit that checks the church. The church in the absence of the indwelling spirit becomes formal and produces servile and weak characters, while the indwelling Holy Spirit, in the absence of the church, runs into individualism, fanaticism and irrelevance. One factor that draws that circularity beyond itself is the notion of divine providence, the presence of the Holy Spirit within human history, holding both church and the individual human soul to account in terms of the promises of God manifest in the coming kingdom.[25]

American society in the early nineteenth century was marked by radical social insecurity, producing in numerous young men like Hecker a sense of rootlessness and a desire for personal authenticity. The personal crisis that marked his trip to Boston and Brook Farm recurred throughout Hecker's life. In its initial stages he was determined to take responsibility for his personal growth and move beyond simple adaptation to the external requirements of middle-class life. Throughout that early period he felt "tossed about on a sea without a rudder," driven forward toward an unknown future. Rebelling almost in spite of himself against traditional social forms, he could not be comfortable with his rebellion. Aware of his own limitations, he could not follow so many of his colleagues in total reliance upon inner inspiration alone. Instead he sought a solid ground for his religious experience and a defined framework for a vocation. Having turned away from marriage, family and a business career, he literally did not know what to do, and he could not be comfortable with that unsureness because of a deeply rooted sense of responsibility. So strong was his sense of isolation that he shied away from physical contact with others and regarded even the desire for food as a temptation against his personal integrity. His confusion in dealing with women during this period reflected anxiety about the forces drawing him back to conventional life and his determination to realize some ideal vision in defining his own life. Women, Brook Farm, the radicalism of George Ripley and Bronson Alcott, all posed choices for Hecker which he was unwilling to make.

Yet he was distinctly uncomfortable with the range of choices constantly set before him and yearned for the security of an intimate personal relationship or of a settled regular community. When the New England reformers were unable to convince him of the permanence, stability and reasonableness of the social forms they advocated, he turned away and explored the churches. Finally, in Catholicism, he found the solid framework that both affirmed his own internal quest for purity and holiness and provided a foundation for a creative and vigorous life's work.

Yet, as his journal kept during the summer and fall of 1844 indicated, conversion to the Catholic church hardly answered all his questions. The desire for purity and holiness remained very strong, and while he took pleasure in the religious affirmation he found within his new church, his personal quest was far from answered. In the seminary, in his early days as a Redemptorist, on the missions, Hecker found work to do which he had always desired, yet he was constantly driven forward by the desire for personal holiness and a vision which would make his work fulfilling and meaningful in light of his deep faith. The freedom he had experienced was a providential revelation of the means by which the Kingdom of God was to be brought about. At the times of his most creative work he had full faith that "history was turning his way" and that his religious order, his church and he himself stood in the center of human history. When that confidence eroded, he fell into personal suffering and malaise. He felt himself alone and buffeted by events over which he had no control; unlike Brownson, however, he never turned away from that basic experience of his early life. "At no time in his life, not even during this final collapse did Hecker turn against his experiences," Michael Fellman writes. "He never completely buried his sense of freedom under the authority he sought. His life was a continual quest for the correct management of freedom within the community; his sense of possibility was not overcome."[26]

After Isaac Hecker died, Elliott, who had known him best in the later years, caught something of Hecker's combination of spiritual inwardness and apostolic energy. "When I look back on Father Hecker's life and character as I knew him well and intimately, I recognize more and more clearly the two motive forces in God's dealing with him," Elliott wrote.

> One is the absolute conservatism of his interior life, his immovable, unalterable adherence to the principle of cleansing the heart by prayer and self-denial, meanwhile looking for God's sanctifying influences and cooperating with them. The other trait was in his external conduct. And this was a marvelously keen outlook for new ways of advancing God's kingdom. Novelties of apostolic zeal, innovations of holy charity, ever selecting works and methods that were greatly needed and yet left undone. He was full of St. Paul's reluctance to do merely what others were doing. . . . Conservative in the interior life, radical and novel in the outward works of zeal, such was Fr. Hecker.[27]

There was truth in this, of course, for much of Hecker's thought on the spiritual life found confirmation in the lives of earlier Christian mystics and spiritual writers, while his advocacy of the press, public lectures, tracts and other techniques of evangelization were new for American Catholics, though widely used by Catholics abroad and non-Catholics in the United States.

But, examined more deeply, Elliott's characterization of Hecker could be reversed. Hecker's evangelizing was highly conservative. Hecker really did believe that all Americans, and ultimately all people, would eventually enter the church and bring about an integral Catholic Christian commonwealth. In seeking to promote that goal in freedom by sending Catholics forth to improve society and create an art, a science, a politics which was modern, American and Catholic, he anticipated ideas of evangelization which would not become common until after the Second Vatican Council, but the goal remained traditional and orthodox: to make the whole of human society and culture Christian and Catholic. His spirituality, on the other hand, was far more radical, however deep its roots in Christian history. His emphasis on freedom, self-determination (even self-actualization), the centrality of the human person and the guidance of the indwelling Holy Spirit all stood in sharp contrast not only to the "externals" so emphasized in the nineteenth and twentieth centuries, but to the whole thrust of modern Catholicism toward institutionalization. As historians of popular religion and devotions have made clear, the piety which came to dominate Catholicism in the nineteenth century, like the ecclesiology and pastoral practice, was designed to bring people to become "practicing Catholics," to emphasize the sacraments, particularly the Eucharist, as the central means to attain union with God and eternal salvation, and thus to build dependence on that class which alone made the sacraments available, the clergy and their episcopal and papal superiors. Hecker's understanding of the presence of God in history blurred the lines between the individual human soul, the church and society at large. The same Holy Spirit was present in and spoke through all three; while the limitations of human nature might find the voice of the spirit confusing, there was in fact no contradiction. The church existed to confirm and correct individual intuitions, to proclaim the Gospel and preserve the deposit of faith, and to make available various aids to the quest for holiness, but in the end, that quest remained personal.

For the Paulists, this meant personal perfection attained through the competent performance of duties defined by discerning the signs of God's presence in contemporary history and their own providential relationship to that history. For lay people it meant a similar struggle to keep an "eye to God" while responding to concrete responsibilities. Missions may have drawn Catholics to the sacraments, but for Hecker the practice of the faith in church was a means, not an end.

As it happened, both with Paulists and people, the means often became substitutes for the end. As he wrote in his later years: "Why is it that we seek to please God . . . by the performance of works or acts of devotion which are not required of us, while neglecting those which he has enjoined, as those duties of our condition of life?" Hecker did not notice it at the time, but his enthusiasm in the last fifteen years of his life for spiritual doctrine that would affirm the inner life of the Holy Spirit was part of a larger pattern in American Christianity to seek "the holy in the midst of the mundane" and "to flee ordinary religion in search of extraordinary religion." Faced with the emergence of new structures of economic and political life, and religion, and cultural attitudes which prescribed adaptation to them, Hecker was not alone in seeking a standpoint for human dignity, one which would allow individuals and the church to direct their lives toward human purposes and by so doing take on real personal responsibility.[28]

For Hecker it was not doctrines or sacraments, councils, popes or bishops that were central to Catholic Christian faith, but "what caused all that." If this was true, would not the whole emphasis of modern Catholicism on doctrine, discipline and sacramental practice seem, not wrong, but simply misplaced? Combined with an optimism about people and a confidence in history, such a shift would constitute a veritable revolution in Catholic consciousness. After his death the explosiveness of his ideas would be evident when they were presented by lesser men than himself. His gentleness, caution and fidelity to the church muted the message a bit, while his good works could easily be directed toward ecclesiastically acceptable objectives. But explosive his ideas were, dangerous to the stability of the church and the Catholic subculture, at times almost unintelligible, even to his friends. Deeply rooted in his own experience as they were, he could not turn away from them without betraying his deepest convictions. He was doomed to disappointment, but there can be no doubt that his vision and his dream would awaken again, when Catholics knew themselves as he had known himself, as earnest seekers in quest of a direction and a destiny, yearning for communion with God, with one another and with their world.

20

Alone at the End

Almost every aspect of Hecker's life in the last decade seemed to end in disappointment. His energetic efforts in the Catholic press left only the *Catholic World* and, in its pages, a stronger denunciation of non-Catholics and narrower definition of Catholic goals. His desire to make America Catholic ended a bit closer to the sectarianism of those he had so long opposed. His evangelical vision of a Catholic America became at times an almost pathetic plea for Catholics to be reasonable and non-Catholics to be fair; the prospects that either side would listen seemed less promising than ever. The dream of a mission to Europe and the church universal never materialized and only one or two people even appreciated why such an effort should be made. His spiritual life was vital, but lonely, shared with no one, enclosed within himself. Yet Hecker remained alert. His writing was sharp and clear; his arguments still flashed with trust in God and confidence in the long-range prospects of the human enterprise.

His deepest disappointment might have been with the Paulists, for none of the factors that had led him to doubt that he could take up his "old work" with them eased; in fact, most of the fathers were more and more invested in projects within the church and most sought more, not less, structure in community life. Yet Hecker remained the leader of the Paulists and took an active role in the community, neither surrendering his own convictions nor seeking to impose them on his brothers. As in the past, he understood that others might have different "lights" and be led in other directions than he was; he could and did respect their independence. He could support their work, even if he did not share their convictions.

In addition to taking up the *Catholic World* and presiding at chapter meetings on his return from Europe in 1875, Hecker gave his attention to the complications that had arisen in building a church for St. Paul's. Initially Hecker had anticipated a massive basilica and had plans drawn up by European architects. While he was away, Deshon and Young squabbled over the design until the Paulist chapter placed Young in charge and chose New York architect Jeremiah O'Rourke to oversee the work. All this, however, was scuttled by the depression which began in 1873. The community wanted to reduce the building projects, but Hecker counselled delay. When he returned, he encouraged the larger plans, now taking the Cathedral of Santa Croce in Florence, with its simplicity of outline and broad spaces, as the model for the church in New York. Architect O'Rourke told Young in February 1876 that Hecker had requested further sketches of the building and decided to draw up a new contract, providing a change in the arrangements to allow insertion of mosaics on the front panels of the church. On June 4, Bishop Corrigan of Newark laid the cornerstone; soon after, O'Rourke complained that specifications were not being met because of Deshon's interference. Hecker responded by placing construction in the hands of a new firm. Construction of the residence was soon finished, but the church construction dragged on into the eighties.[1]

In August 1876 Hecker brought his personal hopes before Hewit. Hewit agreed not to oppose the idea of Paulists in Europe, but he was clearly not enthusiastic. This encounter exhausted Hecker's strength. He was prepared to do all he could for the community but only "on condition that I am left alone in conditions that it is possible for me to live in." Yet, as superior, he could not avoid community problems. Walter Elliott, for example, had found Hecker's absence particularly trying. More than any of the Paulist recruits, Elliott had joined the community under Hecker's inspiration. For a year after Hecker's return he refrained from approaching him with his problems, but on August 21, 1876, he finally wrote from Lake George, giving a full account of his experience of the community. Elliott charged that the community was losing its simplicity of life. He suggested that Hecker begin "a sort of formal visitation to the house at regular intervals."[2]

There is no record of Hecker's response, but he undoubtedly resisted Elliott's plan to have community rules make up for lack of individual self-discipline. For Hecker, the problems of community life reflected deeper issues. His notes in Europe clearly indicated the gap which had developed between his ideas of evangelization and the parochial and missionary preoccupation of the other fathers. Sometime in the mid-seventies, after returning from his brother's house to the Paulist residence, Hecker wrote a detailed memorandum setting forth what he regarded as the problems of the Paulist community. From the beginning, there had been "two tendencies" among the members, he thought. One faction emphasized the "ordinary works of the priesthood in parochial and mission labors, but with the aim of doing these works more perfectly." Parochial and mission work, and other apostolates aimed exclusively at serving Catholics, differed from the direction of Hecker's own disposition and placed a constant strain on him and on other members of the community. His tendency was to regard such works as secondary, providing "a base for the employment of the measures which tend primarily to the conversion of the people of the country." "Instead of multiplying societies, devotions" and parish programs, the community should prepare sermons, lectures and conferences for delivery in New York and around the country. Such measures were needed not only for the conversion of non-Catholics but "for the strengthening and confirmation of the truths of faith in the minds of our young generations of Catholics whose intellects have been quickened by education and by other causes in the communities in which they live." He still believed that this new generation should be aroused to missionary vocation, bringing Catholic truths into the heart of secular life, winning a respect for the church and, eventually, conversion.[3]

Hecker's reservations regarding the community were certainly not without foundation. A chapter was scheduled for 1878 to deal once again with the Rule and constitution. Hewit told Hecker that some members of the community were "tempted to become depressed and anxious on account of the trials which [they had] undergone, the unsettled and undetermined state of the congregation, and the lack of entire harmony even among those who [had] the government in their hands." They should try to give a "more organic unity and better order to the congregation." On the eve of the chapter meeting Hewit again wrote Hecker. "The great difficulty at present consists in a distrust of our having any divine vocation or sufficient principle of unity and growth." Some members wanted the Rule to be more clearly that of a religious community; they were even tempted to move away from the Paulists to an approved congregation which had vows. The chapter's success depended "on knocking in the head any notion that we are trying an experiment of dubious utility which is threatened with failure." The chapter was a success, but the tension between the day to day work of parish and missions and the ideal of working among non-Catholics was unresolved.[4]

In a conference for the fathers at South Orange in October 1878 Hecker attempted to revitalize his ideal for the Paulists. As he saw it, Catholic immigrants had a faith which rested on tradition and "all that they require for their salvation is the faithful administration of the ordinary means of the church." Their children, however, had received some education and required "a more explicit knowledge of their religion." As for the non-Catholics, "the inroads which sectarianism, infidelity, and atheism are making . . . [render] the present moment opportune to present to them the truths of Catholicity." For these reasons, Hecker stated bluntly, "conferences on religion should be chiefly addressed to these last two classes." Work among first-generation immigrant Catholics could be left to the "ordinary work" of the church; the Paulists should concentrate on the new Catholic middle class and on non-Catholics.[5]

In these terms, Elliott, Hewit and some of the other Paulists affirmed the Paulist vocation, for it gave the community a distinctive identity, but they saw the work of conversion in a far more limited way than Hecker. His larger vision of a Catholic commonwealth, the promised land, was too utopian to engage their attention and they were far less restless with the church's inclination toward self-serving righteousness. They were not alone, for beyond the community as well few seemed to grasp the vision of Hecker's *Exposition*. In the spring of 1879 Cardinal Manning wrote Archbishop McCloskey asking him to select someone to prepare an article on the church in the United States for the English magazine *Nineteenth Century*. Apparently McCloskey asked Hecker, but when Hecker submitted the article to the magazine, it was returned. Hecker then sent the article to the biblical scholar Father Ramiere in Paris. Ramiere, who had written for the *Catholic World*, had earlier given cautious approval to Hecker's ideas, but now he challenged some of Hecker's most basic assumptions. Ramiere told Hecker that, in his desire to integrate Catholic principles and the American Constitution, he was confused. The American principle that governments derive their just power from the consent of the governed could not be called "a Catholic doctrine," nor could it be regarded as a "universal principle." Catholic theologians taught that authority came from God; placing that authority in the hands of a given individual might require consent, but once given, that consent did not have to be renewed. Ramiere also disagreed with Hecker's treatment of the relationship between reason and freedom. According to Catholic faith, original sin had "greatly dimmed," though not extinguished, reason and weakened, though not destroyed, freedom of the will. This being the case, it was doubtful that political institutions which supposed that all people were capable of judging rightly the interests of the state and of using political power dispassionately were in accord with the Catholic teaching. He could not understand how Hecker could continue to argue that there was agreement between the tendencies of the American republic and the Catholic church. It was an old problem, of course, the same one which had divided Hecker and his oldest friend, Brownson. Still, coming at a time when Hecker was struggling to find a place for his vision and a direction for his community, it must have been another signal that the promise of the new Pentecost was not to be fulfilled, at least not yet.[6]

Hecker never took criticism well, and this letter undoubtedly intensified his loneliness and made his physical and spiritual suffering even harder to bear. Years later Hewit told Elliott that he had called on Hecker shortly after his return to urge him to shake off his despondency and return to the community. Hecker reportedly told him, "I wish to suffer! I am willing." So transformed was his appearance when he said these words that Hewit felt they arose from a profound spiritual struggle. As a result, Hewit resigned himself to Hecker's absence from the Paulist house. Only in the fall of 1879 did Hecker return finally to live with the Paulists at 59th Street. Under Hewit's direction the house had been put in order for his return. There were ten priests and nine students living in the New York house, and Hecker had a room no different from that of any of the other fathers. Despite his return, he remained relatively inactive in daily community affairs. He rarely said a public Mass or participated in the liturgical life of the parish, although he was often seen standing at the rear of the church or behind a column during one of the high Masses on Sunday or a Holy Day.

Although he always felt better at Lake George, his health remained a source of constant difficulty. As he wrote to Mrs. Ward in the summer of 1881, "I can beat anybody on the score of weakness." He added good-naturedly that God's will "does not leave much room for egoism." Unfortunately such light-heartedness was rare. More often the combination of poor health and inactivity made him depressed; he wrote to a nun in June 1883 that "as for me, ten years ago I died. My present life is only a special prolongation." He did engage in a long correspondence with Bishop McQuaid about sanitariums, hoping that their treatments might improve his health. On McQuaid's recommendation he stayed at one in Dansville, New York, in May 1884. The rest did him good but there was no evidence it improved his health.[7]

While taking a greater interest in the *Catholic World*, and writing occasionally himself, Hecker showed little concern for the Catholic Publication Society. Sustained for years by the generosity of George Hecker, the society had been almost totally directed by Lawrence Kehoe since Isaac Hecker's illness and departure for Europe in 1873. In 1882 George, who had long backed the CPS, offered it for sale to Kehoe. In October 1883 Kehoe completed negotiations, and the Catholic Publication Society passed from the Heckers' control.[8]

In September 1884 another General Chapter meeting was held to elect a superior and consultors.[9] Hecker opened by expressing satisfaction with the community's spiritual condition and with the parish. He reported on the disposition of the Catholic Publication Society, noting a buy-back provision still in effect if any father had the time and resources for the work. He also noted the *Catholic World*'s new publishing arrangements, which would require increased funding. The balloting for superior general then took place. The results showed Hewit with eight votes to Hecker's five. Elliott, whose notes are the sole remaining source on these events, expressed his "utter and unspeakable surprise," while Hewit and Deshon, who had counted the ballots, "were pale and evidently intensely wrought up with excitement." Hecker, for his part, "seemed absolutely undisturbed . . . the most undisturbed man in the room," as he called for another ballot, a two-thirds majority being required for election. The second ballot produced six for Hewit, five for Hecker and one each for Deshon and Wyman.

When the community gathered the next day, Hecker was too ill to preside. Hewit, who had said he would refuse the office, now told the group that Hecker had always been the father and founder of the community, by a special grace from God. Hewit had accepted the office when forced by Hecker's ill-health, but had always returned it as soon as possible. If the fathers now rejected Hecker, all would be lost, for it would call forth suspicion from the hierarchy and the prominent men who identified the community so closely with Father Hecker. Most important, he noted that he had read of many founders who were not appreciated in their own time, often not even by men who lived in the same house with them. Their virtues were not seen and they were often surrounded by men not worthy of them. When reading of such men, Hewit concluded, people say to themselves they would have acted differently, but now the Paulists were showing the same lack of appreciation of Hecker. Hewit's speech moved Elliott deeply but changed few votes; the deadlock persisted.

The opposition group then submitted a formal statement of their concerns, emphasizing Hecker's inability to preside. They denied any departure from Hecker's teaching and rather insisted on their complete devotion to it; they questioned only his ability to conduct community business. Privately, negotiations took place, with the dissidents expressing dissatisfaction with the rectorship of Father Deshon and their desire for change among the consultors. Hecker indicated he could allow no conditions for his election but was willing to accept any consultors the community chose. After asking Hecker whether he truly would allow Hewit and Deshon to be reduced to equal status with the others, Elliott noted his response: "Yes, he says, they have followed me because they believed me the man God had chosen, but they have not actually shared my convictions." After two days of intense discussions, Hecker was elected. He came downstairs from his sickbed, thanked the fathers, and then collapsed, reviving later for recreation with the community. Fathers Searle and Brady replaced Hewit and

Deshon as consultors and, a short time later, Deshon went on the missions under Elliott's superiorship and Searle replaced him as rector at 59th Street. Elliott concluded his notes with these words: "Father Hecker felt distressed over Father Deshon's disgrace, and over the state of things brought about." Elliott found Hecker's calm during the crisis admirable, but Hecker was clearly hurt. On a summer evening almost two years later Elliott found Hecker more talkative than usual, complaining of the lack of kindred spirits. Since the General Chapter, he admitted, he felt even more that he had been deserted by his companions. Elliott's argument that the dissidents were a small minority gave him no comfort.

Shortly after the chapter meeting Hecker was invited to attend the third plenary council of Baltimore. He was determined to make the trip although the condition of his health worried Father Hewit, who wrote secretly to ask Archbishop James Gibbons to make arrangements for Hecker to stay with a priest's family, where he could have the attention he required. Hecker could not be trusted to take "proper measures for his own comfort" and Hewit feared the trip was "running a risk that may be very serious." Gibbons turned the matter over to one of his priests, who placed a carriage at Hecker's disposal, assuring Hewit that "we will do all we can to prolong his valuable life." Hecker enjoyed the honor he received at the council, but returned early to 59th Street.[10]

One of the friendships Hecker renewed during the eighties was with John Keane, at the time the bishop of Richmond and later first president of the Catholic University of America. Keane, who was Irish-born but raised in Richmond, was ordained for the Archdiocese of Baltimore in 1866. While stationed at St. Patrick's Church in Washington, he met Hecker several times and was impressed by his spiritual ideas. Hecker gave him a copy of Lallament's *Spiritual Doctrine,* which Keane very much appreciated. In 1872 Keane asked Archbishop Bayley for permission to join the Paulists. Hecker wrote a strong letter on his behalf, predicting he would make a "perfect religious" and indicating he needed Keane to take over editorial direction of the *Catholic World.* Bayley, faced with a great need for priests, refused to release Keane, who was already slated for larger responsibilities. After Hecker's return from Europe the two men re-established their friendship. At Hecker's request Keane wrote to England's Cardinal Manning to explore establishing a Paulist house in London. Nothing came of this correspondence, adding another disappointment, but Keane remained a warm friend who gave a larger audience for some of Hecker's ideas on providence, the role of the Holy Spirit, and the prospects for the American church.[11]

Even after he had given up on the possibility of new projects and resigned himself to the development of the Paulist community in ways which he did not approve, Hecker did not hesitate to set forth clearly and continually the Paulist ideal as he had formulated it. He knew that few really understood him. Baker had and perhaps Tillotson too; later Father Rosecrans, who had doubted Hecker's orthodoxy and accused him of minimizing Catholic doctrine, was won over while working with Hecker on the *Catholic World.* Hecker shared his disappointment with Elliott, who smilingly suggested that he would have to do "for a disciple for want of a better." Hecker responded by pounding Elliott with his stick. "He often did that," Elliott added, after recording the incident good-naturedly in his notes.

In this conversation with Elliott, Hecker did express pride in the Paulists. Elliott thought that what the community needed was a more rigorous discipline or an invitation "to heroic sacrifice of some sort." Hecker responded that a "fine thoughtful fellow" should be attracted by the "freshness" of their "method." When Elliott responded that they seemed more attracted to the older orders, whose methods, while less adapted to America, were more strict, Hecker became upset and ended the conversation. Hecker certainly favored ascetic practices and submission to community discipline, as was evident in a list of rules he proposed for missionaries, which ranged from modest eating and carrying their own bags to prompt obedience to superiors. But he always held fast to the idea that these practices should be voluntary and subordinated to the great end of religious life, which was spiritual perfection. If poverty, obedience, "liberty of spirit" or any other virtue would lead to this end, each should be free to pursue it. "The one who called you has to do the big work," Hecker told Elliott. If a person was "going to depend on any routine, set form of direction or devotion or study as a substitute for this inward guidance, they had better go where these things are willingly supplied." He delighted in recalling a remark of his friend Sherwood Healy, that the Paulists lived and worked together in harmony, yet each retained "his own individuality of view and of character generally." This was, Hecker said, "just what ought to be."

So there were and remained few rules, few projects and few Paulists, but Hecker felt that small numbers and limited foundations were good. They should be a "corps d'élite" who in the future would return their parishes to the secular clergy. Religious communities should place at their center the pursuit of personal spiritual perfection which, for Hecker, always meant the immediate guidance of the indwelling Holy Spirit. Each member of the community should be free to pursue those particular virtues which led him in that direction: "Great fidelity in action with a great and large freedom of action should be the spirit of the community."[12]

No Paulist tried harder than Elliott to understand and follow Hecker's ideal. In 1886 Elliott wrote an article in the *Catholic World* that contrasted many of Hecker's ideas to the growing parochialism and narrowing imagination of American Catholic culture. Entitled "The True Man of the Times," the article described the typical American whose dominant trait was, like Hecker's earnest seeker, "attachment to the truth." Catholics were in danger of "catching the contagion" of embracing limited, particular truths, Elliott argued, while the times required an emphasis on the "universality of the truth which they hold." The United States, where God was revealing the unity of the human family, could not be satisfied with a religion which was "only personal," like so much Protestantism or one which bore "the marks of a particular race, like ethnocentric Catholicism." The religion needed by the age and nation would have to meet the needs of all and be expounded by persons of "universal sympathies." If in their public practice Catholics "lay too much stress on any but fundamental and universal principles," they would too often confirm the prejudices of others. "Your idiosyncrasy may be just German Catholicity or sound Irish Catholicity," Elliott wrote, "but your neighbor is entitled to know whether it is Catholicity pure and simple."[13]

Elliott's reading of Hecker's evangelical vision clearly reflected problems less apparent in Hecker's own version. From the point of view of an immigrant church still receiving vast numbers of newcomers from Europe, the disdain for racial and national characteristics could only seem insensitive. Pastors alert to the role of traditional faith in immigrant life could easily hear Elliott's plea for "Catholicity pure and simple" as a demand for conformity to Irish-American, if not native American, particularities. Further, the "universal" truth Elliott would proclaim might, like Hecker's, slip easily into a soft liberal denominationalism, especially if combined with Hecker's optimism about history, human nature and the church. Paradoxically, in the absence, or even with the modification, of Hecker's optimism, they could become the "pure and simple" orthodoxies of triumphalist, ultramontane Catholicism, holding fast to a trans-historical and trans-cultural set of dogmas severed from concrete social and cultural circumstances. Hecker's liberalism, in less skillful hands, could thus easily become a crude Americanism or a triumphalist Catholicism or, as it eventually turned out, both. Elliott, as Hecker seemed to understand, had all the words, and all the goodwill his mentor could hope for, but somehow something crucial was lost.

As for Hecker himself, he had no choice but to wait, as God had not shown how he was to respond. In conversion, in the seminary, in the Redemptorists, during the Civil War, at each stage of his life he had experienced new "light" from the Spirit, had struggled and finally found a way to respond, but not so with those lights which had come to him in Europe. He had taken up many of his former labors, directing the building of a massive church, overhauling a leading magazine, writing regularly on religious and political topics, offering guidance to his religious community, but he felt even more distant from his long-hoped-for dream of evangelical triumph.

Elliott by this time was Hecker's constant companion, sleeping in the next room, walking with him and listening to his recollections of earlier years. The younger man was convinced that Hecker's physical infirmity reflected inner spiritual turmoil arising from the depth and intensity of his relationship with God. God had promised him that he would suffer, Hecker said repeatedly, and the promise had indeed been fulfilled. He ate little, joined the community only briefly for recreation, and found it increasingly difficult to say Mass. On occasion he would burst into tears, as when talking with Keane about the Paulist future. Still, he held firmly to the old ideas. When Elliott complained that the aristocratic Madames of the Sacred Heart were spreading a social system which was breaking apart everywhere else, Hecker agreed, stating that he had only visited their convents twice, "and then because he couldn't help it." On another occasion, he was visited by Bishop McQuaid, who complained that some Paulists were supporting radicals on the Irish question. Hecker responded that while he was not strong enough to follow the actions of all the fathers, he himself was "heart and soul" with the Irish and took his ideas from the Irish hierarchy and "those laymen whom the Providence of God has put at the head of the Irish people."[14]

There is no doubt that many around Hecker recognized that pain he suffered, knew that his hopes had been frustrated and worried that he felt alone and misunderstood. Clearly, too, the Paulists honored, even revered him, not only as the founder of their community but as a man of profound holiness, far closer to God than most. For all his inner agonies of spirit, he had always impressed others as calm, reasonable and compassionate. Yet there were dangers in the intense spirituality Hecker practiced, dangers occasionally noted in writing by Hewit, perhaps more often in private conversation. A certain self-centeredness, especially at times of conflict, marked his life from the first spiritual crisis until the last. There was that touch of self-pity Julia Beers had noted when she met him in Rome and the insensitivity to the problems of ordinary people evident to Elizabeth Cullen. Hecker told Elliott in June 1885 that he had always longed for someone to whom he could open his heart, but "God never permitted me to find that longing realized." As this remark indicates, his dealings with Elliott in the 1880s reflected an occasional insensitivity, even selfishness, that stands in marked contrast to the warmth and generous toleration that usually seemed to mark his relationships even with men who clearly pursued a path far removed from his own. Elliott recalled some of these incidents with touching innocence in the notes he kept of his conversations with Hecker during those final months. One in particular stands out. On an evening shortly before Hecker's death, Elliott sat by his bedside. He recalled that "what had been on my mind for a long time came out." He told his friend, "Father Hecker, I am sorry that I did not profit better by your instruction." "So am I," he answered at once, and "I fear that he was altogether in earnest."

Perhaps Hecker's feelings about Elliott arose from his disappointment that this hearty, generous and altogether American priest did not, in Hecker's opinion, grasp the central truth of his message. In any event, his treatment of Elliott indicated something of the distortions which his long loneliness had caused. One might go further and argue that, to a degree at least, Hecker's failures were not entirely the fault of others or of the "times." In his dealing with the other fathers from Europe in the fateful winter of 1857–58, he had not always been candid, sometimes sharing ideas with George that he would not share with the others, even instructing George to "guide their steps." To launch the new community he sought common ground, accepted a statement of purpose which did not include work among non-Catholics, and took on a parish, all of which stood at some distance from his own hopes but also raised the possibility that he was not altogether open with his fellow Paulists. In the 1870s, when he became disillusioned with his Paulist brothers, there is no evidence he confronted them directly. Again and again he would subtly shape his arguments to his audience, telling friends that a project was directed at his ultimate aim of evangelization, but then telling bishops or Roman officials that it was intended primarily to serve the church. Such an approach was understandable; indeed, in his lectures it was part of an intelligent strategy of winning attention for Catholic claims. But it could and sometimes did cross the boundary to mild deception, and others might be forgiven for thinking that they were responding positively to Hecker when he felt they had not heard, or had ignored, what he was trying to say.

Generations of later Paulists would see their mission as involving a balance of personal sanctification, serving the needs of the church, and working for converts, and believe they were fulfilling the Paulist vocation. Few understood the full depth of Hecker's vision, that America, then the world, should indeed become Catholic and that all, absolutely all, of human life should be brought under the direction of God's Holy Spirit. For most of them the promised land of God's Kingdom was simply an expanded version of the contemporary church or a future possibility unconnected to present historical realities, both of which his language sometimes confirmed. That the Kingdom of God, that promised destiny of the human community, was the public side of the personal quest for union with God and, like it, a real, immediate historic possibility, remained outside the imagination of most Catholics of his and later generations. The reasons for that were for the most part beyond Hecker's control, but he was not without some responsibility.

The concrete presence of the promised land, he had decided, was somehow contained in the Catholic Church. To that church he committed himself, fully and completely. As a result, his critical spirit could not extend to the church, his beloved community, the expression and guarantee of that other reality, the Holy Spirit within. Unable, sometimes simply unwilling, to confront that church, he could not break the chains that bound so many Catholics of his generation. Neither could he persuade himself, as Brownson had, that submission need become total. He could not publicly express a docility and obedience which violated conscience. Thus the deepest conflicts of his life remained hidden, in his letters and notes, and even there they were obscured by a language which spiritualized and mystified church affairs. Some sense of that, some sense that his failures were at least in part the result of his personal needs, undoubtedly accounted for his unwillingness to confront and challenge others. Like all virtues in this limited life, his modesty, humility and piety had their price.

Yet Hecker remained close to God and faithful to the spirit within. During the Civil War, on the twentieth anniversary of his own baptism, Hecker had written:

> To me, my life has been one continued growth; and hence I have never had any desire to return to any part or period of it. This applies as well to my life before I was received into the Church as after. My best life was always in the present.

Undoubtedly it was harder to make that affirmation now. He hated being idle, telling Elliott that "next to the evil self-company of the unforgiven sinner, there is no loneliness so sad as that of the invalid." Yet almost until the end Hecker was able to write, to read and to pray. He showed no regret over past decisions and never surrendered his basic convictions. Since coming home he had been open to any sign that his dreams might be realized, but he had practiced the patience and resignation he had preached to others. In the past he may have too quickly identified his own projects with the will of God. Now he had no new projects. He was humbled a bit, more dependent on God, more willing to leave the future in God's hands.

Wednesday, December 19, 1888, was Hecker's sixty-ninth birthday. He received the congratulations of the community, but the next day he became ill. On Friday he was a bit better, but that night he declined. Elliott anointed him with oil and gave him the last sacraments. At his funeral Jesuit Thomas Campbell described the scene. The community gathered in his room and knelt for the blessing of their founder. Hewit leaned over and asked, "Shall I bless them for you, Father?" Campbell went on:

> He aroused himself from the depth of pain and exhaustion, and his ashen lips which death was sealing pronounced the singular words: "No, I will give it in the shadow of death." His feeble hands were raised, and like a soldier dying on the field of battle, he reconsecrated his followers in the name of the Father, Son and Holy Ghost for the struggle in which they had chosen him as leader.

After blessing the community, Hecker slept soundly. Waking briefly on Saturday morning, he lapsed into unconsciousness, and at one o'clock that afternoon, he died. Friends and the public were notified; his body lay in state in St. Paul's; an impressive funeral service was held and his remains were interred in the church. Letters of condolence arrived, commenting on his holiness, his enthusiasm, his leadership. The public press noted his death as it would that of any prominent American known for good works and good citizenship. Catholic papers thought the significance of his life lay in his conviction that only Catholicism consistently and fully taught the dignity of the human person, so that the church, in the words of the *Freeman's Journal*, was "necessary to complete the harmony and beauty of the American people" whom he loved. John Henry Newman wrote that he had always thought there was "a sort of unity in our lives," that they had "begun a work of the same kind."[15] The Paulists mourned, Catholics were saddened, the public wondered why so little had been heard of him in recent years, and life went on. Few would have believed, if they were told, that the greatest controversies about Isaac Hecker still lay ahead.

21

"Heckerism"

During his lifetime Isaac Hecker expressed many views which sharply diverged from the main directions of nineteenth-century Catholicism. His apologetics, based upon an optimistic understanding of human nature, stood in sharp contrast to the arguments from authority with which most Catholics defended their faith. His spirituality emphasized the interior life of the spirit and aimed to liberate Christians from the need for minute direction and undue dependence upon what he called externals, which seemed to include the authority of the church. Nothing could be further removed from the contemporary church's extreme emphasis on sacramental practice and papal power. In the *Exposition* he offered an explanation of modern history that seemed to leave the Latin races behind and make the Jesuits anachronistic. Finally, and more practically, his ideas about the providential mission of America and the missionary responsibilities of the American church raised questions about his relationship to the actual church as it was developing in the United States.

Surprisingly, however, his views sparked little controversy during his lifetime. Brownson questioned his apologetics in the 1850s and raised doubts about the soundness of his democratic ideas after the Civil War. The *Exposition* drew some critical comments as well, but they were rather isolated and again mostly private. Generally Hecker was admired, respected and liked, and he escaped harsh criticism, much less censure. Even those who might have been most suspicious, like John Hughes and Pope Pius IX, seem to have been taken with the man, impressed by his sincerity and convinced of his devotion to the church. While he was disappointed again and again at the failure of others to capture his enthusiasm or take up the banner he raised, he had no reason to feel that he had been persecuted by church authorities or rejected by his fellow Catholics. Yet in the years that followed his death, Isaac Hecker became the most controversial figure in American Catholic history. His ideas provided a central point of contention between parties struggling to control the direction of the universal church; some of these ideas were condemned by the Holy See in an encyclical letter in 1899. As a result the legacy of Isaac Hecker was filtered through the prism of the most bitter disputes, making it hard for later Catholics to understand, much less appropriate, the vision and ideals which shaped his life.

In January 1889 Father Hewit wrote an appreciation of the departed founder of the Paulists in the *Catholic World.* The short article, printed inside black bordered pages, sketched Hecker's life, emphasized his commitment to the conversion of that "special class" who had no positive faith but sought a rational foundation for belief, and pointed to the "Apostolate of the Press," especially the *Catholic World*, as his most important work.[1]

Three months later a longer assessment appeared, written by Hecker's close friend John J. Keane, now the rector of the newly established Catholic University of America. He saw Hecker as an optimist and noted Hecker's love for America and its people and his yearning for an outpouring of the Holy Spirit, first in the American church, then flowing "back upon the old world" to spark enthusiasm in "generous hearts" for "the great things that might be done for helping on the Kingdom of the Lord." Keane's tribute must have seemed unexceptional at the time, but later reading would suggest that Keane's article signalled the problems that would soon surround Hecker's memory, most notably the special role of the Holy Spirit and of the United States.

At the time of Hecker's death the American church was deeply divided. In 1889, as Keane was writing his tribute, division had reached into the hierarchy, and Keane could not help enlisting Hecker in the fight. Despite the absence of any substantial public criticism of Hecker, or even any criticism at all since Brownson's death, Keane wrote:

> Some there were doubtless who thought him a visionary, a dreamer, a dangerous theorizer. There are always whelps to bark at a great man's heels. There are always petty minds to look with pity, or with suspicion, upon what transcends the measure of their small conservatism. There are always little embodiments of precautionary prudence and safe suspiciousness ever eager to whisper or to squeak their wee note of alarm and to cry "down brakes." And it is well, perhaps, that there are such. Their vocation is a pitiable one, but it has its use.[2]

Keane's language sounded partisan, and indeed it was. The American bishops had met in relative harmony at the third plenary council of Baltimore in 1884, but in the aftermath of the council serious conflicts arose. Archbishop Corrigan of New York resented the tendency of Cardinal Gibbons of Baltimore to assume leadership in the American church. When Corrigan clashed with Father McGlynn in 1886, he suspected that McGlynn and his local supporters were receiving encouragement from some bishops, including Archbishop John Ireland of St. Paul. That same year Gibbons, with help from Ireland and Keane, prevented publication of a Vatican condemnation of the Knights of Labor, and he subsequently worked hard to prevent public condemnation of McGlynn's hero, Henry George. The council had approved creation of a national university. Corrigan wanted it located in New York, but the decision was made to locate it in Washington, within Gibbons's jurisdiction. Moreover, Keane was made rector, and he was regarded as a friend of Gibbons.

In 1886 Ireland and Keane met in Rome with Dennis O'Connell, rector of the North American College and a close friend of Gibbons. The three men discovered that they shared a common commitment to reforming the American church in order to overcome its image as a foreign institution in American society. They favored rapid Americanization of the immigrants, more progressive education of the clergy, and positive encouragement of religious liberty and church-state separation. From that point on, they acted as a party in the American church, drawing upon their Roman connections and what they took to be the liberal stance of Pope Leo XIII to forward greater identification with American society, more rapid assimilation of the immigrants and active efforts to overcome the parochialism of the past. Corrigan was joined in opposing their projects by German-American church leaders, who resented Ireland's opposition to foreign-language teaching in the schools of the Western states, and by a number of bishops irritated by what they took to be liberal efforts to interfere within their diocese.

Most important, the liberals shared a body of ideas similar to those of Father Hecker. They believed in the emergence of a new era in world history dominated by personal liberty, political democracy and economic progress, and they believed that the church would have to adapt its message and ministry to ensure its vigorous presence in the modern world. They believed in the providential mission of the United States, the world's leading exemplar of progress and democracy. The American church's evident success was testimony to the possibilities that would open before the universal church when it made its own the modern values of progress and freedom. Corrigan and his supporters, in contrast, feared the many dangers present in modern societies. They wanted to build and strengthen a Catholic subculture, centered on the bishops, which would limit as much as possible the interaction of Catholics and non-Catholics and insure the survival of the church by insisting on the most clear articulation of distinctive Catholic doctrines.[3]

In 1892 these battles intensified, centered now on the reemergence of the school question. Under Roman pressure the American bishops had mandated the establishment of a school in every parish in 1884, but they had left the bishops free to modify that rule if local conditions required. Many priests and bishops were still not convinced that parochial-school education was desirable; far more thought it simply impractical. The underlying differences burst into the open in 1891 when Ireland gave a speech praising the public schools and shortly thereafter entered into an experiment by which a Catholic school was rented to public-school authorities and religious instruction was offered after school hours. This public championing of cooperation with the public schools was strongly opposed by Corrigan, whose diocese had long been committed to Catholic schools; by Bernard McQuaid, one of Hecker's old friends; and by the German-Americans, who had long championed separate school education. In 1893 the Holy See sent the first Apostolic Delegate to the United States to resolve these and other disputes. Ireland and his friends, convinced that they had the support of Leo XIII, welcomed this move, befriended the delegate, Francesco Satolli and, as they had with the university, used their Roman influence to forward their views, further dividing the American bishops. The appointment meant the end of a century of relative independence for the American bishops, whose unity had allowed them to control episcopal appointments and shape national policy to national needs. At first Satolli took the liberal side, residing at Keane's university, approving with conditions Ireland's school experiment and readmitting the excommunicated McGlynn to the church.

All of this lay ahead when Keane wrote his tribute to Hecker, but it would not be long before Keane's quite-innocent identification of Hecker with the liberal cause would become a matter of international significance. In 1890 Father Hewit asked Hecker's most ardent disciple, Walter Elliott, to prepare a biography of Hecker to be printed in the *Catholic World.* At first Elliott demurred, suggesting that one of Hecker's lifelong co-workers, Hewit or Deshon, would be a more appropriate biographer. But Hewit insisted and Elliott took up what was clearly a labor of love. With the help of a research assistant, he gathered materials and began publishing the biography in serial form in the Paulist magazine. The articles were well-received and were brought together in book form and published by Columbus Press, founded in 1891 by Elliott and his Paulist colleague Alexander P. Doyle. Hewit, after reading the proofs, told Elliott he "could not wish for anything better, and it will certainly not give any offense to anybody, but the contrary." Archbishop Corrigan did not hesitate to grant the work an imprimatur while Archbishop Ireland wrote an eloquent introduction, arguing that Hecker was indeed the "typical American priest," combining in his person great holiness, profound loyalty to the church, deep love for his country, and an inquiring openness to the world around him.[4]

Reviews of the book were glowing. Hecker's combination of patriotism, Catholic loyalty and enthusiasm about the future fit the mold of the Catholic reading public, and reviewers noticed no relationship between Hecker and the controversies brewing in the American church. The only worry for Elliott came from an unexpected source, James A. Healey, the Bishop of Portland.

Son of an Irish-American Georgia planter and his mulatto wife, and brother of Sherwood Healey, a prominent Boston priest Hecker had almost persuaded to enter the Paulists, the bishop had been a priest in Boston and a close friend of Bishop Fitzpatrick, the only Catholic Hecker ever publicly criticized by name. Elliott made no mention of Hecker's feelings about Fitzpatrick, but Healy was dissatisfied with his treatment of the bishop's attitude at the time of Hecker's conversion. Fitzpatrick never doubted Hecker's sanctity and always appreciated his "ardent labors" for the church, Healy wrote. But he did "distrust his spirit" and that distrust "was shared in after years by very many friends, lay and clerical, of Father Hecker." Healey feared that Elliott's book would "justify the grounds of that distrust." Healey believed that Hecker's "spirit of liberty, liberty of spirit if you please, led him more than once into words and ways that made his devoted friends tremble." After receiving a response from Elliott he wrote again, characteristically noting that while he and Hecker had "diverged in views," they had never "disagreed in heart." Nevertheless, he told Elliott, he still worried that Hecker's "views will not escape without blame if you blazon them too generously."[5]

These were private opinions, and Elliott had reason to be pleased that no further problems arose with the American edition. In fact, Elliott was a friend of Keane, an ardent admirer of Ireland and a strong champion of their ideas. When Ireland was preparing his introductory essay, Elliott intervened to soften his language, particularly on the subject of religious orders. Ireland said that Hecker had "arraigned" the older religious orders "for servility, for mustiness of weapons, and for Chinese methods." He argued further that Hecker thought new orders were needed and that they should be subject to the direct authority of the bishops. Aside from the last point, Elliott agreed that those had been Hecker's views, "but it was never his method to say such things in public"; he had always kept his criticism of other religious orders "private and good natured." Ireland did modify these passages, but his essay painted Hecker in very liberal colors.

The use of Hecker did not end there. In September 1890 Dennis O'Connell reported from Rome that the pope was reading *Questions of the Soul* and was "delighted with it." Hecker's relationship to the liberal cause did not pass unnoticed by the other side. As early as July 1889 O'Connell noted "insinuations from New York against Father Hecker." Ella Edes, a Roman-based friend of Corrigan, reported to Father Hudson of Notre Dame at about the same time Roman gossip about the "strange" views of the Paulist founder; she thought Hecker's *The Church and the Age* "would not pass muster if submitted to the Index."[6]

In later years Elliott would appear as the innocent victim of internal feuds among Catholics, but he had, in fact, all but enlisted in the liberal cause, and Hecker's biography became more and more a liberal project. In March 1892 he congratulated Ireland on the success of his recent trip to Rome; he rejoiced in the defeat of Ireland's enemies, who were "enemies of a loving church," "adepts at intrigue" and "whisperers by profession." He hoped that the school experiment in Minnesota would be carried out across the nation; it would "save the coming generation" and provide "Catholic schools for all our children." The *Catholic World* had two articles ready for publication defending Ireland on the school question, Elliott reported. However, when two of the fathers called on Archbishop Corrigan on another matter, he warned them that they should take "the orthodox side" on schools, which he identified with an article that had recently appeared in Rome blasting Ireland's position. Hewit immediately withdrew the articles and told Keane he could not accept another he was preparing. Elliott reported to Ireland Hewit's fear that "the Archbishop can ruin us"; in response, Elliott urged the older man to take a more businesslike approach in dealing with Corrigan and perhaps consider removing the magazine's editorial offices to Washington.[7]

Meanwhile plans were being made to publish the biography in France. Even before the American edition appeared, Elliott had written Vicomte Alfred de Meaux, son-in-law of Charles de Montalembert, about that possibility; the vicomte passed the inquiry on to the Count de Chabrol, another acquaintance of Hecker. Both men were publicly associated with liberal Catholicism in Europe. Chabrol reported to Elliott that publishers were uninterested because the book was too long and too "American"; he suggested that a friend, the Countess Revilliaz, translate and "rewrite" the biography, "abbreviate it and rebuild it on a plan more suited to the habits of our French religious public." Work began in the fall of 1893, but four years intervened before the book appeared.

During that period, divisions deepened in the American church. At first the liberal party seemed in control. But Herman Heuser, editor of the *American Ecclesiastical Review*, returned from Europe to tell a friend that the pope was "undeceived about the aims of the men here who, under the pretense of national pride, propagate a vicious liberalism." In 1895 a Roman correspondent told friends that a number of American bishops were counteracting Ireland's influence. Signs of a shift appeared dramatically in 1895, when O'Connell was forced to resign as head of the North American College. The delegate was reconciled with Corrigan and the German-Americans, and that same year Leo XIII sent an encyclical letter, *Longinqua Oceani*, which strongly championed the university but explained the role of the apostolic delegate as strengthening papal authority within the American church. The pope called upon lay Catholics "to associate as much as possible with other Catholics," and he warned against setting up the American system as ideal for the universal church. The following year another blow fell when Keane was forced out of the Catholic University.[8]

By the time the French edition of Hecker's life appeared in the early summer of 1897, the American liberals were in retreat. The French church was even more bitterly divided. The struggle was at its peak as the Hecker biography moved toward publication under liberal Catholic auspices. At the urging of the publisher, the book appeared with a preface by Abbé Felix Klein, who had taken on revision of the manuscript; Klein was a well-known biblical scholar who had edited Ireland's speeches for French publication. All signs seemed favorable as the book sold a thousand copies in the first month and soon went through several editions. Chabrol reported that early reviews, many of which he and Klein had arranged, were positive. Xavier Dufresne, once Hecker's most faithful French disciple, wrote enthusiastically and good-naturedly chided Elliott and Hewit for their failure to take steps to forward Hecker's canonization.[9]

By this time O'Connell and Keane were in Rome, attempting to recover their losses and forward the liberal cause by working with like-minded Europeans to win papal favor and shape Catholic opinion. The *Life* seemed a most valuable instrument. O'Connell reported enthusiastically the beneficial impact of the book at the Vatican and suggested translation into Italian. In the fall he was even more excited, telling Elliott: "Really, it seems that Father Hecker is destined to do after his death what he failed to do, tho he dreamed it, during his life. It almost seems as if a revolution were preparing in religious thought."[10]

The French edition of the *Life* was shorter than the original, which had itself simplified some of Hecker's vague and complex ideas. Many Europeans who would soon argue about Hecker, however, knew him not from the book itself, but from Klein's articles in the Catholic press and, especially, Klein's preface. These set forth the central themes of Hecker's life in the sharpest fashion and with considerable exaggeration. Comparing Hecker to St. Augustine, Klein argued that the Paulist was "one of those great religious figures, those universal geniuses," whose thoughts ranged from the highest conceptions of metaphysics and fundamental theology to a "striking transformation of the religious life." To illustrate, he pointed to Hecker's understanding of the "radical change" taking place in history, central to which was "freedom" and personal independence, which led to the spiritual doctrine that men and women should be led to ever greater reliance on the indwelling Holy Spirit. According to Klein, Hecker believed that the "union of the soul with God is immediate and direct" and confessors should help people rely upon God alone as the director of their souls, an "American idea . . . he knew to be God's will for all civilized people of our time."

He went on to describe Hecker's argument for the adaptation of the evangelical message to different historical epochs, his vision on the Nile of a similar adaptation to different cultures, and his supposed recognition that the "passive virtues" characteristic of the previous age should "recoil before those active virtues without which nothing maintains itself any longer." He noted Hecker's emphasis on the external authority of the church, his respect for tradition and his loyalty to Catholic doctrine, but argued that these could now be taken for granted; the field of present and future activity would be universalizing the Christian message and integrating it with the tendency of the contemporary world toward freedom and progress. When Klein included some of Hecker's references to the dependence of the Latin race on external institutions, to Anglo-Saxon virtues, and to the "obvious coming victory of the northern races," the reasons for suspicion of Hecker and of the *Life* become clear.[11]

In September, with Catholics from all over Europe present for a scientific Congress at Fribourg, O'Connell presented a paper on "A New Idea in the Life of Father Hecker." He distinguished between political and ecclesiastical "Americanism," the term now being used to describe the ideas of Ireland and his friends. Political Americanism, according to O'Connell, had to do with the Catholic response to separation of church and state and religious liberty. The American arrangement need not be hostile to the church. In fact, by assuring the freedom of the church and the independence of the individual, it offered unique opportunities for Catholic evangelization. The union of Catholicism and liberty held great promise for the church: this was Hecker's "new idea." O'Connell added some remarks of his own about American reliance upon common law and the benefits of that tradition in the new era of liberty and progress that lay ahead. Ecclesiastical Americanism, in contrast, while identified by critics with Hecker, was the furthest thing from his mind. He did not favor undue liberty in spiritual matters but always upheld ecclesiastical authority and authentic Catholic doctrine. Following O'Connell's talk, the archbishop of Nancy, whom O'Connell called "the bore of the Congress," demanded time to reply. He described Hecker as "Protestant" because of his emphasis on the interior guidance of the Holy Spirit. O'Connell and his friends consulted with Klein, who then took the floor to rebut these charges, reading sections of the book describing Hecker's argument that the interior life must be held in obedience to the external authority of the church. O'Connell told Elliott that they had filled the hall with people sympathetic to their cause, so Klein's defense was well-received and the chairman of the day, another friend, then declared the discussion closed.

Despite favorable reports from de Chabrol and Klein, Elliott was worried. In June he told Klein he was "still a little nervous" about the book's "reception by the censorious orthodox," though he recognized that Leo XIII had turned Rome away from the "ancient spirit of discipline" toward "Christian liberty." Three months later he admitted to Xavier Dufresne that he remained filled with "foreboding." Well he might, for dangers were building on all sides.[12]

Elliott especially feared the Jesuits and in December Klein reported Jesuit attacks from pulpits and press in Paris. Not all French Jesuits were hostile to Hecker; one, reviewing the French biography, criticized the partisan use to which Klein had put Hecker: "Let us not express a man's character or the tendency of his teaching in theses that are absolute and less comprehensive then they should be, especially when the man is many sided and his teaching somewhat vague." Unfortunately, such fairness was not very common in the French church in the 1890s. Conservatives, with Jesuits in the lead, were determined to turn back the assault of "Americanism," and now they had a vulnerable target.[13]

Critics were at work in Rome as well, although the danger of the index seemed to have passed. Keane was optimistic, attributing the good news to "a good deal of Hecker propagandism" by their friends. In mid-December he urged Elliott to prepare a revised, much-shortened edition, leaving out all that was purely American and making "the great majestic powerful Father" accessible to millions who would never read the longer book. He suggested that this step could remove some of the misunderstandings that had arisen. For example, Hecker's comparison of the Latin and Anglo-Saxon races was "substantially correct," but his friends should "bear in mind the sensibilities of our judges." In addition, he should remove the accusation that Hecker and others wanted to make the condition of things in the United States the norm for the universal church, which Leo had condemned in his 1895 encyclical. In early 1898 Keane again urged caution, reporting that the preamble of the Paulist rule should not be presented in Rome, for it made reference to Hecker's emphasis on the interior guidance of the Holy Spirit, which the Holy See regarded with disfavor when made a general rule. He admitted that "Heckerism" was passing through a crisis, but the controversy would ultimately do good by drawing attention to his ideas.[14]

But the major assault was still to come. In March and April a series of fifteen highly critical articles appeared in the Paris journal *La Verité Française*; in May they were published in book form under the title *Father Hecker: Is He a Saint?* Signed "Martel," they were the work of Charles Maignen, a leading French conservative. Lifting out of context some of Hecker's more extreme statements, most drawn from the prefaces of Klein and Ireland and from Klein's articles, he argued that Hecker's ideas had been condemned by the Holy See. His description of the interior guidance of the Holy Spirit was in fact Illuminism, or the heresy of direct revelation from God to the individual soul. Hecker's emphasis on freedom was described by Maignen as Protestant, while his support of American institutions violated the *Syllabus of Errors* and the teachings of Pope Leo XIII. He took special aim as well at Hecker's treatment of religious vows, active and passive virtues and spiritual direction. Maignen's charges were harsh and his language polemical; he called attention to ideas Hecker had not thought through and surely had not backed with the historical and theological arguments demanded by the dominant theologians of the day. But Maignen's target was larger than Hecker. His book was filled with denunciations of American institutions and bitter assaults on Ireland, O'Connell, Gibbons and others who thought the church could live with them, and by implication, on those French Catholics who thought the church in the United States provided a model for the future.[15]

Maignen's work and the Jesuit assaults worried Chabrol. He reported that the archbishop of Paris had denied Maignen an imprimatur but, far worse, one was provided by Monsignor Alberto Lepidi, O.P., Master of the Sacred Palace at the Vatican. Chabrol told his American friends to enlist the aid of the American bishops. Cardinal Gibbons responded quickly, writing Klein a letter indicating his "high regard" for Hecker and his desire to help "remove wrong impressions regarding him from the minds of ill informed people in Europe." But more help would be needed for powerful forces had gathered in the anti-Hecker camp. Archbishop Satolli, now back in Rome, promised to provide a preface for the English translation of Maignen's book. Archbishop Messmer of Milwaukee and Corrigan sent supportive letters to Lepidi. In April Keane told Elliott that he and O'Connell had decided to postpone an Italian translation of the *Life* because Europe had already experienced "as big a dose of Heckerism and Americanism as it can stand."

In June 1898 war broke out between the United States and Spain, adding fuel to the fire. Many European Catholics, suspicious of Americans to begin with, ignored or were uninformed about Spanish atrocities in Cuba. Given American action, the ardent patriotism of the liberals seemed misplaced, if not disloyal. Pamphlets were published and rumors abounded. In July O'Connell met with Lepidi, who told him there was nothing heretical in Hecker's thought, but much that was unwise. His teachings on the Holy Spirit, for example, were orthodox, but dangerous. "Why make it public for everybody, when it is safe only with a few?" he asked O'Connell. The latter replied that Lepidi should make a list of objectionable passages and he would see to the publication of a new edition of the *Life* incorporating those corrections. Reporting this conversation to Keane, who had returned to the United States, O'Connell described the atmosphere at the Vatican: "a perfect feeling of spite and madness is running wild here just now."

Before Lepidi could give O'Connell his list, the pope announced that he was taking the matter into his own hands. Cardinal Gibbons wrote the Vatican to protest Maignen's insults to the American church, and Cardinal Rampolla of the Propaganda responded sympathetically. Back home the Paulists were naturally alarmed. George Deshon, now superior general, drew up a memorial defending Hecker against Maignen's charges; he arranged for Corrigan to present it to the meeting of the American archbishops in October, hoping they would endorse it and send it on to the pope. Ireland was absent and Corrigan presented the memorial in mild tones, suggesting that it would be best for the Paulists and the American hierarchy to "lie low" during "this war." As a result, the archbishops took no action. Corrigan had also advised silence when Elliott asked for his help in August. Elliott well knew that the New York archbishop was working against the Americanist cause behind the scenes, although Corrigan's Roman agents assured him that the blow, if it came, would be directed at the French edition of the *Life* and the Paulists would be spared. The Paulists had "nothing to fear," Jesuit Salvadore Brandi told Corrigan, "so long as they did not profess the strange principles rightly or wrongly attributed to their Founder." McQuaid was more emphatic, telling Corrigan the Paulists were his "diocesans"; if they were teaching "heresies," they should be corrected but "they should not be made scapegoats for Ireland, Keane and Company."[16]

When the pope took the controversy out of the hands of the Vatican congregations in October 1898, he promised to investigate and then write a letter on the subject of Americanism. O'Connell, Elliott and Keane were optimistic, but when the letter came in February 1899, it turned out to be far stronger than they had expected.[17] Ireland, Keane, O'Connell and Felix Klein had all underestimated the degree of anti-Americanism that existed in Europe and which the Spanish American war brought to a boil. Rome, for its part, faced something of a dilemma. A root and branch condemnation of Hecker and Americanism would call into question Leo's own policies of encouraging rapprochement between the church and the Third Republic in France and his stated thesis that Catholicism favored no particular political system. Equally important, Cardinal Gibbons' unusually strong letter of protest against Maignen's book, clearly a direct attack on the American church and its most visible leaders, made it necessary to protect the vested interest of the American hierarchy in assuring the legitimacy of church-state separation and religious liberty. The way out was offered by Denis O'Connell's distinction, made in a paper delivered at the height of the controversy, between political and ecclesiastical Americanism. The former could be allowed as long as democratic values were not carried into religious affairs. In addition, the American leaders who were stirring up Europe and encouraging divisions would have to be warned once again that American practices should not be set forth as ideal.

The principles of religious Americanism could then be condemned in a way that associated them with the conflict in Europe, accusing no one in particular of holding to these ideas while providing a useful warning against extending democratic values into ecclesiastical affairs. On the one hand, the American bishops could deny that their people believed such things; on the other, papal authority would be reaffirmed, American Catholics would again be reminded of the need to hold fast to the complete corpus of doctrine and to accept the ecclesiastic centralization they had resisted at Vatican I. All would be warned against translating political practices into theological, ecclesiastical or spiritual doctrines which might hamper the work of the church.[18]

The encyclical *Testem Benevolentiae* took the form of a letter to Cardinal Gibbons. It was occasioned, the pope said, by publication of Hecker's *Life* in France and the controversy it excited over "certain opinions . . . concerning the manner of living the Christian life." The pope contended that the "principles on which the new opinions" were based could be reduced to one, "that, in order the more easily to bring over to Catholic doctrine those who dissent from it, the Church ought to adapt herself somewhat to our advanced civilization, and, relaxing her ancient rigor, show some indulgence to modern popular theories and methods." In fact, the pope insisted, the rule of life for Catholics admitted no modifications "according to the diversity of time and place"; the church's teaching office "has constantly adhered to the same doctrine, in the same sense and in the same mind."

The pope then attacked the argument that "a certain liberty ought to be introduced into the Church." He specifically rejected as "preposterous" Hecker's argument that the declaration of infallibility meant that "a wider field of thought and action is thrown open to individuals." It meant the opposite, that no one should wish to withdraw from the church's infallible teaching but all "should strive to be more thoroughly imbued with it and guided by its spirit so as the more easily to be preserved from any private error whatsoever."

The pope then took up specific ideas which had come to be associated with Hecker. He rejected the suggestion that "external guidance" was undesirable because the Holy Spirit acted on souls directly; he criticized as well the suggestions that the natural virtues should be placed before the supernatural, that the active virtues were more suited to the age than the passive, and that religious vows were of less value than in the past. Leo concluded by using the term *Americanism* in a way which allowed O'Connell's distinction between political and ecclesiastical versions.

> We cannot approve the opinions which some comprise under the head of Americanism. If indeed by that name be designated characteristic qualities which reflect honor on the people of America, conditions of your commonwealth or the laws and customs which prevail in them, there is surely no reason why we should deem that it ought to be discarded. But, if it is to be used not only to signify but even to commend the above doctrines, there can be no doubt but that our Venerable Brethren the bishops of America would be the first to repudiate and condemn it, as being especially unjust to them and to the entire nation as well. For it raises the suspicion that there are some among you who conceive of and desire a church in America different from that which is in the rest of the world.[19]

"Alas, it is pretty bad," Keane wrote Father Doyle. Fortunately, the Americanism condemned by Leo XIII was Maignen's "caricature," so they could say it had "nothing to do" with them. Nevertheless, he advised the Paulists to send the pope an "extremely responsible and docile" letter of submission. Ireland agreed with Keane that "the Americanism condemned is Maignen's nightmare." Rampolla had given assurances the letter was written in such a way "as to allow us to say that the things condemned were never said or written in America, not even by Hecker" but were "set afloat in France" by poor translations and interpretations. This was "small comfort, but we must make the most of it," Ireland added sadly.[20]

Small comfort, but there was little the Paulists could do. Father John Hughes, assistant superior general, told one newspaper that the problems arose from bad translations and misquotation of Hecker. If he were alive, Hecker would be the first to disavow any beliefs at variance with the Holy See. Father Doyle, then editor of the *Catholic World*, told the *New York Times* that the Paulists were not disappointed with the letter, "not in any sense. It does not touch us," because "Father Hecker's teaching was always perfectly orthodox."

After conferring with Corrigan, the Paulists wrote their submission to the Holy Father, repeating their claim that neither Hecker nor they had ever held the condemned doctrines. Then, at Corrigan's recommendation, they announced that they would remove the biography from circulation. This upset Ireland, who told Deshon that no one expected this and, by taking the action, the Paulists "give rise to the belief that the book is somewhat condemnable." He argued that instead they should have a new and revised book prepared. Keane disagreed. While theoretically a defense ought to be made, there were influences in Rome who would "distort and discolor it." The Paulists, under Deshon's direction, knew that power had clearly shifted and they could only rely on Corrigan for protection. In March Corrigan told Deshon that the Holy Father was pleased with their submission and extended to them his apostolic benediction.[21]

As for the bishops, Corrigan wrote praising the pope for slaying the "monster" of Americanism, while the bishops of the Milwaukee province wrote admitting the presence of the condemned doctrines in the United States. At the archbishops' meeting in the fall, several bishops protested the Milwaukee letter and demanded that the nation's bishops be surveyed to determine whether they believed the condemned theories were present in the country. This motion was defeated, as was one by Corrigan to add to the praise extended to the Holy Father. All the bishops had sent the pope their thanks and praise, but Cardinal Gibbons was disturbed that enemies of the American church were listened to in Rome, while its friends were ignored. McQuaid and Corrigan, of course, were delighted by the outcome, though the former was anxious to salvage Hecker. He told a congregation in his see city that Elliott's original *Life* had fallen "dead from the press." As for Hecker, he was patronizing. He "had some peculiar notions but was a man of deep earnestness," "childlike simplicity" and "boyishness of soul." "No one who knew him well ever dreamed of his inciting heresy or running foul of the Church," the bishop insisted. Unfortunately, a bad translation had led to severe controversy and the pope's letter. The errors censured arose from Ireland's support for public schools, the liberals' opposition to the ban on secret societies and an appearance of Keane at Harvard University, none of which had any direct connection with Hecker.[22]

Stung by charges that it was the liberals who had been condemned, Ireland struck back with an article in the *North American Review* under the pen name J. St. Clair Etheridge. Political Americanism, associated with Hecker, had to do with the frank acceptance by Catholics in the United States of the American constitution and their conviction that this arrangement best suited the church in their country. It meant little more than that "every good Catholic in America should also be a good citizen," cooperate with others to break down bigotry, and unite behind every good cause for the welfare of the people. This form of Americanism, Ireland insisted, was "approved and blessed" by Leo XIII. Religious Americanism, in contrast, was the "body of crude heretical opinions lately condemned." It had been "foisted off" on American Catholics by Maignen and his supporters, who included an ousted Catholic University professor, the Jesuits and especially the Jesuit periodical *Civiltà Cattolica*, which supported "bigotry, political and theological" and was the "enemy of democracy." Fortunately, Leo XIII had resisted their hatred of democracy and of America and had condemned ideas which had nothing to do with the church in the United States.[23]

By such arguments those who loved Hecker were reassured that what Hecker had believed was not condemned in the letter, for the controversy in Europe had little if anything to do with Hecker's doctrine. The Roman correspondent for the *Freeman's Journal*, for example, charged that "all the hot heads, sore heads and soft heads of Europe" put "into the good Father Hecker's mouth all the dangerous, stupid and damnable notions that swarmed in their own heads." As Dennis O'Connell told an interviewer, "the only condemnations have been the errors which certain fanatics had put in circulation under the name Americanism. They conjured up a phantom of heresy. The pope swept away the phantom." Josephine Hecker, George's widow, told Elliott that she was pleased that all that *Testem Benevolentiae* "condemned had been far from Father Hecker's mind always and that he never had any thought of the Church making concessions to reach those outside her."

Nevertheless, without question, Hecker's reputation was badly damaged. Only a few papers attacked Hecker directly. The *Providence Visitor*, for example, called him "a man so erratic that one of his friends thanked God he died in the Catholic faith." More disturbing were efforts by the friends of "Heckerism" to distance themselves from his ideas. Ireland, for example, admitted to a reporter that he had never understood Hecker's "ambiguous" notions about the Holy Spirit. They were "exclusive and personal with Father Hecker," a man of "strong impulses," Ireland claimed; he had "met no one who could be accused of sharing [his] theory." The *Northwest Chronicle* of Iowa argued that "whatever lapses from the true teachings of the Church may have characterized the closing days of (Hecker's) life," they were "attributable to the mental decay which not infrequently accompanies advanced age." The Catholic *Herald Citizen* of Milwaukee, a paper sympathetic to Ireland and the Americanist cause, admitted that Hecker may have "erred in at least some of his opinions," though "the good that he did lives after him." Worst of all was Dennis O'Connell, who called Hecker a good man with "queer ideas," who was never "held in very high esteem, even by those who were well-inclined to him." Even Xavier Dufresne admitted to Elliott privately that Hecker had his faults. He sometimes "abused his gift for speculation by throwing himself into thoughts too subtle and paradoxical," or expressed himself "in too general a manner" without making his ideas practical and precise enough.[24]

Another result of the controversy was that even Hecker's admirers accepted, without modification, the implicit assumption that lay behind the conservative position, the condemnation of 1899 and the subsequent condemnation of modernism in 1905. This was that Catholic truth extended far beyond the minimum elements of dogma to which Hecker had hoped to confine it and embraced much that he might have considered secondary or accidental. As O'Connell put it,

> the practical lesson which we must all draw from Leo XIII's apostolic letter is that Catholic principles do not change, whether through the passing of the years, or the changing of countries, or new discoveries, or motives of utility. They are always the principles that Christ taught, that the church made known and the Popes and Councils defended. . . . As they are they must be taken or left. Whoever accepts them in all their fullness and strictness is a Catholic; whoever hesitates, staggers, adjusts himself to the times, makes compromises, may call themselves [sic] what name they will but before God and the church he is a rebel and a traitor.

The *Freeman's Journal*, Hecker's strongest newspaper defender, agreed:

> Leo XIII has laid down once and for all, that Catholic truth is absolutely inviolable in the very smallest details as in the most fundamental dogmas, and that this inviolability is to be proclaimed by all Catholics. . . . The dominant note of the church today is what it has always been: devoted adhesion to the whole cycle of revealed truth and no compromise with religious falsehood.[25]

Pius IX and the latter-day Brownson had won.

Deshon was not satisfied simply to withdraw the biography. He ordered Elliott to gather together "Hecker's papers on spiritual doctrine" and send them to him, along with a pamphlet entitled "Paulist Vocation and Mission" which had already been printed. Elliott promised to insure that the latter was not circulated. The manuscript of Hecker's book on the Holy Spirit Elliott preserved by accepting Deshon's decision against printing at present. Elliott was not happy with these decisions. He and Doyle worried about the future of the congregation and its work. "The *Catholic World* is under a scare," Elliott told Klein in 1900. "We are afraid of our shadow. You do not know how near we are to a veritable panic and yet must keep up the appearance of indifference."[26] In later years Elliott carried the Hecker legacy, defending him against attacks, preparing a revised biography to redeem his reputation, promoting Hecker's spirituality within the congregation and fighting to make convert-work the heart of the Paulist enterprise. He was not very successful, for the biography was never published, he had never fully grasped Hecker's spiritual ideas, and the Paulists soon domesticated the convert apostolate.[27]

When Father Deshon died in 1904, the *New York Times* in a friendly notice referred to the "liberal views" of the Paulist founders, which had led them to be called "The Protestant Catholics." Father George Searle protested strongly. While zeal for converts had always characterized the Paulists, they denied the term "liberal" as suggesting that they would pursue converts by "the immoral and un-Christian spirit of compromise which would deny one of the doctrines of Christ's Gospel." The only sense in which they were liberal was that they disliked the "denunciation and bitterness of old time controversy," preferring St. Francis de Sales' dictum that "a good Christian is never outdone in good manners." Thus Hecker's challenging vision of deep evangelization was reduced to gentlemanly decorum. The sharp edges of his vision of a Catholic America were blunted, and Paulist convert-work became one more source of pride and respectability for the Catholic subculture. As John B. Sheerin wrote years later, the condemnation, followed by the modernist controversy a few years later, "caused the Paulists to slow their pace and fall back on defensive apologetics or to devote themselves to other matters." While they did much good, "the Hecker mystique of enthusiastic rapprochement with the American mind was missing."[28]

Among the Americanist bishops, only Keane had been closely associated with Hecker and took seriously his spirituality. None of them were theologians of note, and their basic ideas, while similar to Hecker's, were not drawn directly from his writing. The Americanists shared many of Hecker's assumptions about the providential meaning of history, but they did not necessarily draw them from Hecker. Moreover, while he was generally prepared to work on his own and, when frustrated, to await the action of the Holy Spirit, they entered actively into church politics, building a party to support the cause, arranging the placement of articles in the press, and campaigning to have their program implemented by authority from above.

As to Leo XIII, his encyclical and Hecker were like trains passing in the night. The pope and the Paulist gave the same words different meanings. Leo XIII, his advisors and eventually even most of Hecker's admirers saw the church as a timeless, unchanging entity, and they defined doctrine in static terms. Hecker was different. He instinctively read the signs of the times, searching for God's presence in his own life, in contemporary history and in the life of the church. Like other Catholics, he saw the "saving fulness" of God's presence in the Roman Catholic church, but for him that church was "the living power which animated history and pushed it forward unawares." His opponents saw it as "timeless edifice standing over against history." For them vows, virtues, spiritual direction and much else was to be evaluated in terms of the life and work of the organized church. To Hecker, all were matters of concrete means and ends: how could union with God and spiritual perfection be achieved in the situations in which people lived in the nineteenth century?

Taken in the abstract as "absolute" theses, Hecker's ideas were clearly condemned by Leo XIII. But as Hecker understood them, each had solid support in Catholic teaching, as Lepidi admitted to O'Connell. What was at stake, in the end, had little to do with spirituality or the theology of the Holy Spirit and much to do with the unity, discipline and direction of the church. And on that score, Hecker was clearly rejected.[29]

The best assessment of what had happened came in a letter written to a friend by Dennis O'Connell a year after the publication of *Testem Benevolentiae*. Lepidi, in their interview, had shown that he believed the worst of Americans. Ireland's speeches in France "were regarded as tending ultimately to incite the people or clergy to look to something of a representation even in central Church governments." Hecker and his disciples seemed to want to put "the Holy Ghost in place of the Pope." As O'Connell saw it, the division was clear and irreconcilable, for "the real question" was between two races, "the Latin and the Northern," two legal codes, Roman law and common law, and two concepts of government, "the Caesarian and the democratic." O'Connell, privately at least, went further than Hecker, for beyond the "fixed facts" of having the papacy and hierarchy he believed Christ had left the church free to adapt its government to the circumstances in which it found itself.

As Hecker had discovered, the issues, defined in this way, meant defeat for the American Church and for himself. His historical assessment in the *Exposition* was intended to relativize the two positions by placing them in historical context and to establish a new basis for unity in the combination of the indwelling Holy Spirit and the coming Kingdom of God. In the 1890s his defenders, including Elliott, made neither of these doctrines their own. Instead they grasped the standard of democracy and adaptation in dialectical opposition to Lepidi and Maignen and attempted to force a choice.[30]

This analysis helps explain the European controversy, locating it in a century-long debate which extended from the condemnation of Felicité de Lammenais in 1831 through the *Syllabus of Errors* to the condemnation of modernism in 1905. Hecker was aware of this division and instinctively associated with more moderate liberals. Like John Henry Newman, he disliked partisanship in the church and thought he had located a unifying vision and reconciling strategy. But his almost instinctive belief in human freedom and his providential view of history meant that he was far closer to the left than the right and was hardly innocent of the beliefs which aroused such suspicion in the 1890s.

However useful in locating Hecker in the European debate, the "prophets and guardians" interpretation is less useful in explaining Hecker's relationship to Americanism in America. For one thing, Corrigan, McQuaid and their American allies had almost nothing in common with Maignen, Lepidi or even Leo XIII. Politically, McQuaid bitterly denounced Ireland's public support of the Republican party, but the two men fully accepted American political institutions. Nor were there any serious doctrinal differences, as McQuaid's treatment of the controversy made clear. The American debate had far more to do with personalities, American church politics, pastoral strategies and what Thomas Jonas has described as "sensibilities." The liberals, like Hecker, envisioned a national church, mobilized for mission, though their understanding of that mission had little in common with Hecker's passion for a Catholic America. Their opponents were more parochial, more jealous of their autonomy, more determined to keep Catholics Catholic than to engage the problems of national life.[31]

William Portier has argued persuasively that Hecker's ideas reflected the marginal role played by "Yankee Catholics" like himself. After his conversion, the trickle of American-born, mostly middle-class converts, together with such native-born Catholics as Martin Spalding and John Lancaster Spalding, occupied a marginal role in church and society generally. As Catholics they stood on the fringe of the great American middle class, which stood at the pinnacle of a growing, confident industrial society. As American Catholics they stood outside the heart of that church, which was increasingly dominated by the immigrant masses and Irish-born bishops. In the universal church they stood as American Catholics on the fringe of a church engaged in a headlong rush toward the consolidation of a Catholic subculture bent upon survival rather than the dialogue with modern culture. It was not surprising, then, that Yankee Catholics would articulate a Christianized understanding of American destiny and a modernized version of the universal Catholic ideal that would make their own role central both to the church and the nation. In that sense Hecker can be seen as a prophet who offered an ideal for middle-class, American-born Catholics.[32]

Conservatives appealed to the middle-class concern for private property and social order, but they were more aware than the liberals of the pastoral needs of working-class Catholics and the new immigrants, for whom strong parishes and parochial schools were means of ordering their lives, strengthening their families and developing the disciplines necessary for eventual social mobility. The class divisions were evident, too, in the fact that almost all the liberals were temperance advocates; few conservatives and almost no Germans supported that cause. Hecker almost never explored the pastoral dynamics of American Catholicism; as he told the Paulists, immigrants and uneducated Catholics could be left to the work of the parish priests, while they concentrated on native-born, educated Catholics and those outside the church.

Finally, the liberals were, by temperament as well as choice, adaptationists, who would adjust non-essential matters so that the church could retain the loyalty of its assimilating members and fulfill its responsibilities as an accepted American religious institution. Here they parted company with Hecker, whose focus remained on the American people. Liberal Catholics wanted to keep the assimilating middle class in the church; Hecker wanted to inspire them to convert the country. Conservatives, closer to the immigrant experience, were conservationists, concerned to preserve faith and loyalty by means of a subculture isolated at least to some degree from American life. In need of voluntary support they thought that parochial school education, a variety of organizations to meet social and cultural needs and an exclusive view of the church would be more likely to prevent mixed marriages, indifference and disaffiliation than would rapid assimilation, nondenominational social and cultural activities, public school education, and interreligious civility and cooperation. In these terms, once again, Hecker was an Americanist, but with a difference. He would move beyond the Catholic subculture, endorse American institutions and give attention to the middle class, but he would do all these things in order to bring about a deeper, more intimate union with God and to build a Catholic Kingdom of God, first in the United States. All believed a promised land lay ahead, but only Hecker wanted to make that universal, all-embracing Catholic Kingdom of God the actual, living goal of the church and of all Catholics. Alive to the signs of that promised land, he offered a view of Catholic life which burst the bonds of conventional faith and institutional self-centeredness, for each person and the church itself was tested by its relation to the professed goal of Christianity. Abstracted from that context, his spirituality indeed endangered church order and orthodoxy, and his missionary zeal threatened the defensive priorities of the church in Rome and in the United States.

Almost a century after his death, in the wake of another Vatican Council, American Catholics and their church would once again struggle with questions of meaning and purpose in the larger world beyond the church. Then, once again, many would continue to place either the church or the individual at the center of salvation history. But a few lonely voices would look ahead, as Hecker did, celebrate freedom as a sign of God's spirit at work in the world, and invite everyone, including the poorest who so easily had escaped Hecker's attention, to join in making the church a community of men and women bound together by faith in the promises of a living God, who would renew the face of the earth.

Epilogue

At the Second Vatican Council (1962–65) the Roman Catholic bishops of the world declared that they belonged to a church "truly and intimately linked with mankind and its history." The renewal of Vatican II, begun by Pope John XXIII, arose from the collapse of the Roman Catholic subculture constructed in the nineteenth century. In the wake of the tragedies of the twentieth century, the church attempted to turn away from its internal preoccupations and summon all men and women, not just Catholics, to realize the age-old dream of a single human family. In doing so, Catholicism addressed the central question of Isaac Hecker's life and work: Can the human community, at long last, see its common destiny and join in freedom to help bring it about?

The legacy of Isaac Hecker includes many things. There is his passionate desire for union with God; his confidence in the indwelling Holy Spirit; and his conviction that prayer, contemplation and attentiveness to the voice of God within the human heart is a sure ground of faith and life. Catholics appreciate Hecker's equally strong conviction that the same Holy Spirit speaks through the church, so that the voice of the church, properly understood, corresponds to the voice of conscience. The authority of the church protects personal conscience from self-deception, while the authority of conscience protects the church against an overemphasis on externals and a dangerous identification of itself alone with God's presence in human history. And each is protected from a narcissistic preoccupation with self-preservation, and from a limited understanding of the union with God, which is the destiny of the human race, by the presence of God in history, by Divine Providence.

Many of these ideas have become familiar to Catholics in recent years. The shift of modern theology from classical to historical consciousness, the renewed attention to the subject of faith, the human person, an expanded understanding of religious consciousness, and a belief in God's presence beyond the church, compelling study of the "signs of the times," all have given many of Hecker's insights the support of scholarship and more systematic argument than he ever made. Similarly, changes in the social composition and location of American Catholics have brought a renewed interest in spirituality, particularly in a spirituality appropriate to the life of the laity. The decline of the immigrant church has brought deeper appreciation of the church's dependence upon the free commitment of its members. In this context Hecker's belief in the need for deep interior faith and for spiritual growth that leads to emancipation from external dependence while providing inner sources of purpose and direction have become pastoral necessities and sparked a renewed interest in Hecker's spiritual writings. Of course there was much that Isaac Hecker did not understand. He had little sense of the meaning of industrial society and almost no grasp of the role of economic forces in history. He lacked the precision of language and the discipline of analysis which a better education might have given him. He paid little attention to the life of the masses of immigrant Catholics around him. But as a religious thinker he had some great gifts, and as a man of his times he absorbed modern symbols and meanings and blended them with Christian faith and Catholic tradition in ways which were unique. Some of his most basic ideas came from the combination of Catholicism and Americanism, and thus have particular interest a century later when once again the church in the United States debates its mission, especially as it relates to public life, to other Christians and to other communities of faith in an emerging world church.

But there are elements of the Hecker legacy which are less obvious and less easy to appropriate. First, when Isaac Hecker became a Catholic, he said he had discovered "the promised land of my youth." Yet as Susan Perschbacher has pointed out, this was only the first of a series of conversions. The promised land remained as much promise and future expectation as achieved reality. Other Catholics of his generation looked backward, through a history marked by the supposed tragedy of the Reformation, and yearned for a Catholic restoration. Others were locked into the struggle of the present, as the church universal reorganized itself and cautiously adapted to the demands of pluralism. The poles of controversy within which Hecker found himself were a sectarian Catholicism, which located the institutional church at the center of history, and a liberal Catholicism, which often sought a comfortable position in the world. Hecker was dissatisfied with both. His gaze rested on a different place, on a future in which a Catholic America would usher in a Catholic world. "The eyes of the church are set on a divine vision of things that the world has not yet ever witnessed," he wrote; "this is not in the past but in the future, and it consists in the reign of perfect justice, truth, reason and love."

Isaac Hecker really wanted to convert America and then the world, and his understanding of conversion, at his best moments, was neither a larger membership for the institutional church nor a victory for one group in a competition for power. He wanted a deep conversion to God, fidelity to the inner voice of Spirit, alert responsiveness to Divine Providence, and humble submission to the body of Christ, the church. His evangelization excluded both the alienation of a sectarian Catholicism, whose universal claims served mainly to isolate it from the world, and the comfort of a denomination, which left no one caring much about the destiny of the human race.

Unlike most Catholics, but like many other Americans, Hecker had a sense of the immediacy of God's presence, a conviction that the hand of God was at work in even the smallest events. This was one source of his incurable optimism, which made the Civil War for him a providential opening of the hearts of his fellow citizens to the need for the unity, stability and order God and His church could offer. The same optimism made the First Vatican Council the end of an era of power, authority and domination and the beginning of a new pentecost of freedom, independence and spontaneous movement toward the church. For Hecker, it was simply inconceivable that God would let his church fail, much less that he would allow the human experience to come to a screeching halt. What God intended, and promised, God confirmed in the deepest recess of human hearts and must confirm as well in the arena of human history.

Second, the promised land that lay in the future was to be Catholic. Hecker honestly believed that Christianity contained truths revealed by God about the destiny of human beings and that the Catholic Church was the fullest and richest embodiment of that message. He was not very ecumenical, if that meant that the church had much to learn from other Christians. He did think that it was important to listen to the voice of post-Christians, of Emerson, Channing, Thoreau, though not many after that, but one listened largely to sense the religious yearnings they expressed and better understand how to offer a Catholic answer to the aspirations and questions they revealed. Of course the conversation was mostly one way. So powerful was his Catholic conviction that he could be arrogant and righteous at times; dialogue was not his strength.

But there was a positive, critically important truth in Hecker's Catholicism. Part of it was the absolute conviction that Catholicism has something to say, something critically important to say, to the modern world. Of course the Christian church should preach the Gospel, and of course the church should minister to the human and religious needs of its own members. But the church was essentially missionary, called upon to spread its word and win the people. He understood evangelization in the most modern of terms, as an invitation to be issued from the inside and not the outside, an invitation expressed at the very heart of culture, showing how the culture's best hopes and deepest yearnings could indeed be answered, that humanity had a destiny and that destiny was an achievable possibility. He believed that the Catholic Church, with the richness of its historical tradition, had the tools to make that invitation, and the resources to help bring the future to life.

The promised land of the Kingdom of God was not to be a great big Catholic church presided over by Pius IX, but it would be Catholic in the richest and fullest meaning of that term. It would embrace all men and women; it would integrate all dimensions of human experience; it would have great art and music and science as well as great holiness; and it would be marked by the spontaneous response of persons to the Holy Spirit, expressed in life, worship and love for God and one another. Church and world would be transformed and the boundaries required by human history would dissolve when this Catholic Christian commonwealth appeared. It was not a sectarian vision, in which true believers would be rescued from a pagan world by a God returned in judgment. Nor was it denominational, as if the final and quite reasonable, polite judgment would be that Catholics were right and everyone else was wrong. No, it was a Catholic vision of a time when the claims of Roman Catholicism to unity, universality, holiness and historicity would finally be fulfilled.

As Hecker saw it, the Catholic idea lifted human vision beyond itself, beyond the trying ambiguities of life, and called forth the very best that people had in them. To announce a lesser message, to appeal to fear or anxiety, to concentrate on externals, meant not only to betray the Spirit but to risk submersion in the stream of historical events. He was convinced that Catholics "must either raise up their thoughts and courage to the heights of the aims of Christianity as the absolute and universal religion destined to gain the entire world or cease to be Catholics and content themselves to take the ignoble part of one among a thousand of different religious sects and with them finally disappear." The alternatives facing a free Catholic church in a free society could hardly be better stated. The challenge was real, not easy, a claim indeed that the hopes of humanity for harmony, for peace, for justice, could not be fulfilled without a common religion:

> No nation, as no individual, discovers its divine destination, until it is wholly under the influence of religious inspiration. No people becomes properly a nation, acts as one man, unfolds its highest capabilities, displays its true genius and utmost strength until it becomes not only politically and socially but religiously of one mind and heart.

Hecker also believed in freedom. How was the future triumph of the church to be achieved? Most of Hecker's practical answers to that question did not turn out as well as he hoped. He knew, as much as he knew anything, that it would be the work of God's spirit with which men and women could cooperate, guided by the indwelling Holy Spirit and by the church. Yet he had a conviction, so strong that it only occasionally needed to be asserted, that it would be achieved in freedom. Brownson may have settled for coercion, if possible; his fellow Catholics may have lost confidence in the power of their own faith, so that they could not really believe that others would respond. But Hecker thought that only the truth freely chosen was a truth made real in history. Freedom was also a practical matter: "He who would gain the men of this generation must address their intelligence, acknowledge their liberty and respect their dignity," or get no response.

Once again there is the temptation to filter the idea of freedom through the American lens of denominationalism. Hecker's was a tougher idea, as it always is for true believers. It was the element of Hecker's faith that most accounted for the isolation and loneliness of his later years. To be truly Catholic and to believe truly in freedom was, and remains, extremely difficult. It requires one to believe that what the church proclaims is true, that the truth it proclaims is true for all men and women, and that that truth corresponds with the deepest and most legitimate human hopes and aspirations. Faced with the historical fact that many, indeed most, people do not accept the church or even Christianity, one has two basic options. One can conclude that the truth the church proclaims is not true, or one can conclude that the truth it proclaims, for some mysterious reason, is only evident to members of the church. One either believes in people or one believes in the church. Hecker believed in both; then and now that was no small achievement. For him it meant struggle within the church to get the truth clear, and struggle beyond the church to make the truth heard. The boundaries between church and world became dimmer, the Spirit at work outside the church drew little response within; and the spirit at work in the church seemed to be ignored by church leaders themselves. He steadfastly relied on the inner voice of spirit, anchoring his faith beyond the externals, and sought friendship and community, but it was a lonely task.

In summary, Hecker was a friend of the human race, and he thought the church was too. The end of the story was intended to be a reunion of God with people, all people, a time when the aspirations of nature would be fulfilled and the questions of the soul would be answered. The Catholic Church was God's chosen agency for bringing that day about, announcing the Good News from within, not outside, human history, from a standpoint which made the "joys and the hopes, the griefs and anxieties of the men and women of this age" its own, to use Vatican II language. The process was in the hands of the human race, which meant there could be, in the short run, a different outcome. But faith meant that in the end freedom and destiny would be joined and men and women would choose what they truly needed and wanted.

The vision of the Kingdom of God as a real and compelling objective of human life and apostolic action, the conviction that the Christian message is true for everyone, reliance on persuasion, respecting each person's freedom, optimism about human nature and a bias toward the positive in assessing signs of the times—these remain elements of any authentically American political theology. Isaac Hecker, after so many defeats and disappointments, never let squabbles among Catholics, the hostility of non-Catholics, or the busy-ness of his Paulist brothers take his eyes off that brighter future that lay ahead. In the next century another American, Martin Luther King, in the darkest days of his life, often sunk in depression and near despair, always came back to reaffirm a vision of brotherhood and sisterhood, freedom and fraternity, that lay up ahead but was alive around him. By saying it, he almost made it so. To the extent people have shared in communities of faith and fellowship, they have known the promised land. For Christians to turn back in upon themselves, fleeing to caves or church basements, would be an unworthy outcome of their history and would doom their church to negative answers to the question of friendship with the human race.

Isaac Hecker was the premier American spokesman for the bourgeois age of the Catholic Church. He was a man with many faults. In the midst of the Civil War he did not reflect on the tragedy of violence. Personally kind and sympathetic, he asked few hard questions about poverty and injustice. He was a nineteenth-century American in some of the worst as well as the best ways: complacent about the institutions of his country, over-confident in human progress, heedless of the brutal realities of power all too evident around him. His mystical Christianity and his focus on the interior experience of God too often allowed him to skim over problems and at times led to a certain self-centeredness and self-pity.

Still, every race, age and class has its own experience of God, and each local and particular historic experience of the church adds to the total experience of being Christ's presence in history. If the bourgeois, liberal era in history and, delayed, in the church, were not of themselves a full response to the spirit, neither is any other. The degree of adequacy at any time and in any place is determined by choices men and women make. The Catholic Church today faces choices not unlike those that confronted Catholics in 1830, in 1869, in the 1890s; recent events indicate that the choice of Vatican II of openness, mission, service and love is by no means triumphant over the long powerful options of isolation, aloofness and self-righteousness. In the memory of Isaac Hecker Catholics can celebrate not their past achievements but their present possibilities. His was a vision that would overcome the attraction of sectarian abandonment of the world and recognize and celebrate the promise of this moment, a moment, like any moment, that may stand at the threshold of a new era in human history. Today's Catholics might make their own the confidence expressed by Hecker on the twentieth anniversary of his baptism:

> To me my life has been one continued growth; and hence I have never had any desire to return to any part or period of it. This applies to my life before I was received into the church or after. My best life was always in the present.

Notes

For his work on Isaac Hecker, the late Father Vincent Holden gathered Hecker materials from the major archives in North America and Europe. As a result, the Paulist Fathers' archives in New York contain photocopies of all the major documents needed for a biography of the Paulist founder. In the following end notes all materials unless otherwise noted are in those archives. The bulk of the citations refer to the Hecker papers themselves, although at times special note is made of the papers of other Paulists. The letters to and from Fathers Hewit, Deshon, Walworth and other Paulists are in their own papers, as are the notes and correspondence of Father Elliott, although in the case of his notes copies have been made and inserted into the Hecker collection. I have not felt it necessary to add Paulist archives after each citation. Nor have I felt it necessary to add the word *copy* for a document Holden located elsewhere, such as in the Propaganda Fide archives in Rome. I have added a reference where the manuscript material was drawn by me personally from another source, such as the University of Notre Dame archives.

One invaluable aid to scholars is the correspondence of Hecker with Orestes Brownson, collected and ably edited by Joseph F. Gower and Richard M. Leliaert. I have made only a few references to this volume, as I had consulted the original letters in New York and at Notre Dame, but the reader is referred to this work for a firsthand encounter with these two remarkable converts. (*The Brownson-Hecker Correspondence*, ed. and intro. Joseph F. Gower and Richard M. Leliaert [Notre Dame, Indiana: University of Notre Dame Press] 1979).

As indicated earlier, I am most grateful to the former Paulist archivist Lawrence V. McDonnell, C.S.P., for his gracious assistance.

CHAPTER 1
AN AMERICAN LIFE

1. Bernard Bailyn, *Education and the Formation of American Society* (New York, 1972), pp. 25–26. On the theme of new beginnings see R.W.B. Lewis, *The American Adam* (Chicago, 1955).

2. Gordon S. Wood, "The Democratization of Mind in the American Revolution," in *Leadership in the American Revolution* (Washington, 1974), pp. 73–89. The median age of Americans in 1800 was only 16 (as compared to 30.8 in 1950). See Joseph Kett, *Rites of Passage: Adolescence in America* (New York, 1972), chap. 2.

3. Donald M. Scott, "The Popular Lecture and the Creation of a Public in Mid Nineteenth Century America," *Journal of American History* 66 (September 1980), pp. 791–809.

4. Perry Miller, *Errand into the Wilderness* (Cambridge, 1956).

5. Perry Miller, *The Life of the Mind in America: From the Revolution to the Civil War* (New York, 1965). See also David B. Davis, ed., *Antebellum American Culture* (Lexington, 1979), pp. xix–xxi.

6. Miller, *Life of the Mind*, chap. 1.

7. Nathan Hatch, "The Christian Movement and the Search for a Theology of the People," *Journal of American History* 67 (December 1980), pp. 545–67; Timothy L. Smith, "Righteousness and Hope: Christian Holiness and the Millennial Vision in America, 1800–1900," *American Quarterly* 31 (Spring 1979), pp. 21–45. Here and in later discussions of transcendentalism, I have been greatly aided by an unpublished paper made available by Timothy L. Smith: "Transcendental Grace: Biblical Themes in the New England Renaissance."

8. Perry Miller, "Jonathan Edwards to Emerson," *New England Quarterly* 13 (December 1940), pp. 589–617.

9. William Ellery Channing, *Self-Culture* (London, 1844), section reprinted in Davis, *Antebellum American Culture*, esp. pp. 69–70.

10. Vincent Holden, C.S.P., *The Early Years of Isaac Thomas Hecker, 1819–1844* (Washington, 1939), p. 6.

11. Holden, *Early Years*, chap. one.

12. Hecker to family, September 18, 1845.

13. On Caroline Hecker's religious faith see John Farina, *An American Experience of God* (New York, 1981), chap. 2.

14. Hecker, Diary, April 15, 1843; Holden, *Early Years*, pp. 5–6.

15. Holden, *Early Years*, p. 26n. On Hecker's recollections see Walter Elliott, *The Life of Father Hecker* (New York: Arno Press, 1972), p. 27. By 1860 the company had six mills turning out an annual product of over two and a half million dollars. See Harry J. Carman, "The Rise of the Factory System," in Alexander Flick, ed., *History of the State of New York* 4 (New York, 1934), p. 233.

16. Holden, *Early Years*, pp. 35ff.

17. "Report to Superiors," 1858. This document was written for his spiritual advisors in Rome during the crisis which followed his expulsion from the Redemptorists. He had struck a similar theme in a report for his spiritual director and religious superiors while in the seminary a decade earier, but then he placed far less emphasis on social reform as an issue in his own conversion. See Vincent Holden, C.S.P., *The Yankee Paul* (Milwaukee, 1958), p. 14.

18. Cf. Edward Langlois, C.S.P., "The Formation of American Catholic Political Thought: Isaac Hecker's Political Theory," Ph.D. diss. Cornell University, 1977.

19. On the life of Brownson see Thomas R. Ryan, C.PP.S., *Orestes A. Brownson: A Definitive Life* (Huntington, Indiana, 1976).

20. Hecker and brothers to Brownson, November 14, 1841.

21. Diary, May 17, 1843.

22. Diary, October, 1842.

23. Diary, February 3, 1843; Hecker to mother, December 24, 1842; Hecker to brothers, December 26, 1842.

24. Hecker to brothers, December 28, 1842.

25. Diary, early January 1843.

26. Hecker to brothers, January 3, 1843; Hecker to mother, December 24, 1842; John Hecker to Brownson, January 2, 1843.

27. Hecker to family, January 7, 1843; Diary, January 3, 1843.

CHAPTER 2
ERNEST THE SEEKER

1. On Channing and transcendentalism see Paul F. Boller, *American Transcendentalism: An Intellectual Inquiry* (New York, 1974), chap. 1. The quotes are taken from William Henry Channing, "The Essence of the Christian Religion" in Sydney Ahlstrom, ed., *Theology in America: The Major Protestant Voices from Puritanism to Neo-Orthodoxy* (Indianapolis, 1967), pp. 196–210.

2. William Henry Channing, "A Participant's Definition," in Perry Miller, ed., *The American Transcendentalists* (New York, 1957), p. 37;

Charles Mayo Ellis, "An Essay on Transcendentalism," in Miller, p. 23; Emerson, "The Divinity School Address," in Ahlstrom, *American Theology*, pp. 297–316. See also Miller, "Jonathan Edwards to Emerson."

3. Charles R. Crowe, *George Ripley: Transcendentalist and Utopian Socialist* (Athens, Georgia, 1967).

4. Crowe, *Ripley*, pp. 162–63.

5. The religious struggle is described in William Hutchison, *The Transcendentalist Ministers* (New Haven, 1959).

6. Ora Gannett Sedgwick, "A Girl of Sixteen at Brook Farm," *Atlantic Monthly* 85 (January 1900), pp. 394–404.

7. Crowe, *Ripley*, pp. 170–90.

8. Hecker to mother, January 19, 1843; Hecker to George and John, January 26, 1843; Holden, *Early Years*, p. 100.

9. Diary, no date (near February 3, 1843).

10. Diary fragment, between January 11 and February 3, 1843; Diary, February 3, 1843.

11. Diary, February 3, 5, 1843; Hecker to parents, February 22, 1843; Hecker to George, March 6, 1843.

12. Hecker to mother, January 19, 1843.

13. Hecker to brothers, March 14, 1843; Diary, April 18, 1843.

14. Hecker to brothers, May 2, 1843; Diary, April 13, 14, 17, 1843.

15. Diary, April 24, 1843.

16. Diary, April 28, 1843.

17. Diary, May 9, 1843; Hecker to brothers, May 2, 1843.

18. Diary, April 24, 1843.

19. Diary, April 24, May 8, 1843; Hecker to friends, April 13, 1843.

20. Diary, May 4, 1843.

21. Diary, April 15, 18, May 12, 1843; Hecker to mother, May 16, 1843.

22. Diary, May 14, June 1, 1843.

23. Diary, May 30, 1843; Hecker to George, May 23, 30, 1843.

24. Diary, May 14, 1843.

25. Diary, May 10, May 30, 1843.

26. Diary, June 12, 1843; addresses John in letter to George, May 30, 1843.

27. Diary, June 16, 1843.

28. Diary, June 18, 19, 1843; Hecker to family, June 24, 1843.

29. Diary, June 18, 24, 1843; Hecker to brothers, July 7, 11, 1843.

30. Alcott to Mrs. Barlow, February 15, 1843. See also F. B. Sanborn and William T. Harris, *A. Bronson Alcott: His Life and Philosophy*, vol. 2 (New York, 1965), pp. 303, 384. See also Madelon Bedell, *The Alcotts: A Biography of the Family* (New York, 1980), pp. 210–216.

31. Diary, July 7, 1843.
32. Diary, July 11, 12, 13, 17, 1843; Hecker to family, July 13, 1843.
33. Diary, July 21, 1843.
34. Diary, July 25, 1843.
35. Diary, July 24, 25, 27, August 2, 1843.
36. Diary, August 2, 1843.
37. Diary, July 28, 31, August 8, 9, 1843.
38. Hecker to family, July 31, 1843; Diary, July 31, August 9, 1843.
39. Diary, August 22, 1843.
40. Bradford cited in Sedgwick, "A Girl at Brook Farm," p. 403; Hecker to brothers, July 31, 1843; Diary, July 31, 1843.
41. See Sr. Mary Helen Sanfillippo, "Personal Religious Experience of Roman Catholicism: A Transcendentalist Critique," *Catholic Historical Review* 62 (July 1976), pp. 366–87.
42. Undated fragment in Hecker papers; Diary, August 13, 1843.
43. Diary, July 13, 1843.

CHAPTER 3
SEARCHING FOR THE CHURCH

1. Diary, June 13, 1843; John Hecker to Brownson, August 20, 1843; Hecker to Brownson, August 30, September 14, 16, 1843; quotation is from Brownson to Hecker, September 2, 1843.
2. Hecker to Brownson, September 6, 14, 1843; Diary, October 28, November 5, 20, 23, 27, 1843.
3. Ida Russell to Hecker, September 21, November 7, 1843; George W. Curtis to Hecker, August 18, September 3, 16, October 8, 1843; Charles Dana to Hecker, September 15, 1843; Lane to Hecker, November 11, 1843, June 3, 1844; Hecker to Dana, nd (dated March, 1844 in Dana to Walter Elliott, September 6, 1889, in Elliott Papers).
4. Ripley to Hecker, September 18, 1843.
5. Diary, August 22, 26, September 4, October 17, December 2, 1843.
6. Diary, August 30, September 14, December 31, 1843.
7. Diary, September 15, December 5, 16, 1843.
8. Diary, January 20, 1844; Hecker to Brownson, October 16, 1843.
9. Diary, September 24, December 14, 31, 1843, January 29, February 15, 1844.
10. Diary, January 7, March 8, 10, 22, 1844; Hecker to Brownson, January 21, 1844; Hecker to Brownson, March 9, 1844; Brownson to Hecker, March 11, 1844; Hecker to Norris, March 17, 1844; Norris to Hecker, March 25, 1844; Hecker to Brownson, March 15, 28, 1844.

11. Diary, March 30, 1844; Hecker to Brownson, March 28, April 6, 1844.

12. Diary, March 22, 1844.

13. Diary, April 14, 1844; Hecker to family, April 22, 1844.

14. Hecker to family, April 24, 1844.

15. Diary, April 26, 27, 1844.

16. Diary, April 29, May 4, 1844; Hecker to family, May 2, 4, 1844.

17. Diary, May 4, 1844.

18. Diary, May 6, 1844.

19. Diary, May 6, 7, 8, 9, 10, 13, 15, 17, 1844.

20. Hecker to John and George, May 13, 1844; Hecker to friends, May 28, 1844; Diary, May 30, 1844.

21. Diary, May 31, June 5, 1844.

22. Diary, June 5, 6, 1844; Hecker to Brownson, June 4, 1844 [misdated in original]; Brownson to Hecker June 6, 1844.

23. Diary, June 7, 1844.

24. Diary, June 8, 10, 11, 1844; Hecker to family, June 11, 1844. Toward the end of his life, Hecker wrote that Bishop Fitzpatrick had been inquisitorial, questioning him closely on his views, but there is no evidence of this in his reports of the time. Vincent Holden speculated that the aging Hecker confused this meeting with his earlier visit with Bishop Hughes of New York, which had been unsatisfactory, as we have seen. Fitzpatrick, in a letter of introduction to Bishop McCloskey, spoke of Hecker as "a young gentleman for whom I have conceived much esteem," whose "conviction that the Catholic Church has infallible and divine authority" was "thorough and practical." He did note, however, that Hecker needed "guidance, yet in many respects more for moderation than incitement." The letter is quoted in full in Holden, *The Yankee Paul*, p. 440n.

25. Diary, June 11, 1844; Hecker to family, June 11, 1844.

26. Diary, June 13, 24, 1844.

27. Hecker to family, June 14, 1844; Hecker to friends, June 14, 1844; Diary, June 14, 1844. On his trip with Emerson see Richard Gilman, ed., *The Papers of Ralph Waldo Emerson*, vol. 9, p. 14. Rejoinder to Emerson is in Elliott, *Life of Father Hecker*, p. 89.

28. Hecker to friends, June, 1844; Hecker to Brownson, June 24, 1844.

29. *Boston Quarterly Review*, April 1855, in *The Works of Orestes A. Brownson*, vol. 14, edited by Henry F. Brownson, Detroit, 1982, pp. 538–39; Brownson said the same in a letter to Hecker on the latter's return from the seminary, March 28, 1851. See also Hecker, "Dr. Brownson in Boston," *Catholic World* 45 (July 1887), pp. 464–72. Hereafter cited as CW.

30. On Catholic influences at Brook Farm see Sanfillippo, "Personal Experiences," and Eleanor Simpson, "The Conservative Heresy: Yankees

and the 'Reaction in Favor of Roman Catholics,' " Ph.D. diss., University of Minnesota, 1974, part 1.

31. Simpson, "Conservative Heresy," p. 51.

CHAPTER 4
THE LAND PROMISED ME IN MY YOUTH

1. For an examination of the concept of conversion based on Hecker's experience see Susan Perschbacher, "Journey of Faith: The Conversion and Reconversion of Isaac Hecker," Ph.D. diss., University of Chicago, 1981.

2. Holden, *The Yankee Paul*, p. 440; Diary, June 23, 31, July 5, 1844.

3. Diary, July 9, 10, 1843, June 30, July 5, 6, 9, 10, 1844, January 22, 1845; Hecker to Brownson, July 15, 1844.

4. Diary, August 1, 6, 1844.

5. Hecker to Thoreau, August 1, 15, 21, 1844; Thoreau to Hecker, August 14, nd, 1844. For Thoreau's view of Catholicism see Lawrence Willson, "Thoreau and Roman Catholicism," *Catholic Historical Review* 42 (April 1956), pp. 157–72.

6. George Curtis to Hecker, August 4, 1844; Ora Gannett to Hecker, May 10, July 8, 1844; Diary, March 30, 1844.

7. Diary, July 18, 1844.

8. Diary, July 17, 18, 23, 1844.

9. Diary, July 12, 23, August 11, 1844.

10. Diary, July 12, August 11, 1844.

11. Diary, August 19, September 9, 10, 1844.

12. Diary, September 12, 18, 21, 22, 1844.

13. Diary, November 5, 22, August 10, July 15, October 11, 17, 18, November 27, December 8, 1844.

14. Diary, December 18, nd, 1845.

15. Diary, January 20, 1845. See also Hecker to Brownson, January 14, 1845.

16. Diary, January 2, February 2, July 4, 1845.

17. Diary, January 3, February 16, March 3, 12, 15, April 2, 1845.

18. Diary, April 2, 19, 24, 25, 29, 1845.

19. Diary, May 2, June 21, 28, 1845.

20. Diary, June 29, 1845.

21. Diary, June 26, July 17, 19, 1845.

22. Clarence Walworth, *The Oxford Movement in America, or, Glimpses of Life in an Anglican Seminary*, reissued by United States Catholic Histori-

cal Society (New York, 1974). On the Oxford Movement in the United States generally, see the Introduction to this volume.

23. Diary, June 15, July 27, 1845; Hecker to Brownson, July 25, 29, 1845. See also McMaster to Edgar Wadhams, June 13, 1845.

24. Brownson to Hecker, July 31, 1845.

CHAPTER 5
IN ANOTHER COUNTRY

1. Hecker to family, August 29, 1845; George to Brownson, nd.

2. McMaster to Wadhams, October 30, 1845; Hecker to Brownson, September 18, 1845; Hecker to family, September 18, 1845.

3. Hecker to family, September 18, 1845; Hecker to mother, March 4, 1846.

4. Hecker to John, September 18, 1845; Hecker to mother, January 1, March 4, 1846.

5. Hecker to mother, January 1, 1846; Hecker to family, September 14, 1846.

6. Hecker to mother, October 15, 1846; Hecker to Brownson, November 1, 1846. On the influence of Catholic spiritual writers see Farina, *An American Experience of God*, chap. 7.

7. Hecker to McCloskey, October 15, 1846, in John Cardinal Farley, *The Life of John Cardinal McCloskey* (New York, 1918), pp. 156–58.

8. Hecker to John, October 15, 1846.

9. Hecker to Thoreau, May 15, 1847.

10. Holden, *The Yankee Paul*, pp. 131–40.

11. "Report to Superiors," May 30, 1848.

12. Hecker to mother, December 8, 1848; Hecker to Aunt Betsy, December 8, 1847.

13. Burrell Curtis to Hecker, February 15, 1849; George Curtis to Hecker, February 16, 1849; Burrell Curtis to Hecker, April 8, 1849; George Curtis to Hecker, April 15, 1849; Lane to Hecker, October 13, 20, 1849; Hecker to Thoreau, Summer, 1849, in E. H. Russell, "A Bit of Unpublished Correspondence Between Henry David Thoreau and Isaac Hecker," *Proceedings of the American Antiquarian Society* 15 (Worcester, 1902), pp. 1–14.

14. "Account of Interior State," prepared for superiors while in seminary, May 30, 1848.

15. Heilig to Hecker, March 24, 1847 (misdated, should be 1849).

16. Heilig to Hecker, May 13, 1849.

17. Certificate of Ordination.

18. Hecker to family, September, November 7, 1850; Father Smetana to Hecker, November 2, 1850; Heilig to Hecker, January 11, 1851; Hecker to mother, January 19, 1851.

CHAPTER 6 AMERICAN EVANGELIST

1. Review of *Questions of the Soul* in *Brownson's Quarterly Review* 3 (April 1855), pp. 209–26.

2. Hecker to George, April 28, 1851; Hecker to Simpson, August 6, 1852, in Abbot Gasquet, "Some Letters of Father Hecker," CW (May 1906).

3. Hecker to mother, January 22, 1852, March 22, 1854; list of sermon topics in volume of sermons in Walworth papers; Walter Elliott, notes, undated, in the Elliott Papers.

4. Hecker to Thoreau, nd (dated later July 6, 1851).

5. Hecker to Brownson, July 29, 1851 and September 5, 1851.

6. Hecker to Simpson, January 27, 1853, in Gasquet, "Some Letters."

7. Hecker to Hewit, nd (June 1854); Hecker to Brownson, September 14, 1854. On Hecker's approach to apologetics see Joseph Gower, "The New Apologetics of Isaac Thomas Hecker (1819–1888): Catholicity and American Culture," Ph.D. diss., University of Notre Dame, 1978.

8. Hecker, *Questions of the Soul* (New York, 1855).

9. George Bancroft to Hecker, March 15, 1855; Hecker to C. B. Fairbanks, March 24, 1856.

10. Brownson's review of *Questions of the Soul*, pp. 209–11.

11. Hecker to Brownson, August 22, 1855; Hecker to Douglass, July 29, 1856.

12. Hewit to Brownson, October 13, 1856.

13. Hecker to McMaster, November 23, 1855.

14. Hecker to Brownson, April 16, August 7, 1855; Brownson to Hecker, June 1, 1855. For Hughes' reaction to all this see John R.G. Hassard, *Life of Most Reverend John Hughes, First Archbishop of New York* (New York, 1866), pp. 383–85.

15. On the history of the United States Redemptorists, with another view of the story of Hecker and that community, see Michael J. Curley, C.SS.R., *The Provincial Story: History of the Baltimore Province of the Congregation of the Most Holy Redeemer* (New York, 1963), pp. 1–136.

16. Hewit to Hecker, March 19, 1855.

17. Hewit to Hecker, July 4, 1856; Ruland to Hecker, October 18, 1856.

18. de Held to Hecker, February 6, 1855; Curley, *The Provincial Story*, pp. 125–29.

CHAPTER 7
RISKING EVERYTHING

1. Hecker to Father Duffy, June 18, 1855; Hecker to C. B. Fairbanks, March 24, 1856; Hecker to Brownson, March 22, 1855.

2. Hecker, *Aspirations of Nature* (New York, 1857).

3. Hewit to Hecker, May 31, 1857; Ruland to Hecker, July 7, 1857.

4. Simpson to Hecker, July 28, 1856; Hecker to Simpson, August 30, 1856, June 30, 1857.

5. "Aspirations of Nature," *Brownson's Quarterly Review* (October 1857) in Brownson, *Works* vol. 14, pp. 543–77.

6. Hecker to Brownson, August 17, 1845; Brownson to Hecker, June 25, 1845.

7. Brownson to Hecker, August 5, 1857.

8. William Portier, "Providential Nation: An Historical-Theological Study of Isaac Hecker's Americanism," Ph.D. diss., University of Toronto, 1990.

9. Gower, "New Apologetics," pp. 90–97.

10. Hewit to Hecker, May 31, 1857; Walworth to Hecker, July 23, 1857.

11. Circular Letter to Superior General and Rectors Major, May 9, 1857.

12. Deshon to Ruland, July 30, 1857.

13. Walworth to Hecker, July 25, 27, 1857; Walworth to Deshon, August 2, 1857.

14. McMaster to Barnabò, July 28, 1857; McMaster to Hecker, July 28, 1857; Hughes to Barnabò, August 1, 1857; Bayley to Barnabò, August 3, 1857; Hildegarde Yeager, C.S.C., *The Life of James Roosevelt Bayley, First Bishop of Newark and Eighth Archbishop of Baltimore, 1814–1877* (Washington, 1947), p. 175.

15. Ruland to Hecker, July 31 and August 3, 1857. On Helmprecht see Helmprecht to Hecker, July 15, 1857; Hewit to Hecker, July 30, 1857 and Hewit to fathers, August 5, 1857; Ruland to Mauron, October 12, 1857.

16. Helmprecht to Mauron, August 17, 1857; Ruland to Mauron, July 31, 1857.

CHAPTER 8
CATHOLIC INNOCENT ABROAD

1. Hecker to George, August 18, 24, 1857.

2. Decree of Expulsion, August 30, 1857; Hecker to fathers, August 31, 1857; Hecker to Brownson, September 1, 1857.

3. Hecker to George, September 1, 1857.

4. Mauron to Ruland, September 3, 30, 1857.

5. Deshon to Hecker, September 28, 1857; Walworth to Hecker, September 28, 1857; Walworth to Hecker, October 4, 1857; Ruland to Hewit, October 4, 1857.

6. Hecker to George, Sepember 8, 1857.

7. Hecker to fathers, September 20, 1857.

8. Hecker to fathers, October 3, 1857.

9. Hecker to George, October 3, 1857; Hecker to fathers, October 24, 1857.

10. Walworth to Hecker, October 9, 1857; fathers to Hecker, October 20, 1857; Walworth to Hecker, October 23, 1857.

11. Mauron to Ruland, October 8, 1857; Douglass to Ruland, October 30, 1857; Walworth to Hecker, November 11, 1857; Mauron to Ruland, January 29, 1858; Ruland to Mauron, October 12, 1857; Ruland to Hewit, November 8, 1857; Ruland to Mauron, January 5, 1858.

12. Purcell to Kenrick, September 29, 1857, in Anthony H. Deye, "Archbishop John Baptiste Purcell: Pre Civil War Years," Ph.D. diss., University of Notre Dame, 1959, p. 421.

13. Hecker to fathers, November 13, 1857; Walworth to Purcell, December 25, 1857, in Cincinnati Papers, University of Notre Dame.

14. Purcell to Barnabò, nd; Smith to Purcell, March 4, 1858, in Cincinnati Papers.

15. Kenrick to Spalding, February 22, 1858; O'Connor to Smith, December 6, 1857; Spalding to Kenrick, April 16, 1858; O'Connor to Smith, January 6, 1858; Joseph F. Wood to Barnabò, March 2, 1858; John Barry to Barnabò, February nd, 1858; Louis de Groesbriand to Barnabò, February 27, 1858. On Bayley see Walworth to Hecker, December 5, 1857, and Yeager, *Bayley*, p. 177. On Purcell see Deye, "Purcell," p. 422. On O'Connor see Henry A. Szarnick, "The Episcopacy of Michael O'Connor, First Bishop of Pittsburgh, 1843–1860," Ph.D. diss., Catholic University of America, 1971, pp. 242–43.

16. Hughes to Barnabò, October 30, 1857; Hughes to Mauron, October 31, 1857; George to Hecker, December 28, 1857; Hughes to Hecker, December 29, 1857.

17. Hughes to Smith, December 29, 1857; Smith to Hughes, March 4, 1858, Walworth to Hecker, January 3, 1858.

18. de Held to Hecker, December 9, 1857, February 27, 1858; De Buggenoms to Hecker, September 24, 1857; Deschamp to Barnabò, September 25, 1857.

19. Hecker to George, October 23, 1857; Hewit to Hecker, October 14, 1857.

20. Brownson to Hecker, September 29, 1857; Hecker to Brownson, October 24, 1857.

21. Hecker to Smith, October 13, 1857.

22. Hecker to fathers, November 7, 1857.

23. Hecker to fathers, November 7, 20, 1857.

24. "The Present and Future Prospects of the Catholic Faith in the United States of North America," *Civiltà Cattolica* (November 21, 1857), typescript in Hecker Papers. The second article appeared in Rome December 5, 1857. Both were eventually published at home in the *Freeman's Journal* of McMaster.

25. Hecker report to Barnabò.

26. Memorial and Petition of the American Fathers, November 14, 1857.

CHAPTER 9
ALL WE HAD AT HEART

1. Hecker to fathers, November 12, 1857, January 1, 1858; Hecker to "My Dear Friend" [Sarah King], December 15, 1857.

2. Hecker to fathers, December 9, 1857.

3. Hecker to fathers, November 20, 1857; Walworth to Hecker, October 20, December 6, December 22, 1857, January 3, 11, 1858; Hewit to Hecker, December 22, 1857.

4. Walworth to Hecker, February 8, 1858; Hewit to Hecker, February 9, 1858.

5. Hecker to fathers, January 9, 18, 25, 1858; Hecker to George, January 23, 1858.

6. Hecker to fathers, December 17, 18, 1857; Notes, December 22, 1857. Hecker made frequent but irregular diary-like notations. Some on particular subjects have been gathered together, and those collections will be so noted.

7. "Report" January 6, 1858.

8. Hecker to fathers, January 9, 18, 1858; Connolly to Smith, January

17, 1858; Connolly to Barnabò, January 17, 1858; Connolly to Hecker, January 20, 1858.

9. Hecker to fathers, January 18, 1858.

10. Hecker to fathers, January 25, February 19, 26, 1858.

11. Hecker to fathers, February 26, 1858.

12. Hecker to fathers, March 5, 1858. Similar comments in Hecker to George, March 2, 1858.

13. Hecker to fathers, February 26, 1858; Hecker to George, February 27, 1858.

14. "Position of the Congregation of the Most Holy Redeemer in the United States," nd, no author noted, but presumably Mauron.

15. Mauron to Holy Father, February 11, 1858; Mauron to Archbishop Bizarri, February 11, 1858.

16. Ruland to Mauron, March 2, 1858; Hecker to fathers, February 19, 20, 1858.

17. Hecker to George, February 27, March 2 (postscript March 6), 1858.

18. Hecker to fathers, March 6, 1858: Decree dated March 6, 1858.

19. Hecker to George, March 7, 1858; Mauron to Ruland, March 9, 1858.

20. Hecker to fathers, March 11, April 3, 1858.

21. Hecker to fathers, March 18, 1858.

22. Hecker to George, March 9, 1858; Hecker to fathers, March 27, 1858.

23. Ruland, Circular Letter, April 9, 1858; Ruland to Mauron, April 29, 1858.

24. Ruland to Baker, April 17, 1858; Ruland to Walworth, April 2, 1858; Walworth to Ruland, May 3, 1858; Hewit to Ruland, April 8, 1858.

25. Geisen to Mauron, May 26, 1858.

26. Curley, *The Provincial Story*, pp. 129–35.

27. Hecker to George, February 22, 1858.

28. Hecker to fathers, February 26, 1858; Notes, February 1858.

29. Hecker to George, January 23, 1858.

CHAPTER 10
THE PAULISTS

1. Hecker to fathers, March 27, 1858; Hecker to George, March 11, 19, 1858.

2. Walworth to McCloskey, April 2, 1858; Walworth to Purcell, April 3, 1858; Hecker to fathers, December 9, 1857; Hecker to George,

January 30, 1858. On the early days of the Paulists, including the founding meeting, the early missions, biographical information on the early members and details of parish development see James McVann, *The Paulists, 1858–1970*, vol. 1 (privately printed).

3. For excellent brief biographies of the founding Paulists see Joseph McSorley, *Isaac Hecker and His Friends* (New York, 1952; rev. 1978), pp. 91–153.

4. Hewit to "Father," April 1832; Hewit, "How I Became a Catholic," CW 46 (October 1887), pp. 32–43; Joseph P. Flynn, "The Early Years of Augustine F. Hewit, 1820–1846," M.A. thesis, Catholic University of America, 1945. On Hewit and other early members see M. A. Corrigan, "Register of Priests Laboring in the Archdiocese of New York from Early Mission Times to 1885," United States Catholic Historical Society, *Historical Records and Studies* 5 (November 1907), pp. 409–11.

5. Walworth to Hecker, November 29, 1857.

6. Baker to Theodore Revell, April 6, 1858. On Baker see McSorley, *Friends*, pp. 136–37 and Hewit, *Memoir and Sermons of the Rev. Francis A. Baker* (New York, 1866). See review of latter volume in CW 2 (January 1866), pp. 566–67.

7. Deshon to McMaster, July 4, 1852; Walter Elliott, "Father George Deshon," typescript in Elliott Papers.

8. "Program of the Rule and Constitution of the Congregation of the Missionary Priests of St. Paul the Apostle."

9. Walworth to Hewit, June 26, 1858; Walworth to Deshon, June 20, 1858.

10. Walworth to Brownson, July 6, 1858, in Brownson Papers.

11. Hewit to Bishop McCloskey, June 22, 1858; Deshon to Walworth, June 17, 1858.

12. "Agreement Between His Grace the Most Reverend John Hughes and the Congregation of Missionary Priests of St. Paul the Apostle," July 10, 1858. See also Hughes to Hecker, February 7, 1859.

13. "Circular of the Missionary Priests of St. Paul the Apostle Addressed to Their Friends of the Clergy and Laity of the United States," July 14, 1858.

14. Hecker to Bernard Smith, July 20, 1858.

15. Hassard, *Hughes*, pp. 386–87.

16. See Francis E. Tourscher, ed., *The Kenrick-Frenaye Correspondence, 1830–1862* (Lancaster, Pennsylvania, 1920), pp. 410–11; Kenrick to Purcell, April 9, 1858, Cincinnati Papers. The entire conflict is examined in John P. Marschall, "Kenrick and the Paulists: A Conflict of Structures and Personalities," *Church History* 35 (March 1968), pp. 88–105.

17. Baker to Hecker, July 17, 1858; Kenrick to Hecker, July 19, 1858.

18. Hecker to Smith, July 20, 1858.

19. Hughes to Smith, July 27, 1858.

20. Hecker to Smith, August, 1858; Smith to Hecker, September 11, 1858; Hecker to Smith, September 15, 1858.

21. Copy of "Decision of Congregation of Bishops and Regulars," September 20, 1858; Smith to Hughes, October 1, 1858; Smith to Hecker, October 1, 1858; Barnabò to Hecker, October 6, 1858.

22. Hecker to Smith, October 8, 1858.

23. O'Connor to Smith, October 10, 1858; Smith to Kenrick, October 10, 1858; Smith to Hecker, October 11, 1858; O'Connor to Smith, October 21, 1858; Purcell to Smith, October 28, 1858; O'Connor to Kenrick, November 4, 1858; Hecker to fathers, November 6, 1858; O'Connor to Hecker, November 11, 1858; Hecker to Smith, November 13, 1858.

24. Hecker to fathers, November 15, 1858; Hecker to Kenrick, November 23, 1858; Kenrick to Barnabò, November 23, 1858; Foley to Hecker, November 25, 1858.

25. Kenrick to Hecker, November 26, 1858; Baker to Kenrick, November 30, 1858.

26. Hecker to fathers, November 6, 1858; Thomas Walsh to Hecker, January 31, 1859; George McCloskey to Hecker, December 11, 1858; McCloskey to Hughes, January 16, 1859; McCloskey to Hecker, nd.

27. Hughes to Hecker, February 7, 1859; Hughes to Barnabò, February 11, 1859; Hecker to Barnabò, February 15, 1859; Hecker to Bedini, March 5, 1859; Hecker to Smith, March 15, 1859; Smith to Hecker, April 8, 1859; Barnabò to Hecker, April 26, 1859.

28. On novitiate see "Paulist Fathers Chapter Book." On Tillotson see Tillotson to Hecker, October 27, 1859; Hecker to Tillotson, October, 1859; McSorley, *Friends*, pp. 138–39.

29. Walworth to Hecker, December 15, 1860; marginal notations of Deshon.

30. Paulist Register of Priests.

31. McSorley, *Friends*, pp. 237–53.

32. L. B. Binsse to Barnabò, November 12, 1858; *Tablet*, June 18, 1859; *Tribune*, November 29, 1859.

33. Baker to Dwight Lyman, August 14, 1858; Hecker to Smith, June 21, 1859; *Tribune*, November 29, 1859.

34. *Tablet*, April 14, May 12, 1860; *Freeman's Journal*, June 18, 25, 1859.

35. Hecker, "How to Be Happy," in *Sermons Preached at the Church of St. Paul the Apostle During the Year 1863* (New York: Arno Press, 1978), pp. 58–70.

36. On parish activities see *Freeman's Journal and Roman Catholic Regis-*

ter, December 9, 1865; Chapter Notes, September 25, 1860; *Tablet*, February 3, 17, 1872.

37. Walworth to Hecker, July 15, 1865; Hecker to Walworth, July 17, 1865. On suspension of the missions see Hecker to Archbishop Purcell, May 27, 1865.

38. Hecker to Bernard Smith, April 16, 1861; Hecker to Barnabò, April 30, 1862; Hecker to Connolly, May 21, 1862.

39. Hecker to Rouquette, November 18, 1858, July 24, 1859; Hecker to Anna B. Ward, July 25, 1859.

40. Notes, October 1859.

CHAPTER 11
THE FUTURE TRIUMPH OF THE CHURCH

1. Hecker to Bernard Smith, August 12, 1860, February 16, April 16, 1861; Hecker to Richard Simpson, January 16, 1861.

2. Jane Sedgwick to Hecker, April 11, 1861.

3. Hecker to "Sister," September 14, 1861; Hecker to Bernard Smith, June 26, 1861.

4. Hecker to Bishop McFarland, July 1, 1861; G. W. Muse to Hecker, May 17, 1861, with notation by Deshon.

5. Hecker to Simpson, June 26, 1861, May 21, 1862.

6. *Home and Foreign Review* (July 1862), pp. 249–50 (in Hecker Papers); *Tablet*, February 14, 1863; *Tribune*, February 28, 1863.

7. Hecker to Smith, April 1863; Louis Binsse to Barnabò, July 18, 1863; Hecker to Mrs. King, July 19, 1863.

8. "Sermon on the Outbreak of the Rebellion," typescript with note "not delivered."

9. Hecker to Simpson, May 20, September 12, 1862, May 13, 1864.

10. Hecker to Bayley, February 27, 1863; Hecker to Smith, April 6, 1863.

11. Hecker to Bayley, February 27, 1863; Hecker to Barnabò, July 24, 1863; Hecker to Mrs. King, November 18, 1863.

12. Hecker to Simpson, December 29, 1863; Hecker to Mrs. Ward, January 19, 1864.

13. Hecker to Chatard, November 29, 1868; C. J. O'Flynn to Bishop Lefevre, December 3, 1868; Hecker to Chatard, February 2, 1869.

14. Numerous clippings are in the Hecker Papers, while Paulist reminiscence comes from McVann, *The Paulists*. The undated Syracuse clipping is in the Hughes scrapbooks in the Diocese of Syracuse archives.

15. Hecker to Mrs. King, April 4, July 1, 15, 1864.

16. On the early history of Catholic publication see Paul J. Foik, *Pioneer Catholic Journalism* (New York, 1930), and Thomas F. Meehan, "The First Catholic Magazines," United States Catholic Historical Society, *Historical Records and Studies* 31 (1940), pp. 141–42.

17. E. Rameur, "The Progress of the Church in the United States," CW 1 (April 1865), pp. 1–19. See also Richard Walsh, C.S.P., "Father Hecker and the Press," M.A. thesis, Catholic University of America, 1945.

18. Hecker to Mrs. Tikner, November 24, 1865.

19. Hecker to Mrs. King, January 4, 1865,

20. Hecker to Archbishop Purcell, March 27, 1865, Cincinnati Papers.

21. Fragment, Hecker to Bernard Smith, nd. See also Paul J. Fullam, "The Catholic Publication Society and Its Successors, 1866–1916," *Historical Records and Studies* 47 (1959), pp. 12–77.

22. Hassard, *Hughes*, p. 87; Hecker to McCloskey, March 6, 1866; Spalding to Hecker, January 18, 1866; Hecker to Purcell, April 16, 1866; Hecker to Spalding, March 19, 1866.

23. "The Catholic Publication Society," CW 3 (May 1866), pp. 278–83.

24. Hecker to Simpson, May 29, 1865 and Hecker to Mrs. Cullen, October 29, 1866.

25. Thomas W. Spalding, *Martin John Spalding: American Churchman* (Washington, 1973), pp. 135–160.

26. Hecker to Tillotson, October 18, 1866.

27. Text of "The Future Triumph of the Church."

CHAPTER 12
STEAM PRIEST

1. *Tribune*, October 16, 1866; James Parton, "Our Roman Catholic Brethren," *Atlantic Monthly* 21 (May 1868), p. 559.

2. Report to Baltimore Council, October 7, 1866. The letters to Spalding cited in this chapter are from the Spalding Papers at the University of Notre Dame archives.

3. Hecker to Mrs. Tickner, Sepember 6, 1870.

4. John Hassard, "Catholic Literature and the Catholic Public," CW 12 (December 1870), pp. 399–410; J. G. McGee, "On Catholic Libraries," CW 14 (February 1872), pp. 707–15; Hecker to Spalding, May 17, 1869; Thomas W. Spalding, *Martin John Spalding: American Churchman*, p. 344.

5. Brady to Hecker, September 27, 1868; Hecker to H. A. Anderson, September 10, 1868; Hecker to Spalding, June 20, 1869; J. M. Stone to H. L. Richards, April 11, 1871; Spalding to Hecker, July 2, 1869; Hecker

to Spalding, May 1, 7, 1869; Hecker to Brownson, January 8, 1872; "Report to the Catholic Union," nd; Walsh, "Father Hecker and the Press," chap. 5.

6. Hassard, *Hughes*, pp. 385–86.

7. Hecker to Spalding, July 10, 1866.

8. "Catholic Congresses," CW 5 (July 1867), pp. 433–42.

9. Hecker to Chatard, August 17, 1867; Newman to Ambrose St. John, August 9, 1867, in Stephen Dessain, ed., *The Letters and Diaries of John Henry Newman*, vol. 23 (London, 1973), p. 289; Montalembert to Hecker, June 25, 1868, in R. Lacanuet, *Montalembert*, 3d ed., vol. 3 (Paris, 1905), p. 413.

10. "Report on the Present Religious Condition of the United States," September 6, 1867.

11. De Chabrol to Hecker, November 18, 1867; "Shall We Have a Catholic Congress?" CW 7 (November 1868), p. 227.

12. "Shall We Have a Catholic Congress?," pp. 223–24.

13. See Fullam, "Catholic Publication Society," pp. 40–50.

14. "The Second Plenary Council of Baltimore," CW 7 (August 1868), pp. 618–35; same title, CW 9 (July 1869), pp. 497–503.

15. Hecker to Bayley, February 27, 1863.

16. Purcell to Spalding, October 8, 1868; McCloskey to Purcell, February 6, 1869, Cincinnati Papers.

CHAPTER 13
VATICAN I

1. Barnabò to Hecker, March 1869; Hecker to Spalding, April 2, 1869; Hecker to Chatard, June 7, 1869; Hecker to Spalding, June 19, 1869; Hecker to Chatard, June 19, 1869; Brownson to Frank, August 1, 1869. This last letter and all subsequent Brownson family letters are in the Brownson Papers at the University of Notre Dame.

2. On the background of the Council see Hales, *Pio Nono*; August B. Hasler, *How the Pope Became Infallible: Pius IX and the Politics of Persuasion* (Garden City, 1981); and Dom Cuthbert Butler, *The Vatican Council* (London, 1930).

3. Diary, July 4, 1845; "Father Hecker's Farewell Sermon," CW 10 (December 1869), pp. 289–93. For a detailed account of Hecker's experience at the Council, which argues that during this period his ideas regarding the providential destiny of America crystallized, see William Portier, *Isaac Hecker and the First Vatican Council* (Lewiston and Queenston, 1985). Professor Portier graciously shared his manuscript with me at an earlier date.

4. Hecker to Hewit, November 20, 26, 1869.

5. Newman to William Monsell, December 3, 1869 in Dessain, *Letters and Diaries*, vol. 24, pp. 283, 382; Simpson to Acton, November 9, 1869, in Josef Altholz et al., *The Correspondence of Lord Acton and Richard Simpson*, vol. 3 (Cambridge, 1975), pp. 133, 280–84.

6. Victor Conzemius, *Ignaz Von Dollinger Briefwechsel mit Lord Acton*, vol. 2 (Munich, 1965), pp. 7–8; translation in Hecker Papers. See also James Hennesey, *The First Council of the Vatican: The American Experience* (New York, 1963), pp. 92–93.

7. Hecker to George, December 4, 1869; Hecker to Hewit, December 6, 1869.

8. Hecker to Josephine, January 26, 1870; Hecker to George, December 24, 1869.

9. Hecker to "My Dear Sister [Josephine]," December 19, 1869; Notes, December 29, 1869.

10. On Corcoran's remark see Portier, *Vatican Council*, p. 281n.

11. Rosecrans to Purcell, April 23, 1870; Hecker to George, March 11, 1870.

12. Acton to Dollinger, January 6, 7, 22, 1870, in Conzemius, *Dollinger*, pp. 58, 101–105; Spalding, *Spalding*, p. 296.

13. Hecker to Josephine, December 26, 1869; text of sermon "The Destiny of Man"; Hecker to George, February 8, 1870.

14. Kenrick to H. M. Muhlsiepen, March 6, 1870; Acton to Dollinger, January 22, 1870, cited above.

15. Notes, random, January 1870; Hecker's Roman notes were often undated.

16. Notes, random, December 1869, January 1870; also May 20, 1870.

17. "The American College in Rome," CW 9 (April 1869), pp. 560–64; "The Approaching General Council," CW 9 (April 1869), p. 19; Hewit to Hecker, November 15, 1869, January 1, 1870; "Review of Pastoral Letter of Archbishop Manning," CW 10 (January 1870), pp. 569–71.

18. Hecker to Hewit, January 12, 1870; Hewit to Brownson, February 9, 1870, Brownson Papers; Hennesey, *Vatican I*, p. 117.

19. These articles appeared as "The First Ecumenical Council of the Vatican," CW 10 (February 1870) to 11 (August 1870).

20. Hecker to George, February 8, 1870.

21. Notes, February 24, 1870; Hecker to George, February 8, 24, March 20, 1870.

22. Notes, January 20, 1870. Hecker to George, January 26, 1870.

23. "The Present Condition of Church and State in Europe, 1870" (draft); Hecker to Hewit, February 2, 1870; Hecker to Brownson, January 30, 1870.

24. Notes, April 21, 22, 1870.

25. Notes, May 4, 1870; Connolly to Hecker, May 5, July 12, 1870; Healy to Hecker, June 13, 1870.

26. Connolly to Hecker, September 8, 1870.

27. Hecker to Chatard, June 28, 1870; "Sermon on the Vatican Council, Delivered on the Second Sunday after Pentecost, 1870."

28. "The First Ecumenical Council of the Vatican," CW 11 (September 1870), pp. 840–47.

29. "Infallibility," CW 13 (August 1871), p. 594; "Popular Objections to Papal Infallibility," CW 14 (February 1872), pp. 597–603.

30. Simpson to Acton, August 12, 1870, in Altholz, vol. 3, p. 297; Hecker to Chatard, October 1, 1872, April 4, 1873.

CHAPTER 14
HECKER AND BROWNSON

1. "Doctor Brownson's Road to the Church," CW 46 (October 1887), pp. 1–11. On McMaster see Thomas T. McAvoy, "Public Schools, Catholic Schools and James McMaster," *Review of Politics* 28 (January 1966), pp. 19–46.

2. "Doctor Brownson and Bishop Fitzpatrick," CW 45 (April 1887), pp. 1–7.

3. "Doctor Brownson and Catholicity," CW 46 (November 1887), pp. 222–35.

4. Brownson to Mrs. Goddard, December 20, 1863; Brownson to J. W. Cummings, July 24, 1861, in Brownson Papers; Walworth to Hecker, February 8, 1858. Other Brownson correspondence in this chapter, save that to Hecker, is from the Brownson Papers unless otherwise indicated.

5. Brownson to Simpson, May 2, 1862.

6. Brownson to Frank, April 24, November 30, 1867; George McCloskey to Purcell, December 5, 1864; Cincinnati Papers for information on the annuity.

7. Brownson to Hecker, January 29, 1868; Brownson to Frank, February 18, 1868; Brownson to Hecker, February 12, 1868; Brownson to Henry, April 7, 1868.

8. Brownson to Hecker, March 10, 1868; Hecker to Brownson, March 14, 1868; Brownson to Hecker, March 17, 1868.

9. *Tablet*, June 13, 1868, January 29, 1870; Sadlier to Brownson, July 28, 1868; Brownson to Sadlier, June 3, 1868; Brownson to Henry F. Brownson, June 5, 1868. Last item in Henry F. Brownson Papers, University of Notre Dame.

10. *Tablet*, August 1, October 10, 1868; see also "Rome and the World," CW 6 (October 1867), p. 19.

11. Brownson to Henry F. Brownson, November 3, 1868, H. Brownson Papers; Brownson to children, February 1, April 3, 1869.

12. See also Hewit to Brownson, December 10, 1869.

13. *Tablet*, February 9, 1870.

14. "Review," CW 11 (December 1869); *Tablet*, February 5, 1870.

15. Hewit to Brownson, February 1, 1870; Brownson to Hewit, February 3, 1870, Hewit Papers; *Tablet*, February 19, 1870.

16. "The Future of Catholicism and Protestantism," CW 11 (February 1870), pp. 576–87; "Religious Liberty," CW 11 (April 1870), pp. 1–11; "Church and State," CW 11 (May 1870), pp. 145–60.

17. Hewit to Brownson, March 5, 1870; Brownson to Hewit, March 8, 1870, Hewit Papers; Hewit to Brownson, March 28, 1870.

18. Brownson to Hecker, August 25, 1870.

19. Brownson to Frank, November 22, 1870.

20. Brownson to Frank, March 15, 1871.

21. "Review" of Newman's *History of My Religious Opinions*, in CW 2 (October 1865); Hewit to Brownson, August 2, 1871; Brownson to Hewit, August 3, 1871, Hewit Papers; Brownson to Hecker, January 31, 1872; Brownson to Henry F. Brownson, December 7, 1871, January 28, 1872; Sara Brownson to Henry F. Brownson, January 28, 1872; Hecker to Mrs. Tickner, February 29, 1872; Brownson to Henry F. Brownson, May 23, 1872; Brownson to "Very Reverend Father," nd (1872); Brownson to McCloskey, October 11, 1873. On his daughter's protest see Sara to Henry F. Brownson, January 30, 1876. On the ontology dispute see Wilfred Parsons, S.J., "Brownson, Hecker and Hewit," CW 153 (July 1941), pp. 396–408.

22. Hecker to Sara Brownson, April 5, 1876.

23. *Tablet*, June 18, 1870.

CHAPTER 15
CRISIS

1. Hecker to Mrs. Tickner, July 10, 1871; Hecker to Cullen, January 10, 19, 1872; Hecker to Hewit, July 23, 1872.

2. Yeager, *Bayley*, p. 355; Hecker to Lynch, December 25, 1872; Hecker to Bayley, April 15, 1873; Hewit to Chatard, April 6, 1873; Hecker to Hewit, April 15, 1873.

3. Hecker to Hewit, April 26, 1873.

4. Hecker to Cullen, June 18, 1873.

5. Hecker to Cullen June 10, July 24, 1872.

6. Hecker to Chatard, July 1, 1873; Hecker to George and Josephine, August 19, September 16, October 22, 1873; Hecker to Hewit, August 30, 1873.

7. Hecker to Hewit, September 15, 1873; Hecker to George, October 3, 1873; Hewit to Hecker, September 15, 1873.

8. "Notes on the Interior State," September 11, 1873; Hecker to Walter F. Atlee, October 25, 1873; Hecker to George and Josephine, October 2, 1873. These undated notes were collected under the heading "Notes on the Interior State."

9. Hecker to Archbishop McCloskey, December 9, 1873.

10. Hecker to George and Josephine, December 14, 1873.

11. Notes, December 26, 1873.

12. Notes, December 30, 1873, January 26, 1874.

13. Notes, February 8, 10, 16, 1874; Hecker to George, February 8, 1874; Hecker to George and Josephine, March 26, 1874.

14. Notes, March 30, 1874; Hewit to Hecker, January 15, 1874; George to Hecker, January 15, 1874; Hecker to George, April 8, 1874.

15. Hecker to Hewit, April 10, 1874.

16. Hewit to Hecker, May 3, 1874.

17. Rosecrans to Hecker, April 10, 1874; George to Hecker, April 26, 1874; Young to Hecker, April 25, 1874.

18. Hecker to mother, April 20, May 15, 1874; Hecker to George, May 15, 1874; Mother to Hecker, August 3, 1874, March 3, 1875.

19. Hecker to George and Josephine, June 11, 1874.

20. Hecker to friends, July 2, 30, 1874; Hecker to George and Josephine, August 2, 3, 18, 1874; Hecker to Hewit, August 3, 1874; Notes, September 10, 1874; Hecker to George and Josephine, August 28, September 5, 1874.

21. Hecker to George and Josephine, October 12, 1874; Notes, October 14, 1874.

22. Hecker to Hewit, October 23, 1874; Hecker to George and Josephine, October 23, 1874; Notes, November 10, 12, 19, 1874; Hecker to George and Josephine, June 11, 1874; Hewit to Hecker, November 14, 1874.

23. Notes, November 17, 1874.

24. Hecker to George and Josephine, November 28, 1874.

25. Hecker, *An Exposition of the Church in View of Recent Difficulties and Controversies and the Present Needs of the Church.*

26. Hecker to Hewit, January 15, 24, February 13, 1875; Notes, January 29, 1875.

27. Notes, February 10, 1875; Manning to Hecker, February 1, 1875;

Dufresne to Hecker, March 17, 1875; Joseph Burone to Hecker, April 24, 1875; Hecker to Hewit, February 13, 1875.

28. Newman to Hecker, April 10, 1875, in Dessain, *Letters and Diaries*, vol. 27, pp. 270–72; Hecker to Hewit, April 22, 1875.

29. Hecker to George and Josephine, March 27, April 13, 1875; Notes, March 3, April 15, 1875.

30. Notes on letter to George and Josephine, May 14, 1875.

31. Hecker to McCloskey, March 16, 1875; see Farley, *McCloskey*, p. 309.

32. Julia Beers to Archbishop Bayley, March 11, 1875.

33. Hecker to George and Josephine, March 22, June 16, 1875; Dufresne to Hecker, June 23, 1875; Notes, June 29, July 12, 1875.

34. Young to Hecker, July 7, 1875.

35. Hewit to Hecker, July 9, 1875.

36. Hewit to Hecker, July 13, 1875.

37. Hecker to George, July 30, August 21, 1875; Hecker to Hewit, July 30, 1875.

38. Hecker to Hewit, August 9, 1875.

39. Notes, July 19, August 1, 1875.

40. Notes, August 4, 9, 1875; Hecker to George, August 4, 1875.

41. Hecker to Hewit, August 9, 1875; Hewit to Hecker, August 27, 1875.

42. Hecker to Hewit, September 21, 23, 1875.

43. Notes, September 6, 1875.

44. Notes, September 6, 1875.

45. Notes, September 4, 1875.

46. Hecker to Simpson, September 23, 1875.

CHAPTER 16
MAKING AMERICA CATHOLIC

1. Hewit to Hecker, October 12, 17, 1875; Deshon to Hecker, October 16, 1875; Hecker to Smith, January 3, 1876; Hecker to Hewit, October 13, 1875.

2. On *Catholic World* financial problems see Hecker to Bishop McQuaid, August 15, 1876; on Brownson see McCarthy to Brownson, January 15, 1876, Brownson Papers.

3. Hecker, "Notes on the Church as Representative of Mankind," nd.

4. Preface to *Three Converts* (New York, 1860). See also "Doctor Brownson and Bishop Fitzpatrick," CW 45 (April 1887), pp. 1–7.

5. Hecker to Catherine Beecher, nd; Beecher to Hecker, June 16, 1862; Holmes to Hecker, January 6, 1864.

6. He stated his position clearly to Bishop William Elder, May 5, 1873; Hecker to Simpson, December 29, 1863, in Gasquet, "Some Letters of Father Hecker."

7. "Doctor Brownson and Catholicity," CW 46 (November 1878), p. 231.

8. See John Updike, "On Hawthorne's Mind," *New York Review* (March 19, 1981), pp. 4–7.

9. "Doctor Brownson and Catholicity"; Hecker to George, April 8, 1858.

10. Hewit, "Doctor Bacon on Conversion to the Catholic Church," CW 5 (April 1867), pp. 104–19; Hewit to Brownson, September 12, 1862, Brownson Papers; Hewit, "Nature and Grace," CW 6 (January 1868), pp. 505–27.

11. "The Last Gasp of the Anti-Catholic Faction," CW 7 (September 1868), pp. 848–55; "Pope or People?" CW 9 (May 1869), pp. 212–21; "The Future of Protestantism and Catholicity," CW 10 (January 1870), pp. 433–48; "Free Religion," CW 10 (November 1869), pp. 195–206; Hewit to Newman, July 27, 1868.

12. Diary Notebooks, early 1845.

13. "The Religious Condition of the Country," text in *Freeman's Journal*, April 24, 1869.

14. Hassard, "American Catholics and Partisan Newspapers," CW 16 (April 1873), pp. 756–65; Searle, "Religious Liberty as Understood by the Evangelical Alliance," CW 39 (June 1884), pp. 440–46.

15. Notebooks kept on trip to Egypt; "Leo XIII," CW 46 (December 1887), pp. 251–98.

16. "Introductory," CW 31 (April 1880), pp. 1–4.

17. Editorial, CW 32 (February 1881), p. 721.

18. Hecker, "True and False Friends of Reason," CW 33 (June 1881), pp. 289–98.

19. "Protestantism versus the Church," CW 38 (October 1883), pp. 1–13.

20. "Luther and the Diet of Worms," CW 38 (November 1883), pp. 145–61.

21. "The Intellectual Outlook of the Age," CW 31 (May 1880), pp. 148, 158.

CHAPTER 17
NOT YET THE PROMISED LAND

1. "The Liberty and Independence of the Pope," CW 35 (April 1882), pp. 1–10.

2. Thomas T. McAvoy, "Public Schools," cited above.

3. *Tribune*, October 9, 1875, quoted in John Whitney Evans, "Catholics and the Blair Education Bill," *Catholic Historical Review*, 46 (October 1960), p. 278.

4. "Popular Education," CW 7 (May 1868), pp. 228–35; "The Catholic View of Public Education in the United States," CW 8 (February 1869), pp. 686–97; "The Education Question," CW 9 (April 1869), pp. 121–35.

5. Brownson, "The School Question," CW 11 (April 1870), pp. 91–106; Brownson, "Unification and Education," CW 12 (April 1871), pp. 1–14; Brownson, "Who Is to Educate Our Children?" CW 14 (January 1872), pp. 432–47.

6. Hecker to Bernard Smith, January 30, 1876; Hecker to McQuaid, February 8, 1876.

7. "What Does the School Question Mean?" CW 34 (October 1881), pp. 84–90; Hecker, "New But False Plea for Public Schools," CW 36 (December 1882), p. 419.

8. "Catholics and Protestants Agreeing on the School Question," CW 32 (February 1881), pp. 699–713.

9. "What Does the School Question Mean?" p. 85.

10. "New But False Plea," pp. 412, 422; Hecker, "The Impending Issue of the School Question," CW 36 (March 1883), pp. 849–54.

11. Hecker, "The Intellectual Outlook of the Age," CW 31 (May 1880), pp. 145–58.

12. Hecker, "Two Prophets of This Age," CW 47 (August 1888), pp. 684–93.

13. Hewit, "Episcopacy the Bond of Unity," CW 46 (March 1888), pp. 721–35.

14. Hecker, "The Things That Make for Unity," CW 47 (April 1888), pp. 102–09.

15. Hecker, "Leo XIII," CW 46 (December 1887), p. 293.

CHAPTER 18
PUBLIC CATHOLICISM

1. These remarks are scattered throughout the Elliott notes of his conversations with Hecker during the last years of his life.

2. See Diary, especially May 26, 1843, June 24, 1843, July 28, 1843.

3. Hecker to Mrs. Thompson, July 30, 1868; Notes on Various Subjects, nd.

4. Diary, May 7, 1844.

5. Hecker to Mrs. King, May 28, 1865.

6. Clipping, *Boston Advertiser* (January 13, ny).

7. Hecker, "Who Shall Take Care of the Poor?," CW 6 (February 1869), p. 703, plus the following unsigned articles: "Religion in New York," CW 3 (June 1866), p. 319; "Religion in Prisons," CW 10 (October 1869), p. 108; "Public Charities," CW 18 (April 1873), pp. 1–23; "The Poor You Have Always With You," CW 47 (July 1883), pp. 566–67. Here as so often the *Catholic World*'s early efforts at civility were challenged. A series on the sanitary and moral conditions of New York presented a stinging indictment of tenement slums, noting that the city had the highest death rate in the Western world. The author praised Catholic parishes and reformatories, but also expressed admiration for such Protestant efforts as those of the Methodist Ladies Home Missionary Society. Such Protestants were doing the work "we ought to have attempted long ago," he wrote. This aroused a firestorm of criticism; one writer in the *Tablet*, for example, admitted he had no interest in describing the work of Protestants and regarded articles like those in the *Catholic World* as disloyal. The original author responded vigorously, attacking those who imagined that "no man who is unfortunate enough to be a heretic can possibly do a good deed from a good impulse," but the episode made clear that even mild self-criticism would be difficult in an atmosphere of interreligious competition and discord. See the original series in CW 7 (July 1868 and August 1868); *Tablet*, October 31, 1868; and "Charities in New York," CW 8 (November 1868), pp. 279–85.

8. The six articles appeared from CW 14 (February 1872) to CW 15 (July 1872).

9. Diary, July 26, 1844.

10. Diary, July 27, 1843.

11. Quoted in Langlois, "Political Theory," p. 112.

12. Diary, June 5, 1844; Notes on Various Subjects, nd; Hecker, "Life Is Real," CW 46 (October 1878), pp. 137–38.

13. "Catholic Colonization," CW 31 (May 1880), pp. 273–84.

14. Smith, "The Workingman Should Not Act but Think," CW 47 (September 1888), pp. 838–43; Smith, "Let Us Study the Labor Question," CW 47 (April 1888), pp. 51–58; Smith, "The Children at Work," CW 43 (August 1886), pp. 619–25.

15. Slattery, "The Catholic Church and the Colored People," CW 37 (June 1883), pp. 374–84; Slattery, "Some Aspects of the Negro Problem,"

CW 39 (February 1884), pp. 604–13; Slattery, "The Present and Future of the Negroes in the United States," CW 40 (December 1884), pp. 289–95; J.T., "Is the U.S. Government a Nuisance to Be Abated?" CW 34 (October 1881), pp. 62–69.

16. "The Saint for Our Day," in *Sermons Preached in the Church of St. Paul the Apostle in the Year 1863* (New York: Arno Press: 1978), pp. 90–102.

17. "The Missionary Duty of Catholics," typescript.

18. On Corrigan and McGlynn see Robert Emmett Curran, S.J., *Michael Augustine Corrigan and the Shaping of Conservative Catholicism in America, 1878–1902* (New York, 1978).

19. These scattered notes on McGlynn are undated.

20. "Church Authority and Power," undated sermon text.

21. Hecker, "John R.G. Hassard," CW 48 (June 1888), pp. 397–401; Hecker to Brownson, January 20, 1870; "The German Problem," CW 34 (December 1881), pp. 289–97.

22. Hecker, "Cardinal Gibbons and American Catholicism," CW 45 (June 1887), pp. 330–37.

23. Hecker, "Leo XIII," CW 46 (December 1887), pp. 291–98. See also Elliott notes dated December 27, 1883, Hecker's notes in Rome, January 1870, and Hecker, *The Church and the Age* (New York, 1886), p. 99.

24. Hecker, *The Church and the Age*, pp. 80–87.

CHAPTER 19
THE INDWELLING HOLY SPIRIT

1. Hecker, "Notes on the Spiritual Life," nd; "Spiritual Doctrine," undated notes.

2. Hecker, "Thoughts on the Spiritual Life," nd; Christmas Sermon, 1870; Diary, June 6, 1844.

3. Diary, August 15, 1844, February 2, 1845.

4. Hecker, "Notes on the Perfection of the Lay State," nd.

5. Hecker to Brownson, September 5, 1851.

6. Hecker to King, March 25, 1863.

7. Hecker to King, April 16, 1863.

8. Hecker to King, May 16, 1863.

9. Hecker to King, June 9, 26, 1863.

10. Hecker to King, October 8, 22, November 14, 1863, January 29, March 18, 1864. See also notes in Egypt, November 25, 1873.

11. Hecker to Cullen, January 23, 1863.

12. Hecker to Cullen, February 9, March 16, May 17, 1867; Cullen to Hecker, April 10, June 15, June 19, 1867.

13. Hecker to Sister Magdeline, July 20, 1876.

14. Hecker to Julia Beers, September 17, 1876.

15. Hecker to Elliott, September 1885; Elliott, Notes.

16. "Preface" to Mrs. Sophia Ripley's translation of *The Life and Death of St. Catherine of Genoa* (New York, 1873).

17. Elliott, Notes on conversations with Father Hecker, nd.

18. Hecker, "Notes on the Spiritual Life," May 14, 1875; "God and Man," unpublished manuscript, pp. 119–20.

19. Notes in Rome, March 13, April 21, 1870; Notes on Community Life, nd; Hecker to Mrs. Cullen, May 19, 1873.

20. Notes on Various Subjects, nd; letter to "Sisters," March 28, 1877.

21. Simpson to Hecker, September 10, 1859; Hecker to Simpson, March 26, 1860.

22. Elliott, Notes, most undated but see especially June 24, 1885. See also Hecker to Mrs. Ward, March 15, 1859.

23. "The Guidance of the Holy Spirit," CW 45 (September 1887), pp. 846–47; "Spiritual Guidance," CW 46 (February 1888), pp. 715–16.

24. "Spiritual Guidance," p. 716.

25. George Hagmaier, C.S.P., "The Holy Spirit, the Church and the Individual: Father Hecker's Synthesis," *American Ecclesiastical Review*, 141 (July 1959), pp. 95–102; Hecker to Mrs. A. B. Ward, August 22, 1881.

26. Michael Fellman, *The Unbounded Frame: Freedom and Community in Nineteenth Century Utopianism* (Westport, Connecticut, 1973), pp. 20–41. I am grateful to Father Philip Kiley, S.J., for calling this reference to my attention. See also Susan J. Perschbacher, "Journey of Faith."

27. Elliott, Notes, January 18, 1886.

28. Unpublished manuscript on the spiritual life, 1860. See also Grant Wacker, "The Holy Spirit and the Spirit of the Age in American Protestantism, 1880–1910," *Journal of American History*, 72 (June 1985), pp. 45–62; Timothy L. Smith, "Righteousness and Hope," pp. 40–41.

CHAPTER 20
ALONE AT THE END

1. Hecker to Colonel Hudson, January 24, 1876; O'Rourke to Young, February 1, 1876; O'Rourke to Hecker, June 19, 1876; Hecker to O'Rourke, June 21, 1876; O'Rourke to Hecker, June 24, 1876.

2. Notes, August 26, 1876; Elliott to Hecker, August 21, 1876.

3. Notes, undated; Hecker to Ryder, January 18, 1877.

4. Hewit to Hecker, July 5, 1878; Hewit to Hecker, July 17, 1878; Hewit to Hecker, September 1, 1878.

5. "Notes on Conferences on Religion," October 2, 1878.

6. Ramiere to Hecker, July 5, 1879.

7. Hewit to Elliott, September 3, 1891; Hecker to Ward, August 23, 1881; Hecker to Mother Augustine MacKenna, June 28, 1883; Hecker to McQuaid, May 30, 1884.

8. Information on the Catholic Publication Society is drawn from the Kehoe-Hammond papers in the University of Notre Dame archives. Negotiations can be followed in the Kehoe correspondence with George Hecker from 1881 to 1883.

9. Information on the 1884 congregation meeting is taken from detailed notes of Father Elliott in the Elliott Papers. See also McVann, *The Paulists*, p. 627.

10. Hewit to Gibbons, October 15, 1884; Gibbons to Hewit, October 16, 1884.

11. Keane to Hecker, nd, 1881; Keane to Manning, August 1, 1885; Keane to Hecker, November 23, December 12, 1885, January 15, 1886. On Keane and the Paulists see Hecker to Bayley, October 27, 1871, and Patrick Ahearn, "An Assistant Is Chosen for a Bishopric," in *Records*, 63 (September 1952), pp. 168–69.

12. Hecker to Elliott, September 8, 1885; Elliott to Hecker, October 16, 1885; Elliott, Notes, August 1885.

13. Elliott, "The True Man of the Times," CW 44 (December 1886), pp. 289–96.

14. Elliott, Notes.

15. *Freeman's Journal*, December 29, 1888; Newman to Hewit, February 28, 1889, in Hewit papers.

CHAPTER 21
"HECKERISM"

1. "Tribute of the *Catholic World* to Its Founder, Father Hecker," CW 38 (January 1889), pp. 572–75.

2. John J. Keane, "Father Hecker," CW 39 (April 1889), pp. 1–9.

3. On these disputes see Robert D. Cross, *The Emergence of Liberal Catholicism in America* (Cambridge, 1958), and Gerald P. Fogarty, S.J., *The Vatican and the American Hierarchy from 1870 to 1965* (Wilmington, 1985), chaps. 2–7.

4. Ireland, Preface to Walter Elliott, *The Life of Father Hecker* (New

York, 1891), p. ix. Elliott tells the story of his writing of the biography and quotes Hewit in his own preface to the never-published "Revised Life" in the Elliott Papers. The twenty articles appeared in the *Catholic World* from April 1890 to November 1891.

5. James A. Healy to Elliott, December 1, 10, 1890, Elliott Papers.

6. Elliott to Ireland, July 5, 1890; O'Connell to Ireland, July 23, 1885, Ireland Papers, microfilm, College of St. Thomas. On the Roman comments see Edes to Hudson, nd, Hudson Papers, University of Notre Dame.

7. Elliott to Ireland, March 25, 1892, Ireland Papers.

8. Lawrence V. McDonnell, C.S.P., "Walter Elliott and the Hecker Tradition in the Americanist Era," paper delivered at the meeting of the American Historical Association, December 1984. See also Chabrol to Hecker, November 18, 1867; Chabrol to Elliott, July 21, 1893, Elliott Papers; Keane to Gibbons, July 31, 1894, photostat in Ireland Papers; Heuser to Hudson, August 13, 1893, Hudson Papers, University of Notre Dame Archives; Salvadore Brandi to James Edwards, C.S.C., February 28, 1895, Edwards Papers, University of Notre Dame Archives; "Longinqua Oceani," in John Tracy Ellis, ed., *Documents in American Catholic History*, vol. 2 (Chicago, 1967), pp. 499–510. See also Fogarty, *Vatican and American Hierarchy*, pp. 130–42.

9. Chabrol to Elliott, May 21, July 13, 1897; Dufresne to Elliott, August 24, October 19, 1897, Elliott Papers; Elliott to Klein, July 14, 1897, Klein Papers, University of Notre Dame. The best book on the controversy in Europe is still Thomas T. McAvoy, C.S.C., *The Great Crisis in American Catholic History, 1895–1900* (Chicago, 1957). Hecker had long associated with Europe's liberal Catholics, who were generally sympathetic with his ideas and projects. In 1868 Hecker sent Charles de Montalembert copies of James Parton's laudatory *Atlantic Monthly* articles. The great layman responded: "How desireable it would be if both the lay and ecclesiastical oracles of Catholic opinion in Europe would open their eyes to what is happening over the water, instead of brooding and grumbling and shouting forever about old worn out privileges and prerogatives such as *will* and *must* disappear everywhere as they are now doing in America" (Montalembert to Hecker, June 25, 1868).

10. O'Connell to Ireland, August 12, 1897, Ireland Papers; O'Connell to Elliott, August 17, October 12, 1897, Elliott Papers. See also Fogarty, *Vatican and American Hierarchy*, pp. 143–51.

11. Klein, preface to *Le Père Hecker, Fondateur des Paulistes Américains, 1819–1888* (Paris, 1898).

12. Elliott to Klein, June 18, 1897, Klein Papers; Elliott to Dufresne, September 11, 1897; Keane to Elliott, September 29, 1897, Elliott Papers. Text of O'Connell's paper in Hecker Papers.

13. Chabrol to Elliott, May 21, 1897; Elliott to Keane, July 28, 1897; Ireland to Doyle, December 20, 1893; Klein to Elliott, December 3, 1897, Elliott Papers; A. de Barre, S.J., in *Etudes Religieuse*, in Americanism Papers, University of Notre Dame.

14. Keane to Elliott, December 13, 1897, February 5, 1898.

15. Charles Maignen, *Le Père Hecker: est-il un saint* (Paris, 1898).

16. Chabrol to Elliott, March 28, 1898; Keane to Elliott, April 19, May 5, 1898, Elliott Papers; Gibbons to Klein, May 20, 1898, Klein Papers; O'Connell to Ireland, July 20, 1898; O'Connell to Keane, July 12, 1898, Ireland Papers; Brandi to Corrigan, September 3, 1898; McQuaid to Corrigan, August 30, 1898, New York Papers; Memorial, Americanism Papers, Paulist archives.

17. Gibbons to Elliott, April 14, 1898; Ireland to Elliott, November 6, 1898, Elliott Papers; Corrigan to Deshon, October 17, 1898, Americanism Papers; Keane to Ireland, June 7, 1897, October 18, 1898, Ireland Papers.

18. Keane to Gibbons, November 9, 1898, Ireland Papers; O'Connell to Elliott, November 13, 1898, Elliott Papers; Robert C. Ayers, "The Americanist Attack in Europe," unpublished paper delivered at annual meeting of the College Theology Society, 1984.

19. "*Testem Benevolentiae*," in Ellis, *Documents*, pp. 537–46.

20. Rampolla to Gibbons, February 9, 1899, Ireland Papers; Ireland to Deshon, February 24, 1899; Keane to Doyle, February 25, 1899, in Americanism Papers.

21. *The Irish American* (New York), February 25, 1895; *Baltimore Sun*, February 23, 1899; *New York Times*, February 24, 1899, clippings in Americanism Papers; Deshon to Elliott, February 26, 1899; Keane to Elliott, May 5, 1895, Elliott Papers; Ireland to Deshon, March 14, 1899; Corrigan to Deshon, March 27, 1899, in Americanism Papers. On reaction generally see Cross, *Liberal Catholicism*, pp. 201–02 and Fogarty, *Vatican and American Hierarchy*, pp. 180–84.

22. Spalding to Hudson, August 22, 1899, Hudson Papers; O'Connell to Ireland, June 23, 1900, Ireland Papers; Robert McNamara, "Bernard J. McQuaid's Sermon Against Theological Americanism," *Records*, 90 (March 1979), pp. 23–32.

23. J. St. Claire Ethridge, "The Sources of Americanism," *North American Review* (May 1902), typescript in Ireland Papers.

24. *Northwest Chronicle*, March 3, 1899; *Milwaukee Herald Citizen*, February 25, 1899; Ireland, quoted from *Gazette de Lausanne*, March 10, 1899, quoted in New York *Sun*, November 12, 1899; *Providence Visitor*, February 25, 1899; *Freemans Journal*, March 18, 1899; *Literary Digest* 18 (March 11, 1899), clippings in Americanism Papers; Josephine Hecker to Elliott, February 25, 1899, and Dufresne to Elliott, nd, Elliott Papers. See

also Samuel J. Thomas, "The American Periodical Press and the Apostolic Letter *Testem Benevolentiae*," *Catholic Historical Review* 62 (Fall 1976), pp. 408–23.

25. O'Connell, quoted in *Literary Digest* 18 (March 11, 1899); *Freeman's Journal*, March 18, 1899; William Gibson, "An Outburst of Activity Among Roman Congregations," *Nineteenth Century* (May 1899), Klein Papers.

26. Elliott to Deshon, October 15, 1900; Doyle to Elliott, September 10, 1899; Elliott to Doyle, nd, 1899, in Elliott papers. Elliott letter to Klein is quoted in Thomas Jonas, "The Divided Mind: American Catholic Evangelism in the 1890s," unpublished Ph.D. diss., University of Chicago, 1980, p. 321.

27. See David O'Brien, "Isaac Hecker as Symbol and Myth," Working Papers, Cushwa Center for American Catholic Studies, Series 15 (Fall 1984).

28. Searle quote is in *Catholic News*, January 9, 1904; John P. Sheerin, "The Paulist Apostolate," *Commonweal* 69 (December 26, 1958), pp. 334–46. Even the very best of Hecker's Paulists tended in the context of the twentieth-century subculture to reduce his legacy to a simple matter of Catholic accommodation to America. The mission of the Paulists, according to John J. Burke, was based on the "thesis that not only could a Catholic be a good American, but that he ought to be a better American because he is a Catholic; and secondly, that America, considering the political and economic condition of the world, offered here and now a particular opportunity for the spread and acceptance of the Catholic faith" (John J. Burke, C.S.P. to Peter Guilday, November 19, 1927, in Guilday Papers, Catholic University of America). Somewhat uneasily, later Paulists more or less ignored the theological issues and held to the "phantom heresy" argument that there had been no Americanism heresy, but simply a misunderstanding. See James Gillis, "Americanism: After Fifty Years," CW 169 (July 1949), p. 246, and Vincent Holden, "Father Hecker's Vision Vindicated," *Historical Records and Studies* 50 (1964), pp. 40–52.

29. Thomas Wangler, "Two Generations of American Catholic Expansion in Europe: Isaac Thomas Hecker and John J. Keane," paper delivered at annual meeting of the College Theology Society, 1984; "The Emergence of John J. Keane as a Liberal Catholic and Americanist (1878–1887)," *American Ecclesiastical Review* 156 (1972), pp. 457–58. Margaret Reher has argued that Hecker provided the intellectual underpinning of the Americanist movement, especially by focusing attention on the Kingdom of God. See "Leo XIII and Americanism," *Theological Studies* 34 (Fall 1973), pp. 690ff. My own interpretation has been influenced by the analysis offered by William Portier in his dissertation, and in "Isaac Hecker and

Testem Benevolentiae: A Study in Theological Pluralism," in John Farina, ed., *Hecker Studies*, pp. 11–45.

30. O'Connell to James Moynihan, January 30, 1900, in Ireland Papers.

31. Jonas, "The Divided Mind," pp. 4–10.

32. Portier, "Isaac Hecker and Americanism," *Ecumenist* 19 (November-December 1980), pp. 9–12.

Index